T0244514

This Fierce People

This Fierce People

The Untold Story of America's Revolutionary War in the South

ALAN PELL CRAWFORD

Alfred A. Knopf

NEW YORK

2024

THIS IS A BORZOI BOOK
PUBLISHED BY ALFRED A. KNOPF

Copyright © 2024 by Alan Pell Crawford

All rights reserved.
Published in the United States by Alfred A. Knopf,
a division of Penguin Random House LLC, New York,
and distributed in Canada by
Penguin Random House Canada Limited, Toronto.

www.aaknopf.com

Knopf, Borzoi Books, and the colophon are
registered trademarks of Penguin Random House LLC.

Library of Congress Cataloging-in-Publication Data
Names: Crawford, Alan Pell, author.
Title: This fierce people: the untold story of America's Revolutionary War
in the South / Alan Pell Crawford.
Other titles: Untold story of America's Revolutionary War in the South
Description: First edition. | New York: Alfred A. Knopf, 2024. |
"This is a Borzoi book." | Includes bibliographical references and index. |
Identifiers: LCCN 2023050429 | ISBN 9780593318508 (hardcover) |
ISBN 9780593318515 (ebook)
Subjects: LCSH: Greene, Nathanael, 1742–1786—Military leadership. |
Morgan, Daniel, 1736–1802—Military leadership. | Slavery—Southern States—
History—18th century. | Southern States—History—Revolution, 1775–1783. |
Southern States—Militia—History—18th century.
Classification: LCC E230.5.S7 C73 2024 | DDC 975/.03—dc23/eng/20231214
LC record available at https://lccn.loc.gov/2023050429

Map by Erin Hurley-Brown
Jacket image: *The Battle of Cowpens*, 1781
(detail) by Don Troiani © Don Troiani.
All Rights Reserved 2023 / Bridgeman Images
Jacket design by Ariel Harari

Manufactured in the United States of America
First Edition

For Ned and Tim

We cannot, I fear, falsify the pedigree of this fierce people, and persuade them that they are not sprung from a nation in whose veins the blood of freedom circulates.

—EDMUND BURKE,
SPEECH ON CONCILIATION WITH AMERICA,
MARCH 22, 1775

Contents

Contents

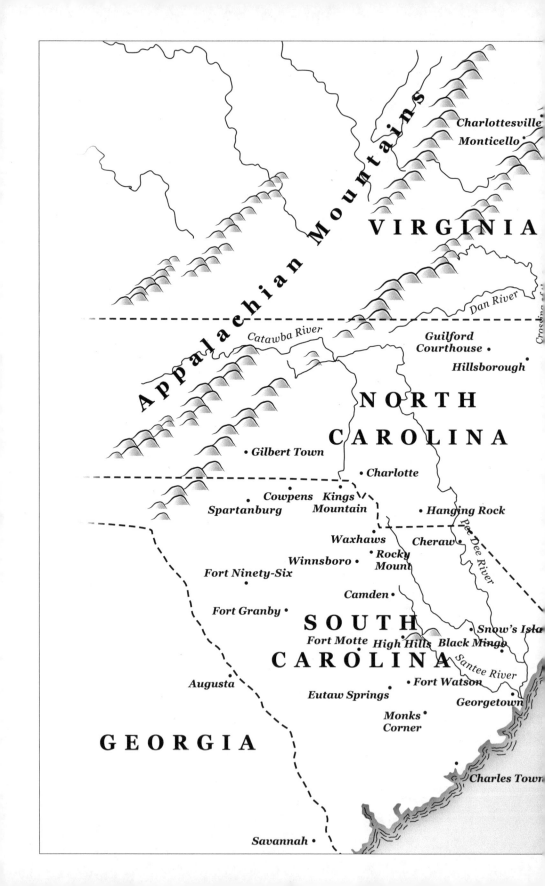

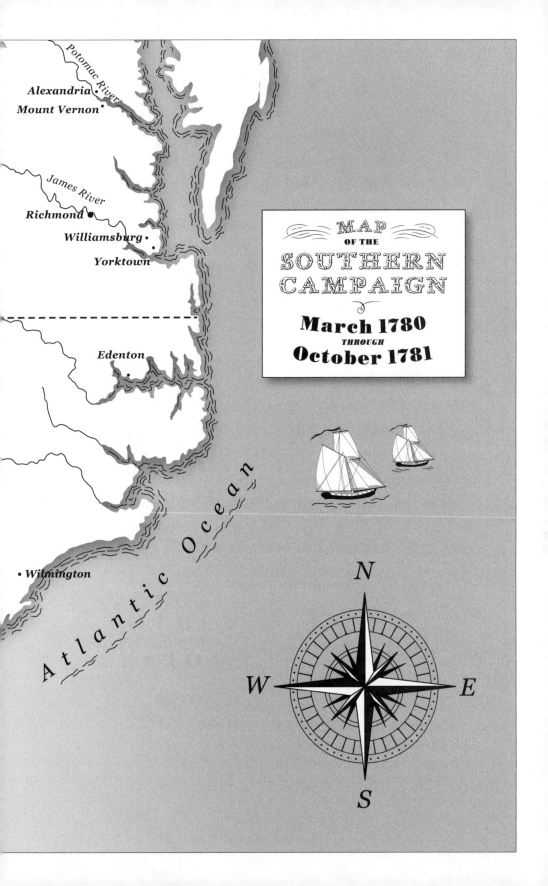

This Fierce People

Introduction

John Adams, with that acidic intelligence of his, was concerned from the get-go. He was "distressed," he said, by "the superstitious veneration that is sometimes paid to General Washington." This was in 1777, when the Continental army under Washington's command was camped for the winter at Morristown, New Jersey. This was before the major battles had been fought at Brandywine, Germantown, Saratoga, and Monmouth. But already even the most accomplished members of the Continental Congress found themselves in awe of the tall and distinguished-looking soldier from Virginia, and with good reason.

Even Thomas Jefferson, who had his disagreements with his fellow Virginian, found Washington uncommonly impressive. After Washington had been dead for more than a decade, Jefferson said the man who led the Continental army to victory over the British "was incapable of fear, meeting dangers with the calmest unconcern. His integrity was most pure, his justice the most inflexible I have ever known . . . his stature exactly what one would wish, his deportment easy, erect and noble; the best horseman of his age, and the most graceful figure that could be seen on horseback."

Never, Jefferson continued,

did nature and fortune combine more perfectly to make a man great, [and] his was the singular destiny and merit, of leading the armies of his country successfully through an arduous

war, for the establishment of its independence; of conducting its councils through the birth of a government, new in its
forms and principles, until it had settled down into a quiet and
orderly train, and of scrupulously obeying the laws through the
whole of his career, civil and military, of which the history of
the world furnishes no other example.

Not for nothing, then, is the Revolutionary War seen even to this
day as "George Washington's War," as a 1992 history of that conflict was
entitled. In part because of his subsequent service as the nation's first
president, Americans find it almost impossible to see the War of Independence except, as it were, in Washington's shadow. General histories
of the Revolution, even in our own time, take the form of accounts of
battles in which the Father of Our Country, as John Marshall called
him, or troops under his immediate command fought. These clashes
were—until Yorktown—those in the North.

Even educated Americans think of the War of Independence almost
exclusively in terms of stirring stories about its beginnings—Lexington
and Concord, Bunker Hill, Washington crossing the Delaware, the
cruel winter at Valley Forge—in which "embattled farmers" and "citizens in arms" led by Washington triumph over the greatest military
power in the world.

There is a problem with the standard narrative, however stirring.
The problem is that much of the war took place not in the North but
in the South, and that is where the most decisive battles—those that
forced the British surrender at Yorktown—were fought. Washington
himself remained in New York and New Jersey, primarily, for most of
the war. It was not until late summer of 1781, en route to Yorktown,
that he crossed the Potomac, more than three years after the last major
battle in the North, at Monmouth, took place. The events that forced
the British to give up the fight are given short shrift, and the surrender
at Yorktown, in most histories of the war, occurs almost as if by magic.

There are understandable reasons that the histories of the war take
the form that they do. The earliest accounts of the war came largely
from biographies of Washington himself, so they focus on events that
he was either directly involved in or closely associated with. Parson
Weems's *The Life of George Washington* (1808), in which he was deemed
a "Demi-god," was wildly popular, and went through several editions,

as did John Marshall's *The Life of George Washington* (1838). Washington Irving followed with a five-volume *Life of George Washington* (1855), which was widely read as well.

Contemporary memoirs of the war published during the first decades of the next century—those of William Moultrie (1802) and Henry "Light Horse Harry" Lee III (1812), for example—were important to later scholars but never achieved the readership of the Washington biographies. Early histories of the fledgling nation—that of Mercy Otis Warren (1805), for example—were written by New Englanders and, for that reason, focused on New England. More scholarly works followed, decade after decade, with Progressive Era historians, for example, having their say about the revolutionary period, its causes and consequences. Each period brings its own concerns and seeks in the Revolution its own "usable past."

More about this in a moment, but the Civil War, of course, is a factor in the historiography of the Revolution, too. Because the South was seen—no great surprise here—as disloyal and unpatriotic, any desire on the part of historians to recognize, much less celebrate, its contribution to the cause of independence itself collapsed. But even in the earliest years of the republic, when self-conscious "nation-building" was taking place, the presence of loyalist elements in the South during the revolutionary period was also a factor in the way historians regarded the region's role in the War of Independence. So, by the turn of the twentieth century, the popular narrative of the Revolution was well established, with Washington dominating inspiring events in the North.

Fortunately, it is possible to correct the record, as it were, with no disrespect to Washington or without diminishing his role in the war. No debunking is necessary, or desired. This is not a political or diplomatic history of the war, and in both areas, Washington's contribution was, of course, immense. But if anything, it can be argued that by giving scant attention to the southern campaign, we have failed to acknowledge one of Washington's most indispensable attributes as a leader: with the notable exception of Benedict Arnold, Washington was a superb judge of character. As the pages that follow should demonstrate, over the course of the war, Washington came to recognize the abilities of largely self-made men—Nathanael Greene, notably, and Daniel Morgan—and trust them to make decisions about how best to conduct the war in the South, where Washington could not be.

Given a fair hearing, however, it should become clear that the events of the southern campaign, during the three-plus years that convinced the British to surrender, are as compelling as any of the most widely publicized events in the North. In battles too few Americans have even heard of, fought by armies commanded by largely unsung heroes, this book seeks to account for the American victory, the reasons for which would otherwise remain a mystery. The South had its "embattled farmers" and "citizens in arms," too. The war, after all, was not only fought between American Continentals and British redcoats; it was also a civil war fought with astonishing ferocity between "partisans" fighting for independence and their "loyalist" neighbors, in battles, skirmishes, and appalling acts of domestic terrorism. The South had its Molly Pitchers, too, and their stories need to be told.

The South also had African Americans who fought in the Revolution, much as Crispus Attucks had in the North—and they fought on both sides of the war. When denied the opportunity to fight, they were servants and laborers. The record here is not as tidy as later generations, including our own, might wish. There were abolitionists in the South as well as in the North, and there were slaveholders in the North as well as in the South. Benjamin Franklin of Boston and Philadelphia—and a member of the Pennsylvania Abolition Society—was at one time a slaveholder himself. So was Philadelphia's Benjamin Rush, a signer of the Declaration of Independence and member of the same abolitionist society. Alexander Hamilton, a member of the New York Manumission Society, also owned slaves.

And there were southerners who were forthright in their belief that slavery was wrong—a violation of the values for which the Revolution was fought—and that it should be abolished. These included some of the most prominent leaders in the drive for independence, and slaveholders themselves, including Thomas Jefferson and Henry Laurens. They were compromised by their ownership of slaves and, for that reason, disappointing to readers today, but they not once defended the institution. It was, as Jefferson said, a "hideous evil," though he never figured out a practical plan for its abolition.

This brings us, finally, to another reason the war in the South had been downplayed in recent years. "How is it," Samuel Johnson asked, "that we hear loudest yelps for liberty from the drivers of negroes?" The sad fact is that the war in the South was fought by armies commanded by slaveholders whose ranks were filled with slaveholders. The political leaders of the cause of independence—in Richmond, Charles Town, and elsewhere in the South—were slaveholders themselves and, in some cases, slave traders. It is not surprising that historians in our own time have had little inclination to chronicle the war in the South, much less to credit the contribution of white southerners to the establishment of the new nation.

To many thoughtful contemporaries, Jefferson's "Empire of Liberty" seems a ghastly imposture that stains anything and everything associated with it. But this is not new. Even in the immediate aftermath of the Civil War, historians were understandably reluctant to honor the southerners who contributed so much to the War of Independence, knowing as they did the direct line from Henry Lee III, for example, to Robert E. Lee. This is why historians have chosen to celebrate the early episodes of the American Revolution—the Boston Massacre, Lexington and Concord, Bunker Hill, and Washington's crossing—and avert their gaze from the later ones—Camden, Kings Mountain, Cowpens—in the South.

That southerners saw little contradiction in fighting for their liberty while keeping others in bondage is itself revealing, a subject that the pages that follow will explore and explain but not attempt to justify. It is difficult—even painful—to acknowledge this shameful reality of our nation's history, but it is long past time to do so.

On a related note, the way the revolutionary generation viewed Native Americans is not how we view them today, a subject touched on in this account of the war. Native Americans were routinely referred to as Indians, and the terms appear interchangeably in the pages that follow.

CHAPTER ONE

"A Spirit of Independence"

The day after Major General Johann von Robais, Baron de Kalb, and his entourage of officers crossed from Virginia into North Carolina, he found time to write to his wife in Paris. "Here I am at last, considerably south," he wrote, "suffering from intolerable heat, the worst of quarters, and the most voracious of insects of every hue and form." It was mid-June 1780, and de Kalb's men, well-trained veterans from Delaware and Maryland, had sweated their way through swamps and pine forests before making camp outside Goshen, a town that cannot today be located on a map. They would pass the night at other long-forgotten settlements as they headed toward Charles Town, hoping to reinforce the garrison there and, if they were too late for that, to defend the rest of the South as the British sought to bring the entire region under their control.

The war, by this time, had dragged on for years, without either the British or the Americans being able to defeat the other and bring it to a close. The first shots had been exchanged at Lexington and Concord more than seven years before. All the great events later generations would teach their children about—the Battle of Bunker Hill, Washington's crossing the Delaware, the victory at Saratoga, the winter at Valley Forge, where de Kalb had suffered with the others—had come and gone, with still no end in sight. The last battle in the North, the inconclusive clash at Monmouth, took place in June 1778, exactly two years earlier. After that, not much had happened, and the cause of independence seemed to have stalled. The British still held New York and Philadelphia, and, in the South, when de Kalb had arrived, they were moving on the port at Charles Town. Starting a war, a cynic might say, was easy. Ending a war—actually winning one—was another matter. If this war was to be brought to a successful conclusion, it would be in the South, and General George Washington, back in New Jersey, hoped that de Kalb could be of more use there than in the North.

This trek to the Carolinas was hard-going even for young men born and raised in the mid-Atlantic colonies. For de Kalb, who was fifty-eight years old and had grown up in Bavaria and spent most of his life in northern Europe, summer in the American South presented daunting challenges. This old campaigner had known nights in rough barracks and drafty tents and on cold ground, but he had experienced nothing like the insects that hummed and buzzed and bit, morning, noon, and night. This was something that his wife, ensconced with their three small children in an elegant townhouse in Paris, could only imagine. "The most disagreeable [of these]," he told his wife, "is what is commonly called the tick, a kind of strong black flea, which makes its way under the skin, and by its bite produces the most painful irritation and inflammation, which lasts a number of days." His body was "covered with these stings," which southerners to this day know not as ticks but chiggers.

It would not get any easier for any of the men—especially those accustomed to the cooler weather of England and northern Europe—as they made their way deeper into the swampy lowlands along the southern coast. There, as the British commander at Savannah told Lord Charles Cornwallis, the heat was "beyond anything you can conceive." Malaria, smallpox, typhus, dysentery, and what were called "malignant fevers," "putrid fevers," and "bilious fevers" would spread through their camps, killing officers and men. This made it "the height of madness and folly," another British officer said, to do much fighting during the summer months. Diseases would sweep through the prison ships and the filthy encampments, and before long, the men were carrying the deadly microbes with them wherever they went. De Kalb had arrived in early summer, when the temperatures were rising, and with them, disease.

De Kalb would never make it back to his wife and children in France. Eight weeks later, when the British commanded by Cornwallis annihilated the main Continental army under General Horatio Gates at Camden, South Carolina, another 175 miles farther away, an enemy soldier struck de Kalb with a saber, opening an alarming gash in his head. Other redcoats then converged on him, and de Kalb was down, his body pierced three times with musket balls. All told, he would be wounded eleven times in the following seconds, and he would have been torn to pieces had not the Chevalier du Buysson, his aide-de-camp, shielded his commander's body with his own. Only when du Buysson told the British soldiers de Kalb's name and rank did they relent. By the time de Kalb was hit, the firing elsewhere in this lopsided battle had more or less ceased, and Cornwallis himself rode over, paying his respects to his fallen adversary, as the unwritten rules of so-called civilized warfare required; these included treating defeated officers with gentlemanly courtesy.

"I am sorry, sir, to see you," Cornwallis told de Kalb, "not sorry that you are vanquished, but sorry to see you so badly wounded." Cornwallis ordered his men to carry de Kalb into Camden on a litter. There he was tended to by British surgeons, but, after three days, he died. The British general saw to it that de Kalb was buried with full military honors, with the other enemy officers attending the ceremonies.

He was born simply Johann Kalb on June 29, 1721, in Huttendorf, just northwest of Nuremburg, the son, official records say, of a "peasant." This was a time of constant warfare in Europe, and, for an ambitious and capable young man, a career as a professional soldier offered opportunities for advancement. Before he was twenty, he had joined the French army, serving in the Chasseurs de Fischer, a corps of partisans—what we would call guerrillas, or irregulars—under the command of Marshal de Saxe, one of the great military theorists to emerge from the War of the Austrian Succession. At twenty-two, Kalb was made a lieutenant in the Lowendahl Regiment, a sophisticated, highly cultured, multilingual unit led by officers from all over Europe, also under Saxe's command. By learning "how to lead troops, and gaining experience in all aspects of the art of military planning and combat," John Beakes Jr., de Kalb's recent biographer, writes, he was making himself into a "very effective officer." Serving under early European masters of mobility in warfare—of the feint, of the hit-and-run, of the surprise attack, in units often far removed from the main army that operated with unusual independence—he was learning the kind of fighting especially suited to the American landscape. By 1747, when Kalb was twenty-six, he had fought in sixteen major battles and was promoted from lieutenant to captain with the designation aid-major. After that, he began to call himself de Kalb, as he would be known thereafter; the Baron would come later.

By the end of the War of the Austrian Succession in 1748, de Kalb had grown into a tall, imposing figure, calm under fire, well regarded by the men who served under him, and admirably humane at a time when his peers could be cruel. He remained with the French army in peacetime, where he became something of a reformer. He proposed— without success—the formation of a special regiment of "marine infantry," trained to undertake surprise attacks on the English coast and its colonies. Any such regiment should include good numbers of Irishmen. "All the world is aware," he wrote, "of the hatred cherished by the Irish against the English."

But de Kalb also attended to matters involving individuals. When a court-martial issued a death sentence for a deserter who then returned to the army, de Kalb successfully argued that capital punishment was applicable only when the deserter was arrested on foreign soil. His efforts to reform some of the harsher protocols of camp life were not always successful, but he tried. Prostitutes were not to enter the barracks, and when they were discovered to have done so, soldiers they were there to entertain could be made to whip the women as punishment. Men who objected to this treatment were hanged for insubordination. Details are sketchy, but Beakes says de Kalb sought "more humane" responses to this too-common occurrence, "and it was his practice throughout his career to try to soften some of the more drastic punishments that prevailed in eighteenth-century armies. He was a firm disciplinarian, but he seems to have tempered this with a genuine concern for his troops." How he dealt with the prostitutes awaits further research.

With the outbreak of the Seven Years' War, which Americans called the French and Indian War, de Kalb was fighting again, as struggles between France and Great Britain spilled over into the New World— where, in Pennsylvania, the twenty-one-year-old Virginia militia officer George Washington, sent with a small force to protect construction of a British fort on what the French claimed was their territory, ambushed a force of Canadians and killed its commander. Again de Kalb was with the Loewendal Regiment and in 1756 was promoted to major. The following year he fought in the Battle of Rossbach, an ancien régime engagement unlike what he and other veterans of European wars would see in the New World.

At Rossbach, Frederick the Great's twenty thousand Prussians defeated forty thousand troops fighting for France and Austria. In the southern theater in the American Revolution, by contrast, it was not unusual for what was considered a major battle to be fought between troops totaling no more than two thousand or three thousand on both sides. Compare that to Leipzig, where, in 1813, half a million men would fight. But Fortune had smiled on America, Alexis de Tocqueville observed in 1840. It had placed its "inhabitants . . . in the midst of a wilderness, where they have, so to speak, no neighbors." Even half a century after the War for Independence, a "few thousand soldiers are sufficient for their wants, but this is peculiar to America, not to democracy."

In 1760, de Kalb purchased a commission in the First Battalion of the regiment Anhalt, where he was appointed quartermaster general of the Army of the Upper Rhine. This further deepened his considerable military education. There seemed almost no aspect of the art and science of war in which he was not experienced, both in theory and practice. For his performance in the Battle of Wilhelmsthal in 1762, he received the French Order of Military Merit. The war ended the following year. De Kalb was forty-two now—no longer a young man—and had spent almost two decades in the French army, fighting in at least twenty major engagements in two wars. During visits to Paris, he met and in 1764 married Anna Elisabeth Emilie Robais, the sixteen-year-old heiress to a cloth-manufacturing fortune. On his pension—and his wife's money—this German peasant who had affixed a "de" to his name retired to what could have been a life of ease. De Kalb could not claim to possess one of the "first-rate fortunes," he admitted, but he need never again fret about money.

Retirement did not suit de Kalb, however, and in October 1767, he was on board the *Hercules,* sailing to the American colonies on a secret mission for France. Bent on revenge for its losses in the Seven Years' War, the court of Louis XV followed the mounting unrest on the shores of the Atlantic and was eager to determine the extent to which troubles there might be exploited to its advantage. The French wanted to know, de Kalb was told, whether the rebels there "are in need of good engineers and artillery officers," the "quantities of munitions of war and provisions they are able to procure," what were "their resources in troops, fortified places, and forts." France wanted to know, too, the rebels' "plan of revolt," if they had one, "and the leaders who are expected to direct and control it," and "the strength of their purpose to withdraw from the English government."

France needed a spy, and de Kalb, with his reputation for courage, sound judgment, and discretion, plus the knowledge a quartermaster general of the Army of the Upper Rhine would possess, was the man for the job. De Kalb landed in Philadelphia in January 1768, and, during his six months in the colonies, he visited Boston and New York, cultivating sources and filing reports, written in code to the Duc de Choiseul, the French foreign minister, who was his handler back home. Six years before the British closed the port of Boston—before de Kalb had even sailed to Philadelphia—he sympathized with the Americans' complaints. England, he wrote, "ought to be content with the profits it derives from selling them worthless goods at high prices, and purchasing necessities for a song." If the colonists made good on their threats to boycott anything manufactured in the mother country, the British economy would suffer, and "if the court should undertake to cure this evil by imposing additional taxes [as it would], sedition will follow, and the break be beyond healing."

These sympathies intensified as de Kalb got to know the colonists and saw the effects of British policies on their lives, all the while eluding English spies who were, in turn, tracking his comings and goings. "All people here," he wrote from New York, "are imbued with such a spirit of independence and even license, that if the provinces can be united under a common representation, an independent state will certainly come forth in time." In Boston, he discovered that the inhabitants "are almost exclusively Englishmen or of English stock." This native of Germany who had spent most of his life in the French army saw in the colonists' heritage a telling paradox: Because they are Englishmen, he wrote, "the liberties so long enjoyed by them have only swelled the pride and presumption peculiar to that people." It was precisely the enjoyment of those liberties and their pride and presumption that made the colonists desire independence and would make them willing to make considerable sacrifices to achieve it.

Before arriving back in Paris in June 1768, de Kalb translated articles from American newspapers from English to French and sent them on to his handler to supplement his personal observations. His reception was not what he had expected. Choiseul had lost interest in the American colonies, and in de Kalb's reports. The foreign minister's attention, for now, was on the conquest of Corsica, and he had no time for his returning spy. De Kalb sought an audience with Choiseul but was repeatedly rebuffed. They finally met the following year at a social event. "You returned too soon from America, and your labors are therefore of no use to me," de Kalb was told. "You need not send me any more reports about that country."

Choiseul might have lost interest in de Kalb's findings, but for the next decade—and with increasing intensity after that—the French continued to seek ways to help what they routinely referred to as the American "insurgents." By 1776, at least a year before the Battle of Saratoga and France's recognition of American independence, French interests were covertly shipping arms, ammunition, and other supplies to the rebels, and the following year, a meeting was arranged between de Kalb and an immensely rich young nobleman eager to risk everything for the American cause. This was Marie-Joseph Paul Yves Roch Gilbert du Motier, or, as he is better known, the Marquis de Lafayette.

Lafayette was nineteen years old when he was introduced to de Kalb, who was described to him as a man "whose experience and counsels might be valuable" to him. The young marquis "is a prodigy for his age," de Kalb wrote, "full of courage, spirit, judgement, good manners, feelings of generosity and zeal for the cause of liberty." De Kalb had developed a "zeal for the cause of liberty," too, although his was also informed by his desire to be of professional service in a war where his abilities would be recognized and rewarded.

The Americans needed more than the idealism of young aristocrats like Lafayette, de Kalb believed. If they had any hope of success against the British, they could not rely on green recruits. What would be required by the colonists, "now in the position of mere children," de Kalb said, "is some foreign troops." They needed battled-tested leaders, of course, and he was eager to make his thirty-two years of experience available. Other European officers were interested in the cause as well—"gentlemen of rank and fortune," as Silas Deane, the Continental Congress's secret envoy in Paris, described them—and they, too, wished to participate. Whispered negotiations ensued, and de Kalb was back and forth between Paris and Versailles, eventually obtaining a two-year furlough from the French army and, thanks to Deane, a commission in George Washington's new army. It was during this winter of intrigue that, for reasons that remain somewhat mysterious, de Kalb was first referred to, in official correspondence, as "Monsieur Le Baron." (Other titles were also questionable. Without proper authorization, Deane signed agreements with both de Kalb and Lafayette, making them major generals in the Continental army—a matter that would have to be sorted out later, when both were actually on American soil.)

Not everyone was enthusiastic about Lafayette's "zeal for the cause of liberty," however. His family was against the scheme. So was the court of Louis XVI. Agents were sent to arrest the young nobleman to prevent his departure but, on the *Victoire,* a ship Lafayette purchased out of his own fortune, he, de Kalb, and several other ambitious French officers slipped away in March 1777. For three weeks, they laid anchor in a Spanish port, while Lafayette, his family, and the court came to terms with the marquis's plans. Learning of their opposition to the scheme, de Kalb "advised him to sell the ship," because "this folly will cost him dearly. But if it be said that he has done a foolish thing, it may be answered that he acted from the most honorable motives and that he can hold up his head before all high-minded men." The adventure was off to a rocky start—Lafayette was seasick when they set out—but they reached open seas in mid-April. Even then, with British men-of-war prowling the Atlantic, they were not out of danger.

It was a "long and painful voyage," de Kalb told his wife, "not entirely without anxiety every time we saw some ships, all the more so since we had decided to defend ourselves, though we were poorly equipped for the purpose." This did not prove necessary, and on June 13, 1777, the *Victoire* reached South Carolina.

CHAPTER TWO

"Proud and Jealous of Their Freedom"

Strong winds prevented the *Victoire* from sailing into port at Charles Town, and the ship moored instead in Winyah Bay, outside Georgetown, some sixty miles to the north. The Marquis de Lafayette, Baron de Kalb, and the others would have to make the trek overland, which would prove arduous for them all. But until the more serious business of war began, the young French aristocrat was enjoying himself, enchanted by his first glimpse of the American South.

The weather the morning after their arrival "was beautiful," he wrote, recording his impressions in third person.

> The novelty of all that surrounded him—the room, the bed covered with mosquito nets, the black servant who came to ask his commands, the beauty and foreign aspect of the country which he beheld from his windows, and which was covered by a rich vegetation—all united to produce on M. de Lafayette a magical effect, and excite in him a variety of inexpressible sensations.

These would give way, soon enough, to a less rapturous response. They couldn't get enough horses to ride the sixty miles to Charles Town, so for much of the trek the men walked, sometimes barefoot, through swamps and over hot sand. It was hard going, but de Kalb did as well as any of the others. "I believe I'll bury all our young men," he said.

When they finally reached Charles Town, according to one of their officers, they looked like "beggars and bandits." Once they had cleaned up, however, there were eight days of "feasts and celebrations," and Lafayette again expressed his admiration for the Americans. "A simplicity of manners, a desire to please, the love of country and liberty" were everywhere. "The richest man and the poorest are upon the same social level, and although there are some great fortunes in the country, I defy one to discover the least difference in the bearing of one man to another"—except, of course, for the institution of slavery, of which Lafayette publicly disapproved.

Charles Town "is one of the most attractive, the best built, and inhabited by the most agreeable people that I have ever seen . . . There are no poor people in America, not even what may be called peasants. Every man has his own property, and each has the same rights with the greatest land-owner in the country." This was something of an exaggeration, though other visitors, accustomed to far more stratified societies of Europe, were similarly impressed by the extent to which a nascent democracy really was operating, even in the slaveholding South.

There was no question, of course, that Charles Town's so-called rice kings enjoyed themselves in a way most residents of this city did not, though even its mechanics and artisans enjoyed a higher standard of living than did those of the big cities of the North. Charles Town was wealthier than any other city in North America, and its fourth-largest port—and the only one still operating unimpeded when those of New York and Philadelphia were in British hands. This made the city especially attractive to the British, who had tried—and failed—to capture it the previous year. It was also a city that foreign officers would love to occupy, for understandable reasons. The people of Charles Town "live rapidly, not willingly letting go untasted any of the pleasures of life," a German visitor at the time observed. Their "manner of life, dress, equipages, furniture, everything denotes a higher degree of taste and love of show, and less frugality than in the northern provinces." There was a "grand dinner" given in Lafayette's honor "that lasted five hours," during which, the young nobleman said, the guests "drank many healths and I spoke very bad English." De Kalb served as his teacher and translator of this language, which Lafayette said, with evident pride, "I am beginning now to use a little."

What seems to have escaped the young Frenchman's notice—early on, anyway—was the extent to which South Carolina's wealth and charm, and especially Charles Town's, were possible only because they were built on an institution he professed to deplore. By the time of Lafayette's arrival, Charles Town was the fourth-largest city in America, behind only Boston, Philadelphia, and New York, and one of the richest. Half of its twelve thousand residents were Black slaves, with thousands of others living and working on the rice and indigo plantations outside of it. Charles Town was also America's largest center of the slave trade, outranking Richmond and New Orleans. An early South Carolina constitution, adopted before the city was established, gave freemen "absolute power and authority over Negro slaves." Even so, the slave owners were utterly dependent on the people over whom they exercised this near-total control. The slaves not only knew more about the cultivation of rice than the planters did but also proved far better able to survive the malarial summers of the South Carolina lowcountry, having developed immunities in Africa. Over time, the colony, as one visitor wrote, came to look "more like a Negro country than like a Country settled by white people."

Charles Town also became a financial and commercial center thanks to the slave trade. The buying and selling of other human beings "required enormous capital outlays, so Charles Town merchants turned to the Caribbean and English connections for credit and made their profits by wharf-side auctions of slaves to Low Country planters, who usually paid in rice," Walter J. Fraser Jr. wrote in his history of the city. "Aggressively expanding their acreage and buying more slaves, planters mortgaged both to Charles Town merchants, who knew, as one Carolinian wrote in the 1730s, that 'Negroes' were 'the bait proper for Catching a Carolina Planter, as certain as Beef to catch a Shark.'"

Those were boom times for Charles Town merchants, for dozens of whom "the profits were enormous." During that decade, almost twenty thousand slaves were imported from Africa, and more than 30 percent of them were brought in by one company. The leading families of the city—who would figure prominently in the drive toward independence—were all dependent, in one way or another, on the slave trade. Henry Laurens, who would emerge as a highly compromised critic of the slave trade, ran a firm that handled the sale of more than seven hundred slaves per year, brought to the wharf in more than sixty cargos. Laurens's family, like the Brewtons, Pinckneys, and Mottes, grew rich from the slave trade, giving a special tone and temper to the city and to the colony. The richest families intermarried, forming "alliances," consolidating their wealth, and buying plantations of their own, all the while living most of the year in elegant houses near the waterfront. They also consolidated their power. To be elected to public office, a man had to own five hundred acres of land or ten slaves, or other forms of property worth at least one thousand pounds sterling. This alone limited potential officeholders and the population that elected them to fewer than five hundred people.

The city's elite, Robert N. Rosen wrote in *A Short History of Charleston,*

> was able to do as it pleased, defying many of the standards of its time, because slavery made it an elite without opposition. Over time the planters, the great merchants and the elite of colonial Charlestown developed a way of life distinguished not only by great wealth but also by the elevation of pleasure and pleasure seeking to the highest of social goals.

Luxury items—including cloth from Russia and Holland and wine from Portugal—were carried in the shops. Dr. Alexander Garden, one of the elite himself, wrote that "the gentlemen planters . . . are absolutely above every occupation but eating, drinking, lolling, smoking, and sleeping, which five modes of action constitute the essence of their life and existence."

This was somewhat unfair, as the Revolution, which tested the mettle of these men, would demonstrate. But it was not without some basis in fact, as everyday life in the city bore out. Whites and Blacks in equal numbers walked the streets of the city, though the laws and customs that governed their actions differed radically. Womanizing was the other great pastime of the planter class, many of whose men seem to have viewed preying on enslaved women—including rape—as acceptable behavior. "The enjoyment of a negro or mulatto woman," Josiah Quincy of Boston observed when he visited Charles Town, "is spoken of as quite a common thing; no reluctance, delicacy or shame is made about the matter." A letter to the editor of *The South Carolina Gazette* noted that Charles Town bachelors and widowers "in a Strait for Women" need only "wait for the next Shipping from the Coast of

Guinny. Those African ladies are of a strong robust Constitution [able] to serve them Night as well as Day."

Charles Wesley, a British clergyman and a founder of Methodism, observed when he visited the city in the 1730s that white children had slaves of their own age "to tyrannize over, to beat and abuse out of sport." White women looked down on domestic chores, which were considered the work of household slaves. Even tradesmen often had slaves do their work for them. Rosen quotes a visitor who saw "tradesmen go through the city followed by a Negro carrying their tools—barbers who are supported in idleness and ease by their negroes who do the business, and in fact many of the mechanics bear nothing more of their trade than the name."

The stench of the slave trade was, in a very real sense, inescapable. "Following the sale of the slave cargoes," Fraser wrote,

the putrid holds of the slavers, awash with excrement, urine, and vomit, would be "smoked" by the crews who plunged heated bullets into buckets of vinegar to clean the vessels for the loading of outward bound cargoes of commodities. Despite these efforts, sailors often refused to serve on slave ships after several voyages as the smells of the human cargoes seem to permeate the timbers. As the common saying went: "You can smell a slaver five miles downwind on the open ocean."

The men who ran these shipments were "a rough set of people," one visitor said, but were nonetheless "caressed" by the slave merchants when they came into port "on account of the great profits of their commissions."

As might be expected, slaveholders, slave traders, and white people generally lived in fear of slave insurrections and passed harsh slave codes in the hope of reducing their likelihood. The bloodiest uprising in the country took place in late summer of 1739 twenty miles south of Charles Town. Slaves hoping to escape to Spanish Florida killed a dozen whites and burned their houses before being overtaken by planters, who shot twelve of them; a year later, slaves north of the city were planning to revolt before their plans were made known by one of their fellows. Nearly seventy of the alleged conspirators were rounded up, with several hanged "to intimidate other Negroes." By one account, the planters "cutt off [the slaves'] heads and set them up at every Mile Post they came to."

City dwellers feared their own domestic workers, and the fact that whites and Blacks lived close together in Charles Town meant their relations were more complicated than on the plantations. A jury found, for example, that the "unrestrained intercourse and indulgence of familiarities" between the two races "are destructive of the respect and subserviency which our laws recognize as due from one to the other." The city allowed police to "break doors, gates or windows" if they suspected that meetings were taking place to teach slaves to read or write, which was illegal. Black-run churches were similarly viewed with suspicion as dangerous "nurseries of self government." Blacks caught in the streets after dark, unless they were carrying a letter of permission from their owners, could be locked up overnight and subject to whipping in the morning. To secure their release, their owners would have to pay a fine.

As troubling as all these attitudes and actions strike us today, and in time offended Lafayette, they were taken for granted throughout much of the American South and in fact figured prominently in the region's drive for independence. "Absolute and unquestioned rule over the lives of other human beings, a rule that included, as a practical matter, life-and-death decisions, gave to the planter class a justified feeling of absolute power," Rosen wrote. These assumptions were especially pronounced in Charles Town but existed in Richmond and New Orleans and Savannah as well and on plantations throughout the South. "Each planter," as Rosen puts it, "was king of all he owned. His friends and neighbors were the government and the courts. In all the history of America, it is doubtful that a more absolutely powerful class or group ever ruled a city, colony, or state." And when the power of that class was challenged by the mother country—after decades in which its members had been left to govern themselves—they were indignant.

When the British tried to enforce the Stamp Act in 1765, Christopher Gadsden, one of the city's elite, led the opposition, declaring the act inconsistent "with that inherent right of every British subject, not to be taxed but by his own consent, or that of his representatives." Mobs calling themselves the "Sons of Liberty" and by some accounts directed by Gadsden rioted, erected a forty-foot-high gallows near the harbor, buried a coffin bearing the sign "American Liberty," and burned in effigy a stamp distributor. A decade later, following Boston's lead,

Charles Town, again with Gadsden leading the opposition, staged its own Tea Party, dumping shipments into the Cooper River.

It was Edmund Burke, the prominent member of the Whig opposition in Parliament, who seems to have best understood the role of slavery in the South's push for independence—which, contrary to current assertions, had nothing at all to do with fear that the British threatened its so-called Peculiar Institution. Great Britain posed no such threat, and there is scant evidence that southerners believed that it did. The Americans rebelled, in large measure, to defend the rights they believed they possessed as loyal subjects of the Crown. They rebelled, too, because their experience of self-government had shaped their character as a people. Having become accustomed to governing themselves, they were increasingly suspicious of attempts to limit their liberty. They were also sensitive to being taxed. This should have surprised no one in Parliament because, as Burke told the House of Commons just weeks before Lexington and Concord, "the great contests for freedom in this country were from the earliest times chiefly upon the question of taxing." Clearly, more than policy was operative here. The very temperament, disposition, and understanding of themselves made it impossible, under the circumstances, for Americans not to rebel.

The colonies, Burke reminded the other members of Parliament, had been settled by Protestants, who are "the most adverse to all implicit submission of mind and opinion. This is a persuasion not only favorable to liberty, but built upon it." This posture of defiance was true in the northern colonies, so long associated with Pilgrims and Puritans, but in the Anglican South as well, where a different set of circumstances made the determination to rebel at any suspicion of British tyranny all the more acute. There was a paradox here, of course. The "spirit of liberty" among the southerners, Burke argued, "was still more high and haughty than in those to the northward," precisely because of the institution of slavery. In Virginia and the Carolinas, "they have a vast multitude of slaves. Where this is the case in any part of the world, those who are free are by far the most proud and jealous of their freedom." Burke in no way intended

> to commend the superior morality of this sentiment, which
> has at least as much pride as virtue in it; but I cannot alter
> the nature of man. The fact is so; and that these people of the

southern colonies are much more strongly, and with a higher and stubborn spirit, attached to liberty, than those to the northward . . . In such a people, the haughtiness of domination combined with the spirit of freedom, fortifies it, and renders it invincible.

Men from the Continent, unlike Burke, often took a less nuanced view of the chattel slavery that they witnessed not only in the American colonies but also, in the case of France, in their own New World possessions. Lafayette, of course, would emerge as an outspoken and imaginative abolitionist. Influenced by the *philosophes* of the European Enlightenment, in 1783, Lafayette would write to Washington of a "wild scheme" he had dreamed up, in which the two of them would buy acreage where the enslaved workers at Mount Vernon and Washington's outlying properties could work as tenant farmers. The project, if successful, would then spread in popularity throughout the United States and, eventually, to the West Indies.

"If it be a Wild scheme," Lafayette told Washington, "I had rather be mad in this way, than to be thought wise in [another] task." Washington responded with praise for his young protégé. The idea "which you propose as a precedent, to encourage the emancipation of the black people of this Country from the state of Bondage [in which] they are held, is a striking evidence of the benevolence of your Heart." Washington found the plan commendable but remained uncommitted. While he supported the idea in principle and would "be happy to join you in so laudable a work," he would prefer to discuss the details when they next met in person.

The plan—without Washington's participation—moved forward, with some alterations. Three years after broaching the subject with Washington, Lafayette wrote again to his former commander about "that Experiment which you know is my Hobby Horse," informing Washington that he had purchased a plantation in French Guiana, intending to free the slaves on it. They would work the land, with the assurance that they could not be sold. The purchase of the estate, Washington told Lafayette, "with a view of emancipating the slaves on it, is a generous and noble proof of your humanity," and he sincerely hoped that "a like spirit would diffuse itself generally into the minds of the people of this country." Even so, like almost all of his countrymen, North and South, Washington believed that the matter could not be rushed. A sudden and immediate emancipation "would, I really believe, be productive of much inconvenience and mischief; but by degrees it certainly might, and assuredly ought to be effected; and that too by Legislative authority."

All that would come later, of course—after the war had been won. For now, Lafayette was enjoying himself in balmy Charles Town, while de Kalb—the more seasoned and less idealistic soldier—set about the serious business of inspecting the city's defenses.

CHAPTER THREE

"The Principal Theater of the War"

Charles Town's defenses, de Kalb learned, held up surprisingly well when the British first tried to establish a base of operations on Sullivan's Island, at the entrance to the city's harbor. That was the previous June, when an armada carrying three thousand redcoats arrived—and Benjamin Lincoln, commanding an army of six thousand Americans, showed up to oppose them. Fear had been building for months, not least that the British were encouraging slave revolts. "Opulent and Sensible" residents of Charles Town would remain loyal to the Crown, the British told themselves, while the "Low and Ignorant" would not. A Council of Safety was created to maintain order, and the Provincial Congress urged people on the way to church to "take with them their Fire-Arms and Ammunition." Residents suspected of conspiring with Blacks to set fires and sow discontent were tarred and feathered.

While the well-to-do fled to the countryside and "half the best houses were empty," Lincoln supervised the construction of defenses, which included an unlikely-looking fortification composed of "Mud & Sand, faced with Palmetto Tree[s]," at the southern end of the island. The British attacked on a morning in early summer of that year, and cannonballs that were fired into the palmettos did little damage. "A breach in the wood is impossible," de Kalb reported, for "it never bursts, and cannonballs and their holes close up again, or better, when the blow has lost its force, the shot is sent back by the elasticity of the wood." By evening, the British flotilla withdrew, battered and badly beaten, and hobbled back to New York. "Thus," one of their officers said, was "the Invincible British Navy defeated by a battery which it was supposed would not have stood one Broadside."

Having failed to take Charles Town, the British turned their attentions to the smaller port 120 miles to the south, at Savannah, Georgia. Here, in late December 1778, they succeeded spectacularly, with only three killed and ten wounded, compared to eighty-three Americans killed or wounded, and more than 450 taken prisoner. The British also seized three ships, forty-eight cannons, and twenty-three mortars when Savannah fell. (A joint effort to retake the port in October 1779 failed miserably, and Savannah would remain in British hands until the war's end.)

De Kalb's inspection of Charles Town's remaining defenses—and the story of how well they had served during the last attack—was cause for optimism, but there were other reasons for hope as well. American troops drilled for the entertainment of their European visitors, and de Kalb was "astonished by their precision, for such new troops." The arrival of the French officers was encouraging in itself, and news that they had come to help the cause of American independence appeared in newspapers as far north as Boston.

After eight days, Lafayette, de Kalb, and their aides were off to Philadelphia, about 670 miles north—on a modern interstate highway—and their troubles began anew. Their splendid carriages broke down after a few days, and the men had to abandon them and much of their baggage. First, they rode on horseback, but the heat proved too much for their mounts, and they too broke down. Then the men walked. One of their traveling companions said that de Kalb, "though approaching sixty," had little trouble keeping up with the younger men. He "pressed forward with firm purpose, not without occasional indignant outbursts about the heat or the insects." By the third week of July, when they departed Annapolis, only Lafayette and de Kalb were healthy enough to continue.

They arrived in Philadelphia a week later, by which time the other members of the party seem to have caught up, "in a more pitiable condition even than when we first came into Charles Town." Again they cleaned themselves up, put on their uniforms, and made their way to Independence Hall. There, to their dismay, they were "received like dogs," in Lafayette's words, ordered to wait in the street, and addressed,

Charles-François, the Chevalier du Buysson, recalled, "as a group of adventurers," which left them "stupefied." Silas Deane, they would discover, had exceeded his authority back in Paris, and appointing foreigners as generals had outraged Americans who had earned their rank on the battlefield, including Nathanael Greene and Henry Knox. Tense negotiations followed, and three days later, Congress made Lafayette a major general. It was September before a decision about de Kalb and the others was finally rendered. While de Kalb waited, Lafayette on September 11 fought at the Battle of Brandywine—and fought admirably, suffering a minor wound. Washington was impressed.

It was not until later in the month that Congress reversed itself, offering de Kalb a commission as a major general. Throughout the difficult negotiations, his demeanor had won over the politicians. The more they saw, the more they liked, and James Lovell, who had greeted the foreign officers rudely when they arrived at Independence Hall, was now an admirer. "Baron de Kalb speaks English well," he told a New Hampshire congressman. In "manners and looks," Lovell said, de Kalb resembled Washington himself.

By this time, Philadelphia had fallen to the British, Congress was meeting in York, Pennsylvania, and Washington's army had again been beaten, this time at Germantown, just outside Philadelphia. Prospects seemed bleak then and there, but the victory at Saratoga in September 1777, under Horatio Gates, raised hopes (even as it made Washington's leadership seem increasingly suspect). Most of all, Saratoga persuaded France that the American army was more formidable than they imagined and that the likelihood of the rebellion succeeding was better than the French had imagined. Always eager to weaken its longtime enemy in London, and possibly regain American territories that it had lost in the Seven Years' War, France recognized American independence and signed the formal treaty of alliance in February 1778, clearing the way for the French to enter the war openly, without subterfuge.

De Kalb was with Washington at Valley Forge when the treaty was signed, and for the celebration that followed. Mostly, though, he performed routine but important administrative duties to help prepare the Continental army for the coming campaign. Washington had come to appreciate de Kalb's experience in logistics but also in military engineering, so he was put to work inspecting outlying fortifications. De Kalb was with Washington, too, for the winter encampment at Middlebrook,

New Jersey, in 1778–79, and at Morristown, New Jersey, too, the next year—where it was "so cold the ink freezes in my pen," he wrote, and the ice on the Passaic River was six feet thick. "Those who have been only in Valley Forge and Middlebrook during the last two winters, but have not tasted the cruelties of this one, know not what it is to suffer," de Kalb said. Again, he was doing routine duty, with no opportunity whatever for military glory.

"It is odd," he told his wife,

> that in the two years I have been in service here, constantly with the army, the troops under my command (and I have always had very strong divisions) have not taken part in any battle or engagement, and that I myself, so to speak, have not seen a gun go off. Were I a braggart I might go on to say that since I have been with the army the enemy have had little success, and that they are afraid to attack us because they know I am here, but the coincidence is really singular.

The enemy had racked up no significant successes, and those divisions under de Kalb's command really were first-rate. The last major confrontation in the North had been at Monmouth, in 1778, and while that engagement ended in a draw, Washington's Continentals, drilled by Baron von Steuben since Valley Forge, had put up a far more impressive fight than the British had bargained for. Since then, things had ground to a halt. Washington had managed to pen the British army in at New York, preventing its breaking out, but beyond that, the war had become a kind of stalemate, and was recognized as such by both sides.

De Kalb had been given command of troops from Delaware and Maryland, and they were considered among the best trained in the Continental army. Two years earlier, at the Battle of Long Island, the Maryland line saved Washington's army from annihilation. But there was not much for them to do in the North, given the impasse that had been reached, so Washington dispatched de Kalb and his 1,400 or so troops to the South, where the British now showed every indication of concentrating their energies. In mid-February 1780, another flotilla of British warships, this one carrying several thousand redcoats, had appeared outside Charles Town, and the city was under siege. The fall of Charles Town, should it occur, Washington feared, would "involve the most calamitous consequences to the whole state of South Carolina," and possibly the entire region. If the city fell, he told General Lincoln, still in command of the garrison at Charles Town and the highest-ranking Continental officer in the entire South, "there is much reason to believe, the Southern States will become the principal theatre of the war."

With that likelihood in mind, Washington had ordered de Kalb and his troops toward the Carolinas, though the commander in chief thought they might not arrive in time to save the city. Lafayette, meanwhile, would head north, to link up with Washington's main army. De Kalb sent his troops on ahead and left Philadelphia shortly thereafter. This time, the British knew better than to waste their fire on the palmetto walls. They would approach by land and sea, and by early April, their siege lines were creeping closer to the town's defenses.

CHAPTER FOUR

"Great Guns Bursting and Wounded Men Groaning"

The siege of Charles Town began on March 29, 1780, a Wednesday. The commander of the garrison inside the city had done what he could—given the shortages of everything—to build new fortifications and repair those that had been damaged during the attack the year before. Even so, as George Bancroft wrote in the tenth volume of his 1879 history of America, the city "had neither citadel, nor fort, nor ramparts, nor stone, nor materials for building any thing more than field-works of loose sand, kept together by boards and logs."

There was work to be done, and their struggles were real, but conditions were better in Charles Town than they were for the army in the North. For the second year in a row, General Washington had established winter quarters outside Morristown, New Jersey, about forty miles due west of New York City. From Morristown, Washington's men, protected by a range of hills, could block any British move up the Hudson or, marching through New Jersey, toward Philadelphia, where the Second Continental Congress met. His troops could also ambush enemy foraging parties, which they did to great effect. Above all—unlike the troops in South Carolina—they could rest until spring. They would not break camp until June. But that was not as easy as it might at first appear. The ten thousand to twelve thousand soldiers camped at Morristown hunkered down in crude log shacks, enduring record cold and rarely getting enough to eat.

The commander of the garrison at Charles Town was Benjamin

Lincoln, who, at five feet nine and weighing more than two hundred pounds, looked like he never missed a meal. In the autumn of 1778, at the age of forty-five, Lincoln had been made commander in chief of the Continental army's entire Southern Department. One of the first major generals appointed by Congress, Lincoln was a Massachusetts native, no more comfortable in the climate of the Carolinas than any of the other northerners who found themselves in the South, and probably a good deal less so. Some of these men were gaunt by this time in the war, but not Lincoln. Unlike Washington and de Kalb, who were six feet tall or taller and looked like giants on horseback, Lincoln was "so uncommonly broad a person," William Maclay, a senator from Pennsylvania, said, "as to seem of less stature than he was."

Also, he limped, the result of being shot in the ankle in the action at Saratoga, in an embarrassing episode typical of what can happen when uniforms are not uniform. He was riding through the woods that morning when he spotted a knot of soldiers impossible to identify. "At first," Lincoln said, "I could not distinguish them by their dress from our own troops, two of them having scarlet clothes, others being in blue"—like the Hessians—"and some being clad like our militia." A few of the patriots, moreover, wore British uniforms, captured from the enemy. The Continental troops wore blue, "while our militia resembled in dress the people of the country who had joined the army," meaning they had no uniforms at all.

By the time Lincoln realized that the men he was approaching were the enemy, two in proper British redcoats opened fire. Carried into Albany, Lincoln underwent the first of a series of surgeries that continued for two years. Pieces of broken bone would be removed with alarming regularity. Sometimes fragments worked their way to the surface and punctured the skin. When it was all over, Lincoln's right leg was two inches shorter than the left.

Lincoln also suffered from narcolepsy or, as Maclay called it, "somnolency." During meals—which he otherwise enjoyed immensely—or "when driving himself in a chaise, he would fall into a sound sleep." He was known, while dictating dispatches in battle, to nod off. He "slept between the sentences," but would then snap to, and continue as if he had never fallen asleep at all. People found amusement in this condition of his, but William Jackson, who served as his aide and was later secretary to the Constitutional Convention, defended him. "Sir," he said to one such jokester, "General Lincoln was never asleep when it was necessary for him to be awake."

Lincoln did not seem like much of a soldier in other ways, too. A pious New Englander, "he always frowned on profanity and impropriety." He was also more methodical than decisive, which struck some as evidence of sloth. Although he could be the object of ridicule, he avoided duels, which would also—to some—suggest cowardice. Once, when provoked at dinner by another officer, Lincoln said, "I apprehend, Sir, you are disposed to take too much liberty. If you repeat any thing of this kind, I shall be obliged to tell this company facts, which I know respecting you, that will make their hair stand on end." This ended the matter.

Lincoln was also a man of greater strength and stamina than one might assume. In the cities of the South, manual labor was the work of Black people, not white, and in Charles Town, Lincoln's men were reluctant to toil on the fortifications. The army was always in need of soldiers, and Lincoln tried, unsuccessfully, to persuade the South Carolina Legislature to allow Black men to enlist. Bancroft pondered the shortsightedness of this policy as well as its injustice. "The system of slaveholding," Bancroft wrote, "kept away from defensive service not only more than half the population, whom the planters would not suffer to be armed, but the numerous whites needed to watch the black men, if they were to be kept in bondage while war was waging." Men "deriving their livelihood from the labor of slaves ceased to respect labor, and shunned it as a disgrace." Slaveholders not only opposed permitting slaves to fight; many of them resisted allowing their precious property to labor on the defenses lest they contract smallpox.

Even so, slaves could be rented, and Lincoln did his best under these impossible circumstances. "Setting the example of labor," Bancroft wrote, "he was the first to go to work on them in the morning, and would not return till late in the evening." Knowing these Black men to be hardworking and reliable, he "would spend whole days with the work details, sometimes handling pick and shovel himself," Clifford K. Shipton wrote in *George Washington's Generals*. "Considering the climate and his weight, this was heroism."

Lincoln's efforts, while commendable, were inadequate. In early April, as batteries from both armies opened up, British warships under the direction of Admiral Mariot Arbuthnot easily swept past the forts that guarded the entrance to the town's harbor. As they did so, the siege lines drew closer, and the inhabitants of Charles Town were at once terrified and strangely defiant. Saying he regretted "the Effusion of Blood, and the Distresses which must now commence" should his proposal be rejected, Sir Henry Clinton, commander in chief of the British force, offered Lincoln and the people of Charles Town terms of surrender. Sensible as always, Lincoln took these overtures seriously, but the city fathers did not. On the morning of April 13, after hearing that their offer was rejected, the British bombarded the town for two hours straight, with predictable results.

As the cannonballs began to hit their targets, Johann Ewald, a Hessian officer serving under Clinton at Charles Town, could hear a "loud wailing of female voices." Fires broke out, and buildings were burning. When packs of dogs began roaming the streets, soldiers were ordered to "kill all the dogs they shall find," but refrain from shooting them; this was not to spare the poor animals but to conserve ammunition. At Lincoln's recommendation, South Carolina Governor John Rutledge, with a handful of aides, managed to flee the city, but one of them—the governor's brother Edward—was promptly taken prisoner. The British drained a moat that Lincoln's men had dug, crossed it on foot, and completed their siege lines.

Lincoln continued to negotiate, asking Clinton for a ten-day truce that would enable him to get his troops safely out of the city, which enraged what passed for municipal officials. They vowed that if he even tried to depart, they would destroy any boats that could transport his withdrawing army and open the gates to the enemy.

Out in the countryside, Lieutenant Colonel Banastre Tarleton's British Legion patrolled the river crossings to prevent the arrival of reinforcements from the North and to make it impossible for Lincoln's troops to withdraw safely from the city. This was the kind of assignment at which Tarleton, since sailing to America with Lord Cornwallis in 1776, excelled. He was twenty-five, highly intelligent, by some accounts merciless, and perfectly willing to make independent decisions on the fly. Tarleton believed, as Euripides is to have said centuries earlier, that "the god of war hates those who hesitate." The men under Tarleton's command—Americans all—found his spirited leadership infectious, making the British Legion a formidable foe. (He would have relished the idea of taking on de Kalb, but he would not get the opportunity; de Kalb, through no fault of his own, made it no farther than Hillsborough, North Carolina, three hundred miles away, when the British assaulted Charles Town.)

On the evening of April 13, when fires from the two-hour bombardment still burned in Charles Town, Tarleton captured a slave who was acting as a messenger for the patriots. The slave was carrying a letter from Lieutenant Colonel Isaac Huger (pronounced *you-GEE*) that was intended for Lincoln back in Charles Town. Tarleton bribed the messenger, who revealed the whereabouts of Huger's camp and agreed to lead them there. Huger, with five hundred men who were reinforced by Continental cavalry under William Washington (a second cousin of the commander in chief), waited at Biggin Bridge on the banks of the Cooper River, about thirty-five miles north of the besieged capital.

Guided by their captive, Tarleton's dragoons set out in the night, quietly picking their way through dark swamps and dense forests, and arrived outside the Continentals' camp several hours before sunup. At 3 a.m., they burst out of the woods, scattering the cavalry who were to guard the bridge and the supply train. Tarleton's cavalry did their work with sabers, and the Legion's infantry finished the job with bayonets. A reputation for cruelty that would dog Tarleton for the rest of the war was already building. An officer's attempts to surrender were ignored, and the British horsemen "mangled [him] in the most shocking manner." But it could have been worse, Clinton argued in his memoirs. "The precipitation with which the enemy had fled and the swampiness of the ground . . . prevented the slaughter which might else have ensued," he noted, and allowed some of the other enemy soldiers to get away altogether. Although the battle ended quickly, the scene was far from quiet. There were, of course, the groans and screams of the wounded and dying, and at about 7 p.m. the following night, a storehouse containing two casks of gunpowder caught fire. The building exploded with a tremendous roar.

Tarleton's British Legion took a hundred or so prisoners as well as more than forty wagons loaded with supplies. They also seized more than eighty dragoon horses. A shortage of mounts had been a problem for Tarleton's men since the flotilla carrying their horses had first sailed out of New York Harbor four months earlier. All the way from

New York to Georgia, the ships encountered "blustering, disagreeable Weather," Tarleton said. Storms that the ships had struggled to plow through were so severe that hundreds of the trained horses on board were injured or too sick to be of any future use and had simply been thrown overboard. Only three hundred made the journey successfully. On one of the transports, just roughly thirty horses managed to survive. "The horses of both officers and men, which had been embarked in excellent order, were destroyed, owing to the badness of the vessels employed to transport them," Tarleton said, "or to the severity of the weather on the passage."

The mounts Tarleton and his men captured in the engagement would go far to replace those lost at sea. Some of these proud horsemen—until now—had been reduced to walking or riding inferior animals. And they had come at very low cost: none of Tarleton's men had been killed and only three wounded. This compared to fourteen Continentals killed and nineteen wounded. Huger got away, and so did William Washington, but a key supply line to Charles Town had been cut, and an important river crossing was now under British control. Benjamin Harrison, the chairman of the Board of War, told George Washington, who was still in Morristown, that Tarleton's unfortunate victory at Biggin Bridge had "cut the communications" with Charles Town, which "must in time surrender for want of provision."

The commander in chief was appalled by the news but expressed his disgust with frigid restraint. "I am sorry to hear of Hugers misfortune— on many accts," Washington wrote to James Duane of the Continental Congress. An officer "may be beaten and yet acquire honor, but disgrace must for ever accompany surprizes."

Over the next few days, Tarleton's charged-up dragoons enjoyed themselves, but they did so in ways that were likely to make more Carolinians than ever before turn against the Crown and support the cause of independence. One morning, "three ladies came to our camp in great distress," Lieutenant Anthony Allaire, serving with the loyalists, wrote in his diary. They said they had been "most shockingly abused by a plundering villain," who had ridden up to Fair-Lawn Barony, the plantation of "Lady Jane" Colleton, a widow. They ransacked the house, and when the "plundering villain" tried to rape her, she fought back, and was "badly cut in the hand by a broadsword." A doctor in the camp dressed her wound, and then an officer and twelve other soldiers rode to the plantation of a Mrs. Fayssoux, "whom this infamous villain had likewise abused in the same manner." There they found "a most accomplished, amiable lady in the greatest distress imaginable," though once the doctor drew blood, "she was more composed." The next morning, the women went to the camp "to testify against the cursed villain that abused them in this horrid manner," and he was "secured and sent to Headquarters for trial." The day after that, as Allaire and the doctor were escorting the women back to their plantations, they were met by a servant who told them that "there were more plunderers in the house." Their "melancholy," he said, "was truly deplorable."

What became of the "cursed villain" remains a mystery, but Washington Irving, in his writings on the American Revolution, claimed that the episode caused a permanent rift between Tarleton and Patrick Ferguson, a well-regarded Scottish commander of loyalist troops. According to Irving, Ferguson wanted the "cursed villain" hanged on the spot, but Tarleton, overruling him, had the charges dismissed. Ferguson was outraged, and, from that day forward, he disapproved of "Bloody Ban" and the way he allowed his men to conduct themselves, vowing never to serve with him again. If the story is true, come October, when he would need Tarleton's help, Major Ferguson might have come to regret the high-minded position he had taken.

Three weeks later, in early May, what was left of Huger's men joined forces with a regiment of Continental dragoons under Colonel Anthony Walton White on the Santee River near present-day Jamestown, South Carolina, about forty miles north of Charles Town. Across the river, another American force—newly recruited Virginians under Colonel Abraham Buford—had been desperately trying to get to Charles Town while there was still hope that it could be saved. Huger's troops had camped at Lenud's Ferry, sometimes spelled Lenneau's and Lenew's and pronounced *LEN-oo's*; Lenud, like Huger, was a Huguenot name. While Buford remained on the north side of the river, some of White's dragoons had taken eighteen British soldiers prisoner and brought them back to the crossing.

Tarleton, who happened to be headed toward Lenud's Ferry himself with 150 of his own dragoons, was not pleased with this news and urged his mount forward. Again, the Americans were caught by surprise. Tarleton's men charged at 3 p.m. on May 6, and White had no time to get his 350 troops across the river to meet the threat. The fight was over in minutes. The divided forces of the patriots were almost immediately overcome, the eighteen prisoners were released, and one hundred of White's men, including twelve officers, were killed or wounded, while Buford and his troops watched from across the Santee. White and at least one other officer managed to swim to safety, but others "who wished to follow their example," Tarleton wrote, "perished in the river."

Buford was admirably forthright in his report to the commander in chief. Again the patriots were surprised, and a lack of preparation cost them "the loss of every horse" and the "greatest part" of the men. Tarleton's dragoons "rush'd on them before a single horse could be bridled, Cut & hack'd many of them in a most shocking manner[.] Some were [killed] and many made prisoners." A few of the officers had taken to the water to get away, "which is little bet[t]er than being kill'd or taken." The action, Cornwallis reported, "totally demolished [the enemy's] Cavalry," gave the British control of all the relevant waterways, and closed off the last of the routes by which Lincoln's troops could get out of Charles Town.

Three days after the British victory at Lenud's Ferry, Clinton decided to bring the siege of Charles Town to a conclusion. Two hundred artillery pieces encircled the city, and he ordered them to pound it day and night. The efforts its inhabitants made to defend the town seem in retrospect to have been pathetic. They painted the steeple of St. Michael's Church black, for example, thinking this would make it harder for the British gunners to spot. It had the opposite effect. A cannonball that hit the church ricocheted, hitting the statue of William Pitt and tearing off its right arm. This was unintentional irony: the statue had been erected ten years earlier to honor the former prime minister for his support in the colonies' opposition to the Stamp Act.

The ensuing bombardment horrified even seasoned veterans like Brigadier General William Moultrie, who had led the successful defense of Charles Town in 1776 and in whose name the original palmetto fort had been renamed. It was "incessant," Moultrie said, with "cannonballs whizzing, and shells hissing continually amongst us; ammunition chests and temporary magazines blowing up; great guns bursting and wounded men groaning along the lines." The effect was like that of "meteors crossing each other, and bursting in the air; it appeared as if the stars were tumbling down." Some of the cannonballs had been heated so they would start fires when they landed, which they did. By this time, the Americans inside the city were so low on ammunition that they began to load their muskets with anything that was handy. This included shards of glass from broken bottles, which could inflict horrific damage but did nothing to hold off the enemy.

Three days later, the forty-two-day siege ended. At 11 a.m., on Friday, May 12, as a "Turkish march" played, 5,500 weary soldiers shuffled out of Charles Town, their colors cased, and, with their commander, were made prisoners of war. They were "thin, miserable, ragged, and very dirty," a German officer serving with the British said, "the most ragged Rabble I ever beheld." Considerable numbers of militiamen hid in the bombed-out town but trickled out over the next few days. One Hessian said the residents who had stayed in the city throughout the siege "looked greatly starved," and the houses were "full of [the] wounded."

The prisoners stacked their muskets—thousands of them—near the Charles Town arsenal, and while a strict accounting was never made, the British also took nearly four hundred cannons, more than thirty thousand rounds of ammunition, and "Large Quantities of Musket Cartridges, Arms, and other small Articles." They also seized four thousand pounds of "fixed ammunition," meaning that the shot had already been attached to the casing and was ready to be fired. This, as the British soon discovered, made them extremely dangerous to handle and store. Some of the muskets, moreover, were loaded, too, as the prisoners tried to warn their captors.

Almost two thousand of the Continental soldiers, with several hundred others captured a few months later in other engagements, would end up on prison ships, where, according to Bancroft, in "thirteen months one-third of the whole number perished by malignant fevers." Other prisoners "were impressed into the British service as mariners; several hundred young men were taken by violence on board transports, and forced to serve in a British regiment in Jamaica, leaving wives and young children to want. Of more than three thousand confined in prison-ships, all but about seven hundred were made away with." Over the course of the occupation, two thousand of the slaves who had sought asylum within the British lines "were shipped to a market in the West Indies." This was not official policy; much of the shipment was the work of individual British officers who stood to profit from the slaves' sale.

General Washington was still unaware that the city had fallen and said, on the day after its surrender, that he was "exceedingly anxious for the fate of Charles-Town." On May 29, *The Royal Gazette*, a loyalist newspaper in New York, reported the news, adding that it was the "DESIRE OF THE INHABITANTS" that they be rescued from "the tyranny" of those who supported independence. By June 11, Washington said he now had "no doubt" that Charles Town—and the only American army worthy of the name left in the South—had been lost.

On the afternoon after Charles Town's surrender, Hessian Captain Ewald was visiting a sick friend in the city when "an extraordinary blast" shook the house and all those around it, with window sashes rattling "as if they would tumble out of their frames." Rushing into the street, Ewald saw that the storehouse in which the captured muskets and ammunition were stored had blown up, and above what was left of it floated a "thick cloud of vapor." Johann Hinrichs, another Hessian officer, said he had watched as muskets "flew up into the air [and] ramrods and bayonet were blown onto the roofs of houses," while muskets continued to go off, on their own, for hours.

The townspeople were stunned by what was happening. Ewald recalled how "dreadful cries arose from all sides." As he made his way toward the storehouse, he passed the bodies of what he estimated to be sixty people, "burnt beyond recognition, half dead and, suffering from burns [who] writhed like worms on the ground." American militia, slaves, and even some British soldiers were frantically trying to put out fires, and many of them, Ewald said, "were killed or wounded by the gunshots which came from loaded muskets" in the storehouse cellar. When the fire spread toward the city's powder magazine, and someone claimed—mistakenly—that it too was on fire, panic ensued. People were running as far away from the structure as they could, and although they were "confoundedly frightened," as one of the American officers said, they "could not help laughing, to see the confusion and tumbling over each other." The body of one man, thrown in the initial blast, had been hurled into a church steeple, and Ewald saw "a number of mutilated bodies hanging on the farthest houses and lying in the streets."

People were stepping over charred and severed arms and legs. The gaol, where "lunatics and negroes" were chained "for trifling misdemeanors," burned down.

It was hours before the fires were brought under control and an assessment of the damage could be made, although it was only a guess. Major General William Croghan, a Virginian, estimated that "near a hundred" had lost their lives in the explosion and resulting fires. Among these, besides civilians, were British soldiers and officers, which was a blow to the loyalists. The loss of so many muskets was also distressing. The British had intended to use them, Hinrichs said, "to arm the back-country people, all of whom are loyalists, or at least pretend to be."

With Charles Town firmly in British hands, Lord Charles Cornwallis, second in command to Clinton until the latter returned to New York in early June, could now secure South Carolina, as Clinton had ordered him to do, and then sweep through North Carolina and into Virginia. As they did so, they could rouse the loyalist population to fight back against their independence-minded neighbors, putting down the rebellion once and for all. They could get the Americans to fight the war for them. Charles Town would be their base of operations, and if they had to find other weapons to put into the hands of the Americans loyal to the Crown, that would be an annoyance, a temporary setback only.

All the momentum now, as George Washington feared, was with the British. And the only other battle-ready Continental soldiers left in South Carolina were Buford's Virginians, which had just retreated from Lenud's Ferry. There were only four hundred of them, and they were rapidly losing men to illness and desertion. This was no great surprise given the demoralizing drubbing their cavalry had taken—and the news of Charles Town's fall.

CHAPTER FIVE

"The Blood Be Upon Your Head"

After Lenud's Ferry, when it had become clear that Charles Town was lost, Brigadier General Isaac Huger, now in command of American forces in the South Carolina lowcountry, ordered Abraham Buford's Virginians to withdraw into North Carolina. At Salisbury, they were to join up with de Kalb's soldiers, marching south from Washington's camp at Morristown. Buford and his men, battered and dispirited, did as they were told. As spring turned into early summer, they trudged their way toward Camden, which—a hundred miles north of Lenud's— was about halfway to their intended destination at Salisbury. There had been four hundred of them when they broke camp, but now there were only about 350, and it was impossible to know how many more they would lose along the way. There were North Carolina militia with them now, too, as well as Governor John Rutledge, who had managed to get out of Charles Town before its surrender. They were all headed away from the unpleasantness there, hoping to recover from their wounds and figure out what to do once they were out of immediate danger.

That, anyway, was the plan. But on May 22, a week after Huger, Buford, Rutledge, and all the others set off north along the Santee River Road, Lord Cornwallis and his army of 2,500 began their own march up that same road, accompanied by Banastre Tarleton and his British Legion. Somewhere along the way, Cornwallis sent Tarleton and his dragoons off to capture Georgetown on the coast, which they accomplished in short order—another significant victory for the British—and promptly returned. At Nelson's Ferry, about halfway to Camden, Cornwallis gave Tarleton another special assignment. He was to overtake—and, they hoped, destroy—Buford's Continentals and, if possible, capture Governor Rutledge in the bargain. Cornwallis knew that Buford had a ten-day head start on Tarleton, and given the "impracticality of the design," as Tarleton wrote in his memoirs, success "appeared to be doubtful." Even so, they agreed, it would be worth it to try.

This was the kind of challenge that Tarleton found irresistible. Even though Buford was hemorrhaging men, the British Legion was still outnumbered. It was also outgunned, as Buford brought two six-pound fieldpieces to Tarleton's one three-pounder—pounds referring to the weight of the shot the cannons fired. Buford's men spent the morning of May 27 at Camden, loading wagons with gunpowder to prevent its capture, which would add to the considerable supply of provisions that the Continentals were transporting, along with the troops themselves. By this time, Buford was burdened with twenty-six freight wagons, pulled by workhorses, and freight wagons do not roll easily through swamps, bogs, and sand. That afternoon, the rains came, turning carriage trails to mud. By this time, only twenty-five miles separated the two forces, and Tarleton was closing in.

Even so, with only 270 men in his small force, Tarleton faced challenges of his own. Still short of horses, he double-mounted his soldiers, with an infantryman seated behind a cavalryman. Awkward but not impractical, this arrangement was wearisome, especially since they traveled this way, through the same sweltering bogs and swamps and sandy trails, for more than a hundred miles.

Tarleton's mission required quick thinking, independent judgment, bold action, and a streak of meanness, and Tarleton possessed them all. He was, it might be said, born to it. He had the advantages of wealth but, unlike most British officers, was not really wellborn, and so went through life with that gnawing determination to prove himself to his social betters characteristic of so many ambitious men. One of his forebears, in 1682, had been elected mayor of Liverpool, which was where Banastre was born. That forebear, Edward Tarleton, had outfitted and commanded the man-of-war *Dublin,* and shipping, and then slave trading—an all-too-common offshoot of shipping—became the family business. Before long, the family owned plantations on several islands in the West Indies. Banastre's father also became mayor of Liverpool.

This Tarleton's political career ended in 1768, when he tried to run for Parliament and, as Robert D. Bass wrote in *The Green Dragoon*, "rioting whalemen from the Mersey used their long-handled skinning knives to prevent his appearance upon the Liverpool hustings." (Whatever he did to offend the whalemen is probably the subject for a different book, but a younger brother, John, who managed to avoid the controversies that doomed their father, would be elected to the House of Commons.)

A good cricket batsman, Banastre also enjoyed acting, but at fifteen, his father enrolled him at Middle Temple in London for a respectable career in the law. At University College, Oxford, Tarleton became friends with Francis Rawdon, soon to be Lord Rawdon, a young Irishman who would also serve in the American War of Independence. Somewhere along the way, Banastre would also befriend John André, another well-bred and well-educated young Englishman who would sail to the colonies to fight, ending up as the legendary Major André, hanged for his role in the Benedict Arnold conspiracy.

In 1773, two years before he purchased a commission as a cavalry officer in the First Dragoon Guards, Tarleton inherited five thousand pounds. This bequest he promptly blew through, though Maria Elizabeth Robinson, the daughter of his future mistress, the stage actress Mary Robinson, put the matter more delicately: "With a volatile disposition and a lively genius, he was drawn by gay companions into a vortex of fashionable amusements, and by the eager pursuit of them, exhausted his finances." (When he was in America, Tarleton's own family stopped covering his debts and chastised him for his irresponsible habits. He acknowledged his "folly and Dissipation" as well as his "cursed Itch for Play," but urged them to bail him out anyway. If they failed to do so, he said, "Ruin is Inevitable.")

Tarleton's favored hangout was the Cocoa Tree on London's St. James's Street, where, a few years later, Edward Gibbon and Lord Byron would be members. Here he cavorted, caroused, and gambled, and, with an "almost femininely beautiful face" and a "form that was a perfect model of manly strength and vigor," Tarleton had his way with women and enjoyed it immensely. Sir Joshua Reynolds would paint his portrait, though Tarleton would not have seemed out of place in almost any Hogarth.

It was when Tarleton had "exhausted his finances," Maria Elizabeth Robinson wrote, that he "turned his thoughts to the military line." He expressed "a desire to go to America," where, five days before he purchased his commission, British troops had clashed with local farmers at Lexington and Concord. As *The London Chronicle* put it a few years later, Tarleton had decided that, "with his natural activity and courage," in an army at war, "he would be sure of making his fortune or dying in the pursuit of it." Tarleton hankered after military glory, and he had no use for the ungrateful troublemakers in the colonies. Treating the rebels with leniency only demoralized the thousands of Americans who remained loyal to the Crown. A policy of moderation "did not reconcile enemies," he said. It only "discouraged friends," declaring that "nothing will serve these people but fire and sword . . . and pox."

After a farewell party at the Cocoa Tree and several months of training, Tarleton sailed out of Cork, Ireland, with Lord Cornwallis and five regiments of infantry on the *Bristol,* bound for Cape Fear, North Carolina. Tarleton had been present for the first and failed attempt to take Charles Town but then headed for New York. There, in December 1776, he distinguished himself by capturing General Charles Lee.

Capturing Lee was a significant achievement. Born in England, the son of a British major general, Charles Lee was something of a soldier of fortune, having fought under Edward Braddock in the Seven Years' War. Lee returned to Europe to fight for Portugal and Poland under King Stanislaus II, then sailed back to America in 1773, bought a plantation in Virginia, and made his services available to the Continental army. It was Lee, as first commander of the Continentals' Southern Department, who was in charge of the defense of Charles Town when, in the summer of 1776, the British failed to take it. After his succeful defense of Charles Town, Lee was ordered back to the North. In the winter, as the rest of Washington's army was retreating across New Jersey, Lee—commanding a separate detachment that Washington urgently needed—settled in with his army nearby at the Widow White's Tavern in Basking Ridge, New Jersey. There, by one critical account, he passed the time catching up with his correspondence. On a snowy morning in mid-December, while writing to Major General Horatio Gates to complain about how "a certain great man is damnably deficient" (he meant George Washington), Lee heard gunfire.

Peeking out his second-floor window, Lee discovered that the tavern was surrounded. Cornwallis had dispatched his dragoons—his "eyes and ears," he said—to find Lee and his troops, ordering Tarleton to investigate the rumor that they were at White's. Upon their arrival at the tavern, they took Lee's bodyguards by surprise, and, after Tarleton himself fired two shots through the front door, he ordered his men "to fire into the House thro' every Window & Door, & cut up as many of the Guard as they could." If the general "does not surrender in five minutes," Tarleton announced, "I will set fire to the house," and "every person, without exception," will be "put to the sword."

When some of Lee's guards tried to flee through a back door, they were shot dead. Lee surrendered and was strapped onto a horse, his legs tied to the stirrup leathers, and paraded the twenty-five miles back to camp. "This is a most miraculous Event," Tarleton said, "it appears like a Dream." (He even told his mother, somewhat optimistically, that capturing Lee would bring the war to a successful conclusion. This "*coup de Main*," he declared, "has put an end to the campaign.")

After that excitement, it was two years of more or less routine camp duties for Tarleton, which he told his mother was "stupid." The only excitement was in January 1778, when he attempted without success to capture Captain Henry Lee III (no relation to Charles) at Spread Eagle Tavern outside Philadelphia, about six miles from Valley Forge. Henry Lee was more successful when Tarleton's men approached than Charles Lee had been. Firing from the tavern's windows, his handful of men fought off a much larger number of Tarleton's British dragoons, shooting some of them from their saddles. Before Tarleton called off the raid, three shots hit his horse, one pierced his jacket, and one hit his leather riding helmet. (About that helmet: he designed it himself, as he had his Legion's uniforms. They wore green jackets, which is why Tarleton himself was called "the Green Dragoon." The jackets were trimmed with gold, and fur or an ostrich feather topped the helmet, though soldiers of lower rank made do with woolen plumes. The Tarleton helmet, as it became known, would be used in the British army until the Napoleonic Wars ended at Waterloo.)

While Washington's army hunkered down at Valley Forge, Tarleton spent the rest of the winter and spring of 1778 in the comforts of Philadelphia society. There he and John André entertained themselves with contrived amusements, taking over an abandoned South Street playhouse to stage regular theatrical performances, "for the benefit of the widows and orphans of the army." They outdid themselves in May in an extravaganza celebrating the return to England of Sir William Howe, commander in chief of British armies in America, who would be succeeded by Sir Henry Clinton. Tarleton and André called it the "Mischianza," from the Italian *mescere* ("to mix") or *mischiare* ("to mingle"). It featured a regatta with fireworks and gun salutes on the Delaware River, followed by a jousting tournament, performed "according to the laws of ancient chivalry," for the entertainment of the ladies of the town, who "excel in wit, beauty, and every accomplishment, those of the *whole world.*" Astride a black charger, carrying a device with the motto "Swift, Vigilant, and Bold," Tarleton was the sixth Knight of the Burning Mountain.

Tarleton was back in the South during the successful siege of Charles Town, and, after thrashing the Americans at Monck's Corner and Lenud's Ferry, he was now pursuing what was left of the enemy's army, under Abraham Buford, toward Camden and however much farther the chase would lead them. Tarleton's dragoons had covered more than one hundred miles in just over two days, losing several horses to the heat, but they were steadily gaining ground. It was when he was camped for the night at Hanging Rock that Buford got the sobering news: only twenty-some miles now separated predator from prey.

Tarleton, Buford was told, had already reached Camden, whose citizens had sent representatives to him, begging him to spare their town from destruction. Tarleton agreed and then moved on, riding through the night to the Waxhaws, an area along the border of the two Carolinas, named for an Indian tribe that had lived there but was wiped out shortly after the white settlers arrived. Buford, for his part, stumbled on, trying to lighten his load by abandoning one wagon full of gunpowder but making little progress.

As Tarleton urged his Legion forward, he sought to capitalize on such opportunities as presented themselves along the way. Approaching the plantation of the increasingly troublesome Thomas Sumter, a former Continental officer now operating, more or less, as an independent partisan, Tarleton dispatched one of his captains to capture Sumter, who managed to slip away before the British dragoons arrived. Undeterred, they raided Sumter's house, the pantry, and other outbuildings. Sumter's wife witnessed all of this. A well-to-do widow when he married her, Mary Sumter had suffered from infantile paralysis, "which withered her left side, leaving a [lame] leg and shortened arm." She had trouble walking, so Tarleton's men picked up the chair she was sitting in and carried it—with her in it—into the yard. Then they burned the house. One of the dragoons, feeling some sense of pity for her and the Sumter children, put a smoked ham under the chair, which she concealed under her skirts.

Tarleton and the bulk of the Legion had ridden on, and in the morning of the next day, May 29, they had drawn so close to Buford's rear guard that Tarleton sent a messenger ahead, with a grim message. "Resistance being vain, to prevent the effusion of human blood," he offered terms of surrender and made the case for their immediate acceptance. "You are now almost encompassed by a corps of seven hundred light troops on horse-back, half of that number are infantry with cannon, the rest cavalry: Earl Cornwallis is likewise within a short march with nine British battalions." This was false. Tarleton had at most 240 men total, with only one fieldpiece, and Cornwallis was nowhere near the Waxhaws. But the situation was nonetheless dire, and Buford was given half an hour to accept these terms; if he failed to do so, "the blood be upon your head." Buford did not need half an hour to ponder the offer. He consulted his officers and sent along his response. "Sir," he wrote, "I reject your proposals, and shall defend myself to the last extremity."

Buford continued to march his men into a pine forest up the Rocky River Road, some five miles south of the North Carolina border. They had gotten only about two miles farther when, in the middle of the afternoon, Tarleton's men overtook the detachment of Virginians that formed Buford's rear guard. One of Tarleton's dragoons slashed its commander with a saber, and as he sprawled on the ground, he was hit again. His nose, lips, tongue, and jaw were split open and, while he survived, he was never again to "articulate distinctly." Now only three hundred yards separated the two armies, and Buford's rear guard had been taken out of the battle.

Buford sent his cavalry, artillery, and wagons on ahead, but turned the rest of his men—foot soldiers all—to face south, deploying them in a battle line, two ranks deep, just east of the road. Tarleton moved his men into position, too, squaring off against the Virginian enemy's main force. Aware that a cavalry charge was coming, Buford told his men to hold their fire until the British horses were within ten yards of them.

At three thirty, the trumpets sounded, Tarleton ordered his men to charge, and they galloped headlong into Buford's line. Tarleton's dragoons were accomplished and battle-tested horsemen, and they rushed on so fast that some of Buford's men, under orders to wait, didn't fire their muskets more than once. They were completely overrun, and Tarleton's dragoons, swinging their sabers, hacked their way through the American lines, and then wheeled about and came charging through from behind with the same lethal result. By this time, Tarleton's light infantry had closed in, and their bayonets also found their targets. Some of Buford's men who had not fallen bloody and maimed managed to scramble a few hundred yards up the road, where they tried to regroup and return to the fray, but with little effect.

The British dragoons continued to slice their way back and forth among their enemy's disordered lines, and for those on the receiving end of the assault, the battle seemed to last longer than it did. It was all over in minutes. Buford's men never once unleashed a coordinated volley at the British, and one of their officers said his men never fired their muskets at all. The British made no use of their muskets, either. All that was needed to thoroughly rout the Americans was galloping horses, the saber, and the bayonet.

What else did or did not happen during the battle and its immediate aftermath remains a matter of considerable controversy to this day. But there was no doubt in the minds of outraged patriots at the time about what occurred. Buford had tried to surrender, sending a flag of truce, which Tarleton refused to recognize. By some accounts, Tarleton had struck down the man who carried it. Individuals had also tried to surrender, throwing down their arms and begging for mercy, but these efforts were also rebuffed. In wanton defiance of the accepted—if as yet uncodified—rules of war, Tarleton's infantrymen "went over the ground plunging their bayonets into every one that exhibited any signs of life," according to a surgeon serving under Buford, and "where several had fallen over the other, these monsters were seen to throw off at the point of the bayonet the uppermost, to come at those beneath." This slaughter went on for fifteen minutes.

Those who managed to live through what was routinely called a massacre—Tarleton called it a "slaughter" in his own memoirs—were also treated with criminal neglect. A captain who "received twenty-three wounds" told the surgeon "the manner and order in which they were inflicted." His right hand was sliced off with a single blow and his head "was then laid open almost the whole length of the crown of his head to the eye brows." Tarleton's surgeon, though busy attending to the Legion's injuries, grudgingly agreed to dress the enemy captain's head wounds. He stuffed rough cloth into them, "the particles of which would not be separated from the brain for several days." (This resilient soldier also survived; a decade later, nominated by President Washington, he served as a federal judge in North Carolina.)

The grim statistics supported the idea of a slaughter. Some 113 of Buford's men were "killed on the spot," with another 150 so badly maimed they could not be moved. Only about fifty were taken prisoner. This compares to five of Tarleton's Legionnaires who lost their lives in that brief engagement, with fourteen wounded. The British also seized twenty-six wagons that day, with the supplies they carried.

Accounts of the battle appeared in the British newspapers, and Tarleton was now a hero back home. A vain and ambitious man, he wanted fame, not in the classical sense that Washington sought it— for noble deeds performed selflessly and well—but in a newer sense, which meant notoriety in almost any form. And he achieved it. The gallant young horseman in the green jacket and plumed helmet had performed "the duty he owed his country," *The London Chronicle* proclaimed, which was "to fight and conquer."

Such notoriety as he had achieved before the war now made this new burst of acclaim even gaudier. Even Horace Walpole and Richard Brinsley Sheridan, who had known Tarleton in his student days, talked about him. "Tarleton boasts of having slaughtered more men and lain with more women than anyone else in the army," Walpole supposedly said. "Lain with! What a weak expression!" Sheridan replied. "He should have said ravished. Rapes are the relaxation of murderers."

Tarleton did nothing to minimize the lopsided nature of his victory at the Waxhaws. He did, however, offer what might be regarded as extenuating circumstances, and these are taken seriously by Jim Piecuch in his careful analysis of the documentary evidence in *The Blood Be Upon Your Head: Tarleton and the Myth of Buford's Massacre*. Tarleton himself scarcely participated in the battle, as he admitted. When his men charged the American lines, his horse had either stumbled or fallen or it had been shot out from under him, and he was momentarily incapacitated, pinned under a thousand pounds of sweating, snorting, trembling horseflesh. But when the other Legionnaires saw or were told that their commander was down, this unleashed in them what Tarleton in his history of the war in the South called "a vindictive asperity not easily restrained." If a flag of truce was in fact sent, it is entirely possible that Tarleton never received it; if it was taken to his officers, they might have felt they had no authority to either accept or reject it.

The surgeon's account appeared forty years after the battle, by which time the American public's understanding of what happened that day was already settled and might well have been tailored to support the conventional version of events. The pension applications of more than fifty of the veterans of the battle "do not contain a single accusation of improper behavior" by members of the British Legion, Piecuch found, and General William Moultrie, incarcerated in Charles Town with the prisoners Tarleton's men had taken, also said nothing about any such atrocities in his memoirs.

Tarleton in his own account attributed the lopsided nature of the battle mostly "to the mistakes committed by the American commander." And survivors, he insisted, were not murdered. "The wounded of both parties were collected with all possible dispatch, and treated with equal humanity," Tarleton wrote. "The American officers and soldiers who were unable to travel, were paroled the next morning, and placed at the neighbouring plantations and in a meetinghouse not far distant from the field of battle: Surgeons were sent from Camden and Charlotte town, and every possible convenience was provided by the British." This was "strange behavior," Piecuch wrote in the *Journal of the American Revolution,* "for someone who wanted to kill them all."

But the damage had been done, whether the claims were based on fact or not. Americans "could not afford another military disaster after Charles Town's surrender," Piecuch concluded, "so they created a mythical massacre that successfully inspired people to continue resistance." And as propaganda, it worked. From this point forward, Tarleton was known from Georgia to Massachusetts as "Bloody Ban" or "Bloody Ben," and Tarleton's own brash statements and his record of ruthlessness made the characterization stick. The name of Tarleton, Mercy Otis Warren wrote in her 1805 history of the war, became "the terror of one side and the triumph of the other," his actions marked by "boldness and barbarity."

The battle itself became known as the "Waxhaws massacre," and after that, when a defeated loyalist or British soldier tried to surrender, they would routinely be reminded of "Tarleton's Quarter"—and summarily killed. ("Quarter," as a noun, was the promise, routinely given, not to kill an enemy soldier who surrenders.) This rallying cry—or "Remember Buford!"—inspired hundreds of Americans to join the fight for independence and others, who had tried not to take sides, to turn against the British. And while the savagery of what was becoming a civil war did not begin at the Waxhaws, what had been a brushfire now spread with alarming speed.

None of this would have been evident in the immediate aftermath of the battle, of course, which was in military terms a complete disaster. And it was only the most recent in a string of disasters. Savannah was already in British hands when this series of dispiriting reversals started. Just two weeks after the siege of Charles Town began came Monck's Corner and Lenud's Ferry, with Charles Town six days after that, and now the Waxhaws—all in six weeks.

CHAPTER SIX

"We May as Well March On and Starve"

By mid-July, six weeks after Charles Town fell, de Kalb was on the Deep River in North Carolina about 120 miles north of Camden. Here, in another month, his troops from Delaware and Maryland would arrive. They had been sent to reinforce the Continental army in the South, but after Charles Town and the shellacking that Buford had taken from Tarleton, there was no Continental army to reinforce. But this did not mean there would be nothing for de Kalb and his men to do. Horatio Gates had been picked as the new commander of the Southern Department—part of his job was to rebuild an army—and when he arrived later that summer, they could take on the British under Cornwallis, which de Kalb was eager to do.

It would be the first real combat de Kalb would see since joining the American army more than three years earlier. This lack of action had surprised and annoyed him, and when he did face enemy fire again, it would be mid-August and even hotter than it already was. He was still getting used to the climate in the South, which took its toll on him and his men, and to the insects that bedeviled them day and night. For the British, the French, and the Germans who had come to fight here, it was another world. "Of the violence of the thunderstorms in this part of the world," de Kalb told his wife, "the Europeans cannot form any idea."

Wars were also fought differently in America, as de Kalb was coming to understand and develop strong opinions about. "What a difference between warfare in this country and in Europe!" he told Anna Elisabeth Emilie back in France. "Those who do not know the former know not what it is to contend against obstacles." He had come to some recognition of these peculiar challenges as early as 1768, on his secret mission to the British colonies. What he had seen as an officer in George Washington's army, first in New York and New Jersey and now in the South, only convinced him all the more of how difficult it would be for either side to win. Anyone who thought this war would end quickly was a fool.

The "immense extent of the country, the want of ready money, the discord among the governors of the various provinces, all independent of each other" made the formation of a national army almost impossible in itself. In the event of "an insurrection," which is how de Kalb referred to what of course it was, "the colonies . . . have nothing but their militia to depend upon, which, though very numerous, is not the best disciplined." A national army had been established, against considerable odds, and it had been remarkably well organized and even well trained, thanks to Washington, and von Steuben, and Gates, but those troops were still up North. In Virginia, the Carolinas, and Georgia, it was a different story. "I meet with no support, no integrity, and no virtue in the state of Virginia," de Kalb reported on his march south, where Thomas Jefferson's government in Richmond was unable to provide the assistance that any army on the move required. For days, de Kalb found himself stuck, "for want of Saddles, Bridles, horses, Waggons and forage," and conditions did not much improve once he could proceed.

In late June, on the day he turned fifty-nine, de Kalb wrote to General Washington from Hillsborough, North Carolina, of "the Scarcity of Provisions [which] have rendered my march very tedious, and disagreeable." His men were forced to "live from hand to mouth," so it was "next to impossible to engage the Enemy's when all the troopes must be employed in hunting Provisions through a vast extent of Country." Feeding the men was especially difficult because, as Colonel Otho Holland Williams, one of de Kalb's most capable officers, said, "marauding parties of militia" had already moved through the same countryside, and "swept all before them." But whatever hardship "the men suffered, and whatever they thought, the example of the officers, who shared with them every inconvenience, repressed the murmurs which were hourly expected to break forth." For several days, de Kalb reported with evident pride, they all "lived on nothing but peaches; and I have not heard of a complaint; there has been no desertion."

All of this weighed heavily on de Kalb, who, as a former quarter-master general of the Army of the Upper Rhine, had faced administrative frustrations before. He was also a realist, blessedly free of the pettiness that afflicted so many of the officers and would-be officers in the Continental army. An exasperated Washington more than once bemoaned the jealousies that pitted one officer against another, which he called "truly alarming." Among the Virginians—men from Washington's own state—the competition over rank resembled "an epidemical disease." John Adams was "wearied to death with the wrangles between military officers, high and low. They quarrel like cats and dogs. They worry one another like mastiffs, scrambling for rank and pay like apes for nuts."

De Kalb, maybe because he was older and more experienced, was not like that. He welcomed help when it was available to him and, in mid-June, when Gates was named commander of the Southern Department—replacing Benjamin Lincoln, who had been captured in the fall of Charles Town—de Kalb was heartened by the news. He was eager for Gates to arrive, even though it meant that he himself would no longer be the most senior officer in the South. When Gates notified de Kalb of the change in command, the latter offered his sincere congratulations. But he also did his best to inform his new commander of the challenges awaiting him.

"I am happy for your arrival," de Kalb wrote, "for I have struggled with a good many difficulties for provisions" since arriving in North Carolina. Although he had put the troops "on short allowance for bread," he wrote, "we cannot even get that: no flour laid in, and no disposition made for any but what I have done by military authority [which meant simply taking it from hard-pressed civilians]; no assistance from the legislature or executive power; and the greatest unwillingness in the people to part with anything." De Kalb hoped to give Gates a "more particular account" upon his arrival, adding that he had been forced to leave three pieces of artillery at the Roanoke River near the Virginia border and sent six others to Hillsborough because he lacked the ability to bring them with him. This left only eight, which he considered "sufficient for so small an army." They would have their work cut out for them, but de Kalb seemed confident that the two of them would be able to do as well as anyone could expect of them.

De Kalb was eager to relinquish administrative responsibility, and the sooner the better. The "hero of Saratoga," as Gates had come to be known, was not only a capable battlefield commander; he was also an able administrator who, although born in England, was an American. He was not a European for whom English was a second or, in de Kalb's case, third language. Finally, Gates had good relations with Congress and, having served as president of the Board of War, understood how decisions about the war were made at the highest levels. His appointment, de Kalb believed, was a wise and encouraging move.

Gates, like de Kalb, was not a young man. He was fifty-three and looked it, and sometimes acted older than that. He was small and stooped, and what was left of his hair was gray. He needed thick glasses, and these tended to rest on the end of his nose, frequently requiring him to push them back in place. He was "Granny Gates" to a lot of the men who served under him—but not all. Most of them felt a good deal of affection for him because he tended to their wants and needs in ways that more supercilious commanders did not. This might have been because, from a poor and undistinguished family in England—his mother was a housekeeper for Peregrine Osborne, the Second Duke of Leeds—he always felt in many ways more like them than he did like the other officers. His family was not of the peerage, but Gates's parents knew how to use the opportunities available to them through their association with the family of his mother's employer. Horace Walpole, later to distinguish himself as an author and Whig member of Parliament, agreed to be young Horatio's godfather, while his father, a minor government official, put up the money for his first commission in the British army.

Gates, also like de Kalb, fought in the War of the Austrian Succession and, coming to America, in the Seven Years' War, where he served alongside George Washington. He fought the French in Canada, too. Upon his return to England, Gates concluded with great reluctance that his advancement in the British army was blocked by his lack of a distinguished pedigree and an independent fortune, and retired. Gates was in his mid-thirties then, and for a time, he tried to forget his disappointment by engaging in "guzzling and gaming," which was followed by a religious conversion and then political activity. By 1770, Gates had become a "red hot republican," and two years after that he wrote to Washington about moving to the colonies, which he did, buying and settling with his wife at a Virginia plantation, Traveller's Rest, near what is now Kearneysville, West Virginia.

Five years later, Gates joined Washington's Continentals, agreeing to go to war against the British army he had once served, as an adjutant general. His organizational abilities helped impose order on the new army, and Washington repeatedly tried to lure him back into that vital, if unglamorous, administrative role. By 1776, Gates was promoted to major general, a rank that he would never have been able to attain in his homeland. The following year, at Saratoga, he defeated the British twice in a three-week period, forcing John Burgoyne to surrender his 5,700-man army. It was the most decisive victory for the Americans to that time, persuading France to enter the war against its longtime enemy, in a development traditionally regarded as a turning point in the war.

That Gates failed to report these victories to his commander in chief, taking the news directly to Congress, irked Washington, and their relationship never recovered. Coming so soon after Washington's losses at Brandywine and Germantown, Saratoga positioned Gates as a winner and Washington as something altogether different; the former's failure to return troops that he had borrowed from the main army also riled Washington, who, as thin-skinned as he could be, knew an insult when he was its object. The simmering hostility between the two would be remembered in the so-called Conway Cabal of late 1777, a supposed conspiracy to replace Washington with Gates, who, for a short time, actually became the commander in chief's superior, when he served briefly as president of the Board of War.

Unmoved by any of this personal animosity, de Kalb welcomed Gates to his camp on the banks of the Deep River in late July 1780, greeting the new commander with a thirteen-gun salute, which is all his limited artillery could offer. The newcomer had few illusions about the difficulties he would encounter, including sweltering temperatures that sapped an army's vitality. Earlier that month, Gates had written to Benjamin Lincoln that he would be taking over "an Army without strength—a Military Chest without money, a department apparently deficient in public spirit, and a climate that increases despondency instead of animating the soldier's arm."

Two weeks later, on the road to Deep River, Gates wrote to de Kalb offering some comfort and encouragement. He too was "astonished at [the] distress and difficulties" that they faced, but reassured de Kalb that he had already written to Congress, to Governor Jefferson in Virginia, and to North Carolina's Executive Council "to describe our real situation, so that no mistake may be entertained on that head." But Gates remained optimistic, telling the troops in his first general orders to them that there "is every reason to hope that this Campaign will decide the war and give peace and freedom to the United States as Great Bodies of Militia are in full motion marching from all Quarters to join the Army."

Gates put the troops in motion the day after his arrival, heading directly to the British base at Camden, about 130 miles due south, where three thousand redcoats were now stationed. De Kalb and others familiar with the territory and its people recommended a more circuitous route, through farmlands populated with patriots who would be generous with their produce, but Gates, eager to save time and thereby prevent reinforcements from reaching the enemy at Camden, overruled them. Yes, he said, they would have to push their way through areas inhabited by unfriendly loyalists, but "we may as well march on and starve, as starve lying here."

Within days, however, Gates admitted that the situation might have been more dire than he had anticipated. In a letter to the commanding officer of the Virginia militia, he called the countryside his men were slogging through a "Desart [that] affords Nothing, therefore the sooner we get through it the better." Before long, the men were reduced to plucking green ears of corn, which they boiled with lean beef taken from emaciated wild cattle they would capture in the woods and then butcher.

Otho Holland Williams, who had been with the Continental army since the siege of Boston, been a prisoner of war for a year, and witnessed almost every distress a soldier can experience, said this concoction of green corn and stringy beef was "not unpalatable to be sure, but which was attended with painful effects." Green peaches "were substituted for bread, with similar consequences." Some of the officers figured out that their hair powder "would thicken soup, and it was actually applied." Others used candle wax. Soon the men were getting sick, and their numbers were further depleted when Thomas Sumter, the fiery former militia officer, informed Gates that he was in a position to raid a supply train delivering ammunition to Camden but would need more men to do it. So, in accordance with the plan to isolate the British garrison at Camden, Gates sent four hundred men to Sumter, which left him with about 3,700. This would hardly have qualified as an army in the North—Washington commanded almost fifteen thousand at Brandywine—but in the Carolinas, this was a substantial fighting force.

Gates would be facing troops under Lord Francis Rawdon, an Irishman in his mid-twenties who was not nearly as experienced as de Kalb or Gates, but by reputation was no less coldblooded and ruthless than Banastre Tarleton. Support for this notoriety, deserved or not, came from his own pen, in a letter written from camp at Staten Island early in the war. "The fair nymphs of this isle are in wonderful tribulation," Rawdon wrote,

> as the fresh meat our men have got here has made them as riotous as satyrs. A girl cannot step into the bushes to pluck a rose without running the most imminent risk of being ravished, and they are so little accustomed to these vigorous methods that they don't bear them with the proper resignation, and of consequence we have the most entertaining courts-martial every day.

On the battlefield, at Bunker Hill, Long Island, and Monmouth, Rawdon had proven himself to be calm and, when the situation called for it, capable of making quick and intelligent decisions. An important consideration was how many troops he would have to work with at Camden and, of course, how many Gates and de Kalb would bring to oppose him. And these questions were far from settled as any engagement, which seemed more and more inevitable, drew near. Gates felt confident but had yet to determine where such a confrontation should take place, if it did. What Gates did not learn until hours before the battle was that he would be facing troops under Cornwallis as well as Rawdon. Informed of Gates's movements, Cornwallis and his staff arrived from Charles Town in just four days, while Rawdon called in outlying detachments to concentrate his force. Upon establishing his headquarters in Camden in mid-August, Cornwallis promptly arrested Joseph Kershaw, a well-known supporter of independence, and moved into his house, which was the finest in town. He allowed Kershaw's wife and children to stay but banished Kershaw himself to far-off Bermuda.

Cornwallis now had about 2,200 men under his command—about eight hundred British soldiers were too sick to fight—which meant they were still outnumbered by what Gates called his "Grand Army." This was a disadvantage that the British high command always believed would be overcome as "large numbers of the inhabitants [will] flock to the King's standard," in the words of Lord George Germain, the British secretary of state for the American colonies. Such was the basis for the Crown's strategy for the campaign in the South, although the anticipated uprising of thousands of loyalists seemed increasingly doubtful as the war dragged on. Cornwallis had no illusions about the enemy's numbers, unlike Gates, but decided to take the fight to the rebels anyway. He would make his stand a few miles north of Camden, planning to attack as soon as the sun came up on August 16. Cornwallis had "little to lose by a defeat," he said, "and much to gain by a victory."

CHAPTER SEVEN

"The Most Tremendous Firing I Have Ever Heard"

Gates established his camp about twelve miles outside Camden, at Clermont, the plantation of Colonel Henry Rugeley, a loyalist who had joined the British army after Charles Town fell. The troops arrived at Clermont on the afternoon of August 13, exhausted from forced night marches, which, however arduous, seemed preferable to slogging through the oppressive heat of day. They ate and rested, and then at 10 p.m. on August 15 they were on the move again, heading toward Camden. The men had not eaten well in days, and Gates attempted to rectify the situation with as hearty a breakfast as could be provided. It was routine before battle to fortify the men with rum, but there was none. So they were served molasses instead, which, because it contained no alcohol, lacked rum's encouraging effects.

The men were fed fresh-killed meat, raw corn, and green peaches, "with a dessert of molasses mixed with mush or dumplings," a meal they soon enough came to regret. Some who felt good beforehand got sick, and those who were already sick got sicker. "There is a theory," one historian has written, "that corn meal mush mixed with molasses and wolfed down with campfire-baked bread and fresh-killed beef will act as a charge of explosives in the stock of a famished army." Evidence from the march toward Camden supports this hypothesis. As the temperature rose, men were breaking ranks, racing into the woods, and then scrambling to get back into line.

Ordered to maintain the "profoundest silence" along the way, they were also told that any one of them who fired his gun "without the command of his officer must be instantly put to death." Keeping quiet was difficult, with all the running in and out of the woods, and, because Gates had placed his cavalry in the front, the clattering of the horses' hooves made more of a racket than the sounds of foot soldiers on the march.

By the time Gates finally reached the spot he had selected and put his men into position on both sides of the road, a quarter of them were too ill to fight, and many had not been properly trained for what lay ahead. Members of the various militias, who were considered unreliable at best, had been issued bayonets only the day before, and the only time they had used them was for roasting their meat over campfires. Their inexperience had been a consideration in Gates's planning. He had hoped to establish a solid defensive position, placing the militia companies in the front. They might not be able to mount a credible assault, but they could—he hoped—defend a position when attacked.

What Gates did not know—besides the fact that Cornwallis had arrived at Camden and taken command of all British forces—was that he had only about three thousand men under his command, not counting officers, who were able to fight, when he thought he had seven thousand. Otho Holland Williams had to disabuse Gates of that mistaken notion, showing him independent reports from the senior officers with accurate numbers of men they, individually, had under their respective commands. But in the last council of war before the fighting began, Gates had already told them—because he still believed it—that he had more than twice as many men in his army than was the case.

He was also unaware that the enemy had started out from its camp at precisely the same time as he had put his army on the move. Cornwallis was determined to surprise Gates, pushing his redcoats north on the same road Gates was on, meaning that the two armies were going to run smack dab into each other, and neither knew it. There were advance guards, of course, moving well ahead of the main army, and—this, too, Gates did not know—performing that role for Cornwallis was Banastre Tarleton and his British Legion. At about 1 a.m., sounds of gunfire popped and whistled through the night air, though no one in the main forces marching toward each other knew the source. Here too happenstance played a role. Tarleton's dragoons spotted Gates's advance guard and galloped forward, yelling, "Charge!," which was heard, Guilford Dudley of the North Carolina militia said, "in every direction through the pine forest." Tarleton opened fire, and some of the men "began to fall back in much disorder upon the first meeting of the cavalry," when Colonel Charles Porterfield, commander of the Virginia militia, "ordered halt, face to the road, and fire," according to Dudley. "This order was executed with the velocity of a flash of lightening, spreading from right to left, and again the piney forest resounded with the thunder of our musketry."

Because Tarleton was preoccupied with the cavalry immediately in front of him, he was surprised by the fire from the light infantry in its rear and on his flanks but quickly regained the initiative. They "returned upon us heavy fire," Dudley recalled, "which enveloped us from our right to left," and the "unbroken, undismayed" redcoats sustained the attack. The resistance of Gates's men, after finding themselves surrounded, collapsed. Porterfield suffered a "horrid wound in his left leg, a little before the knee, which shattered it to pieces." He slumped in his saddle, and Dudley led Porterfield's horse away from the action, with the blood "gushing out of his wound in a torrent." Feeling "weary after long marches in the hot season," Dudley found a place to hide near a swamp, and the men lay down together. There they spent the night. Besides taking Porterfield out of the battle, Tarleton bagged at least two prisoners, who reported that Gates was heading south on the same road, and Tarleton scampered back to report this intelligence to Cornwallis. What was left of Gates's advance guard made it back to relay what had just taken place, and both commanders had to make quick decisions.

It was only then that Gates learned that he would face Cornwallis as well as Rawdon, and Williams said, "The general's astonishment could not be concealed." Even so, Gates told his senior officers—discouraging any dissent from them—that it was too late to turn back. He was ready, and they should be, too. At the first sound of the skirmishing, in fact, he had ridden to the front of the line, despite being urged to hang back, telling one of his aides "that it was his duty to be wherever it was most necessary to give orders." He watched as men from his advance guard pulled back, remaining in this exposed position until the firing died down and his officers were able to reform their ranks to prepare for the battle to come.

They were a few miles north of Camden when Gates settled his

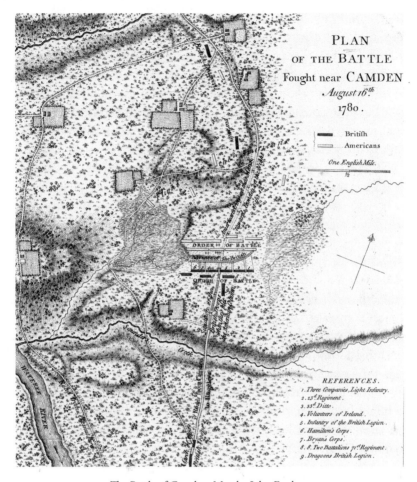

The Battle of Camden. Map by John Fawkes

Grand Army in a spot where there were swamps on both sides of the road but plenty of room to array his forces in the open pine forest between them. Cornwallis made his stand in the same spot—the armies could see each other facing them—which did not allow for much maneuvering, but confined the action. This positioning also made it difficult for the inexperienced men under Gates to flee. He established his skirmish line, about eight hundred yards wide, on both sides of the road, with only a few hundred yards separating him from his enemy. Then he waited.

At dawn, when movement by the British indicated that they were forming up to attack, de Kalb and his Maryland and Delaware regiments received orders from Gates to move now, which they did. Dudley, who had been taking care of Porterfield all night, suddenly heard "the most tremendous firing I have ever heard, accompanied by the continued roar of cannon." Smoke was everywhere, and, as Cornwallis recalled, the morning mist over the swamp prevented the smoke from rising, which "occasioned so thick a darkness, that it was difficult to see the effect of a very heavy and well-supported fire on both sides."

When the British could see well enough to move, they rushed forward with their bayonets; when they were within two hundred yards, Gates ordered the Virginia militia to answer with their bayonets. This they did, but the sight of the steel ends of the enemy's weapons, pointed at them from ranks moving shoulder to shoulder and firing as they advanced, Williams said, "threw the whole body of militia into such a panic, that they generally threw down their loaded arms and fled, in the utmost consternation."

Garret Watts, a twenty-four-year-old private with the North Carolina militia, was positioned just to the right of the Virginians when they engaged with the enemy, and "the loud roar soon became general from one end of the line to the other." Watts opened fire, too, convinced that he might have been the first of the North Carolina boys to do so, "notwithstanding the orders: for we were close to the enemy who appeared to maneuver in contempt of us & I fired without thinking except that I might prevent the man opposite me from killing me."

Watts was not only the first who fired, but—by his own admission—he was "amongst the first that fled—the cause of that I can not tell except that every one I saw was about to do the same. It was instantaneous," and there was no effort made to prevent their flight, "no encouragement to fight. I threw away my gun," and skedaddled. He realized that having discarded his weapon, he might be punished for being without arms, so he picked up a drum. But the drum made such a racket when touched by the smallest tree branch that he threw it down as well.

The British had quickly cleared the battlefield on one side of the road, but the Continentals from Maryland and Delaware on the other side—on the patriot right, to the west—held strong, and the resistance they were putting up was impressive. Some of the Marylanders had straddled the road and actually moved forward against the tide of the fleeing militia, eventually taking a position near de Kalb. "When we had gone," Watts said, "we heard the roar of guns still, but we knew not why. Had we known, we might have returned," because it came from "that portion of the army commanded by de Kalb fighting still." De Kalb had rallied his men, first on horseback, but then his horse was shot from under him, and he fought on foot, wielding his saber. There were now maybe six hundred Continentals left to fight off some three thousand redcoats, and whatever odds might have seemed to favor the more numerous patriots under Gates the night before were shifting rapidly against them. Cornwallis sensed this and rode confidently among his troops, but both times Rawdon's men charged through the smoke and haze, the troops under de Kalb pushed them back.

By this time, however, Tarleton's cavalry, stationed in the rear, were sweeping around to the left and hit Gates's Continentals from behind, and even the men from Delaware and Maryland were trying to flee. Only de Kalb and a few of his men held on, and the British swarmed over them. It was then that de Kalb was mortally wounded, providing a note of dogged heroism to what would nevertheless constitute a staggering setback for the Continental army.

In little more than an hour, some nine hundred men in Gates's army had been either killed or wounded, with a thousand captured, and it was not over. Two days later, in Gates's words, "Fortune seem'd determined to continue to distress us." Cornwallis was aware that Sumter was nearby. The British commander also knew that the men Sumter had with him were the only battle-ready troops in South Carolina, such as they were. Sumter had failed to seize the supply train he told Gates he could bag, though he was transporting a good deal of other booty he had taken from the British and was moving up the Wateree River, where he was close enough to have heard the guns from the Battle of Camden. Now, though Sumter did not know the disaster that had befallen the Americans there, he was nonetheless trying to get his own troops out of danger.

Cornwallis ordered Tarleton to go after Sumter, and the race began. Still lacking horses, Tarleton again double-mounted his men, and for a time, the two small forces—Tarleton's and Sumter's—marched north, on opposites sides of the river, though Sumter never seemed to realize he was being pursued. At noon on August 17, Tarleton's hundred dragoons and sixty infantrymen splashed across to the other side, and that night they overtook Sumter's rear guard. Sumter heard the commotion but, told that this was only the sound of the camp butchers killing beef cattle, went back to sleep.

Tarleton's men rode on, and at about noon the next day, at a point overlooking Fishing Creek, they saw to their amazement that their prey was camped below, oblivious to the peril they were in. Their arms were stacked. Some were cooking. Some were asleep under trees. Some were drunk from puncheons of rum they had seized along the way. A few were swimming in the river. Sumter himself had taken off his coat and hat and boots, put a blanket beside a wagon, laid down, and gone to sleep.

"The decision and the preparation for the attack were momentary," Tarleton wrote in his memoirs. "The cavalry and infantry were formed into one line, and giving a general shout, advanced to the charge." The camp erupted in "universal consternation," and except for some opposition "made from behind the waggons, in front of the militia," the rout was complete. "Colonel [Sumter], who had taken off part of his clothes on account of the heat . . . amidst the general confusion," climbed onto the back of a wagon horse and, after failing to rally his men, galloped toward the safety of the swamp, and "made his escape."

The losses were appalling. Only sixteen of Tarleton's men were killed or wounded, but 150 under Sumter lost their lives and a hundred were wounded. Another three hundred were taken prisoner, and one hundred redcoats who had been captured along the way were released. The British Legion, by Tarleton's account, also took eight hundred horses, "two three pounders, two ammunition wagons, one thousand stand of arms, forty-four carriages, loaded with baggage, rum, and other stores."

Within a week, the British were back at Camden, and the garrison there was now stronger by far than it had been before. Lord Germain informed King George of the triumphs at Camden and Fishing Creek, and His Majesty passed along, in Germain's words, his "approbation of their judicious and spirited Conduct," which included "a double Claim of Praise for [Tarleton's] great Alertness in overtaking General Sumter's detachment before they were apprized of [Gates's] defeat, and by their destruction rendering the Victory at Camden still more decisive." *The Royal Gazette,* the loyalist newspaper in New York, reported a "perfect victory" for their cause.

When, exactly, General Washington got a report from Gates is difficult to determine, but he seems to have taken the news with his characteristic, generally unflappable resignation. First, Gates wrote to Samuel Huntington, president of the Continental Congress, reporting that the militia "ran like a torrent, and bore all before them," which accounted for the disaster. Then he wrote to the commander in chief, again attributing the loss to the militia, which "broke so early in the Day, and scattered in so many directions" that, offering as favorable an interpretation as possible of the debacle, "very few have fallen into the Hands of the Enemy." Thanks to the "Firmness and Bravery of the Continental Troops, the Victory is far from bloodless on the part of the Foe," Gates went on, arguing that he did not think Cornwallis would "be able to reap any Advantage of Consequences, from his Victory."

Gates certainly reaped no advantage from his defeat. His report to Washington was sent from Hillsborough, North Carolina, nearly two hundred miles from Camden. Gates had ridden into Hillsborough just two days after the battle, having retreated back toward the camp at Rugeley's with some of the militia men as soon as their resistance crumbled. He was seen fleeing toward Charlotte on the day of the battle itself, covering sixty miles that afternoon and another 120 the next day, astonishing officers in the Carolinas and elsewhere with the speed by which he fled the scene—and also by what they interpreted as his cowardice.

Gates left Camden with a plan, however, which he explained to Washington and to anyone else who would listen. At least some of them found it persuasive. He would rebuild the shattered Continental army, reinforced with militia, from the relative safety of North Carolina, where troops on the march from Virginia would join him. At Hillsborough, he told Washington, "I shall continue my unwearied Endeavors, to stop the Progress of the Enemy, to reinstate our Affairs, to recommence an Offensive War, and to recover all our losses in the Southern States." But under the circumstances, Gates was well aware that his defeat at Camden and his decision to ride on to Hillsborough might be viewed with disapproval. If the misfortunes that had come his way were "Reason sufficient for removing me from Command, I shall most chearfully submit to the Orders of Congress" and resign. This was a possibility that Congress, and Washington, would have to consider, and it did not look good for Gates.

Nathanael Greene, who would be a worthy successor if Gates were fired as commander of the Southern Department, could not resist a chuckle at the erstwhile Hero of Saratoga's expense. Gates's retreat, said Greene—drawing on his knowledge of Greek history and the retreat of the Ten Thousand—"is equal to that of Xenophon, but only a little more rapid." Alexander Hamilton, then an aide to Washington, was more direct in expressing his disapproval.

"Was there ever an instance of a general running away as Gates has done from his whole army?" Hamilton wanted to know. "And was there ever so precipitous a flight? One hundred and eighty miles in three days and a half. It does admirable credit to the activity of a man at his time of life. But it disgraces the General and the Soldiers."

CHAPTER EIGHT

"Independence Is All I Wish"

Among the nine hundred Continentals killed or wounded at the Battle of Camden was an aide-de-camp to General Gates. This was twenty-nine-year-old Thomas Pinckney, a Charles Town native and scion of one of South Carolina's richest and most important families. Educated at Oxford and at London's Middle Temple, Thomas was the son of Charles Pinckney, the former attorney general of South Carolina who had also studied law in England. Like so many prominent southerners, the Pinckneys were Anglophiles. They had lived for several years in the mother country when Charles had served as the colony's agent there. In the 1750s, Charles and his wife, the former Eliza Lucas, bought what they called a "villa" in Surrey, twenty-five miles southwest of London, bringing with them slaves from their Charles Town mansion.

Shortly after their return to South Carolina, Charles Pinckney died at Mount Pleasant, a plantation owned by the Mottes, a Charles Town family as politically prominent and well-to-do as the Pinckneys and with whom they had intermarried, knitting the two families together in that baffling way so characteristic of the southern gentry. One such clan, as a chronicler of a comparable Virginia family put it, had intermarried "with such regularity that it become impossible for all but the most devoted family historian to keep them all straight, a veritable 'tangle of fish-hooks so ensnarled together that it was impossible to pick one up without pulling three or four others with it.'"

The Pinckneys and Mottes owned several rice plantations outside

Charles Town as well as townhouses within the prosperous port city, plus rental properties. The Mottes' King Street townhouse was sufficiently grand that when the city fell in May 1780, Sir Henry Clinton made the residence his headquarters. When Clinton moved out, Lord Cornwallis moved in. The family's friendly ties with England had not prevented them from supporting independence, but their connections to the mother country did save Thomas's life. When he was shot in the leg at Camden and nearly bled to death, one of his schoolmates, fighting for the British, spotted him lying on the battlefield and persuaded his own army's understaffed and overworked surgeons to treat his old friend's wounds.

"My Treatment," Thomas reported to General Gates, "has been humane, Politic, and attentive from the British officers into whose Hands I have fallen," and he remained as a prisoner of war. Even so, according to Lorri Glover, author of a biography of Eliza Lucas Pinckney, Thomas's mother, for weeks "the wound remained a purulent mess." The year before, he had married the former Betsey Motte, who was nine months pregnant when he was shot. Betsey, like so many other women, fled Charles Town when the British took over, seeking permanent shelter elsewhere. This meant they were on the move for months, while the redcoats, depending on need and convenience, took over one plantation after another. Betsey tended her husband's wounds while caring for their newborn son, at least once fainting when digging bone fragments from Thomas's shattered leg. As Thomas told his sister, Harriott, "My legs are literally no thicker than a Stout Man's Wrist," but the surgeons had concluded that amputation, for now, would not be necessary. He tried to keep his sense of humor throughout the ordeal. "I suppose you are curious to know the Situation of my Leg," he wrote to a ten-year-old nephew, and enclosed a shard of bone that Betsey had managed to extract.

It was not supposed to be this way for Pinckneys and Mottes and Laurenses and other South Carolina families of their station, and especially not for their women. Until the war came, they had enjoyed money, status, and power, which many of them assumed would continue in perpetuity. They had led lives of high privilege, though hardly lives of leisure. Their husbands were planters and lawyers and public officials and merchants—slave traders, some of them—who had grand mansions in Charles Town and on their plantations, where enslaved people toiled nearly year-round, planting, cultivating, harvesting, and milling the rice that made their owners rich.

It is a myth, born of the Civil War era, that these planters' wives were fragile and delicate ladies, unaccustomed to work themselves. Almost none of the women of the American South during the decades leading from settlement of the colonies to the Revolution spent their days sipping mint juleps under fragrant magnolias. They did not labor as their slaves did, but they labored nonetheless. Pioneer women were hardly hothouse flowers, and the wives of the men whose forebears had established the big plantations had duties to perform, which increased in the years before the war and grew in intensity as it was fought. Plantations were businesses, and the women more often than not helped their husbands run the business. This was especially the case when the men left the farm to be in Charles Town or Savannah or Richmond or even Philadelphia, which—being civic leaders, merchants, and lawyers—they were often required to do. Sometimes, for months at a stretch, they would be back in England.

When the British came and the fighting started, women were left to manage the plantations, more or less on their own. The wartime letters between plantation mistresses and their soldiering husbands "often resembled the correspondence of overseas merchants," one scholar has noted, and the women who had helped their husbands manage their far-flung properties and extensive businesses rose to the occasion. As fathers, husbands, sons, and brothers went off to war, "many women found themselves left to run the family farm or business," the late Betty Wood of Girton College, Cambridge, wrote in *The Blackwell Encyclopedia of the American Revolution*. "For those who had worked alongside the men in their family, and in the process acquired invaluable knowledge and expertise, this might have been an unwelcome prospect, but was certainly not daunting." When the men were killed in battle, "this meant not only the trauma of bereavement but also the psychological and sometimes material problems of adjusting to widowhood." When the townhouses and plantations of well-to-do women were ransacked, and their husbands did not return from the war, they could be reduced to penury.

"War in itself however distant is indeed terrible," sixteen-year-old Betsey Ambler, later Chief Justice John Marshall's sister-in-law, wrote, "but when brought to our very doors, when those we most love are personally engaged in it, when our neighbors are exposed to its ravages, [the challenges could be] overwhelming." Even so, these women were often better prepared for the hardships of war than many of their less well-situated counterparts. They were more likely to be educated and to have had a wider experience of the world; they were capable managers and, as their recipe books indicate, "had to assume responsibility as ministering physician as well as housekeeper," Catherine Clinton wrote in *The Plantation Mistress: Woman's World in the Old South*. They "made daily rounds either to the cabins of sick slaves or to the buildings set aside for the invalid and infant members of the slave community," doctoring the slaves "both as humane plantation mistresses, seeing to the needs of their black charges, and in their capacity as slaveholders' wives, looking out for their husbands' property interests."

More and more of these women were also following what we would call "the news" than they had been before the war. In the summer of 1774, a special session of the North Carolina General Assembly, in response to the Boston Tea Party of December 1773, voted to boycott British tea. They would forgo importing British cloth as well. In October, a few months after the North Carolina legislature's action, women in Edenton, which had been the colonial capital until it was relocated to New Bern in 1766, met and called themselves the Edenton Ladies' Patriotic Guild, and eventually prevailed on several dozen others to sign a petition of support for the assembly's declaration. Fifty-one names appeared on the document, as reported in *The Virginia Gazette* in Williamsburg and dated October 25, 1774.

> As we cannot be indifferent on any occasion that appears nearly to affect the peace and happiness of our country, and as it has been thought necessary, for the public good, to enter into several particular resolves by a meeting of members deputed from the whole Province, it is a duty which we owe, not only to our near and dear connections, who have concurred in them, but to ourselves, who are essentially interested in their welfare, to do everything as far as lies in our power, to testify our sincere adherence to the same; and we do therefore accordingly subscribe this paper, as a witness of our fixed intention and solemn determination to do so.

Reprinted in *The Morning Chronicle and London Advertiser* in January 1775, the petition was introduced by a letter from one of the Ladies' Patriotic Guild organizers. This was Penelope Barker, who had been twice widowed before marrying an Edenton attorney, and managed the properties that had been those of her first two husbands, making her one of the colony's richest women. "The Provincial Deputies of North Carolina, having resolved not to drink any more tea, nor wear any more British cloth," the letter reads,

> many ladies of this province have determined to give memorable proof of their patriotism, and have accordingly entered into the following honourable and spirited association. I send it to you to shew your fair countrywomen, how zealously and faithfully, American ladies follow the laudable example of their husbands, and what opposition your matchless Ministers may expect to receive from a people thus firmly united against them.

Although the petition itself does not mention tea, and there was no actual Edenton Tea Party, as some have claimed, with the women assembling at the Barker House to write and sign the document, the event is nonetheless of considerable historic significance. "This apparently simple statement had unprecedented implications," Mary Beth Norton writes in *Liberty's Daughters: The Revolutionary Experience of American Women, 1750–1800.* "The Edenton women were not only asserting their right to acquiesce in political measures, but they were also taking upon themselves a 'duty' to work for the common good. Never before had female Americans formally shouldered the responsibility of a public role, never before had they claimed a voice—even a compliant one—in public policy." Their statement "marked an important turning point in American women's political perceptions," the start of a "process through which they would eventually come to regard themselves as participants in the polity rather than as females with purely private concerns."

Their action received more coverage in England than at home and, apparently, caused sufficient consternation as to elicit sarcasm and scorn. James Iredell, who had come to North Carolina from England at seventeen and worked at the Edenton custom house, had a brother, Arthur, in London who read the petition, and wrote to James, taking a sardonic view of the whole situation. "Is there a female Congress at Edenton?" Arthur asked.

> I hope not, for we Englishmen are afraid of the male Congress, but if the ladies, who have ever, since the Amazonian Era, been esteemed the most formidable enemies, if they, I say, should attack us, the most fatal consequence is to be dreaded. So dexterous in the handling of a dart, each wound they give is mortal; whilst we, so unhappily formed by nature, the more we strive to conquer them, the more we are conquered!
>
> The Edenton ladies, conscious, I suppose, of this superiority . . . are willing, I imagine, to crush us into atoms, by their omnipotency; the only security on our side, to prevent the impending ruin, that I can perceive, is the probability that there are but few places in America which possess so much female artillery as Edenton.

A 1775 cartoon in the Hogarth manner by the London satirist Philip Dawe is entitled "A Society of Patriotic Ladies, at Edenton in North Carolina" and depicts the women as grotesques neglecting their maternal duties to sign the petition. They are waited on by a Black slave, and one of the women, with a man whispering in her ear, is clearly acting at his direction.

There is no evidence that Eliza Pinckney—the wounded Thomas's mother—was at the meeting, but she was as formidable as any of the women who were. She was born Eliza Lucas in Antigua, where her father's family had settled in the 1660s. Sugar was the cash crop of the British-held island, and the Lucases were prosperous, politically active slaveholding planters. Sent to a boarding school in England at ten, she studied the usual subjects expected of well-bred young ladies, such as dancing and French, but also botany—which she loved—and bookkeeping. She read widely the classics of Greece and Rome as well as Milton. She thanked her parents for "the pains and money you laid out for my Education."

After five years, Eliza sailed back to Antigua, only to learn that her father, George Lucas, was left insolvent when a hurricane, an earthquake, and a bloody slave uprising wrecked the island's economy—and that he was moving the family to South Carolina. There in the low-country he owned land the knowledge of which, as Eliza's biographer, Lorri Glover, wrote, "he had kept from his increasingly impatient creditors." Serving as lieutenant governor of Antigua, George would go back and forth between the family's new home, on a rice plantation outside Charles Town, and the Caribbean island. In 1739, when her father was back in Antigua and her mother fell dangerously ill, seventeen-year-old Eliza found herself "imployed in business, of which my father has left me a pretty good share." The family by this time owned and operated three South Carolina plantations, and she was now responsible for them all.

"I have the business of 3 plantations to transact," she told a friend back in England, which "requires much writing and more business and fatigue of other sorts than you can imagine." This kept her on the plantations, though she did find time to visit Charles Town and enjoy the city's "giddy gayety." Corresponding with merchants, lawyers, and government officials in Charles Town and London, she was "secure in her knowledge of agriculture and finance," Glover writes.

Her competence and initiative earned the respect of her correspondents, who sold her supplies on credit; she signed and received bills of exchange. Eliza paid her accounts on time and shipped quality commodities to her English factors. None of her business contacts appeared to question her legal standing to operate first as [their] proxy and then on her own.

On her own, Eliza also pursued what she called her "schemes." She read law books, including Thomas Wood's *An Institute of the Laws of England,* required of students at the Inns of Court, and helped neighbors with legal problems. "What can I do if a poor creature lies a dying and their people take it in their head that I can serve them?" she wrote to a friend in Charles Town. "I'll trust you with a secret. I have made two wills already." But this was a sideline. Her father hoped that her interest in plants "might produce something of real and public utility," and she made every effort to do so.

She experimented. She planted oak trees at one of the plantations, "which I look upon as my own property, whether my father gives me the land or not." They will be valuable, she said, "when we come to build fleets." She planted a fig orchard, hoping to dry and export the fruit. She also cultivated silk. Eager to lighten the lowcountry's dependence on rice, she planted ginger and alfalfa. "Out of many" of the experiments, she figured, "surely one may hitt."

One did. This was indigo, a crop that Eliza had greater hopes for, she told her father, "than any of the rest of the things I had tryd." She had "no doubt Indigo will prove a very valuable Commodity in time," and she was right. The cultivation of the plants and production of the dye was a labor-intensive ordeal, far more so than with rice, but there was a constant demand for it, especially among the English. When European wars involving the West Indies severed global trade routes, the rice economy fizzled, but the British demand for indigo from its American colonies boomed. "In 1746," Glover writes, "Carolinians exported 5,000 pounds of indigo. The next year the figure jumped to nearly 150,000 pounds." It was not of the finest quality, but perfectly acceptable for dyeing military uniforms. Four years later, the Charles Town merchant and planter Henry Laurens called South Carolina "Indigo Country."

It was in 1744 that Eliza married Charles Pinckney, and in their years in England, she arranged to meet the Dowager Princess Augusta and present the mother of future King George III with a silk dress, dyed with Carolina indigo, "in order that her highness might see what the province was capable of producing." Meeting the dowager princess, Eliza said, was "pretty extraordinary for an American," not a loyal British subject—not a Carolinian even, but an American.

Charles Pinckney also owned lowcountry plantations, and together they used their wealth to build the grandest mansion on the Charles Town waterfront and owned rental properties in the port city. They also made money renting their slaves to other planters. In February 1746, Eliza gave birth to Charles Cotesworth Pinckney, carrying forward his maternal grandmother's family name. Another son was born in 1747, but died shortly thereafter. Their only daughter, Harriott, was born in 1749, followed in 1750 by Thomas, who would later be wounded at Camden. (There was another change in Eliza's domestic life: In 1746, her father—then acting governor of Antigua—had sailed for England to appeal for military aid to help defend the island from the Spanish and French in the War of the Austrian Succession. When his ship was seized en route by a French warship, he was taken prisoner and died in their custody the following year.)

By the late 1750s, by which time the Pinckneys returned from

England, the Seven Years' War had led to a recession in South Carolina. In 1758 Charles died, leaving his widow with new challenges. Their plantations, left in the hands of Charles's brother William, had fallen into unprofitable disrepair, which Eliza blamed on "ignorant and dishonest overseers." There were now nine of these farms, and it fell to Eliza to once again make them pay, and she did it. By the early 1770s, thanks largely to the shipment of rice and indigo to England, the colony's economy was booming. But there were troubles ahead. The South Carolina legislature had joined with those of the other colonies to protest the Stamp Act and other increasingly burdensome British tax policies. After the fighting at Lexington and Concord, the royal government in Charles Town had collapsed, and members of the colonial legislature pledged their "lives and fortunes" to "resisting force by force." And with trade with England and the European countries shutting down, South Carolina's economy again ground to a halt. Eliza's sons Charles Cotesworth and Thomas, interrupting their law practices in Charles Town, enlisted. So did Daniel Huger Horry, whom Harriott had married in 1768. Horry, rich and well connected like the Pinckneys, Mottes, and Laurenses, also owned several rice plantations.

Charles Cotesworth, who served as an aide-de-camp to George Washington at Brandywine and Germantown and was president of the South Carolina Senate, was taken prisoner when Charles Town fell and held on parole in Philadelphia. There conditions for gentlemen prisoners were ridiculously comfortable. He was not exchanged until February 1782, however, six months after Cornwallis surrendered at Yorktown. Horry, on the other hand, swore allegiance to the Crown when taken prisoner at Charles Town, and, as a result, he was freed and his Hampton Plantation mansion was spared.

It was son Thomas that Eliza worried most about—even before he was shot at Camden. In the spring of 1779, the British burned his plantation home, called Auckland, "and everything in it that they could not carry away," taking slaves with them. In mid-May, she wrote to him, in an attempt to comfort him in what she called his "almost ruined fortunes by the enemy, a severe blow!" The enemy had plundered some of her properties, too, but this concerned her less than what the losses meant for her "dear Tom." Hers, she wrote, "affect me little but that it will deprive my dear children of my Assistance, when they stand most in need of it. One happiness however I have ever enjoyed, that of being free from Avarice, which will lighten the present evil with regard to my self, and a very little at my time of life will be sufficient. I can't want but little, nor that little long." She would turn fifty-eight that year, a fairly advanced age for women in the early eighteenth century, and she had come to understand that the riches of the world, which took considerable effort to amass, could be lost in a matter of minutes.

Charles Cotesworth had made a "truly generous offer to devide what remains to him among us," but she refused to accept money from him. "I am greatly affected with, but not suprized at his liberallity I know his disinterestedness, his sensibility and affection." Even so, she "could not take a penny from his young helpless family. Independence is all I wish, and a little will make us that." She was writing from Hampton, which the British had left alone, and she and Harriott were throwing open the doors to their women friends and family.

Eliza was still in occupied Charles Town when she learned of the action at Camden. "After a thousand fears and apprehensions for my greatly beloved [Thomas]," she wrote in August,

> I am at length made acquainted this day . . . of your leg being shattered and you yourself a prisoner. Gracious God support me in this hour of distress! You can more easily conceive my feelings than I can express them, alas! My child, 'tis saying little at my age to tell you how readily I would part with life, could it save your limb; but how little is in my power to do for you, situated as I am, and not allowed to give you that attendance or pay you those tender attentions which might in some measure aleviate your distress and which are so justly due to you from me.

She wanted to visit Thomas in Camden, where he was being held, but he hadn't allowed it. Camden was 120 miles north of Charles Town, and such a trek in the malarial heat of the lowcountry summer could risk her life in a vain attempt to help save his. Tom was well aware of the dangers of making such a journey "to such a place of sickness, filth, and wretchedness," she wrote, and she decided to stay where she was, to save her son "the pain which [he] would suffer on my account."

As soon as he was strong enough to travel, Thomas was allowed to move to Mount Joseph, one of the Motte family's plantations, about fifty miles south of Camden. A number of the Motte and Pinckney women had moved to Mount Joseph, which they turned into a hospital for wounded soldiers, and he recuperated there. For a full year, Glover writes, he "was too weak to mount his horse," and then Thomas, like brother Charles Cotesworth, sailed to Philadelphia, where other gentlemen who had been taken prisoner were held while waiting to be exchanged for British soldiers of comparable rank. The brothers took their wives and children with them, and by the end of 1781, nearly six hundred Carolinians—most of them women and children—had moved to Philadelphia. There they could be near their captured loved ones—and under the protection of the enemy. Other families, however, chose not to "Sully their honour & Conscience by taking protection." Eliza stayed behind, at Hampton, while Thomas's mother-in-law, Rebecca Brewton Motte, remained at Mount Joseph, hoping it would be spared. The following spring, the British would show up at Mount Joseph, and what happened then would test her loyalty to the cause.

CHAPTER NINE

"It Rained Militia from the Heavens"

The summer of 1780—with the notable exception of the disaster at Camden—brought some faint flicker of hope. In July, the Comte de Rochambeau sailed into the harbor at Newport, Rhode Island, with some five thousand troops, in what was the latest and most public expression of French support for the American cause. The French had furnished supplies to the Continental army for four years already, and Washington's successes at Trenton and Princeton had been possible only, it was widely acknowledged, with French aid. But it was the victory at Saratoga in the fall of 1777 that brought France into open alliance with the Americans, with the Continental Congress ratifying the relevant treaties a few months after that.

Most of the requisite diplomatic maneuvering took place in the colder months when the troops in the North were in their winter encampments. The war in the South, of course, continued more or less year-round, and in the weeks that preceded Cornwallis's victory at Camden, the British and their "friends," as they called the loyalists, continued to move steadily through South Carolina.

There they would try to convince the locals to swear allegiance to the king or face reprisals if they did not. From their outpost at Rocky Mount, loyalists under the command of Lieutenant Colonel George Turnbull, born at Blackadder Mains in Scotland, were also determined to confront and destroy pockets of armed resistance. They were especially keen on putting an end to the activities of those irregulars fighting for and with Thomas Sumter. Because he moved his camp so often and so quickly, it had proved maddeningly difficult—at least until Tarleton caught up with him at Fishing Creek in August—to know where Sumter was at any given moment and when he might strike next.

But Turnbull's intelligence was getting better by the week—the loyalists functioned as spies as well as soldiers—and by early July he had learned something of possibly vital importance: Sumter was allowing some of his men to go home to their farms for the wheat harvest. That meant they would be on their own, or with at most a few other irregulars, and were therefore vulnerable to capture or to being killed outright.

To track down Sumter's men, Turnbull chose Christian Huck, who made little effort to endear himself to the people who favored independence or even to those who wished to be left alone and avoid all the unpleasantness. Born in present-day Germany, Huck—sometimes spelled Hook, Houck, and Haulk—had emigrated to Philadelphia, where he practiced law, bought and sold real estate, and became an outspoken loyalist. In May 1778, eight months after the defeat at Brandywine gave Philadelphia to the British and a month before the Americans regained it, *The Pennsylvania Packet,* an organ of the rebellion, published a statement by the Pennsylvania Supreme Court pronouncing Huck and a number of other residents of the city guilty of "High Treason." Their crime was having "knowingly and willingly aided and assisted the enemies [of] the United States of America, by having joined their armies." In addition to being subjected to all the "pains and penalties" the charge of high treason carried, they would be forced to give up all their property, which, in the real estate speculator Huck's case, was considerable. A month after the proclamation, he reported to the British army in Philadelphia, and a company of thirty men he had raised fought at Monmouth. He and his troops, under Tarleton, also fought at the Waxhaws, but within weeks, though formally reporting to Turnbull, Huck was pretty much on his own. As he and his men marauded their way through the upcountry, they made more enemies than friends.

Huck had a tendency to swear, though before long, this was the least of the grievances the Presbyterians of North Carolina's Catawba Valley had against him. People were outraged that he blasphemed, examples of which were repeated, in hushed tones, whenever and wherever pious farmwives talked. Huck said, or supposedly said, that "God Almighty" seemed to have joined the cause of independence, but "if there were 20 gods on that side, they would all be conquered." Even "if the Rebels were thick as trees, and Jesus Christ himself were to command them," Huck would prevail.

But Huck did more than curse and blaspheme. On a Sunday morning early in the summer, "the Swearing Captain," as locals called him, went looking for the Reverend John Simpson, the well-regarded, well-educated Presbyterian clergyman who, the loyalists had been told, had been made a captain in the patriot militia. On their way to the Fishing Creek Meeting House, where Simpson officiated, Huck and his men brought their horses to a halt at the farmhouse of Jenny Strong, a widow whose two sons had also joined the militia. By Colonel Turnbull's own account, while his men patrolled the road from Strong's farm to the church, they saw "two men with Rebell Uniforms" running through a wheat field, and shot and killed one of them. This turned out to be Jenny Strong's seventeen-year-old son, William.

Turnbull's loyalists then rode on to the church, which was known to be a gathering place, and possibly a drilling ground, for rebel militia. Finding no one inside the church, they proceeded to burn it down. From there they went to Simpson's house, determined to "burn the rascal out." Upon their arrival, they discovered that Simpson was not there either, but his wife, in her thirty-sixth week of pregnancy, and their four children were at home. Trumbull's men told her she would never see her husband again, at least not alive, because they would hang him. One of them said he would bring her the clergyman's scalp. The loyalists "rifled the house of everything valuable," by one account, "took out four featherbeds, and ripped them open in the yard; collected all of the clothing, from which they selected such articles as they fancied for their own keeping, and having exhausted their invention in devising mischief," they burned the house. They also set fire to a smaller dependency that functioned as Simpson's study. Before it was completely destroyed, however, the clergyman's wife rushed into the building and managed to carry out "two aprons' full of books. She could save no more, and in doing this was much burned and had nearly lost her life." She and the children took refuge in a neighbor's house, remaining there until after her confinement.

About this time, Huck's men rode to William Hill's ironworks, about twenty-five miles north of the church. The ironworks was also a known gathering place for the rebels, and, Turnbull told Huck, "a Refuge for Runaways," meaning deserters from loyalist militias. There was a forge and a blast furnace at the site, as well as a gristmill, sawmill, and general store. This bustling commercial complex, worked by almost one hundred slaves, turned out plows and other tools used by farmers. Since 1776, however, it had also kept busy "casting swivel guns, cannons and cannonballs," first for the defense of Charles Town but in recent months for Sumter's partisans.

Turnbull told Huck he should "destroy this Place," which Huck was determined to do. Hill, like so many of his neighbors, had also joined Sumter's little army, leaving only about fifteen or so white men, plus the slaves, to defend the works. Upon the appearance of Huck's troops, numbering about five hundred that day, most of the defenders fled. A few volleys were exchanged, with seven of Hill's employees killed and four taken prisoner. Once the prisoners were stripped "of everything even to the rings some of them wore on their fingers," Hill wrote in his memoirs, the loyalists burned the forge, furnace, gristmills, and sawmills "together with all other buildings even to the negro huts." They also "bore away about 90 negroes," some of whom, back at their camp at Rocky Mount, were made personal servants to Turnbull's officers. Two of Hill's "very valuable young negroes" Turnbull "kept to wait on him."

After laying waste to the church, the Presbyterian parsonage, and Hill's ironworks, Huck returned to Turnbull's camp at Rocky Mount. It was there, in early July, that they learned that Sumter had allowed some of his officers to return to their farms to oversee the harvest. Away from the rest of the rebel army and on their own, Turnbull reasoned, were two troublemakers of special interest, so he turned Huck loose once again, this time with about 120 men, to round the rebel leaders up. The first was twenty-five-year-old John McClure, who had fought in the Charles Town campaign and become active again after learning of Tarleton's "shocking massacre" at the Waxhaws. McClure had raised a small force of maybe thirty of his neighbors. There had been some brief but fiery exchanges with the loyalists but nothing even qualifying as a skirmish. McClure's men had managed to retake some of the horses that the loyalists had taken from rebel farms; at least three of them, returned to their rightful owner, had belonged to McClure's mother.

The other rebel that Huck wanted to capture was William Bratton, a native of Ireland whose family, like many who settled in the Carolina backcountry, had first arrived in Pennsylvania. In 1780—already in his mid- to late thirties—Bratton had married Martha Robertson (possibly Robinson), fathered at least some of the eight children he and his wife would raise, and built a two-story log house on two hundred acres on the south fork of Fishing Creek. Bratton also commanded a regiment of partisans under General Sumter, then camped on the east side of the Catawba River. In the summer of 1780, when Huck came after them, McClure and Bratton had merged their little armies. With a few from other detachments, they commanded some 250 men when, with Sumter's blessing, they had gone home for the harvest. While on leave, they were to recruit more men, if possible, and, should the need arise, protect themselves and their families against loyalist threats.

They would not have to wait long to do so. On the morning of July 11, Huck's men appeared at John McClure's farm, hoping to find him there. McClure, who was single at the time, lived on the family farm, though he was not at home, as his mother, Mary Gaston McClure, told them; whether she told them he was with Sumter at the Catawba is not clear. But McClure's younger brother, James, was in the house, and when the loyalists entered it, they caught James and Edward "Ned" Martin, Mary McClure's son-in-law, melting Mrs. McClure's pewter plates to be fashioned into bullets. The loyalists also found the bullet molds and two finished bullets in the frightened young men's pockets. The loyalists immediately seized these two "violent rebels," vowing to hang them as traitors when the sun came up the next day. Mrs. McClure protested, and one of Huck's men hit her with the flat of his sword. Then Huck took the two prisoners and rode away. Once they were well out of sight, Mrs. McClure sent their daughter, Mary, away, hoping she could warn John and the other rebels at Sumter's camp that Huck was in pursuit.

Next Huck rode to the home of William and Mary Adair, another Scots-Irish family who had moved from Pennsylvania. Three of their sons—James, John, and William—were fighting with the rebels, but none of them were home, and neither was their father. So Huck's men pocketed whatever they wanted, which included Mrs. Adair's shoe buckles and rings. They also raided the pantry and smokehouse; when a group of rebel scouts stopped by later that day, William Sr. was back home and told them he had nothing for them to eat because the loyal-ists hadn't left him enough "to make himself a hoe-cake."

By late afternoon, a large detachment of Huck's men showed up at William Bratton's farm, some wearing the green jackets that identified them as members of Tarleton's British Legion. There were redcoats, too, Bratton's youngest son, William Jr., would remember years later, and some loyalists who had on the same clothes they wore when working in their fields. Martha Bratton met her visitors on the front porch, and in "deliberate and measured tones" told them the "simple truth" that her husband was not at home, and even if she knew where he was, she wouldn't tell them. This enraged one of the loyalists, a "red-headed ruf-fian," who grabbed a sickle from a peg on the wall, held it to her neck, and said that if she didn't tell them William's whereabouts, he would "cut her head off and split it."

This was too much for one of the other Tories, identified later as John Adamson, who kept a tavern in Camden. Adamson struck the "red-headed ruffian" and, after kicking him headlong off the porch and standing over him, beat him with the flat of his sword. Adamson apologized to Martha and offered the family his protection. Then the loyalists got on their horses and rode away. When night fell, Martha, like Mary McClure before her, took action. She dispatched an enslaved man named Watt to ride to Sumter's camp and tell her husband that the loyalists were looking for him.

Later in the day, the loyalists returned to Bratton's, and this time Huck himself was with them. He "asked for an interview with my Mother," William Jr. recalled, "and was, at first, very courteous and polite," even taking the boy on his knee. After offering a commission in His Majesty's Service to William Sr., Huck asked Martha to use her influence to persuade her husband to accept it. At first, she simply told Huck that she "had no influence with her Husband in such matters," but when he persisted, she cut him off. "It is useless to prolong the interview if that is its purpose," she said. "My husband is in Sumter's Army and I would rather see him die there, true to his Country and cause," than have him live out his years as a "traitor."

At this, Huck stood up, and the boy sprawled on the floor, break-ing his nose ("an honorable scar," he would later call it) against the fireplace. Huck then demanded that Martha prepare dinner for him and his officers, which she did. When dinner was over, he confined her and her children to the attic for the night. Three elderly neighbors, who had come to help gather in the wheat, were also taken prisoner and, with James McClure and Ned Martin, told that they too would be hanged at sunup. When Huck settled in for the night at the plantation of James Williamson, about a quarter of a mile from Bratton's, the five prisoners were locked up in a corncrib. Huck made his headquarters at Williamson's two-story log house. His men pitched their tents on two sides of the trail leading to the plantation, with split-rail fences on both sides of the trail. By this time, William Sr. and John McClure, having been informed that Huck was pursuing them, set off from camp and began to go after him. The chase was on.

Bratton and McClure, leading about 250 men, set off on the night of July 11, "as light as day." A rare appearance of the aurora borealis made it possible for the men to see with remarkable clarity, and one of the sights that greeted—and inspired—them when they reached the Catawba River was the crowd of families huddled on its banks, burned out of their homes by the loyalists. Their plight "excited in every bosom a sympathy for the distressed, and an indignation against the hard-hearted foe who could perpetrate such an inhuman deed," John Craig, who fought that day, wrote in his memoirs. "We received our orders to set these distressed people over the river which we did. Then we received orders to turn our horses out to graze, and meanwhile the offi-cers called a council and soon determined to risk all consequences and attack the inhuman ruffians."

Then they rode on through the night, stopping at the farm of Edward Lacey Sr., the father of Edward Lacey Jr., one of their captains. Lacey Sr. was a loyalist, so, to prevent word of the rebels' movements from getting out, his son posted four guards around the house. But the old man slipped out anyway and was on his way to alert Huck's troops at Williamson's plantation when he was caught. This time Lacey Jr. had his father tied to his bed.

The officers settled on a plan that, while not complicated, would nevertheless take some doing to pull off. Before dawn, Bratton's men were to position themselves for a charge up the road that led from his farm to Williamson's—and Huck's headquarters—and the loyalists' camp alongside the road and in front of the farmhouse. There were other buildings on the property, and behind these was a peach orchard. As Bratton's men took their positions, McClure and Lacey were to lead their troops around where the loyalists were camped, so they could attack down the same road at the same time, except from the opposite side. A third band of partisans would attack from a third side, from out of the peach orchard. The question was whether the three groups would be able to assemble in time to mount the coordinated attack. As soon as they had found their posts and the first shot was fired, no matter by whom, they were "to raise the war-whoop" and attack.

At daybreak, the northern lights were no longer visible, and clouds covered the moon. As quietly as possible, the rebels crept through the swamps and woods toward their assigned positions, intending to subdue any enemy sentry unfortunate enough to get in their way. Bratton's men came across one such picket and left a man to guard him, with orders "to shoot him if he should move." He moved and was shot. A second sentry, at the west end of the lane, was also shot to death. McClure and Lacey's men, making their way around to the other end of the road, came across a third sentry and killed him, too. Most of the loyalists, scouts reported, were still asleep. Bratton's men had little trouble settling in behind the rail fence, but those under McClure and Lacey had to pick their way through the dark swamps, which impeded their progress and made them late. The men headed for the orchard were also struggling, but when they had come within sight of the log house, they dismounted, hitched their horses, and began their approach on foot.

One of the men in the orchard was sixteen-year-old James Potter Collins, whose family's plans for a college education had been derailed a few years earlier, when, as he would write, "times began to be troublesome." When Collins expressed a desire to join the militia, his father consented with some reluctance, telling him that if he "went to battle, he stood as fair a chance" of getting shot as he did if he stayed home. So far, he had seen no action, but, on this July morning, that was about to change.

Armed with a "blue barrel shot gun," Collins found his spot in the orchard when one of the remaining loyalist sentries caught sight of movement among the peach trees, fired in the general direction of the movement, scrambled back into the camp, and alerted the others. The sleepy camp sprang to life, and before Collins knew what was happening, redcoats had mounted their horses and charged. "This, I confess, was a very imposing sight," Collins said, having "never seen a troop of British horse before, and thought they differed vastly in appearance from us—poor hunting shirt fellows." As soon as the rebels opened fire, "Our rifle balls began to whistle among them," and as clouds of smoke spread over the scene, loyalists jerked back in their saddles, reeled, and dropped to the ground.

McClure and Lacey, who were supposed to be attacking down the same road as Bratton, became mired in the swamp. Bratton moved up the road anyway, and opened fire. Distracted by the action from the orchard, the loyalist dragoons concentrated their efforts on Collins's "poor hunting shirt fellows," leaving the opposition to Bratton's oncoming rebels to the infantry with their bayonets. Ordinarily, the steel of the bayonets terrified the rebels, but this time, the rail fences stood in the way, forming a "kind of breastwork," according to Maurice Moore, a South Carolina physician who fought that day. This gave the rebels "some little protection against the enemy's musketry, and afforded a good rest for their rifles, with which they took unerring aim." The fences also made it almost impossible for the loyalists to make any impression with their bayonets. They would make their move, and the rebels would fire, and the onrushing redcoats would be knocked backward. They would then regroup, with the same result. They tried three times before their lines were so thinned out that they called it off.

Huck, who had remained in the house during the first moments of the battle, emerged shortly after the shooting started, but not before telling the family on whose hospitality he had imposed that his troops would prevail even "if it rained militia from the Heavens." The moment he left the house, the Williamsons barricaded the doors, preventing him from retrieving his dragoon jacket. He climbed on a horse and "began to storm and rave," as Collins recalled, exhorting his men to keep up the fight and yelling at the enemy to "disperse you d—d rebels, or I will put every man of you to the sword."

Huck's white shirt made him a readily visible target, and one of the sharpshooters—John Carroll of nearby Fishing Creek took credit— loaded and fired two balls from his rifle, nailing Huck in the back of his head, behind the ear. He jerked about and, clinging to the saddle so tightly that it came off with him, "fell at full length," his sword slipping from his hand and landing "at some distance" from his horse. By this time, the men under McClure and Lacey had arrived, hurried forward by a cry that would be repeated in one form or another throughout the southern campaign and just might contain the kernel of wisdom that made independence imaginable and ultimately achievable: "Boys take the fence, and every man his own commander!"

With Huck down, the loyalists panicked, and the onrushing rebels made quick work of the few who did not flee. "We was in full possession of the field in five minutes," one of their officers said, "without a single man" killed or wounded. This was an exaggeration, but not by much. Of the 140 or so rebels who fought that morning, only one was killed and another wounded. The loyalists' losses, by contrast, were horrendous. Of the 120 or so of them who participated, well over half were wounded or captured. More than twenty other loyalists managed to escape to the surrounding swamps and forests. These were pursued by the rebels "for thirteen or fourteen miles, wreaking vengeance and retaliating for their cruelties and atrocities," with "many carcasses found in the woods some days after." What some historians call the Battle of Williamson's Plantation was known locally and for the rest of the war by a different name. It was, and is, called Huck's Defeat.

The tidying up took several days, but the rebels began to celebrate immediately. When they went to the corncrib where Huck had locked up young James McClure and Ned Martin—the young men who had been melting down pewter plates to make bullets—and the three older men who had come to Bratton's to help with the harvest, they were astounded to see that it was empty. When a guard had been distracted during the battle, one of the prisoners had grabbed the man's musket and held him at gunpoint, while another "pushed off the top of the crib & gave a hurra for the Whigs," releasing them from their captivity.

The victorious rebels auctioned off the spoils of battle, and there was a lot of it. John Carroll, who got credit for killing Huck, was awarded with the Swearing Captain's sword. John Adair bought "a fine silver-mounted gun, and a roan horse," and some of the men claimed swords, pistols, powder and lead, and Huck's watch. Huck's cap and holsters went to Bratton. Some of the slaves the loyalists had taken were returned to their owners, and John Nixon, one of the rebels, bought Sam, an African who, until the battle, belonged to the loyalist Matthew Floyd. Young James Potter Collins got none of the spoils, and, it appears, did not think he deserved any. "For my own part," he would write, "I fired my old shot gun only twice in the action. I suppose I did no more harm than burning so much powder."

By noon on the day of the battle, Martha Bratton and her children were released from their captivity on the second floor of their house, came downstairs, and stepped outside. Dead loyalists lay everywhere, and the wounded of both sides were being helped into the first floor of the house, where the women of the neighborhood were gathering to care for them. When Martha ventured outside, she saw her husband and another officer, with swords drawn, standing over an enemy officer. In time they called her over, where a tense conversation was taking place between Bratton and the downed loyalist, who was bleeding from a wound in the chest.

When the shooting had ended, Martha would learn, Bratton had looked for the "red-headed ruffian" who had terrorized her the day before, and he believed he had found the scoundrel. When the man denied it, Bratton and the other officer called him a coward and threatened "to cut him into mincemeat." Struggling to speak, he begged the men to call Mrs. Bratton herself "before you perpetrate such a wrong," and when she arrived, she recognized the voice, if not the grimy face, as that of John Adamson, the officer who had in fact saved her life. Realizing the mistake, Bratton had the man carried into the house, which by now was filled with the wounded. To make room, Bratton and another rebel picked up wounded redcoats, "one by the head and the other by the heels," Bratton's son recalled, "and threw them out of the house like dead hogs."

Adamson, it turns out, would recover and live a long and productive life among his rebel neighbors back in Camden, with the animosities of the past put behind them. But all that was years in the future. For now, the war in the South was only beginning to heat up, and the engagement at Williamson's Plantation represented a serious setback for Cornwallis, for Sir Henry Clinton, and for the British cause. Less than two weeks before the battle, Cornwallis had assured his commander in chief that he and his loyalist allies had "put an end to all resistance" in South Carolina. This was clearly not the case now. Huck's Defeat, at least for now, dashed any plan Cornwallis had of moving forthwith into North Carolina and from there to Virginia.

CHAPTER TEN

"Huzzah for King George!"

On the night of August 18, Isaac Shelby, James Williams, and Elijah Clarke—leaders of an odd assortment of armed men, some of whom were attached to no organized or officially recognized army—pulled their mounts to a halt about a mile from Musgrove's Mill on the south banks of the Enoree River. Musgrove's Mill was about thirty miles below the North Carolina border, not far from present-day Spartanburg, which did not at that time exist. A clutch of some two hundred loyalists was camped at the mill, roughly the same number of men as Shelby, Williams, and Clarke led. But—as they were soon to learn—the loyalists had been reinforced by at least that many seasoned British regulars who had not only been there for a few days already but were getting a good night's sleep as the rebels arrived.

Their horses were rested, too, unlike those of the rebels, who had been on the move all night. They had covered the forty miles from their camp at Smith's Ford on the Pacolet River and were, as might be expected, exhausted. The night march spared the horses from the heat of a late-summer afternoon but was hard on man and beast all the same. They "never stopped to even let their horses drink," Shelby said.

Clarke's men were Georgians, tough partisans who had attached themselves to Sumter's South Carolina militia once Georgia had been subdued. The men commanded by Williams were South Carolinians. Shelby's were more difficult to categorize.

Many of the men now commanded by Shelby took such weather

Isaac Shelby.
Portrait by Matthew Harris Jouet,
ca. 1816–1820

for granted. It was all they had ever known. Unlike so many of the rebels fighting the British and the loyalists, they were not from the Carolina lowcountry; their forebears, who had come down the Great Wagon Road from Pennsylvania, might have lived a few years east of the Blue Ridge, but their descendants were "Overmountain Men," as they called themselves. They had crossed the Alleghenies and settled, much as Daniel Boone's followers had done when they reached Kentucky, where they could find flat, fertile land along the Holston and Watauga Rivers that in years to come would become Tennessee. They were not mountaineers, most of them, but small farmers, with all the ornery independence, resolve, and resourcefulness that small farmers have possessed since time immemorial.

Some of them, or their fathers, had been associated with the Regulator movement. The Regulators, who lived in the western reaches of the Carolinas, had clashed repeatedly with the planter aristocracy back in the lowcountry over lack of representation in the provincial assemblies. The Regulators had also grown impatient with the legislatures' refusal to address the rampant lawlessness that characterized frontier life in the upcountry and, losing patience, threatened to invade Charles

Town if their demands were not met. "We are Free Men—English Subjects—not Born Slaves," they declared in 1767, and attempted to raise troops to fight those representing Crown officials. These ongoing disputes led to the Regulators' defeat at the Alamance River near Hillsboro, North Carolina, in May 1771, considered by some historians to be the first true battle of the war. Although their two thousand men outnumbered Royal Governor William Tryon's troops by two to one, many of the Regulators were unarmed and proved to be easily dispersed. Twelve of them were convicted of treason, six of whom were hanged. More than six thousand locals were made to sign oaths of allegiance to Tryon's provincial government, and many of those who did not wish to do so moved across the mountains, settling there.

Their backgrounds reflected that of the Shelby family, which had moved from the Atlantic colonies across the Appalachians into what would become the states of Kentucky and Tennessee. The men Shelby commanded had also migrated to the west, where they fed their families from what they could raise on their own farms, without slave labor, and what they could bring down with their rifles. They were not soldiers, if by soldiers one meant that they had been trained to follow the British manual of arms of 1764, or even von Steuben's *Regulations for the Order and Discipline of the Troops of the United States,* adopted in 1777.

But these men had hunted their entire lives, and if they had yet to face the shining steel of the redcoats' bayonet charge, they had fought Indians in the gloomy shadows of the dense forests that covered the hills where they settled. This was a different kind of training and valuable experience in its own brutal way. Being attacked by the bayonet was terrifying, but so was the prospect of being scalped. This experience served them well in the civil war that had erupted in the Carolinas, where personal animosity between neighbors and an unseemly appetite for retribution was proving to be as effective, under favorable circumstances, as disciplined drilling in the European tradition.

Shelby's family, while more entrepreneurial and business-minded than most of their neighbors, had sailed from Wales to Philadelphia in 1735 but moved four years later to Maryland, where, in 1750, Isaac was born. Evan Shelby, Isaac's father, fought for the British in the Seven Years' War, where he was reported to have killed an Indian chief with his bare hands. Shelby *pere* also sold goods to the Indians, who bought their war paint, which was "manufactured in Germany and shipped by

England and sold by colonial traders" at the door of Fort Pitt, where he operated a trading post. In 1771, Isaac's father established Fort Shelby, near what is now Bristol, Tennessee, through which more than 100,000 settlers are believed to have passed on their way west.

Although Isaac Shelby received only what he called "the rudiments of an English education," he was made sheriff of Frederick Town, Maryland, before he turned twenty. Within three years, he was serving with his father in the Virginia militia, answering Royal Governor Dunmore's call to subdue the Indians on the western frontier. After the decisive battle at Point Pleasant in present-day West Virginia, when Dunmore's militia in October 1774 routed Chief Cornstalk's Shawnees and drove them back farther into the interior, Isaac in a letter to his family described "a Very hard day, its really impossible for me to Express or you to Conceive . . . the Hideous Cries of the Enemy and the groans of your wound[ed] men lying around it was Enough to Shud[d]er the stoutest hart."

The victory at Point Pleasant, which made settlers of the Kentucky and Tennessee territories less vulnerable to attack from the Shawnees, had other significant ramifications. Daniel Morgan, whose role in the coming War of Independence would soon loom large, had been at Point Pleasant, too, and he and many of the others who fought there were aware of what was happening, that same year, hundreds of miles away in Boston. The British had closed Boston Harbor in July—and the First Continental Congress had convened in Philadelphia a few weeks after that. It was at Point Pleasant, Morgan would write, that some of the men took a solemn oath. "We as an army victorious," Morgan recalled, "formed ourselves into a society pledging our word of honor to each other to assist our brethren of Boston in case hostilities should commence."

The hostilities Morgan mentioned had not only commenced but had erupted into full-fledged war, here in the backcountry as well as along the Eastern Seaboard. Christian Huck had been unleashed on the rebels in the Carolinas, but so was a considerably more formidable commander of militia who proved to be as accomplished at raising troops as he was at protecting loyalists from their independence-minded neighbors. This was a duty Lord North's government and George III took seriously. The man Cornwallis had selected to oversee the British push through the upcountry, of far more consequence than Captain Huck, was Patrick Ferguson, and from the moment of his arrival in the American South, he and Isaac Shelby seemed fated to meet.

Born in Aberdeenshire and raised in Edinburgh, Ferguson was the second son of a prominent barrister with claims to the lesser nobility, and nephew of Patrick Murray, the fifth Lord Elibank, an author, economist, and patron of the arts. A product of the Scottish Enlightenment—the philosopher David Hume, the novelist Tobias Smollett, and the painter Allan Ramsay were family friends—Ferguson began his military career at the age of fifteen. As a junior officer in the Royal North British Dragoons, he fought in the Seven Years' War; service in Germany left him with a leg injury that troubled him for the rest of his life. In 1768, he bought a captaincy, and for three years he was stationed in the Caribbean. In Tobago, he helped put down slave rebellions.

Ferguson was, by all accounts, a young man of considerable wit and charm. Unusual among British officers, he believed that volunteers who were not professional soldiers, as he was, could be effective on the field of battle. Almost all of the thousand or so men under his command in the Carolinas were loyalists, and he was effective in his efforts to recruit others. Inspired by the "boasted skill of the American marksmen," Ferguson designed a breech-loading rifle—the first used by the British army—and when he demonstrated it for the army's leaders, one witness reported, he "astonished all beholders." In heavy rain and driving winds, Ferguson fired his rifle while standing still and while advancing, getting off as many as ten rounds a minute. Next, he "poured a bottle of water into the pan and barrel of the piece when loaded so as to wet every grain of the powder, and in less than half a minute he fired with it as well as ever without extracting the ball." Finally Ferguson "hit the bull's eye lying on his back on the ground, incredible as it may seem to many, considering the variations of the wind and the wetness of the weather." Only three times during the entire demonstration did Ferguson miss his target. In December 1776, after George III witnessed a demonstration, Ferguson was granted a patent. In 1777, when the Crown called for volunteers to put down the rebellion in the North American colonies, Ferguson was given command of a special, one-hundred-man Experimental Rifle Corps equipped with rifles of his own design.

That fall, when Isaac Shelby, acting as Virginia's commissary agent in the Kentucky territory, was rounding up provisions for Continental troops fighting the Indians, Ferguson's Experimental Rifle Corps was stationed outside Philadelphia, making ready to fight at Brandywine Creek. The day before the battle, Ferguson and three of his marksmen were on patrol when they came upon two unsuspecting enemy officers, almost certainly of high rank, to judge from their uniforms. Both were mounted. One appeared to be a French hussar. The other was probably an American. He was a large man—he seemed especially so in the saddle—with a decidedly stately bearing. Ferguson whispered to his men to inch forward, maintaining their silence, and bag their prey. Before they could do so, however, he had second thoughts and ordered his men to hold their fire. It would be ungentlemanly to shoot an enemy officer in the back; the idea, he later wrote, "disgusted" him. Instead, in a gesture of sportsmanship, Ferguson called out to the dignified American, alerting him to the danger he faced. The American calmly glanced his way, and Ferguson called out again. This time, he leveled his rifle and took aim, and the enemy officer urged his horse forward. The two men disappeared into the woods. "It was not pleasant to fire at the back of an unoffending individual who was acquitting himself very cooly of his duty," Ferguson wrote, "so I let him alone."

It was not until the next day, after Ferguson's men were commended for their "gallant and spirited behaviour" at Brandywine that he learned the identity of the two officers whose lives he had spared. One of the surgeons who treated Ferguson for an injury he sustained in the action the day before said the man wearing the uniform of a French hussar was Casimir Pulaski, the Polish dragoon who was a volunteer aide-de-camp to General Washington. The American was Washington himself.

Historians have been reluctant to credit this too-good-to-be-true story, and their reluctance is understandable. But a letter to Congress from Lieutenant Colonel Robert Hanson Harrison, who as Washington's military secretary was responsible for his correspondence, confirmed at least some of the details. "His Excellency" was in fact out "reconnoitering" the day before the battle, and Pulaski, who had only recently arrived from France, did wear a hussar's uniform. Ferguson admitted that he was not sure how he would have acted had he known that he could have killed the commander in chief of the Continental army, thereby changing the course of the war and of human history. "I am not sorry," he said, "that I did not know at the time who it was."

The injury for which the surgeon treated Ferguson after Brandy-wine was a serious one. A bullet had passed through his right elbow, and he would spend months in Philadelphia, suffering through a series of ghastly operations to remove bone splinters, trying to recuperate and to keep his sense of humor. Surgeons had wanted to amputate, but he argued against it, joking in a letter to his family back in Scotland that the question was whether the mangled limb should belong to him or to "the worms." Ferguson prevailed, the arm was saved, and while he rested in Philadelphia he taught himself to shoot and brandish a sword with his left arm. In his absence, his rifle corps—experimental from its formation—was disbanded, and its men returned to the light infantry units from which they had been drawn. (Used only at Brandywine, the Ferguson rifle, however impressive, proved prohibitively expensive, costing three times as much to manufacture as a conventional musket.)

When the war moved south, Ferguson and his new troops, known informally as Ferguson's Rangers, fought with Tarleton's Legion at Monck's Corner. In that skirmish, Ferguson sustained another injury. One dark night, Ferguson and his men stumbled into some of Tar-leton's. Both thought they had encountered the enemy and opened fire. In the ensuing carnage, Ferguson's left arm—his good one—was slashed with a bayonet. Here, too, he avoided amputation, and for three weeks, he rode with his reins clenched between his teeth.

Ferguson understood, as Huck did not, the importance of reassur-ing people in the backcountry of British intentions. "We come not to make war on women and children," he told them, "but to relieve [your distresses]." Men were eager to serve under him, and as many as two thousand joined his militia. Throughout the summer of 1780, Fergu-son's Rangers played a game of cat and mouse with Sumter's partisans, disrupting their efforts to disrupt the British, but never quite putting them out of action. In a pattern coming to define the American way of war, the rebels would strike, inflict annoying damage, then disappear. The rebels did their best in small engagements, but Ferguson's relatively large but nonetheless mobile force was proving capable of making a hit-and-run campaign like that of Sumter and Shelby more difficult than they might like. Even so, the rebels continued their raids on loyalist outposts with remarkable success.

In late July, Sumter learned that Ferguson had moved beyond the Broad River. He detached Shelby and Clarke, with about six hundred men, to follow, hoping to take out a loyalist camp about fifteen miles northeast of Spartanburg, at Thicketty Creek, at a fort built to fight the Indians. The fort was formidable, but the garrison inside was seriously outnumbered and, once surrounded, gave up without a shot fired. Shelby and his men took ninety-four prisoners and 250 muskets. Two weeks later, the rebels tangled with a detachment of Ferguson's own men. This was at Cedar Springs, about four miles from Spartanburg, with—Shelby and Clarke did not know this—Ferguson's main army of at least fifteen hundred and by some accounts 2,500 men a few miles to the rear. A foraging party composed of British soldiers as well as loyalists was gathering peaches in an orchard when Shelby and Clarke approached. They were driven off by British cavalry, but this was only temporary. They regrouped and returned, and the battle seesawed back and forth, in and out of the peach orchard, before rebel reinforcements arrived and the loyalists withdrew. But this too was temporary.

An 1842 account of the skirmish says that Clarke

astonished Shelby by the energy and adroitness with which he dealt his blows. Shelby often said he stopped in the midst of the engagement to see Clarke fight. The Liberty Men drove back their foes, when the whole British Army [meaning Ferguson's main force] came up. A retreat was now a matter of necessity as well as sound policy. Shelby and Clarke had taken fifty prisoners, most of them British and some of them officers. These Ferguson was extremely anxious to retake, and his antagonists by no means willing to lose. Hence the pursuit was pressed for miles with great vigor and the retreat managed so skillfully as to render the great superiority of the royal army of no avail. A kind of running fight was maintained for five miles, until the prisoners were entirely out of reach.

Ten days later, on August 18, Shelby, Clarke, and Williams were ready to strike again, this time on the banks of the Enoree River, at Musgrove's Mill. To get there, they had to sneak by Ferguson's camp, which they managed to do, but received distressing news when they arrived. Hundreds of reinforcements from the loyalist camp at Fort Ninety Six had arrived the night before, and the rebels were now outnumbered by more than two to one. Worse than that, scouts had exchanged fire in the dark, dashing any hope they might have had of surprising the enemy. Ferguson's army was in their rear, and once news of a battle got back to the Scotsman, he would be headed their way.

This would increasingly be the case in the battles in the South: "There was no overall commander, an arrangement frowned on in official military circles, and admittedly it carries the potential for turmoil," John Buchanan wrote in *The Road to Guilford Courthouse*. But it was "often the case when militia took the field and was quite workable when men of reason were involved." Whether that would be the case this time, of course, remained to be seen. There was no room to retreat, in any event, and Shelby and Clarke felt they had no choice but to attack. Even so, they would have to be on the defensive, even if, or when, they started the fight.

Preparing for the inevitable, Shelby and the other officers put the troops to work, preparing defenses—or what would pass for them. They threw together a breastwork of fallen logs and brush that extended in a semicircle three hundred yards long. The soldiers then took their positions behind this makeshift barricade, and twenty-five men— led by a Georgian named Shadrack Inman, who volunteered for the assignment—were to climb into the saddle, cross the river, and creep as close as they could to the enemy camp. There they were to open fire, in the hope of provoking a counterattack. Inman and his party rode off, and the men behind the logs and brush, with their horses secured in the rear, held their breath and waited. Shelby's men were behind the barricade, such as it was, and Clarke had his men positioned in the rear, as reinforcements.

They did not have to wait long. Inman's dragoons fired, and the redcoats charged, splashing across the river and into the makeshift defenses. The men there were to hold tight until Shelby had fired his rifle, then let loose. At about 150 yards from the breastwork, the loyalists opened fire with their muskets, but with little effect. They tended to overshoot the mark, but this was hardly decisive. What followed were onrushing infantry with fixed bayonets, led by their commander, Colonel Alexander Innes, on his horse, yelling, "Huzzah for King George!," which managed to dislodge some of the terrified rebels. The others held their ground, awaiting Shelby's signal. That came when the loyalists had covered about seventy yards or so, cutting the distance in half. The rebels fired, smoke enshrouded the field, and the British fell back, but only for a moment. Another bayonet charge followed, and the rebel lines "slowly began to bend," as Buchanan put it, "like a sapling under pressure." That's when Clarke's reinforcements, about forty in all, came on, and in smoke "so thick as to hide a man at twenty yards," as Shelby described it, Innes went down. Screeching like the Indians they had fought on the far side of the mountains, Shelby's men charged over the breastwork, and then Clarke's also surmounted the flimsy defenses, and in the smoke, screams, and crackling of the muskets, the loyalists "broke in great confusion," Shelby would recall, and "dead men lay thick on the Ground over which our men pursued the enemy." Inman, who led the charge that provoked the counterattack, was among the fallen. He had been shot seven times, an inspection of his wounds revealed, once in the forehead.

The loyalists lost not only Innes but nearly half of their entire force as well. Out of the five hundred in camp, 223 were either killed, wounded, or taken prisoner. The rebels suffered just eleven casualties, four killed and seven wounded. Emboldened by the decisive victory, Shelby, Clarke, and Williams were eager to head off twenty-five miles south, to the loyalist stronghold at Ninety Six. (No one seems sure why the fort there had the name it did, though it was supposedly that many miles from the nearest Cherokee town, frequently visited by traders; the town that remains is still called Ninety Six.)

Ninety Six was the next post that, at the moment, looked like easy pickings for the rebels. They were about to leave for it when they received the distressing news from Camden. Two days earlier, the entire Continental army under Horatio Gates had been destroyed or taken prisoner, and the position of the British in South Carolina had never been stronger. Under Cornwallis and Rawdon, the redcoats were on the move, ready to subdue the entire state, and in that larger effort, the troops under Shelby, Clarke, and Williams could be easily eliminated. Cornwallis told Ferguson, with his now considerably larger force, to take care of that backcountry nuisance, and he was already on his way. The rebels, meanwhile, were under orders to get away as fast as they could and forget, for the moment, any hope of further action. They would meet Ferguson head on, six weeks later. And this time, it would be decisive.

CHAPTER ELEVEN

"No Longer an Englishman"

On September 3, 1780, two weeks after Camden, the *Mercury*, a brigantine owned by the Continental Congress and called "as fast a sailor as any in America," was overtaken off the coast of Newfoundland. After a five-hour chase, the *Vestal*, a twenty-eight-gun British frigate, fired three warning shots, and the *Mercury* promptly surrendered. The *Mercury*, its captors quickly discovered, was bound for Holland, where one of its passengers had been sent to arrange for a sizable loan from the Dutch Republic, at that time the financial center of Europe.

The Netherlands played no favorites, ideologically, in these international squabbles; their interest was business, and here their own trade with other countries had suffered through competition—and conflict—with the British. The Dutch had wanted to remain neutral in the rest of Europe's ongoing disputes, but, when France entered the war on the American side, England was able to use Dutch declarations of neutrality against them, forbidding them from selling and shipping supplies directly to its rebellious Atlantic colonies. For a time, the Dutch shipped goods, as contraband, to France, and from France to America. The British put a stop to this practice, however, and by September, when the *Mercury* was seized, hostilities between England and the Netherlands were boiling over.

The capture of the *Mercury*, and its most notable passenger, would provide the occasion for the British to declare war on the Dutch, with the war—far from a small matter of a mother country attempting to control her bothersome colonies—spreading with alarming momentum.

This notable passenger was Henry Laurens, who, the previous year, had been named by Congress as its minister to the Netherlands. Another Huguenot whose forebears had emigrated from France, sailed to New York, and settled in Charles Town, Laurens was the son of a prosperous saddler and merchant whose business grew to include the manufacture and sale of carriages. In 1744, in line to inherit the family business, Henry was sent to England to work in a Scottish counting-house and further his understanding of international business practices. "He went to London, lured and intoxicated by the grandeur of the English capital," David Duncan Wallace, Henry's earliest biographer, wrote in 1915. He "left it a British subject still and long to remain a proudly loyal one; but there was a new feeling in him too, the first evidence of that strong love for the spot of earth that bore and nourished him which was in time to make him no longer an Englishman," but an American. "I shall once more ship myself to Carolina," he wrote to a brother back home, "where, please God I shall arrive safe, I shall pitch my tent."

In 1747, when Henry was twenty-three and back in Charles Town, his father died, and over the next few years, his heir built the family business into the largest slave-trading house in the American colonies, selling more than eight thousand slaves in the 1750s alone. When that decade began, he married the daughter of a family that owned rice plantations, and in 1754, their first son, John, was born. Hardly a rabble-rouser, Henry Laurens was so identified with the still-loyalist Charles Town establishment that in 1765, after the Stamp Act went into effect and self-described "Sons of Liberty" went on a rampage, they showed up at his house in the belief that he was hiding the detested stamps. He was no fan of these men, who, he once declared "under the guise of Patriotism," had "committed unbounded acts of Licentiousness & at length Burglary and Robbery." These Sons of Liberty ransacked his house and, in Laurens's words, "cursed me and threatened . . . to carry me away to some unknown place and punish me." Finding no stamps—but ransacking his wine cellar—they moved on.

By 1771, a year after his wife died, Laurens retired, devoting himself to politics and the supervision of his sons' educations in England. Selected by his fellow Carolinians to serve in the Continental Congress, in 1777 he succeeded John Hancock as its president. It was three years later, when he was sent by Congress to the Netherlands, that his ship was seized. By this time, son John had joined the Continental army, served as an aide-de-camp to General Washington, wintered at Valley Forge, and fought at Germantown, where he was injured, and at Monmouth. John fought at Charles Town, too, and, when it fell, he was captured and sent to Philadelphia. He was able to visit with his father there, before the *Mercury* sailed away.

The nature of Henry Laurens's mission was not immediately apparent, but it became so once the *Vestal*'s crew retrieved a cache of documents that their panicked *Mercury* counterparts had thrown into the sea. Among these papers was the draft of a proposed treaty between Congress and the Dutch Republic. Discovery of the treaty prompted Great Britain in December to declare war on the Dutch. This expanded a conflict that over time had become global in nature, with the British attempt to put down the rebellion in the colonies forming only one part of a larger, international struggle. England's longtime adversary France had entered the war following the stunning American victory at Saratoga late in 1777. The entry of the French added to the mounting challenges the English seemed almost overnight to be facing in the West Indies, in the Mediterranean, India, and Africa. Spain, having made a secret treaty with France, had entered the war in 1779, and now Holland was drawn into the struggle.

"A compleat history of the American war," John Adams would write in 1784, would constitute "nearly the History of Mankind for the whole Epoch of it. The History of France, Spain, Holland, England, and the Neutral Powers, as well as America are at least comprised of it." The international nature of the struggle is easy for Americans to overlook. But doing so makes it almost impossible to understand their own war for independence, and the extent to which the British were stretched thin in their prosecution of it. The English supply lines extended for more than three thousand miles, and manpower would always be a challenge, which helps explain why it would be possible for the Americans— by waging a war of attrition in the South—to defeat such a militarily superior enemy.

For a time, of course, Great Britain's power in the world seemed unassailable. At the conclusion of the Seven Years' War, when British flags flew throughout the world, Horace Walpole wrote that the empire's triumphs "come so tumbling over one another from distant parts of the globe that it looks like the handiwork of a lady romance-writer." Cannons fired in celebration "will never have time to cool," while bells "are worn threadbare with the ringing for victories." It took Rome three hundred years to conquer the world, Walpole said, but the English had done it in a fortnight. England emerged from the Seven Years' War, as Don Cook wrote in *The Long Fuse: How England Lost the American Colonies, 1760–1785,* "sure of her power in the world, and determined to run the British Empire as she damn well pleased."

Beneath the surface, however, there were signs that all was not right. At the end of the Seven Years' War, Great Britain faced serious economic difficulties and, deep in debt, was "borrowing more money," Cook writes, "than it had in all its past history." When Parliament attempted to raise revenues by increasing taxes on the American colonies, the Americans were quick to respond. Non-importation agreements were signed, merchants canceled orders, merchant ships ceased to sail, and the English economy suffered still more, with poverty—especially in London—deepening. Americans like to picture the English society against whose government they rebelled as stodgy, placid, and complacent. This is inaccurate. In the spring of 1768, after the rabble-rousing John Wilkes, that radical journalist and on-again, off-again member of Parliament, was imprisoned for "seditious libel" of George III, London was the scene of the worst civil unrest in its long history.

This city, "the residence of the King," Benjamin Franklin reported, "is now a daily scene of lawless riot and confusion." Mobs patrolled the streets in the middle of the day, making the bloodless Boston Tea Party five years in the future seem a model of decorum. Rioters, Franklin wrote, attacked everyone

> that will not roar for Wilkes and Liberty, courts of justice afraid to give judgements against him; coal heavers and porters pulling down the houses of coal merchants that refuse to give them more wages; sawyers destroying sawmills; sailors unrigging all the outward bound ships and suffering none at all to sail until merchants agree to raise their pay; watermen destroying private boats and threatening bridges [across the Thames]; soldiers firing among the mobs and killing men, women and children, which seems only to have produced a universal sullenness, that looks like a great black cloud coming on, ready to burst in a general tempest.

Wilkes, who as mayor of London called the war against the American colonies "bloody, expensive, and a threat to liberty" and as a member of Parliament denounced it as "unnatural, unjust and barbarous," was adored by the Americans. John Adams, Samuel Adams, and other American patriots sent letters and petitions in his defense; supporters in Virginia and Maryland shipped him forty-five hogsheads of tobacco to cover his expenses. South Carolina's provincial legislature voted to allocate fifteen hundred pounds sterling to help pay the high-living Wilkes's personal debts, which Henry Laurens, suspicious of its intended recipient's radicalism, opposed. Lord North's ministry intervened, opposing the appropriation, which effectively ended legislative government in South Carolina, restoring royal rule.

Two years later, in the summer of 1780, London was again rocked by what James Boswell called a weeklong orgy of "barbarous anarchy." During the so-called Gordon Riots, named for Lord George Gordon, the head of the Protestant Association that had whipped up anti-Catholic hysteria, Catholic chapels were burned, as the townspeople exhibited what Edward Gibbon called "a dark and diabolical fanaticism which I had supposed was extinct." On the morning of Black Wednesday, Samuel Johnson found Newgate Prison "in ruins with the fire yet glowing." When a distillery near the prison was torched, Stanley Weintraub wrote in *Iron Tears: America's Battle for Freedom, Britain's Quagmire: 1775–1783*, "the fetid gutters ran with alcohol. The rabble, even women and children, sopped up the slimy spirits in rags, shoes, caps, and buckets, drinking themselves insensible. Lurching for more drink too close to the burning buildings, some died in the flames." The rioters attacked the Bank of London, too, and when order was finally restored, work gangs had to whitewash its walls to cover the bloodstains and bullet holes. Several hundred people died in what one member of Parliament called the "Wild and savage insurrection."

There was "an edge to life" in Britain that "is hard for us to recapture," J. H. Plumb wrote in *England in the Eighteenth Century*. "In every class there [was] the same taut neurotic quality—the fantastic gambling and drinking, the riots, brutality and violence, and everywhere and always a constant sense of death." There was horrifying poverty and, among the aristocracy, "grotesque extravagance." London, as Johnson put it, was "a city famous for wealth, commerce and plenty, and for every kind of civility and politeness, but abounds with such heaps of filth as a savage would look on with amazement." The most popular forms of entertainment were public hangings.

Through it all, however, the American colonists remained proud British subjects. Twenty-five thousand of them had joined militias to fight alongside the redcoats in what Americans called the French and Indian War and expressed no desire for independence. The colonies had grown in population and prosperity under a regime that Sir Robert Walpole called one of "salutary neglect." Trade boomed, and the Americans—left, for the most part, to govern themselves—had grown strong and confident in their ability to manage their own affairs. But when the British tried to replenish the king's coffers by raising taxes on the colonies, and the Americans resisted, the response—as critics within Parliament warned—was utterly predictable: the Americans rebelled, and the British cracked down. The colonists had not reacted "in all things with prudence and temper," William Pitt the Elder, who had been prime minister from 1766 through 1768, reminded his colleagues in the House of Commons. But the Americans had "been wronged" and "driven to madness by injustice." They had been perfectly reasonable subjects, but what they could not tolerate was bullying British soldiers patrolling their streets, disbanding their legislatures, and "taking money out of their pockets without their consent."

It was in March 1775—less than a month before Lexington and Concord—that Edmund Burke issued his warning, which was as stern as Pitt's. Britain's meddling was resulting in the "incurable alienation of our colonies," kindling a flame "that is ready to consume us," Burke warned, in the same speech in which he had pointed out the role of slavery in the southerners' desire for independence. Burke understood, as George III and Lord North's ministry did not, that the Americans had rebelled, initially, to defend what they saw as their rights as loyal English subjects.

And it was in the very nature of the colonists—developed as part of their heritage as proud English subjects but also as a result of their experience in self-government—to resist any attempts to limit their liberty. As British subjects, even without their slavery, the Americans were intensely aware of their rights. "This fierce spirit of liberty," Burke said, "is stronger in the English colonies probably than in any other people of the earth," and is "unalterable by any human art. We cannot, I fear, falsify the pedigree of this fierce people, and persuade them that they are not sprung from a nation in whose veins the blood of freedom circulates."

Burke understood, finally, that the colonists' discontent drew heavily on a tradition of dissent voiced for a century by the English Whigs. Well before the Americans took up the cry, the English Whigs—and dissenters like John Wilkes—claimed that Parliament had become grievously corrupt. This tradition of dissent and its rhetoric were readily taken up by the colonists. Those who supported independence did not call themselves "patriots" but "whigs," a term that dated back at least to the Glorious Revolution of 1688. American whigs, as Gordon S. Wood wrote in *The American Revolution,* "insisted that they were rebelling not against the principles of the English constitution but on behalf of them." Those who fought for reconciliation—or sometimes merely prayed in secret for it—were Tories.

Even Franklin, who came late to the cause of independence, contrasted that "old rotten state" of England and its political structures with the "glorious public virtue so predominant in our rising country." In England, "numberless and needless [public sinecures], enormous salaries, pensions, perquisites, bribes, groundless quarrels, foolish expeditions, false accounts or no accounts, contracts and jobs, devour all revenue, and produce continual necessity in the midst of plenty." Any reconciliation, Franklin reluctantly concluded, will only "corrupt and poison" the colonists, too. Alexander Hamilton was even more direct, likening the British system of government to "an old, wrinkled, withered, worn-out hag."

Henry Laurens, like Franklin, came to support independence reluctantly as well. He felt affection for his king and, as many of the colonists did, blamed Parliament—or assumed that George III was the victim of bad advice. On June 4, 1775—the king's birthday, no less—Laurens told the other members of South Carolina's First Provincial Congress that even then he still considered himself "one of his Majesty's most dutiful and loyal subjects, willing at all times to do my utmost in defense of his person, crown, and dignity." Laurens did "not wish the Monarch's death nor to remove him from the throne, the crown from his head, or the sceptre from his hand." Unfortunately, George III was being badly misled by malicious courtiers. And if his administration persisted in its attempts to subvert the liberties of its own loyal colonists, Laurens declared himself ready

> to bear arms and to repel force by force in any command suitable to my rank, whenever such shall appear in hostile acts against my country. Against every invader of our rights and liberties, I shall be ready to make all possible opposition. I shall do so with the greater cheerfulness from a strong hope of being instrumental in restoring to his Majesty his undoubted right of reigning over a vast empire of freemen, of recovering to him the possession of the hearts of millions of his faithful subjects of which he has been robbed by the machinations of a few wicked men who falsely call themselves his friends.

But this was much too generous. George III, as the record would show, remained zealous about prosecuting the war even when his own prime minister urged him to consider the costs and the consequences—and the good chance that England would lose. There was the three-thousand-mile supply line, for starters. There was the problem of manpower—British soldiers were needed elsewhere, to safeguard the empire's other far-flung possessions. But the king would not listen to reason. Even Saratoga, in 1777, which brought the French into the war, George III considered a "misfortune . . . very serious but not without remedy." In 1778, as the king recorded their conversation, Lord North told him the condition of the country's military, including its vaunted navy, "is deplorable; it is totally unequal to a war with Spain, France and America, and will . . . be over-matched."

England could win the war, Lord North argued, only at "an enormous expense, which will ruin her and will not in any degree be repaid by the most brilliant victories." But the king would not be persuaded. Once the Americans had made their stand in Massachusetts, back in 1774, George III's mind was made up. "I am not sorry" that a war was to follow, he told Lord North. "The New England governments are in a State of Rebellion. *Blows must decide* whether they are to be subject to this country or independent," a position from which he would never budge. The following year, Parliament made it official, announcing that the colonies were in "a state of rebellion," which constituted a declaration of war against England. That is why the news that the colonies had issued a Declaration of Independence, received in London in August 1776, was viewed with sniffish disdain. Parliament, in its summer recess, remained in recess. Thomas Jefferson's bold words stirred his countrymen and alerted other countries to their intentions, but they meant almost nothing back in London.

Laurens, slow to lose faith in George III, remained an optimist. Even when the *Vestal* had overtaken the *Mercury* and seized its crew as prisoners, he expressed confidence that, although he would not be able to fulfill his mission to negotiate a loan from the Dutch, he still believed he would be able to accomplish something of value, whatever awaited him. Moses Young, on board the *Mercury* as Laurens's secretary, was frightened and despondent, but Laurens would have none of it. "I feel a satisfaction [in] being Captured by a British ship," he told his aide. "I shall now be sent to England where I shall be of more real service to my own Country than I could possibly be in any other part of Europe."

Laurens was in for an unpleasant surprise. He was taken first to St. John's, Newfoundland, where—as he had assumed would be the case—he was treated more as an ambassador than a prisoner of war. He was then shipped on board *The Fairy* to Dartmouth. From Dartmouth he was taken to London, arriving on October 5. There, despite his insistence that he was a legitimate diplomatic representative of the Continental Congress, his "treatment immediately became rigorous to the point of absurdity," Wallace wrote in his biography. After being interrogated, Laurens was promptly locked in the Tower of London, the highest-ranking American prisoner and the only one confined to that walled city inside London. He was being held on suspicion of high treason, an allegation so serious that it would deny him the possibility of release, even as part of a general prisoner exchange.

And there he remained.

CHAPTER TWELVE

"I Surmount Every Difficulty"

A few days before Camden, while Horatio Gates still had an army to command, a small, beak-nosed, pointy-chinned man of middle or late middle age appeared at the general's camp at Rugeley's plantation, eager to put the pitiful handful of followers he brought with him to the service of the cause. This was Francis Marion, a Continental soldier who commanded a small force of militia. First impressions of the man were rarely favorable. "He was below the middle stature of men," recalled William Dobein James, who joined "Marion's Men," as they would be known, at the age of fifteen. "His body was well set, but his knees and ankles were badly formed," and he "limped upon one leg." Even so, there was something oddly compelling about the man. "He had a countenance remarkably steady," James said, and his eyes were "black and piercing."

Colonel Otho Holland Williams reserved judgment. The men Marion brought with him were "distinguished"—"distinguished" seems a stretch—"by small leather caps, and the wretchedness of their attire," Williams said.

> Their number did not exceed twenty men and boys, some white, some black, and all mounted, but most of them miserably equipped; their appearance was in fact so burlesque, that it was with much difficulty [that] the diversion of the regular soldiery was restrained by the officers, and the General himself

was glad of an opportunity of detaching Col. Marion, at his own insistence, towards the interior of South Carolina, with orders to watch the motions of the enemy and furnish intelligence.

A more forthright way to put it is that Gates encouraged Marion and his ragamuffins to get away from the rest of the troops as quickly as possible, go somewhere else where they might possibly be of some use, and leave the real soldiering to others.

But this was probably fine with Marion, whose dedication to independence was not in theory only. He was at his best when he answered to no one, and, understanding the difference between well-drilled Continentals and raw militia, he made allowances for the latter's lack of discipline. He was also content to harass the enemy, an activity that made better use of his men's abilities than major engagements would. If he could swing south of Camden, disrupting the redcoats' ability to move men, provisions, and intelligence back and forth from Charles Town, as well as cutting off the enemy's ability to retreat to safety, he would be happy to oblige. Peter Horry, who served under Marion throughout the campaign, remembered the assignment they were given with admirable candor: "Col. Francis Marion & Myself was ordered to go Down the Country to Destroy all boats & Craft of any kind, we found on Santee River in Order to prevent Cornwallis & his Troops Escaping him." This they proceeded to do with characteristic élan.

Much has been made of the feisty temperament of the Scots-Irish who fought in the War of Independence, but Francis Marion, like others whose heritage has been given short shrift, was a Huguenot. Marion was born, it is believed, in 1732, the same year as George Washington, on a plantation on Goose Creek, about twenty miles northwest of Charles Town. His grandparents on both sides had come to America with thousands of other French-speaking refugees in the late seventeenth century, after the revocation of the Edict of Nantes made Protestantism once again illegal in France. John Crockett, who would settle in Tennessee, fight for the rebels at Kings Mountain, and father Davey Crockett, was a Huguenot; his surname at birth in Virginia was John Crocketague. Marion's lifelong friend and fellow partisan Peter Horry was a Huguenot, too; Horry was pronounced *or-EE*.

"I have it from good authority," Horry said of Marion, "that this great soldier, at his birth, was not larger than a New England lobster, and might easily have been put into a quart pot." But he was an adventurous boy, ill-suited to such rudimentary schooling as would have been available to him, and was never glib. Whatever indoors education he was made to endure, James said, "seemed to dispose Marion to be modest and reserved in conversation; to think, if not to read much; and, above all not to be communicative." He also seems to have been bored by the routines of the farm—planters grew rice and indigo in the lowcountry—and dreamed of a life at sea. Against his mother's wishes, he set sail at sixteen with a crew of six for the West Indies. Their ship sank, and they clamored onto an open boat, without anything to eat or drink. But, "providentially," as James put it, "a dog swam to them from the ship," and its blood "served them for drink, and his raw flesh for food, for six days." Two of the men died on the boat and were thrown overboard; on the final day, the survivors reached land. Safely back at the farm, Horry wrote, Marion's "constitution seemed renewed, his frame commenced a second and rapid growth, while his cheeks, quitting their pale, suet-colored cast, assumed a bright and healthy olive."

For the next ten years or so, Marion farmed his own place, called Pond Bluff, and in 1761, he joined a militia company fighting the Cherokees; in the one attack he is known to have led, twenty-one of the thirty men under his command were killed or wounded, but he achieved the objective nonetheless. He managed to remove the Cherokees who had blocked the rest of the company's advance. Once they were out of the way, the main force pushed through, burning fifteen Cherokee villages and their crops. Then Marion went back to the farm and, in 1775, was sufficiently well regarded by his neighbors to be elected to represent them in South Carolina's Provincial Congress. By this time, all of the colonies were indignant about the closing of Boston Harbor, which had taken place the year before, and incensed South Carolinians announced an embargo on British goods. Those who were even suspected of engaging in trade with the mother country, whether guilty or not, were subjected to what James called "intemperate" punishments. Without the benefit of trial or public hearing, they were tarred and feathered, or worse.

The following year Marion joined the Continental army; fought with Colonel William Moultrie in the first, and successful, defense of Charles Town; and in 1779 participated in the failed effort to retake Savannah from the British. He was helping build Charles Town's defenses the second time the British came, and why he was not taken prisoner forms an important episode in the Marion mythology. This upstanding Calvinist did not drink wine or hard liquor and looked with some disapproval on those who did. An abstemious sort, he carried water infused with vinegar in his canteen and was never known to carouse in any way. So in March 1780, when he accepted a dinner invitation at the home of Captain Alexander McQueen at the corner of Charles Town's Orange and Tradd Streets, he found himself in an uncomfortable situation.

When the dinner dishes were cleared, McQueen locked the doors, preventing his guests from putting an early end to the festivities. When the toasts began, Marion escaped by jumping from a second-story window and broke his ankle when he hit the ground. "When the story got about in Charles Town," Peter Horry recalled, "people said he was a great fool for his pains, but the event proved that Marion was in the right, and that there is no policy like sticking to a man's duty." To avoid being captured, Marion—now forty-eight years old—"was obliged to sculk about from house to house among his friends," Moultrie wrote, "and sometimes hide in the bushes until he grew better," though the ankle would afflict him for the rest of his life. In time, he "crept out by degrees, and began to collect a few friends; and when he got ten or twelve together he ventured out."

When Gates sent Marion away, he continued to increase his ranks, and he had about seventy volunteers with him, according to Moultrie, who had known Marion ever since they fought the Cherokees. None of his men were paid, and they received no provisions—meaning weapons, clothing, blankets, or food—from Congress, the Continental army, or the states. They subsisted on cornmeal, sweet potatoes, hominy, and the meat of feral hogs or scrub cattle they could run down and kill. Young William Dobein James "had the honour to be invited to dine with the general" one day in camp. Oscar, who was Marion's servant, set the dinner before the company, "partly on a pine log, partly on the ground; it was lean beef, without salt, and sweet potatoes." James "had left a small pot of boiled homminy" where he had slept the night before, which he fetched and shared. "The homminy had salt in it, and proved, though eaten out of the pot, a most acceptable repast. The general said but little," which was to be expected, and the party "had nothing to drink but bad water."

Most of Marion's men were usually "quite unarmed," Moultrie

said. Whatever weapons they carried they supplied themselves. If they had swords or sabers, those they had not taken from the enemy were cut from wood saws by friendly blacksmiths. They carried their own hunting rifles or shotguns, and, according to Henry Lumpkin in *From Savannah to Yorktown,* their favorite ammunition for fighting at close range "was number 2 goose shot," which at twenty or thirty yards "would tear a man apart." Men came and went, but they proved remarkably loyal to Marion and often returned. His "little party would sometimes be reduced to five and twenty men," Moultrie said, but they did not disband.

After Gates's army was destroyed at Camden and Sumter's men were routed two days later at Fishing Creek, there was nothing left of an organized military resistance not just in South Carolina but in the South itself. As of August 1780, Gates had an army in name only. Partisans like Isaac Shelby, Elijah Clarke, and (after regrouping) Thomas Sumter were doing what they could to bleed the British and their loyalist proxies from Camden to the mountains in the west. And in the lowcountry outside Charles Town, there was no one left but Marion to challenge British control, even if this challenge took the homely form of disrupting their supply lines, harassing their foraging parties, or simply burning boats, as Gates had instructed him to do.

Marion learned of the defeat at Camden before his men did, but he kept this demoralizing information to himself. From a British deserter, he also learned that 150 rebel prisoners captured at Camden were being escorted back to Charles Town by a detachment of ninety escorts. This was about thirty more men than Marion had, but transporting prisoners was a burdensome and distracting job that made anyone with that assignment vulnerable to surprise. They had camped at Sumter's old plantation—which Tarleton had burned earlier in the summer—near Nelson's Ferry, on the upper Santee River.

On August 25, Marion and his men attacked the loyalist camp at night, managing to kill or capture more than twenty of the escorts and freeing all the prisoners. Some of them, however, refused to acknowledge such a shabby liberator as Marion. Continental regulars said they would not obey his commands and, rather than be led by him or his pathetic-looking men, would prefer to go to Charles Town on their own. The ones who were happy just to be released from their captivity left with Marion to go to his camp in the swamps, but only three of them made it the whole way. The others wandered off. Even so, reports of the victory made it back to northern newspapers, bringing Marion to the attention of the rest of the country for the first time, and offering some faint flicker of hope after the dispiriting news from Camden.

Marion struck again during the first week of September. A force of between two hundred and two hundred and fifty loyalists had been sent with explicit instructions to destroy him and his troops, and, with five times as many men as Marion had, the odds were clearly with the enemy. Marion decided to attack anyway. Major John James—the father of William Dobein James—routed their loyalists' forty-five-man advance guard, and at dawn on September 4, Marion himself came on, galloping toward the main force of two hundred or so loyalists on the Little Pee Dee River. When Marion saw that the loyalists were forming for battle, he knew he could not surprise them. And so, James said, not wishing "to expose his men, by an attack on equal terms," he "feigned a retreat, and led [the loyalists] into an ambuscade," where they were routed, with scores of the enemy fleeing into the swamps. "This was the first manoeuvre of the kind, for which he afterwards became so conspicuous."

Battle of Black Mingo.
Illustration from *The Life of Francis Marion* by W. Gilmore Simms, 1857

Three weeks later, on September 29, a still-limping Marion and his men attacked the loyalists again. This time it was at Black Mingo Creek, a tea-colored tributary of the Black River that winds its way through the cypress swamps northwest of Georgetown and was named for the Chickasaw word for "chief." About fifty Tories under Colonel John Coming Ball were camped a mile or so downstream from Willtown, at Dollard's Tavern, also known as the Red House, some twenty miles from the coast. The plan was for Marion and about fifty of his men to set out under the moss-draped live oaks early enough to surprise the camp at midnight. They made good progress, especially considering the fact that they had to get across the Little Pee Dee, which meant plunging their horses into the water. Marion couldn't swim and, by one account, clung to the pommel of his horse's saddle and "floated across beside the swimming animal." There were two other rivers to cross, but there were flatboats waiting for them at the Big Pee Dee and a ferry at Lynches, so those crossings were less worrisome.

They had ridden thirty miles since starting out at daybreak, and crossed three rivers, and still managed to get to Mingo Creek when they had hoped. But when their horses clattered across the wooden plank bridge at Willtown, the loyalist sentries heard the racket, and, hearing a gun fired to alert him to the enemy's approach, Ball deployed his loyalists and prepared for the fight. They were not going to mount their defense from a nearby tavern, as Marion had assumed, and he discovered this as soon as his men charged the building. Ball positioned his troops in the moonlit field west of the tavern, and they held their fire until the rebels came within thirty yards of their muskets. Then they sent forth a crackling volley that dropped three officers. This caused the rebels to retreat, but only temporarily. They re-formed and returned, at which point the loyalists' resolve crumbled. This fight, too, seemed to end almost as soon as it began.

It was over in fifteen minutes, and about half of the loyalists were killed on the spot, mortally wounded, or taken captive. Others, dropping their muskets, managed to flee into the darkness of the swamps. Only two of Marion's men lost their lives in the dark of night at Mingo Creek, and among the spoils of battle were a number of horses, including John Coming Ball's sorrel gelding. Marion renamed the charger "Ball" and rode it throughout the rest of the war. They also picked up guns, ammunition, and a few new men: at the close of the battle, five of Ball's loyalists changed sides and went on to fight with Marion. Afterward he said he learned never to charge across a bridge like that again without covering it with blankets. This was an admirable goal, but a problem insofar as his men often had no blankets at all, much less enough to share with a bridge.

After the battle, Marion turned his attention to his men. They had heard that the loyalists were routinely burning houses throughout the lowcountry and worried that theirs too had been put to the torch. Marion sympathized. "Go to your families," he told them, and then he sought to counter stories about how his own men had been conducting themselves. British Major James Wemyss, rampaging throughout the lowcountry near Georgetown, told Cornwallis that the rebels were "burning houses and distressing the [loyalists] in a most severe manner." Such rumors disgusted Marion, especially when there was good reason to believe they might be true. One of the rebels romping about in the lowcountry at the same time was Maurice Murphy, a captain operating even more independently than Marion and from whom Marion kept his distance. Murphy was a hard and abusive man, and when his own uncle tried to talk to him about his treatment of loyalists, Murphy shot him to death.

In early October, Marion reported the victory at Black Mingo Creek to General Gates, and in addition to telling him the good news, he included some details that distressed Gates severely. "I am sorry to Acquaint you," Marion wrote, "that Capt. Murphy's Party have burnt a Great Number of houses [along the Little Pee Dee] & intend to go on in that abominable work—which I am Apprehensive May be Laid to me; but I assure you, there is not one house Burnt by my Orders or by any of my People, it is what I detest to Destroy poor women & children."

But Marion ended his report on an optimistic note. Major James Wemyss was another formidable Scotsman, like Patrick Ferguson. An Edinburgh native, Wemyss had entered the British army at seventeen, fought in the Long Island campaign, and in late 1779 sailed south with Sir Henry Clinton. There, after the fall of Charles Town, Wemyss developed a well-deserved reputation for torching rebels' plantations. Marion was hardly alone in not knowing how the name was spelled (he wrote it as "Whimes") or even pronounced (the correct pronunciation was *weems*). But he was well aware of the man's notoriety. Wemyss had been burning and plundering "everything in their way," in the countryside around Georgetown, but with less abandon than in weeks past, and he was beginning to seem less intimidating than before.

"The Torys are so affrighted with my little Excursion that Many's moving off to Georgia with their Effects, Others are rund into Swamps," Marion said. He had no more than sixty men now, but if he could raise forty more, he "shou'd certainly pay a visit to Georgetown" and retake that port. "I have great fatigues," he said, "but I surmount every Difficulty."

CHAPTER THIRTEEN

"Shout Like Hell, and Fight Like Devils"

The Carolina foothills, some two hundred miles from Charles Town, are a world away from the swamps of the lowcountry. There are no palmettos and few cypress swamps, and by October 1780, when Patrick Ferguson and the eleven hundred loyalists under his command reached Kings Mountain, the leaves of the thick-trunked oaks and hickories had just begun to turn. It was cooler here, and the higher they got on the mountain, the cooler it would become. The air was also fresher, and the trees provided a welcome shade, where, back east, they mostly trapped the heat.

The hardy souls who lived on the far side of the mountains liked it where they were and seldom found good reasons to go back east. But when Ferguson was stirring up trouble, pitting neighbor against neighbor, a lot of these "Overmountain Men" had viewed the situation differently and decided to take action. The haughty Scotsman was trying to snuff out any opposition in the west, and the backcountry rebels would have none of it. They had been playing cat and-mouse for some weeks now, and with Elijah Clarke as well as Isaac Shelby, these Overmountain Men had beaten the loyalists at Thicketty Fort, Cedar Springs, and Musgrove's Mill, and trudged back home.

But then Gates had lost his army at Camden, and Cornwallis, confident that he had subdued South Carolina, was preparing to enter North Carolina; once North Carolina had been conquered, he figured he could roll right on up to Virginia and end the war. With that in

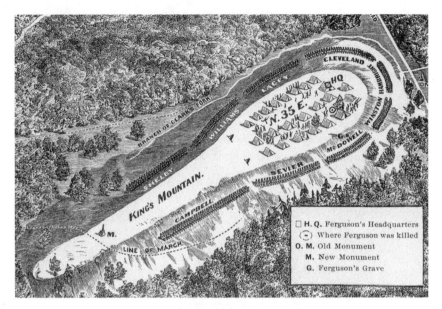

King's Mountain.
Diagram by Lyman Copeland Draper, from *King's Mountain and Its Heroes*

mind, he had dispatched Ferguson to snuff out the rebellion in the west, even if it meant crossing the Blue Ridge himself and eradicating pockets of resistance there. When Ferguson reached Gilbert Town, he sent a messenger to the far side of the mountains. A paroled prisoner who happened to be a kinsman of Shelby's, the messenger carried a warning to all those who might be following Shelby or felt a misguided temptation to do so. They must "desist from their opposition to the British arms," Ferguson announced, and accept protection from the Crown and its representatives. Should they refuse, he "would march his army over the mountains, hang their leaders, and lay their country waste with fire and sword."

Upon receipt of the warning, Shelby rode fifty miles to meet with John Sevier, another Huguenot who, like Francis Marion, had raised and commanded his own militia. They and other men of standing in this rough country agreed that they had toyed with Ferguson long enough. Rather than wait for Ferguson to come to them, they would combine their forces, cross back over the mountains, and go after him.

Shelby commanded six hundred men, and Sevier would bring another 240 or so.

But another frontiersman said he could produce even more men than that. This was Benjamin Cleveland, and Shelby and Sevier knew him as the kind of character they could depend on. Born in Virginia in 1738, unburdened by education, Cleveland was a large—ultimately obese—backwoodsman and, by all accounts, fearless. He had known Daniel Boone, and as a young man had heard Boone talk about his adventures in the Kentucky wilderness. He and a few friends had gone there themselves to hunt and trap. On that outing, they were ambushed by Cherokees, who made off with the furs they had gathered and the horses they rode. But they let the men themselves go free to find their way home, if they could, which they did. Once Cleveland had rested, legend has it, he assembled a party of riflemen, recrossed the mountains, stole back the horses, and rode home again.

Cleveland fought the Cherokees as a North Carolina militiaman, burning thirty-six of the tribe's towns, and before long, he was fighting loyalists, too. In addition to being a colonel in the militia, he also served as a judge and, despite his lack of schooling, managed to get himself elected to the North Carolina legislature. By the time of his death in 1806—at the breakfast table—he was said to weigh 450 pounds. His men, who called him "Old Round-About," were known as "Cleveland's Devils," and with good reason. Their commander's attitude toward loyalists was without nuance, apology, or embellishment. He believed in swift and decisive judgment. "Give them hell," he would tell his men. When captured, if loyalists would take an oath of allegiance to the cause of independence, they were free to go; otherwise, "to get them out of their misery," they would be hanged. This approach did not always sit well with such authority as existed in the backcountry at that time. In the fall of 1779, Cleveland's men strung up two loyalists, and the Superior Court of the town of Salisbury indicted their commander for murder. He received a pardon. This was the kind of man Shelby and Sevier felt could win a war.

They agreed to meet later in September, this time at Sycamore Shoals, near present-day Elizabethtown, Tennessee. When the day came, more than eighteen hundred men showed up, most on horseback with their own rifles. Many of these volunteers came from the wild country west of the Appalachians, but not all. Colonel William

Campbell arrived with four hundred fellow Virginians, but they too were frontiersmen. Most had fought Indians, as the Reverend William Doak, a Presbyterian who preached to them the next day, was well aware. Doak, who kept a rifle close by when he delivered his sermons, was known to stop services to drive off meddlesome Cherokees.

"My countrymen," Doak said in his sermon to the Overmountain Men,

> you are about to set out on an expedition which is full of hardships and dangers, but one in which the Almighty will attend you. The Mother Country has her hands upon you, these American Colonies, and takes that for which our fathers planted their homes in the wilderness—OUR LIBERTY . . . Your brethren across the mountains are crying like Macedonia unto your help. God forbid that you shall refuse to hear and answer their call.

The enemy, Doak continued,

> is marching hither to destroy your homes. Brave men, you are not unacquainted with battle. Your hands have already been taught to war and your fingers to fight. You have wrested these beautiful valleys of the Holston and Watauga from the savage hand. Will you tarry now until the other enemy carries fire and sword to your very doors? No, it cannot be! Go forth then in the strength of your manhood to the aid of your brethren, the defense of your liberty and the protection of your homes. And may the God of Justice be with you and give you victory.

After Doak ended his peroration, he led the men in prayer, and then they set off across the mountains. This "swarm of backwoodsmen," as Banastre Tarleton called them in his history of the southern campaign, marched for ninety miles, often through a snowstorm, and when they pulled their horses to a halt at present-day Morgantown, North Carolina, Benjamin Cleveland joined them, with another 350 men. By this time, Ferguson, who had been alerted to their approach, moved his men east from Gilbert Town, which the Overmountain Men entered during the first week of October, joined shortly thereafter by

Colonel James Williams with four hundred more men from the Carolinas, and the chase began.

"I arrived today at King's Mountain," Ferguson informed Cornwallis two days after the Overmountain Men entered Gilbert Town, "and have taken a post where I do not think I can be forced by a stronger enemy than that against us." Ferguson had eight hundred loyalist militia with him and one hundred provincial infantry, with another two hundred or so who, on the morning of the battle, were out foraging. Ferguson also expected reinforcements from John Harris Cruger's post at Fort Ninety Six and from Tarleton, who was with Cornwallis at Charlotte. What Ferguson did not know was that Cruger had barely enough men to garrison his own fort and that Tarleton was just recovering from malaria, and in no mood to help Ferguson after their disagreement over the so-called Waxhaws massacre. Cornwallis himself was incapacitated in the first weeks of the fall with a "feverish cold."

Ferguson had his men at the top of Kings Mountain, which rises little more than a thousand feet above sea level in the foothills of the Blue Ridge and is imposing only compared to the rolling hills of the surrounding countryside. Mount Mitchell, about sixty-five miles to the northwest, a little past Asheville, by contrast, is almost seven thousand feet in elevation. Even so, Kings Mountain was, in significant respects, a formidable fortress, with commanding views of the entire area around it. The way to its top is rugged and forbidding, with boulders up and down the heavily wooded slopes. Once the pinnacle has been reached—and Ferguson got his men positioned there in plenty of time to rest from their travels—a sense of security is understandable.

The top of the mountain, where Ferguson made his camp, is relatively flat and even, with the shape of an upturned shoe, pointed to the northeast; at its widest, it is only about 120 yards across, and toward the heel, no more than seventy feet wide. Field fortifications in such a ragged and rock-strewn setting seemed almost superfluous, and Ferguson dispensed with them. He placed his seventeen wagons in an arc facing northeast, at the wide end of the summit, and positioned his men around the entire perimeter of the mountaintop. There, with their muskets loaded and their bayonets fixed, they would wait.

A few miles before they reached Kings Mountain, Shelby's men stopped a fourteen-year-old boy whose brother, it turned out, was with the loyalists. The boy carried a message from Ferguson, intended for Cornwallis. Unfortunately for the rebels, it was in code. The terrified youngster provided valuable intelligence nonetheless, telling them exactly where Ferguson and his loyalists were, and also how to identify their commanding officer. They wouldn't be able to see Ferguson's uniform, the boy said, because he would be wearing a checked shirt over it.

And there was more: A woman who said she had delivered chickens to Ferguson's camp corroborated what the boy said about the loyalists' whereabouts, and two enemy scouts, when captured, offered additional information. They too said Ferguson liked to wear a "duster" over his uniform. He had a crippled arm, of course, and he carried a silver whistle. He used it, they said, to direct his troops. It might be unsporting to a British gentleman to target an enemy officer for assassination, but this meant nothing to the men from the other side of the mountains. One of their officers—they elected theirs, not leaving such life-and-death decisions to a monarch across the oceans—told his men to "mark [Ferguson] with your rifles."

The rebels had been marching all night when they finally reached Kings Mountain. Much of that time it had rained, and even when dawn broke, it continued to drizzle. The men were exhausted, but Shelby kept them moving, sending nine hundred of his "best horsemen" ahead, leaving the rest to follow. About a mile from the foot of the mountain, they hitched their horses, and at two in the afternoon, the officers met, agreed on a countersign for use in battle, and finalized their plan of attack. The men would be divided into four columns, each assigned to a different approach up the mountain.

Knowing his role in what was to come, Benjamin Cleveland waddled back to his men, who would begin their ascent at the northernmost base of the mountain, just west of where Ferguson had stationed his wagons. "My brave fellows," Cleveland told his troops, "we have beat the Tories, and we can beat them again. They are all cowards; if they had the spirit of men they would join their fellow citizens in supporting the independence of their country." Then he gave them specific instructions. They were to "fire as quick as you can. When you can do no better, get behind trees, or retreat; but I beg of you not to run quite off. If we are repulsed let us make a point of returning and renewing the fight; perhaps we may have better luck in the second attempt than in the first." If any of them were afraid, they were free to go, but they should go immediately.

Because all the men on the mountain would be Americans—Ferguson was the sole exception—they should not expect to be able to spot the enemy based on their uniforms. There would be no readily identifiable "redcoats" in this engagement. Everybody would be dressed more or less the same. The loyalists were known to put evergreen sprigs in their hats, so some of the rebels, to help their own colleagues identify them, decided to put pieces of cloth or paper in theirs. Of course, some of them dispensed with headgear altogether and would fight as they had known the Indians to do, and it was crucial that the men understood all that this might mean.

"When you are engaged," Cleveland told them, "you are not to wait for the word of command from me. I will show you by example how to fight: I can undertake no more. Every man must consider himself an officer, and act from his own judgment." They were on their own, in a sense, and any collective success would depend not on a grand strategy handed down from above, but on their own initiative and ingenuity, and, of course, personal courage. How well this approach would serve them would soon make itself known.

The men in their four divisions, some of whom had not slept in thirty-six hours, dutifully prepared for the ascent, checking their rifles one last time. For ready access, some of the men carried five lead balls in their cheeks. "My feelings were not the most pleasant," sixteen-year-old James Potter Collins said. "They may be attributed to my youth . . . but I could not well swallow the appellation of coward."

At about 2 p.m., the different units under Cleveland, Shelby, Sevier, Williams, Charles McDowell, and William Campbell were told to move out. Their "Indian war-whoops" echoed through the woods, as they began to make their way up the wooded, rock-strewn slopes. Boulders were everywhere, and underbrush, and ditch-like crevices. Because it had rained, the ground was slippery, which also made for tough climbing, but all the boulders, trees, and crevices were also handy for concealing yourself. How long it took the men to reach anywhere near the summit is hard to know, but Shelby's got there first, and were within a quarter mile of the summit when the loyalists started shooting. Cleveland's men made it shortly thereafter, closing in from the opposite side. As soon as Sevier's appeared, the loyalists pushed them back with the bayonet. Before long, the Virginians scrambled up the ridge, and when they first saw the enemy, Campbell yelled, "Here they are my brave boys; shout like hell and fight like devils." Once again they were driven back, then returned once more. But this time, gasping and coughing as smoke settled in over the entire scene, they held their ground and continued their ascent.

From their lines at the mountaintop, Ferguson's loyalists sent volley after volley toward the onrushing rebels, and some of the rebels realized something that the loyalists had not anticipated. Firing a musket downhill was a challenge because the shot, more often than anyone might guess, sailed over the target's head, falling harmlessly in the underbrush behind them. This allowed the rebels to reach the summit, and when they did, what followed was hand-to-hand combat, with gun butts, knives, and tomahawks serving as weapons.

When Charles Bowen, one of Campbell's men, heard that his brother had been killed, he rushed frantically about and was within fifteen paces of the loyalists before realizing the danger he was in. He had slipped behind a tree and was cocking his gun when Cleveland spotted him. Cleveland rushed over and, as confused as everybody else, demanded to know the countersign. When Bowen could not remember it, Cleveland assumed he was the enemy, leveled his rifle at the man's chest, and pulled the trigger. The gun misfired, and Bowen lunged at his commander and grabbed his collar. As Bowen said in his pension application years later, he "took his Tomahawk and would have [sunk] it in Cleveland's head," had a third man, who knew both parties, not separated them. After Bowen finally remembered the countersign, Cleveland lowered his gun and clasped Bowen in his arms.

Sixteen-year-old Thomas Young made it to the summit, positioned himself behind a tree, and "fired until the bark was nearly all knocked off, and my eyes pretty well filled with it. One fellow shaved me pretty close, for his bullet took a piece out of my own gun stock." Williams was not so fortunate. His horse "was shot under the jaw when [the animal] commenced stamping as if he were in a nest of yellow jackets," Young said. No sooner had Williams dismounted than he too was shot. He was carried into a tent, where he declared, "I am a gone man," and died.

Within moments, all of the rebel divisions had reached the top, and Ferguson's men found themselves surrounded. In a kind of cockpit of destruction, the loyalists were driven back toward the wagons. They were also running out of ammunition. Some of them began to raise white flags, but when they did, Ferguson used his sword to cut them down. By now, the rebels were within pistol range, and loyalist resolve was rapidly collapsing. They had been fighting like this for about an hour, and Ferguson's attempts to rally his troops, while valiant, were without effect. The loyalists could hear the shriek of his silver whistle over the cacophony of battle, and they could see him rushing about on his horse, but not for long. When the rebels had a better view of him than the loyalists did, they opened fire. Ferguson was hit, and as he fell, a foot got caught in the stirrup. Some of his men managed to help him down and prop him up against a tree while the fighting continued. Then and there, he died.

Abraham de Peyster, Ferguson's second in command—they called him "the Bull Dog's pup"—realized that their efforts were coming to nothing and, charging about on his gray horse, raised a white flag. Other white flags went up as well, and loyalists on the ground began frantically signaling their desire to surrender, waving white handkerchiefs and, in some cases, their shirts. Shelby ordered the loyalists who had huddled near the wagons "to throw down your arms." Most of them did. But when the Overmountain Men continued to shoot them, de Peyster, riding up to Colonel Campbell, told him such behavior was "damned unfair!" and Campbell did what he could to put a stop to the slaughter. "For God's sake, don't shoot!" Campbell told his men. "It is murder to kill them now, for they have raised the flag!"

Just as order was about to be restored, however, a foraging party sent out by Ferguson returned, assessed the situation, and sent a volley into the rebels, which killed one of them. This unfortunate turn of events was interpreted as a counterattack, and Campbell responded by ordering his riflemen to fire into the prisoners, lest they take advantage of the chaos and escape. "We killed near a hundred of them," he said, "and hardly could be restrained from killing the whole."

"It was some time before a complete cessation of the firing on our part could be effected," Shelby reported. "Our men who had been scattered in the battle were continually coming up and continued to fire, without comprehending in the heat of the moment what had happened." Some of them were well aware that the loyalists were surrendering but didn't care. They had heard tales about Tarleton at the Waxhaws and, giddy for retribution, continued to fire into the clumps of panicked loyalists.

Death of British Major Ferguson at the Battle of King's Mountain,
by Alonzo Chappel, 1863

"Owing to these causes, the ignorance of some, and the disposition of others to retaliate," Shelby said, "it required some time and some exertion on the part of the officers to put an entire stop to the firing." Once that was accomplished, and the enemy had clearly given up any further resistance, "our men gave spontaneously three loud and long shouts."

The men who had heard that Ferguson had been shot to death wanted to see the proof of it. Collins said that by the look of things, "almost fifty rifles must have been leveled at him at the same time; seven rifle balls had passed through his body; both of his arms were broken, and his hat and clothing were literally shot to pieces." One of the men turned Ferguson's body over and took his pistol from his pocket. There were two whistles, it turned out, and Shelby took the larger one as a souvenir. Sevier got Ferguson's silk sash, and Cleveland, whose own horse had been killed in the fighting, got the Scotsman's white charger.

Then they stabbed his lifeless body repeatedly, and—it was alleged—some of them urinated on his corpse. After the men were finished having their fun, Ferguson was given a "decent" burial: his body was wrapped in a raw beef hide and deposited in a ravine. The bodies of two women camp followers, known to history only as Virginia Sal and Virginia Paul and assumed to be Ferguson's mistresses, were buried with him. How they met their deaths no one seems to know.

The battle lasted little more than an hour, and darkness fell over Kings Mountain. The survivors slept as best they could, "amid the dead and the groans of the dying, who had neither surgical aid, nor water to quench their thirst," fifteen-year-old Robert Henry recalled. Henry was in serious pain as well, having been slashed in the hand by a loyalist bayonet, which then penetrated his thigh. The general cleaning up, it was agreed, could wait until morning, and the wounded lay "weltering in their Gore," in Shelby's words, through the damp and the cold. Uzal Johnson, a loyalist from New Jersey and the only surgeon on the mountain, worked through the night, treating gunshot wounds and amputating limbs by candlelight.

Dawn came. The sun rose in the sky, and Shelby, "exposed to the cold dew of the mountain all night," recalled "enjoying the warmth of the sun, for I had been very wet the day before." What the light of day revealed, however, was "really distressing," James Potter Collins recalled. "The wives and children of the poor Tories came in, in great numbers. Their husbands, fathers, and brothers lay dead in heaps, while others lay wounded or dying." A cursory examination of the dead revealed something startling, which gave a vivid testament to the lethal effectiveness of the rifle in close-quarter combat. "An unusual number of the killed were found to have been shot in the head," David Ramsay wrote in his 1789 history of the war. "Riflemen took off riflemen with such exactness" that it was clear they had killed each other while taking aim; one eye would be open and the other shut, "in the usual manner of marksmen when leveling at their object."

The rebels buried the dead, Collins recalled,

> but it was badly done. They were thrown into convenient piles and covered with old logs, the bark of old trees and rocks, yet not so as to secure them from becoming a prey to the beasts of the forest, or the vultures of the air; and the wolves [later] became so plenty, that it was dangerous for anyone to be out at night for several miles around.

And not just wolves:

> Also the hogs in the neighborhood gathered into the place to
> devour the flesh of men, inasmuch as [many locals] chose to
> live on little meat rather than eat their hogs, though they were
> fat. Half the dogs in the country were said to be mad and were
> put to death. I saw myself in passing the place, a few weeks
> after, all parts of the human frame . . . scattered in every direc-
> tion.

All that would come later, of course. The immediate concern of
the rebels, after burying the dead, was dealing with the prisoners. They
did find time to divvy up the spoils: Potter and his father came away
with two horses and two guns, as well as powder and lead, and articles
of clothing. Prisoners were a burden no officer wanted to assume since
it was difficult enough to feed, clothe, and provide some kind of crude
shelter for their own men. The problem of prisoners was more easily
disposed of in the religious wars of the previous century, before European noblemen adopted a largely unwritten code of honor designed to
render warfare "civilized." Before the Treaty of Westphalia in 1648, most
prisoners after a battle were simply put to death. Sieges were worse.
"The populations of fortified cities and towns that resisted an enemy's
conquest could expect the worst when the city's defenses failed," T. Cole
James wrote in *Captives of Liberty: Prisoners of War and the Politics of
Vengeance in the American Revolution*. They could expect "pillage, rape,
and murder on a massive scale."

Now there were exchanges and paroles and a reasonable expectation that, after a battle, prisoners would be treated with a modicum of
humanity; it was assumed, in European wars, that officers who had surrendered or been taken captive would be regarded as guests. But England
did not consider America a sovereign nation at all, which meant that
any colonists fighting the British were simply outlaws engaged in an
insurrection against their government. They weren't soldiers, so they
did not deserve the consideration owed to soldiers. And because the
rebels of the backcountry were unfamiliar with (or contemptuous of)
the gentlemanly codes that supposedly governed the conduct of European wars, they were happily unrestrained by them. A neighbor who
turned out to be a loyalist could be hanged on the spot. How to treat
the prisoners captured at Kings Mountain had yet to be determined.

With Cornwallis and the redcoats little more than thirty miles away, near Charlotte, the rebels had to move on, and quickly. So they burned Ferguson's wagons, and to transport the wounded who could not walk, litters were rigged up and attached to the horses.

The battle had taken place on October 7, a Saturday. By 10 a.m. on Sunday, the weary rebels—those, that is, who had not begun to return to their homes on the other side of the Alleghenies—were going back down the mountain and heading toward Gilbert Town. There were now seven hundred prisoners for whom the officers were responsible, which almost doubled the number of men on the move. Regular armies under regular commanders have some understanding of what to do under these conditions, but the Overmountain Men clearly did not. "I must proceed on with the prisoners," Campbell wrote, "until I can find some way to dispose of them." Until then, they could be made to carry the fifteen hundred rifles that had been captured, two to a prisoner with the firelocks removed. One way to thin their ranks, of course, was to execute them, which had the added benefit of gratifying their captors.

On Sunday night, the army slept at a plantation near Gilbert Town, selected because its rail fences could be used for firewood and, according to one of the men, for its "sweet potato patch sufficiently large to supply the whole army. This was most fortunate, for not one in fifty of us had tasted food" for the previous two days and nights. The prisoners would have to wait another twenty-four hours before they ate. Come Monday night, each was given an ear of raw corn. They were routinely being stripped of personal belongings, and some were hanged, without even the pretense of a trial—and without Campbell's knowledge. Rumors had spread that several rebels had been hanged by the British at Fort Ninety Six, about 115 miles south of Kings Mountain, which gave some of the men license to retaliate, or so they thought.

Four days after the battle, at a camp south of Gilbert Town, Campbell issued the following general order: "I must request the officers of all ranks in the army to endeavor to restrain the disorderly manner of slaughtering and disturbing the prisoners. If it cannot be prevented by moderate measures, such effectual punishment shall be executed upon delinquents as will put a stop to it."

Tensions were mounting. The march away from Kings Mountain was arduous, and more and more of the men, tired and hungry, were wandering off. They came "near to starving to death," one of them said. "The country was very thinly settled, and provisions could not be had for love or money. I thought green pumpkins, sliced and fried, about the sweetest eating I ever had in my life." The prisoners were thrown raw corn and pumpkins, John Buchanan wrote in *The Road to Guilford Courthouse,* "just as farmers throw feed to their hogs."

Eventually, there were trials, of a kind. On October 14, under pressure from his own soldiers, Campbell convened a court to try loyalists said not only to have violated their paroles but also to have been "breaking open houses, killing the men, and turning the women and children out of doors and burning the houses." At ten o'clock on a rainy morning, the trials began and—without any access to a defense—thirty-six loyalists were convicted of treason, among other crimes, and sentenced to death. One was found guilty of verbally abusing the wife of one of the rebels and whipping the man's son with a switch cut from a tree for refusing to feed loyalists' horses.

The executions took place at night, with torches held aloft so all of the rebels—gathered four deep around an old oak tree—could watch. In groups of three, the condemned men were taken to the tree, strung up, and left to hang there. "They were either mounted and the horses walked out from under them or stood on logs that were kicked away," according to J. David Dameron's *King's Mountain.* In either case, "the fall was not enough to break their necks," so they "kicked a while as they strangled to death, before the upraised faces of the victors, as the pine knot torches cast dancing lights and shadows across their tortured features."

Nine met their deaths before Shelby called off the executions, though why he did so remains something of a mystery. That he was a man of impressive character might account for his decision, but there is another explanation. Word had spread—untrue, it would turn out—that Tarleton and his Legion were in hot pursuit of the rebel army and closing in fast. It was that day or the next that Campbell, Shelby, and the other officers were told what to do with the remaining prisoners. Gates wanted them brought to his camp at Hillsborough, and Cleveland was entrusted with their delivery.

At two o'clock on the morning of October 15, the wounded, according to Shelby, were "sent into secret hiding places in the mountains and the line of march taken up." As Sevier led most of the remaining Overmountain Men back across the Blue Ridge, Cleveland left with the prisoners, marching them all day through a drenching rain, during which one hundred of them managed to escape. (All but sixty of the prisoners who were delivered to Hillsborough would eventually escape from there as well.)

Campbell and Shelby also headed off to Hillsborough, where they would meet with their commander in chief. Their victory at Kings Mountain, Gates declared, "gave me, and every friend to liberty, and the United States, infinite satisfaction. I thank you gentlemen, and the brave officers and soldiers under your command, for your and their glorious behavior in that action."

Such figures are forever being recalculated, but the loyalist losses at Kings Mountain were horrendous. Of the eleven hundred or so who fought that day, about 157 were killed and 163 were too badly wounded to carry off the ridge top; 698 were taken captive. About nine hundred rebels fought there, with twenty-eight killed and sixty-four wounded. The battle's significance, however, cannot be reduced to such numbers. There were other ways to calculate its effects. "No sooner had news of [Ferguson's defeat] spread through the country," Sir Henry Clinton would write, "than multitudes of disaffected flew to arms from all parts and menaced every British post on both frontiers." Cornwallis was astounded by the outcome, Tarleton said, which spread "depression and fear" among the loyalists in the western Carolinas and to the south, presenting a "gloomy prospect" for his commander's plan to carry the war into North Carolina and from there to Virginia. Instead, he crept back to Winnsboro.

Something seemingly impossible had occurred: an outnumbered gaggle of utterly untrained volunteers—that "swarm of backwoodsmen," in Tarleton's words—had whipped a larger force of well-disciplined, well-supplied provincials and militiamen under the command of one of the most experienced and capable of British officers. Over the course of one afternoon, the momentum seemed to have shifted from the loyalists to the rebels, and, with Gates soon to be relieved of his duties and a new head of the Southern Department succeeding him, the war had entered a new phase.

CHAPTER FOURTEEN

"The Rawest . . . Most Untutored Being I Ever Met"

The new commander of the Southern Department of the Continental army, replacing Horatio Gates, would be Nathanael Greene. His appointment to that position only five years earlier would have seemed unimaginable, not least to Washington, who chose him. That Greene would pursue a military career was also unlikely, and that he had performed with distinction would have appeared—at least to those who knew him early in his life—slightly ridiculous. That is how Greene's rise in the ranks of the Continental army struck the other members of the volunteer militia company with which he attempted to serve, formed in the fall of 1774, just six months after the British had closed the port of Boston.

Born in 1742 in Rhode Island, Greene was the son of a reasonably prosperous merchant (his company operated an iron forge), "a man of industry," Greene said, who "brought up his children to business. Early, very early, when I should have been in pursuit of Knowledge, I was digging into the Bowels of the Earth after Wealth." His father "was over shadow'd with prejudices against Literary Accomplishments," and—what might be more significant, considering Greene's career as a soldier—the Greenes were Quakers. As such, many of them were pacifists.

The militia company that he organized called themselves the Kentish Guards, for their home county of Kent, and they drilled in East Greenwich, the county seat. Greene, who shared his neighbors' mounting indignation over British interference in the colonists' economic affairs, was thirty-two that season, and he had spent a good deal of his time preparing himself, he believed, for such a moment as this. The Kentish Guards wore "red coats with green trim, white waistcoat and pantaloons, and hats with a black cockade," and Greene—five foot ten and tall for his time—looked splendid in his.

And he was a sturdier specimen than might first appear. He was a good-looking man, though not without flaws. His right eye was scarred, the result of inoculation against smallpox, and he suffered from asthma, which could keep him up at night and, presumably, anyone else in the room who had to hear him cough. He also had a slight limp brought on by an infection in his right knee. It was this limp that troubled the other members of the Kentish Guards. They had been drilling regularly and making sufficient progress that in October of that year, they successfully petitioned the Rhode Island assembly to recognize them as the county's official militia. Greene was made a private, and, given his commitment to their cause and his position in the community, it was widely assumed that he would be one of their officers, although he would insist that he never expected any such honor. Later in the month, however, his fellow militiamen, without bothering to take him aside, informed him that because of his limp, he was a "blemish to the company." It embarrassed them, and for that reason it was highly unlikely that he would ever be one of the company's officers, assuming he was even allowed to remain a member.

"I confess it is the first stroke of mortification that I ever felt from being considered, either in private or publick Life a blemish to those with whom I assosiated," he wrote to James Varnum, the Kentish Guards' captain who seems not to have been present when Greene was given the bad news. He was "too suseptible of pride, and my sentiments too delicate," he admitted, "to wish a connexion where I am considered an inferior point of light."

He need not be reminded of his handicap. He was well aware that it was his "misfortune to limp a little but I did not conceive it to be so great," Greene admitted, "but we are not apt to discover our own defects." Evidently the problem was more noticeable than he had realized, and for that, he felt "more mortification than resentment." He wished the others in the Kentish Guards had "given me their opinions in private" than in such a public manner, "for nobody loves to be the subject of ridicule however true the cause."

Having gotten that unpleasant business out of the way, Greene wanted Captain Varnum to know that his commitment to the company and to the cause of independence remained unchanged. Greene had established the Kentish Guards because he was convinced that "the cause of liberty was in danger; and as it was attackt by a military force, it was necessary to cultivate a military spirit amongst the people, that, should tyranny endeavor to make any other advances, we might be prepared to check it in its first sallies." He still held to these beliefs, and, whether he remained in the company or not, he would bear his proportion of the cost of its maintenance until the state of Rhode Island assumed those costs. Greene was permitted to remain with the Kentish Guards, and at dawn on April 20, the day after British troops had fired on American militiamen at Lexington and Concord, the company set off for Massachusetts, where they hoped to defend their fragile, fledgling country. Greene, it turned out, would prove to be far better equipped to do so than his skeptics had imagined—far better, in fact, than they.

If Nathanael Greene was an unlikely soldier, he was an even more unlikely Quaker. Not only did he reject his family's pacifism; he rejected as well its disapproving attitude toward the pleasures of the flesh. Limp or no limp, he learned to dance, and when he was known to have gone out at night to engage in this unseemly recreation, when he got back home, his father would beat him. "You dance stiffly," one partner told him. "Very true," Greene replied. "But you see I dance strong." Where he would go to dance is not known, but the year before he joined the Kentish Guards, the Quaker meeting removed him from its rolls for frequenting a "Public Resort," where he had "No Proper Business." The summer before his humiliation by the other militiamen, he married Catharine Littlefield of Block Island, twelve miles off the Rhode Island coast. Known as Caty, she was by no means a pious Quaker. Twelve years younger than her husband—twenty to his thirty-two—Caty was "a small brunette with high color, a vivacious expression, and a snapping pair of dark eyes," with a "form light and agile." She too liked to dance. (Four years later, at an officers' ball at Valley Forge, General Washington danced with her for three hours.)

Although his father scorned "Literary Accomplishments" and considered schooling a distraction from business, Greene took pains to educate himself. He enjoyed *The Drapier's Letters,* by Jonathan Swift, for example, and worked his way through John Locke's *Essay Concerning*

Human Understanding. He kept a copy of Euclid's *Elements* at his side when he worked at his father's forge and tried to master the theorems. Like many of his fellow colonists, he pored over law books, including Sir William Blackstone's *Commentaries on the Laws of England,* which gave the people of the Atlantic colonies a remarkably sophisticated understanding of British common law, strengthening their sense of their rights as subjects of the king. But what Greene seems to have enjoyed most were books on military strategy and tactics. He read, at the very least, Frederick the Great's *Instructions for His Generals* and Maurice de Saxe's *Mes Rêveries.* Both were highly influential contributions to the development of European ideas about war and how it should be waged.

The Kentish Guards would not figure in the defense of Massachusetts. When they reached Pawtucket, Governor Joseph Wanton ordered them to return to East Greenwich, and most of the militiamen did so. Greene, however, trudged on, returning only upon learning that the British had pulled back into Boston. In early May, however, the Rhode Island General Assembly announced the formation of an "Army of Observation," and, recognizing ability where the members of the Kentish Guards did not, the legislators offered command of the 1,500-man force to the asthmatic man with the limp. He was now General Greene.

By the end of the month, Greene and his men, still loyal subjects of the king, were back on the road to Roxbury. There they would join forces with thousands of other colonists laying siege to British-occupied Boston. In June, Congress adopted this unlikely agglomeration of volunteers into the new Continental army and gave George Washington of Virginia the unenviable task of turning it into an effective fighting force. On July 4, Greene and Washington met. "Though raw, irregular, and undisciplined," Washington noticed, Greene's Rhode Islanders were "under much better government than any around Boston." The way they conducted themselves was a noticeable improvement, Washington said, over most of the "dirty & nasty" New Englanders.

Washington, while a realist about such matters, was a stickler for orderly appearance, and this was not merely a matter of personal idiosyncrasy. He had served under Major General Edward Braddock in the Seven Years' War, and his ambition in life—until the drive for independence—was to be a proper British officer. Orderly appearance

was the mark of an orderly army, and Washington took his new responsibilities seriously. By the time he and Greene met, Washington had
developed sturdy notions about how to staff an army worthy of the
name, and these notions looked more to Old Europe than to the New
World. In late September 1776, after having retreated from Long Island
and made his headquarters in Harlem Heights, Washington wrote to
John Hancock about the kind of army he hoped to produce and the
leadership it would require.

"To place any dependence upon Militia, is, assuredly, resting upon
a broken staff," he told the president of the Continental Congress.

> Men just dragged from the tender Scenes of domestick life—
> unaccustomed to the din of Arms—totally unacquainted with
> every kind of Military skill, which being followed by a want of
> Confidence in themselves when opposed to Troops regularly
> train[e]d—disciplined and appointed—superior in knowledge
> & superior in Arms, makes them timid, and ready to fly from
> their own Shadows.

Even when there is no immediate danger, he said, they are unaccustomed to camp life and long for their homes, which results in "shameful, & scandalous Desertions," encouraging bad habits among regulars.
"Again, Men accustomed to unbounded freedom, and no controul,
cannot brooke the Restraint which is indispensably necessary to the
good Order and Government of an Army; without which Licentiousness, & every kind of disorder triumphantly reign."

This war will drag on, Washington told Hancock, and to see it
through required men of strong character and of generous and liberal
impulses. The general wanted men of sound reputation, with significant stature among their countrymen. He sought men, that is, like
Washington himself, a substantial landowner and planter with a solid
sense of the duties that went with his position, which included public service, such as holding local office and representing his county in
the Virginia legislature. Men like Washington and those he believed
should serve as officers in the Continental army would need to be paid
well enough to compensate for the sacrifices they would make over the
course of long campaigns. An officer should not be expected "to ruin
himself and Family to serve his Country, when every member of the

community is equally Interested and benefitted by his Labours." Maintaining a real army "upon a permanent footing" and paying them well "will induce Gentlemen, and Men of Character" to serve, and until "the bulk of your Officers are composed of Such persons as are actuated by Principles of honour, and a spirit of enterprize, you will have little to expect of them."

A few days later, still at Harlem Heights, Washington expressed similar concerns to Governor Patrick Henry, who was then assembling battalions from Virginia. Washington had no confidence in mere militiamen, for good reason. Militias were composed of men on short enlistments and, lacking proper training, were forever "impatient to return to their own Homes; & who from an utter disregard of all discipline and restraint among themselves" were "too apt to infuse the like Spirit into others." Inexperienced in battle, they would tend to flee. They were "altogether unfit for the Service," and costly, as well, given their comings and goings. Up against the enemy's regulars, he told Henry, there was no substitute for a "permanent Body of Forces."

As for officers, Washington had strong opinions as well. Militiamen often elected their commanders from their own ranks, which can invite problems. "One Circumstance, in this important Business ought to be cautiously guarded against, and that is the Soldier & Officer being too nearly on a level—Discipline & subordination add Life & Vigor to military movements," and the absence of both can prove calamitous. Unfortunately, the United States (they had declared their independence six months before) lacked anything resembling a long military tradition, and its men lacked experience in camp, much less in battle. Washington believed it was critical that officers be selected with great care. And it was here that the commander in chief sounded far more European than American. The "true Criterion" by which a candidate for military office should be evaluated is whether that man "has a just pretension to the character of a Gentleman, a proper sense of Honor, & some Reputation to [lose]."

But over time, Washington would find the traits he sought in the officers of the Continental army in unlikely places. Men of substantial wealth from established families such as New York's Philip Schuyler (and, certainly, Benedict Arnold of Connecticut) would repeatedly disappoint him; and, as the war dragged on, he began to see merit in largely self-made men such as the rotund but rugged bookseller Henry

Knox of Massachusetts, the barely literate teamster Daniel Morgan of Virginia, and, most notably, the self-educated Nathanael Greene of Rhode Island. In time, Washington would even come to admire the contributions of such independent partisans as Francis Marion and Andrew Pickens, whose men lacked even the organization of militias.

Knox, who had risen rapidly to become Washington's trusted commander of artillery, was astounded by Greene's ability to absorb information and ideas and put them to practical use. He "came to us, the rawest, the most untutored being I ever met with," Knox said. But within a year, Greene was as knowledgeable about military matters as "any General officer in the army, and very superior to most of them." Tench Tilghman, soon to be one of Washington's aides-de-camp, called Greene "a first-rate military genius and one in whose opinions the General places the utmost confidence." He had already established himself, on a smaller stage, as a man of character, worthy of others' trust. Named to a committee advising the Rhode Island legislature on the colony's defense, Greene was soon shuttling back and forth between Providence and Washington's headquarters outside Boston, developing political skills that would serve him well over the course of the war. That summer, as Washington organized his army, Congress appointed Continental officers, including eight brigadier generals. Greene, at thirty-three, was the youngest.

His early service, once the siege of Boston ended and the Continental army left for New York, was not without problems, however. Greene was ill when the British overran Long Island and took New York City but had sufficiently recovered that Washington assigned him to the defense of Fort Washington in Upper Manhattan and Fort Lee across the Hudson River in New Jersey. Both also fell to the British. Some three thousand Continental soldiers were lost when Fort Washington surrendered, and Greene sought solace from Knox. "I feel mad, vext, sick, and sorry," he told the artillery commander. "Never did I need the consoling voice of a friend more than now."

Despite these losses, Washington stuck by the man who was becoming increasingly recognized as one of his protégés, blaming the lamentable turn of events on the vicissitudes of war rather than any failure on Greene's part. They were together as the Continental army retreated across New Jersey and into Pennsylvania. Greene crossed the icy Delaware with Washington and his troops in December and commanded the left wing of the army as it converged on the Hessians at Trenton; Washington marched with Greene's division. He told Caty, with evident satisfaction, that it "rained, hailed and snowed," but that the battle was over in less than an hour. "We killed, wounded, and took prisoners of the enemy between eleven and twelve hundred. Our troops behaved with great spirit."

In March 1777, Washington dispatched Greene to Philadelphia to confer about military matters with Congress. The commander in chief did not need to go, he said. "This Gentleman is so much in my confidence—so intimately acquainted with my ideas—with our strength, and our weaknesses—with everything respecting the Army," Washington said, "that I have thought it unnecessary to particularize or prescribe any certain line of duty or enquiries for him." Washington left the details to his surrogate, in whom he now placed such confidence that other offices sometimes grumbled about favoritism. Once, when Washington declined to praise Greene's actions while praising those of other subordinates, the thin-skinned Greene brought it to the older man's attention; Washington offered reassurances. "You, sir," he said, "are considered my favorite officer," and praise might backfire, which neither of them wanted. Washington would "be charged with partiality; jealousy will be excited, and the service injured."

That exchange took place after the Battle of Brandywine in the fall of 1777; in December of that year, the army moved into winter quarters at Valley Forge, and Washington made Greene his quartermaster general, with the impossible task of provisioning the troops. Greene accepted the assignment grudgingly. "No body ever heard of a quarter Master in History [when relating] any brilliant Action," he said. Other officers would gain fame on the field of battle, while he found tents, blankets, and canteens for them. "All of you will be immortallising your selves in the golden pages of History," he told one major general, "while I am confined to a series of dru[d]gery to pave the way for it."

Even so, Greene did his job. Understanding early on the importance of mobility in the colonies—something of far less consequence in the set-piece battles in Europe—he established what one military historian has called a "comprehensive system of grain depots capable of supplying forage to Washington's forces wherever they might be." Because of "the ever-present possibility of a shift in the theater of operations, Greene established a number of small magazines rather than a few large ones," limiting grain stocks to a three- or six-month supply, lest larger stores rot. By the time Washington left Valley Forge in June 1778, these depots contained hundreds of thousands of bushels of grain, and the likelihood of starvation, by man or beast, plummeted.

That summer, when Washington moved his army to White Plains, New York, he was able to report to Congress that the Quartermaster Department under Greene "has undergone a very happy change, and such as enabled us, with great facility, to make a sudden move with the whole Army and Baggage, from Valley Forge" to New York "in pursuit of the Enemy."

By September, however, Congress wasn't supplying the Quartermaster Department with money, the horses were beginning to starve, and Greene said he had no idea how to proceed. "What to do or which way to turn I know not," he told one of his deputies. "We can no more support the army without cash, than the Israelites could make bricks without straw. The impolicy of Phar[a]oh brought death upon the first born in Egypt, and this of the Congress will have the same effect on themselves." Greene was determined "to resign as soon I can get out of the business without exposing myself to ruin or disgrace," he told another deputy. He continued in the job for nearly three years nonetheless, finally relinquishing his duties in August 1780.

By this time, more than a year had passed since he had led troops in battle at Monmouth, and the war in the North had reached its stalemate. Savannah, Augusta, and Charles Town had fallen, Gates had been annihilated at Camden, and the British under Cornwallis had begun their push through South Carolina. Washington was pleased with the work Greene had done and said so. "When you were prevailed on to undertake the Office in March 1778," he wrote,

> it was in great disorder and confusion and by extraordinary exertions You so arranged it, as to enable the Army to take the Field the moment it was necessary, and to move with rapidity after the Enemy when they left Philadelphia. From that period to the present time, your exertions have been equally great, have appeared to me to be the result of system and to have been well calculated to promote the interest and honor of your Country. And in fine I cannot but add, that the States have had in you, in my opinion, an able, upright, and diligent Servant.

Washington was looking ahead, of course, and not back, conferring with Congress on the disaster at Camden and learning what lessons could be drawn from it. The loss he attributed to "the fata[l] consequences of depending on Militia" in an engagement of that magnitude. Militia at best can be useful only "as light Troops to be scattered in the woods," he told Samuel Huntington, the president of the Continental Congress, "and plague rather than do serious injury to the Enemy—The firmness requisite for the real business of fighting is only to be attained by a constant course of discipline and service," i.e., that of a regular army, properly trained. "I cannot but remark," Washington wrote, "that it gives me great pains to find the measures pursuing to the Southward still turn upon accumulating large bodies of Militia instead of once for all making a decided effort to have a permanent force. In my ideas of the true system of war to the Southward—the object ought to be to have a good army rather than a large one." They would need no more than six thousand men, he figured, "exclusive of Horse and Artillery."

When Washington rode off to Hartford, where he would confer with the French commanders in late September, leaving Major General Greene in charge, he took Hamilton, Knox, Lafayette, and a few others, plus guards and forty horses. "In my absence," he wrote to Greene, "the command of the army devolves upon you. I have so entire confidence in your prudence and abilities, that I leave the conduct of it to your discretion, with only one observation, that with our present prospects, it is not our business to seek an action or accept it, but on advantageous terms."

This hardly needed to be said. It was not in Greene's nature to take rash actions; he was always "cool and collected," as Mercy Otis Warren wrote in her history of the war, his decisions marked by "remarkable coolness and intrepidity." Had his thinking been radically different from Washington's, he would probably not have been left in command. Greene was honored by the trust the commander in chief had shown in him but managed to keep things in perspective all the same. "This makes me a great man for a few days," Greene told Caty, adding a plaintiff note: "O this war! I would to God it was over! But, alas, I fear this is but the middle of the horrid scene."

CHAPTER FIFTEEN

"I Rely Upon Your Abilities and Exertions"

After Congress made its decision, Washington informed Greene of his new responsibilities, and Greene in turn told his wife. "What I have been dreading has come to pass," he wrote to Caty in Newport. "His Excellency General Washington by order of Congress has appointed me to the command of the Southern Army." Greene had been suffering from a fever for several days, and the prospect of being even farther from his wife—and in a theater of the war where he had serious doubts about the likelihood of success—dampened his spirits all the more. Two hundred miles separated them already, and the family was growing. Martha Washington Greene and George Washington Greene, their first children, born in 1776 and 1778, respectively, had since been joined by two more. North Carolina, where their father would be headed in a matter of days, might as well have been in another country. Caty had visited her husband at Valley Forge, but a trip south seemed unthinkable.

Greene asked Washington if he could go to see his wife and children before he left for Charlotte, where Gates and what was left of the Continental army were camped, but Washington would not allow it. "Your presence with your command as soon as possible is indispensable," Washington said, which settled the matter. "I am rendered unhappy beyond expression," Greene told Caty, "that fatal necessity obliges me to take my leave of you in this way."

This was no doubt true, but there were good reasons Greene might have been eager for a new post with new responsibilities—and to be out of New York. In early October—he would be on his way to Philadelphia and points south by month's end—he had the unpleasant duty of presiding over the trial and execution of Major John André, the British officer who had conspired with Benedict Arnold in his efforts to surrender West Point to the enemy the month before. It was the kind of experience even a seasoned soldier such as Greene was not likely to forget—especially since the American traitor himself was still at large. André had asked to be executed the way an officer and a gentleman would be, by being shot, not hanged like a common criminal. Major General John Stark, one of the jurors in the trial, said six jurors voted for André to be shot, and six said hanged, as a spy; Greene, Stark said, cast the deciding vote for hanging.

While rows of hushed Continentals gathered to watch the solemn ceremony, the young British officer conducted himself with grace and equanimity. André "betrayed no want of fortitude [and] politely bowed to several gentlemen whom he knew, which was respectfully returned," an American army surgeon recalled. Accompanied by a servant, André stepped into the wagon that waited beneath the gallows, and, "instantly elevating his head with firmness he said, 'It will be but a momentary pang.'" Then he produced two white handkerchiefs from his pocket; one was used to bind his arms, and, with the other, he "bandaged his own eyes with perfect firmness, which melted the hearts and moistened the cheeks, not only of [André's] servant, but of the throng of spectators." He "slipped the noose over his head and adjusted it to his neck, without the assistance of the awkward executioner." Offered the opportunity to speak, André said, "I pray you to bear me witness that I meet my fate like a brave man." The wagon was then rolled away from under him, "he was suspended, and instantly expired."

Greene and a small contingent of aides arrived in Philadelphia, his first major stop on the way to North Carolina, in late October. There he and the men who would accompany him to Virginia conferred with Congress. He accepted such advice as these civilians offered and impressed on them the importance of their support when he arrived in the South. Traveling with Greene was Friedrich Wilhelm Augustus von Steuben, the inspector general of the Continental army who had done so much to train the troops at Valley Forge. Born in Germany, von Steuben had served in the Prussian army before coming to America, and Washington believed that he could instill discipline in the South's unruly volunteers as well. Von Steuben's "talents, knowledge of service, zeal and activity," Washington told Greene, "will make him very useful to you in all respects and particularly in the formation and regulation of the raw troops, which will principally compose the southern Army."

Washington was also sending a young neighbor of his from Virginia's Northern Neck who had distinguished himself as a cavalry officer in New York and New Jersey and could be of great service in the Carolinas. This was Henry Lee III, the same promising officer whom Banastre Tarleton had tried unsuccessfully to capture in early 1778. As soon as Lee was ready, Washington told Greene, he promised to send the young Virginian Greene's way. Lee by twenty-two was already a major. His mixed force of infantry and cavalry—"Lee's Legion," it was called—"is an excellent one," Washington told John Mathews, who represented Charles Town in Congress, adding that Lee "has great resources of genius." Daniel Morgan, another Virginian but of a much rougher cast than the highborn and well-educated Lee, would also be sent south. Morgan, that accomplished commander of riflemen in his mid-forties, had been persuaded to come out of retirement by Gates, and William Washington, a kinsman of the commander in chief and, like Lee, a capable cavalry officer, was already in the South, though compromised: his cavalry had been torn to pieces by Tarleton during the operations around Charles Town, and he had withdrawn to North Carolina to rebuild his battered regiment.

Washington was able to offer Greene little guidance on how to prosecute the war once he took over from Gates and assumed command of what remained of the shattered Continental army. "Uninformed as I am of the enemy's force in that quarter, of our own or of the resources which it will be in our power to command for carrying on the War," Washington wrote, "I can give you no particular instructions but must leave you to govern yourself [e]ntirely according to your own prudence and judgment and the circumstances in which you find yourself."

Washington was well aware, he said, "that the nature of the command, will offer you embarrassments of a singular and complicated nature; but I rely upon your abilities and exertions for every thing your means will enable you to effect." Washington would not presume—in today's parlance—to micromanage the war in the South. It would be up to Greene and his own officers to figure out how to win the war down there, or not. If a strategy were to develop, they would have to determine what it would be and to give it form; Washington had the good sense to delegate authority—again drawing on the language of a later day—when the situation required it.

But Washington was beginning to detect a spark of hope that, properly exploited, might burst into flame. The movements of the British army into the Carolina backcountry might actually represent an advantage to the cause of independence, "rather than an evil," he told Mathews, "for they have not a stamina of force sufficient for such extensive conquests, and by spreading themselves out as they are now doing, they will render themselves vulnerable every where." That of course depended on the resources brought to bear on such an overextended enemy. Washington had sent Greene to the South, as Mathews and others in Congress hoped he would, but this was only a start. "You have your wish in the officer appointed to the Southern command," Washington told Mathews. "I am giving you a General; but what can a General do, without men, without arms, without cloathing, without stores, without provisions?"

Even the enemy was well aware of how dire the prospects for the cause of independence seemed. "The common soldiers are exceedingly disgusted with the service," Benedict Arnold reported to his new superior, Lord North's Secretary of State George Germain. Recruiting soldiers, except for short-enlistment militias, was proving difficult for the rebels, and it might prove impossible for them to sustain an army of any kind for another year. The "distress and discontents of the people are daily increasing," the treasury "is entirely empty and the finances are the lowest Ebb," Arnold wrote. The Americans are beginning to "feel their error and look back with remorse to their once happy condition and most ardently wish[ed] for a reconciliation" with the Crown. Without credit, the only way the Continental army could be supplied at all was "by force and terror," which acted "against itself by creating internal enemies and by making friends to Great Britain. It is one of the principal saps hourly undermining the strength of the rebellion."

Then things changed. It was in Philadelphia that Greene, von Steuben, and the Congress got word of momentously encouraging news from the South. There had been a victory, and an unlikely one at that, at a place in the Carolinas called Kings Mountain—a victory over a larger force of well-trained troops under one of the enemy's most capable commanders. In General Orders to the troops in New Jersey, Washington had "the great pleasure to congratulate the army on an important advantage obtained in North Carolina over a corps of 1,400 men, British troops and new Levies commanded by Colonel Ferguson. The militia of the neighbouring country under Colonels Williams, Isaac Shelby, and others having assembled to the amount of 3000 men detached 1600 of their number on horseback to fall in with Ferguson's party at a place called King's mountain, advantageously posted and gave them a total defeat." Ferguson and one hundred fifty of his men had been killed on the mountaintop, with some eight hundred taken prisoner, and fifteen hundred stand of arms captured. "On our part," Washington reported, "the loss was inconsiderable." The victory "will in all probability have a very happy influence upon the successive operations in that quarter. It is proof of the spirit and resources of the country."

Buoyed up by the news, Greene, von Steuben, and their aides pushed on to Annapolis. From Annapolis, they made their way to Alexandria, Virginia, on the Potomac River, and a few miles south of Alexandria, they stopped over at Mount Vernon, General Washington's Potomac River plantation. There they were welcomed by Martha Washington, after whom Nathanael and Caty Greene had named their firstborn daughter. (Von Steuben was unimpressed by the Mount Vernon mansion. "If General Washington were not a better general than he was an architect," he said, "the Affairs of America would be in a very bad condition.")

All along the way, Greene and von Steuben asked elected officials for their support in materiel and manpower but did not expect much to come of it. "They promise me all the assistance in their power," Greene told General Washington, "but are candid enough to tell me, that I must place but little dependance on them, as they have neither money or credit; and from the temper of the people are afraid to push matters to extremities."

The sense that there would be little help from the states only deepened a few days later when Greene and von Steuben arrived in Richmond. There they met with Virginia governor Thomas Jefferson, who seems to have been admirably forthright about his state's determination to keep as many of its soldiers within its own borders, protecting its own people and property. A few weeks earlier, in late October, a British fleet had appeared in the Chesapeake Bay off Portsmouth. There had been landings on both sides of the James River, but except for seizing cattle, little damage was done. In four weeks, the ships were gone, but the state was now on notice, and, if possible, Jefferson wished to confine the war to the Carolinas and keep it out of Virginia. Jefferson would dispatch to the South only such troops as Virginia could spare, and told the Virginia General Assembly of his desires, though the legislators were no more eager to send troops elsewhere than he was.

Virginia was expected to supply the Continental army with 3,500 men but had succeeded in turning out about 1,500, and of those, Jefferson admitted, not a one of them "ever saw the face of an enemy." Some of them wandered off; others might be too sickly, Greene feared, to be of any use at all. And sentiment in the state had wanted to keep them in Virginia in the event of future invasions—which would come—rather than send them to the Carolinas. Jefferson provided some supplies and promised a hundred wagons to transport these supplies but could round up only eighteen. "Our prospects with respect to supplies," Greene told Washington, "are very discouraging." Finding that the quartermaster's department in Virginia was "totally deranged," Greene left von Steuben in Richmond to bring some order to the state's defenses, which included raising and training troops. Then he rode on, arriving in Charlotte on December 2. The transfer of command from Gates to Greene took place without awkwardness or difficulty. Washington had told Greene he could begin a formal investigation of Gates's performance at Camden—and of his flight from the battlefield—but Greene chose not to do so, "a magnanimous gesture," Terry Golway writes in *Washington's General*, his biography of Greene, "at a time when Congress was looking for scapegoats."

Greene sent a note almost immediately to Francis Marion, whom he had not yet met. The new commander of the Southern Department clearly had a strong sense of how the war might be won, and that victory could well depend on contributions from unlikely sources whose methods, while unconventional—and decidedly un-European—were nevertheless proving to be effective. Itching to attack the British outpost at Georgetown, South Carolina, Marion wanted to be reinforced with a modest contingent of Continental regulars. While this would be impossible for now, it did not mean that Greene failed to appreciate what Marion had already accomplished and no doubt would accomplish in coming days.

"I have not the honor of your acquaintance," Greene wrote to Marion, "but am no stranger to your character and merit. Your Services in the lower part of South Carolina in aiding the forces and preventing the enemy from extending their limits have been very important." But as long as he was unable to dispatch some of his own troops to Marion, it was Greene's "earnest desire that you continue where you are" and await further notice. Marion should keep harassing the enemy, without risking his small force—wise guidance that Greene would follow himself as he settled into his new duties. "I like your plan of frequently shifting your ground," Greene told Marion. "It frequently prevents a Surprize and perhaps a total Loss of your Party. Until a more permanent army can be collected than is in the field at present, we must endeavor to keep up a partisan war and preserve the tide of sentiment among the people in our favor as much as possible."

Settling on a partisan war, at least for now, might have seemed an acceptance of the inevitable, but there was more to it than that. Greene came south with a mounting appreciation of the possibilities of what later generations would call guerrilla warfare—and of a recognition of how unlikely it would be, in the Carolinas, to defeat the British and their loyalist allies in conventional, European-style battles. He also realized, upon his arrival in the South, that he had stepped into what a later generation would also call a civil war. Neighbors were killing each other with horrifying regularity, and whatever notions of "civilized" war English settlers might have brought with them over the past century had been abandoned with the first confrontations with Indian "savages" on the frontier. But the British themselves, when sent to the colonies to suppress the rebellion, had for the most part thrown over such ideas, too.

In late December, just weeks after his arrival, Greene moved the army to Cheraw, South Carolina, on the far banks of the Pee Dee River, about seventy-five miles southeast of Charlotte. He made the move, he told Samuel Huntington, president of the Continental Congress, because he was "fully convinced" that the army could not be supported at Charlotte, "the whole Country [around it] being in a great degree laid waste." The loyalists were to blame, but so were those who favored independence, and "the spirit of plundering which prevails among the inhabitants adds not a little to our difficulties." Both sides in the back-country war "pursue each other with as much relentless fury as beasts of prey." Men and boys who had enlisted in neither army "are frequently murdered as they ride along the road," and "great numbers of Tories are way laying the roads," waiting for unsuspecting victims to appear. He told Alexander Hamilton, then an aide-de-camp to Washington, that the "division among the people is much greater than I imagined, and the Whigs and Tories persecute each other, with little less than savage fury. There is nothing but murders and devastations in every quarter."

And then there were the Cherokees. Egged on by the British, they had "murdered a number of Inhabitants" along North Carolina's western border, Greene reported. Cornwallis had instructed his agents to bring the Indians into the war against the rebels, which they did, and Greene had received reports that the militia had retaliated by burning Cherokee towns.

It was all Greene could do to provide for the Continentals under his command, drill the recruits arriving from Virginia and points north, and prepare the lot of them for battle; the militia and the local hooligans were beyond his control—or anybody else's, really, since civil government had almost broken down by this point in the war. Some of these more enterprising freebooters—partisans or "irregulars," they were called—could be useful. Men like Marion and Thomas Sumter, as Greene knew, led small, highly mobile, almost always mounted units; they could make decisions on the fly, sting the enemy, and disappear into the swamps. This made them ideal for gathering intelligence and—this would prove increasingly important as the war dragged on— for harassing the enemy. They could disrupt its lines of supply, wearing down its ability to wage war and its will to win. This was the best Greene could hope for, while rebuilding the main army.

Washington, even with his limited knowledge of conditions in the Carolinas, seemed to understand this reality as well. "It would answer no good purpose to take a position near the enemy," Washington told Gates even before Greene took over, "while you are so far inferior in force. If they can be kept in check, by the light irregular troops under Colo. Sumter and other active Officers," the British "will gain nothing by the time which must be necessarily spent by you, in collecting and arranging the new Army," and replacing the weapons and other provisions lost at Camden.

"Tho' in general I dislike independent Corps," Washington told Congress, "I think a Partizan Corps with an Army useful in many respects." And Henry Lee III could be particularly helpful. Lee "possesses so many talents for commanding a corps of this nature" that it would be a disservice to the cause to try to fold Lee's Legion into someone else's regiment. The kind of hit-and-run escapades that the enterprising young cavalry officer seemed especially partial to would also be of great value in the South, whose geography put a premium on mobility. Also, Greene needed eyes and ears, and small mounted troops under independent commands were ideal for intelligence gatherings. Natives such as Marion and Sumter were also suited to such duties, because they knew the terrain—and a challenging terrain it was.

"There is no single vital river such as the Hudson to defend at all costs," in Golway's words. There were, instead, "dozens of smaller rivers, streams, and tributaries, not to mention disease-infested lowland swamps and rugged backcountry mountains to consider when moving the army and supplies." For that reason, among others, a large army could constitute a liability. The open fields of Europe were ideal for pitched battles, but North America, with its streams, forests, and small farms, was different, as the British discovered during the Seven Years' War. Here, a different kind of warfare was called for, and even if Washington and his generals could field a southern army as large as those that fought in Europe, there would be little if any advantage in doing so.

Xenophon claimed that, at Thymbra, the combined armies of Croesus and Cyrus totaled 616,000. At Borodino in 1812, casualties alone numbered 124,000; at Gettysburg in 1863, 51,000 men would fall. The most Washington could muster at Long Island in 1776 was 10,000—against twice that number of redcoats—and in the South, until Yorktown, it was unusual if more than 1,200 or so Continentals fought in one battle. Gates fielded 4,000 men at Camden, and lost most of them. At Kings Mountain, 900 Overmountain Men had defeated Patrick Ferguson's 1,200 loyalists.

Some of the British commanders had glimpsed the form the war eventually would take as early as 1775, after Bunker Hill, where 2,400 colonists fought three thousand redcoats. Adjutant General Edward Harvey warned Sir William Howe, then commander of all the British troops in the colonies, that if Bunker Hill was any indication, absent great changes of strategy, "our army will be destroyed by damned driblets." Five years later, the 1781 edition of *The Annual Register* in London would report that most of the battles in North America "would in other wars be considered but as skirmishes of little account," though "it is by such skirmishes that the fate of America must necessarily be decided."

This was not by choice, on the rebels' part, but by necessity. When Greene arrived in North Carolina, the only forces opposing the British were small bands of irregulars led by Marion, Sumter, Andrew Pickens, and a few others. They were doing admirable work making life difficult for the enemy, though nothing they could accomplish would be decisive. A decisive victory, as even Washington had come to understand, was increasingly improbable. In November, North Carolina governor Abner Nash, bemoaning Gates's incompetence at Camden, told Washington that the militias of the two Carolinas "had had nine Skirmishes with the Enemy & had been successful in every one," and that the "Enemy's destruction was inevitable had not the General determined unfortunately for us, to risk the fate of the Campaign & with it the two Carolinas on the Event of a single Battle."

Gates had made a grievous mistake, and by this time Greene and everybody else knew it. Greene, in fact, was developing a strategy for the southern campaign even before he arrived in North Carolina, and it was one Washington would approve. It was also one with a distinguished, if unappreciated, pedigree. A war that was largely defensive in nature, relying on stealth and surprise, avoiding pitched battles until circumstances made victory overwhelmingly probable, was thought of as "Fabian" in nature, after Quintus Fabius Maximus Verrucosus, the third-century BCE Roman dictator who employed a strategy of this kind in resisting Hannibal's considerably larger army of Carthaginian invaders. Romans who desired a more aggressive approach called Fabius, sardonically, "the Cunctator," which was translated "the Delayer." He got this nickname for waging a war of attrition, in which he bled the enemy's army while avoiding risk to his own. The Cunctator deployed his forces in raids that would sever Hannibal's supply lines, attack his flanks and foraging parties, and besiege its isolated outposts. Fabius waged a "war of attrition," and Greene realized early on that such a campaign was suited as well to the American South, at least until he could rebuild his own army to the point that it could challenge the British and the loyalists in their ranks in conventional battle.

Although Greene had read widely in military strategy and tactics, he was by no means doctrinaire. He never believed that militia alone could defeat a larger force of well-trained British regulars, but he had no doubt of their ability to sap its strength. He realized, for example, that the defeat of Gates at Camden possibly "rendered the embodying of the Militia absolutely necessary," but that the "evil" of such dependence "should be remedied, as soon as possible," as he told Governor Nash. Greene's familiarity with Fabius the Cunctator is a matter of conjecture, but we know he read Marshall Saxe, the eighteenth-century German who fought for France, and Frederick the Great and was influenced by both of them. Saxe championed the use of skirmishers who "have spent their life firing at a greater distance, who are not drawn up in close order, and who fire at ease, without waiting for the word of command," and not in volleys. Saxe, who argued against "pitched battles," was "convinced that a skillful general can make war all his life without being forced into one." Frequent small engagements "will dissipate the enemy until he is forced to hide from you." Frederick the Great said the "greatest secret of war and the masterpiece of a skillful general is to starve his enemy." And while Greene was establishing a "permanent army," as he called it, he would employ the very tactics that Fabius, Saxe, and Frederick espoused.

And Greene was also determined to construct an army better suited to the conditions of the South than those he had left behind in New York and New Jersey. He wanted a "flying army," he told Washington, a mobile force of eight hundred men on horseback and one thousand infantry, that would prevent Cornwallis from making further inroads, all the while making it increasingly difficult for him to provision the troops under British command.

"I [entirely] approve of your plan for forming a flying army," Washington replied, revealing a more sophisticated understanding of the terrain of the Carolinas than he might have been expected, back in New Jersey, to possess. The commander in chief recommended building "a number of flat-bottomed Boats, of as large a construction as can be conveniently transported on Carriages," enabling Greene's troops to cross all those rivers, "which would otherwise be impassable." Washington had written to Governor Jefferson on the need to send boats to Greene. Except for that, there was little more Washington could do, beyond giving Greene the authority to use his best judgment as opportunities arose.

And, although Washington did not know this yet, Greene was about to make a decision that would defy the settled wisdom of all the scholars of military strategy and tactics since time immemorial.

CHAPTER SIXTEEN

"Our Greatest Plague in This Country"

The unlikely rout of Patrick Ferguson's troops at Kings Mountain, while a shock to Lord Cornwallis, did not cause him to panic. Greene had to build a new army before he could do anything else, and that would be a formidable task. Until Cornwallis believed that was accomplished, he could devote his energies to keeping up the morale of the loyalists in the backcountry, all the while rebuilding his own forces. To make up for the loss of Ferguson's men, Cornwallis ordered General Alexander Leslie to bring his troops from Virginia to South Carolina. Together, they would seek to eradicate the only two enemies of note in the whole of the Carolinas. Even the word "enemies" might be overstating the case, however: Francis Marion, with his gang of irregulars, was more of a pest than anything else, and Thomas Sumter—though given full command of the South Carolina militia in the fall of 1780—might have been more than a nuisance, but, if so, not much more than that. Although he was now commissioned as a brigadier general, Sumter commanded only about three hundred men. He seemed always to be up for a fight, but the last time out, at Fishing Creek in late summer, he had been surprised—he was sleeping, it was said—and soundly routed.

Sumter had been thrashed by Tarleton's British Legion, no less, further swelling that brash young cavalry officer's already impressive conceit. "I had the Honor of a great Command" in the early going at Camden, Tarleton wrote to his brother in England. Later action that day "was wholly entrusted to me—I received a Slight Wound which did not require a dressing. Two days afterwards [at Fishing Creek] I fought with every success and Honor my best Friends would Wish," as he was certain Cornwallis's reports would attest. And they did. To Lord Amherst, organizing British defenses against an anticipated invasion from France, Cornwallis described Tarleton as "one of the most promising officers I ever knew; I have no private connexion with him nor any motive for recommending him but the desire of seeing extraordinary merit rewarded and of placing him in such rank as may enable him to render the most essential services to his King and Country." At both Camden and Fishing Creek, Cornwallis told Germain, the "capacity and vigour of Lieutenant Colonel Tarleton, at the head of the cavalry, deserve my highest commendation."

Tarleton was riding high as his next engagement with Sumter drew near, and it could be dangerous to underestimate the man. Sumter was brash, too, and, for a man with the most rudimentary of backwoods educations, he had seen much more of the world than had someone like Marion or Shelby, or, for that matter, like Washington himself. Sumter was born in 1734 in the foothills of the Blue Ridge Mountains in that part of Virginia that also produced Thomas Jefferson and Patrick Henry, though they became lawyers, and Sumter had little or no formal schooling. Sumter's father, from Wales, came to the English colonies as an indentured servant. He fought the French under General Edward Braddock, helping take Fort Duquesne, renamed Fort Pitt.

Sumter fought the Indians, too, living for a time with friendly Cherokees. He learned their language and gained the confidence of Chief Ostenaco, who accompanied Sumter and his aides back to Williamsburg to prevent their being ambushed by hostile tribes. Ostenaco spent several weeks in the Virginia capital with Sumter, entertained by, among others, Lieutenant Governor Francis Fauquier. At a dinner at the College of William & Mary, Ostenaco was shown a portrait of George III and expressed a longing "to see the King my father." It was arranged. Ostenaco and two other Cherokees, with Sumter and a handful of other colonists, sailed for England, where, Sumter's biographer Robert D. Bass writes, they "became the social rage." They visited Westminster Abbey, Kensington Gardens, St. Paul's Cathedral, and the Tower of London. Sir Joshua Reynolds painted Ostenaco's portrait. At St. James's Palace, the Cherokees were introduced to the king, and, according to *The Gazetteer and London Daily Advertiser,* "their Behaviour was remarkably humble and meek. There seems to be a Mixture of Majesty and Moroseness in their Countenances."

When they returned, Sumter accompanied the Cherokees back to their towns and, for the rest of the year, lived with them. While there, he managed singlehandedly to capture an officer in the Canadian militia who was recruiting Indians to fight against the British. Once Sumter had subdued and arrested the French agent, he was promptly put on a frigate and dispatched to England, where authorities there could deal with him. For this bit of derring-do, Sumter, not yet thirty years old, was feted by Royal Governor Thomas Boone in Charles Town and written up as a hero in *The South Carolina Gazette.*

But Sumter was not a hero for long, at least by conventional standards. A man who had loaned Sumter sixty pounds for the trip to Indian territory, where he first met Ostenaco—a loan he had not repaid—had taken out a warrant against him, and when Sumter got back to Virginia in 1763, he was tried, found guilty, and thrown in jail. There he was visited by a friend named Joe Martin, who left him with ten guineas and a tomahawk, and "with one or both of these," Martin's son said, Sumter escaped. Three weeks later, when Sumter was back in the no-man's-land between South Carolina and the Cherokee territory, Martin received a letter. "Pray excuse my going away and Not leaving your money," Sumter wrote, "but I greatly hope it ante make any great odds as I inter in again Very Early in the Spring," adding: "What Ever is between you and me keep it to your selfe till I return and I am for Ever your Honest Friend."

Military discipline was good for Sumter. So was marriage. His wife was a well-to-do widow, and, with her money, he opened a general store near Eutaw Springs, South Carolina, about four miles from Pond Bluff, Francis Marion's plantation. This was a coincidence, though the two would cross paths in the future. By 1774, Sumter owned fourteen thousand acres, which he once tried to sell but failed to find a buyer. His general store did well enough that he opened a second one. He was a passable farmer, sufficiently well regarded by his neighbors that they sent him to represent them in South Carolina's Provincial Congress. But Sumter's real gifts seemed to lie in soldiering. He served in both the Virginia and South Carolina militias, helping in the successful defense of Charles Town in 1776, but, except for fighting the Indians years earlier, saw little action. This frustrated him, and, in 1778, he resigned his commission as a colonel in the South Carolina Continental line (one of his regiments of militia had been absorbed by Washington's army of regulars) almost as an act of protest. For two years, Sumter "had marched his men hundreds and hundreds of miles," Bass wrote, "and yet they had never fired their rifles in action."

But in the spring of 1780, when Tarleton's men burned his house, Sumter came out of retirement. He raised his own independent command of some six hundred men, who agreed to furnish their own arms and horses. In early August, before Camden fell, they assaulted the British outposts at Rocky Mount and Hanging Rock. At Rocky Mount, three hundred of Sumter's men, assaulting twice that number of loyalist militia, rolled a burning wagon against the cabins where the defenders had been putting up a fierce resistance. But just as the loyalists were raising a white flag, a downpour extinguished the flames, denying Sumter his victory. At Hanging Rock the following week, Sumter commanded eight hundred men, but, while they were again outnumbered—there were fourteen hundred loyalists at the outpost—the rebels carried the day. In four hours, the loyalists lost nearly two hundred men, to about fifty of Sumter's. Then came Camden two weeks later and, after Camden, Fishing Creek, where Tarleton's British Legion ambushed Sumter's camp and annihilated his small force. Sumter barely escaped capture or death by climbing onto the back of an unsaddled draft horse and fleeing with the others. Now, with the Continental army under Gates also obliterated, Sumter and what was left of his troops were—with Marion's small command—the only rebel forces left in South Carolina.

In October, Cornwallis in his camp at Winnsboro received reports that Sumter was headed his way with three hundred men. Major James Wemyss asked to go after "the Gamecock," as Sumter would come to be known, cutting him off before he could arrive, and Cornwallis gave his permission. Sumter by this time had reached Moore's Mill, about thirty miles northwest of Winnsboro, and the plan—Cornwallis was explicit about this—was for Wemyss to attack Sumter at dawn on November 9. He would have forty of Tarleton's British Legion with him, but he was under no circumstances to risk these valuable cavalrymen by deploying them at night. Cornwallis also assigned a squad of five dragoons whose sole job was bring back Sumter, dead or alive.

Wemyss set out, and, to his surprise, saw that Sumter had moved five miles closer to Cornwallis's camp, at Fishdam Ford on the Broad River. Wemyss and his men stumbled into Sumter's pickets at 1 a.m. The pickets were surprised, too, but managed to get off five shots before they withdrew. At least two of these shots hit Wemyss, who fell from his saddle. At three in the morning, a young and inexperienced Lieutenant John Stark took over from Wemyss and, unaware of Cornwallis's orders or choosing to ignore them, led his horsemen—including Tarleton's—on a headlong charge into Sumter's camp. The attack "was as precipitate and violent as can be conceived," Sumter would report. His campfires silhouetted the oncoming loyalists, who were cut to pieces. Wemyss's foot soldiers followed with their bayonets, ran into a rail fence obscured by the darkness, and were chewed up too. In twenty minutes, the fight was over. "Wemyss forgot that he is an infantry officer," Cornwallis said, "and rode into battle."

Sumter missed most of the action, if not all. He was still inside his tent when the dragoons showed up outside of it, but he scrambled out the back, barefoot and without hat or coat. Outrunning his pursuers, he jumped a fence and skedaddled through a briar patch, eventually reaching the river. He crawled under an overhang and, shivering in the November night, waited until the shooting stopped. Then he made his way back toward the camp, found a horse, climbed onto its back, and held on tight until morning. He told one of his officers that, "being in his shirt sleeves, he verily believed he would have perished from the cold" had he not hugged the horse's neck for warmth.

Sumter reported that British losses at Fishdam Ford numbered seven killed and twenty-five taken prisoner. Historians estimate that at most five of Sumter's men might have lost their lives; it is also possible that none did. One of the prisoners was the unfortunate Wemyss, who was paroled and later exchanged. Maimed for life, he would never see action again. It could have been worse: found among Wemyss's papers was a list of men he had hanged and houses he had burned. "Knowing that should his militia read this incrimination," Bass wrote, "it would become the death warrant for Wemyss," Sumter—who barely escaped assassination himself—"generously tossed the paper into the flames." As news of Sumter's victory swept through the Carolinas, men rushed to enlist. "The enemy on this event cried 'victory,'" Cornwallis told Clinton, "and the whole country came in fast to Sumter."

Now Cornwallis was afraid that a reinvigorated Sumter, with a force of one thousand men, might threaten Fort Ninety Six. With spies reporting that the Gamecock was only fifteen miles from that important British post, Cornwallis just days after Fishdam Ford sent Tarleton after Sumter. Tarleton would have far fewer men with him—his Legion, some members of a Scottish regiment, and what was left of Wemyss's men—but he would have the advantage in experience. Tarleton's men, including the loyalists in his Legion, were regulars; Sumter's men, especially those who had joined since Fishdam Ford, were militia. Tarleton would also have speed and mobility on his side. If he could push Sumter back toward Ninety Six, he might be able to squeeze him between his own small force and the larger numbers, under John Harris Cruger of New York, garrisoned there.

With Tarleton closing in, Sumter on November 20 decided to make a stand at Blackstock's plantation, which was situated on a high hill that sloped down to the Tyger River a few miles from present-day Cross Anchor. There was a farmhouse with a creek running in front of it and a lane that led to the river, in case he needed to retreat. About a quarter mile down the hill in front of the farmhouse, as Colonel William Hill recalled, "there was a very large and strong fence made not with common rails but with small trees notched together one on the other." There were outbuildings made of oak, too, and these were solid structures, with this inviting feature: they had never been chinked, meaning Sumter's men could prop their rifles and muskets on the sturdy oak logs and fire through the openings between them, as they might in a medieval castle's loopholes. Tarleton's men would have to get through the fences and over the creek, and as they tried to do so, they would face the fire from men in the outbuildings.

Sumter liked what he saw at Blackstock's, but not everybody approved of what was planned for the property. Mary Blackstock, whose husband had joined the South Carolina militia but was serving elsewhere, made her way up to Sumter and made her wishes known. "General," she said, "I won't have any fighting around my house." But it was much too late for that. Sumter took over the house, stationed some of his riflemen in the outbuildings, and placed the rest of the men under William Hill, Edward Lacey, and William Bratton—all of Huck's Defeat fame—near the creek and behind the fence. Colonel Richard Winn, at the top of the hill, ordered his men to lie down so if the British got that far, they would never know the men were there.

Tarleton, with some expectation that reinforcements would arrive, decided not to wait. With dusk coming on, he sent eighty members of the battle-tested 63rd Regiment forward, with bayonets fixed, and the Battle of Blackstock's Farm was on. Sumter responded by sending five hundred of his men toward the oncoming redcoats, but they stopped halfway to the creek, unleashing a volley that—fired too soon and too far away from their targets—did no damage. Unfazed, Tarleton's men charged on, but then ran headlong into Sumter's riflemen, positioned in the outbuildings. These sharpshooters looked for the epaulettes and stripes of enemy officers and aimed accordingly. Major John Money, waving his sword as he led the 63rd, went down in a heap.

Tarleton and his dragoons, meanwhile, were mounted and monitoring the action from the woods to Sumter's right, which presented an opportunity. Sumter sent Lacey and some of his men around behind them, hoping to ambush the unsuspecting horsemen. Lacey crept within fifty yards of the dragoons and opened fire. Twenty of Tarleton's men, riddled with buckshot, went down before a counterattack drove Lacey's detachment back at the point of the saber, but serious damage had been done.

Realizing that his infantry was also getting torn to pieces in the action to his front, Tarleton led a cavalry charge up the slope toward the house—and right into the teeth of Sumter's men behind the fence. Both "men & horse fell so fast," Colonel William Hill reported in his memoirs, "that the way was nearly stopt up." Those that got to the top of the hill had a surprise waiting for them, too. Winn's men jumped up, gave a rousing shout, and chased them back down the hill, firing as they ran, "with bullets in their mouths and powder in their pockets." Tarleton's horse was shot from beneath him, and "with so many falling either by wounds or stumbling over the dead horses or men," a retreat was ordered. The British "quitted the field in great disorder, and retired with the utmost precipitation," Colonel Charles Myddleton reported, pursued by the Americans—Hill's words here—"with loud shouts of victory."

What most of Sumter's exuberant men did not know was that their commander had been shot. An alert platoon of the 63rd Regiment had spotted him riding with his aides, trying to get as accurate a picture as he could of the enemy's flight, and opened fire. Sumter rode on, and it was not until he was back at the farmyard that one of his captains saw blood draining down his coat. "General, you are wounded," the captain said. "I am wounded," Sumter replied. "Say nothing of it."

He was carried into Blackstock's house, where a field surgeon stanched the flow of blood and pulled out the buckshot. A crude litter was assembled by stretching a bull hide between two poles. These were suspended between two horses, and Sumter was lifted onto the bull hide and carried across the Tyger to safety. Colonel John Twiggs took over command, drove what remained of Tarleton's once-fearsome army from the field, then rounded up the wounded and tended to their injuries. "It is but doing bare justice to General Sumter to declare that the strictest humanity took place upon the present occasion," Lieutenant Roderick Mackenzie of the 71st Highlanders would write. The wounded "were supplied with every comfort in his power."

Determined to avenge his losses, Tarleton spent the evening after the battle about two miles from Blackstock's, planning the next day's action. It rained that night, and Colonel Twiggs ordered the men to light campfires and keep them burning as a way to mislead Tarleton about their intentions. Then Twiggs sent them all across the Tyger. Once they were on the other side of the river, the men were allowed to go home, and as Bass writes, Sumter's "powerful corps disintegrated. Many of his militiamen did not return to the field again during the Revolution."

Sumter lost about eight men of the one thousand who fought that day; three were killed and at least two wounded. According to Tarleton, of his original 270 men, fifty were killed or wounded, but Sumter's men put the figure at ninety-two killed and another one hundred wounded. But this was only part of the story. For the first time, American militia had defeated British regulars, and Tarleton was no longer so fearsome—at least among the Americans.

Tarleton's reputation was untarnished, however, among his superiors. This took some effort on his part. He put the best possible face on his defeat, though it took some stretching to do so. When Tarleton returned to Blackstock's the morning after the battle, he found that the enemy had stolen away in the night and, in that sense, had abandoned the field of battle. This allowed him to claim victory, as he did in his report to Cornwallis. In his history of the southern campaign, Henry Lee III found this account ludicrous. Sumter did what any competent commander would do. Having soundly defeated the British, he got his men out of danger, let them go home, and went away to nurse his wounds. Sumter "did not wait until Colonel Tarleton might return with a superior force," Lee wrote, "and as Tarleton *did* return and occupy the field of battle on the day following, therefore Tarleton was the victor. Such logic does not merit refutation."

Cornwallis was none the wiser, at least for now. Two days after the battle, Tarleton told his commander in chief of his great triumph, and added the glorious news that Sumter was incapacitated—maybe forever. "Sumter is defeated, his corps dispersed, & himself dangerously wounded," he reported. Supposedly, Tarleton said that he had "fought like a gamecock," giving Sumter the nickname that endures to this day. The evidence that Tarleton said any such thing is sketchy at best; the origins of the moniker can more plausibly traced to a couple of cockfighting backcountry brothers whose feisty blue hen they called "Tuck." Sumter delivered a rousing recruiting speech that reminded the brothers of Tuck, and the legend grew from there.

In any case, Sumter had a nickname, but by this time his days as a menace to the British and their loyalist allies were numbered. To make sure of it, Tarleton told Cornwallis, three young men who had fought with Ferguson at Kings Mountain "have promised to fix Sumter immediately." Tarleton in turn had promised them fifty guineas if they could only capture him.

Cornwallis was understandably delighted. "I have no doubt that your victory will be attended with as good consequences to our affairs as it is with honour and credit to yourself," he told Tarleton, "but I wish it had not cost you so much." He would be "very glad to hear that Sumter is in a position to give us no further trouble; he certainly has been our greatest plague in this country." Cornwallis then informed Clinton of the great British victory at Blackstock's. "It is not easy for Lt. Col. Tarleton to add to the reputation he has acquired in this Province, but the defeating [of] 1,000 men posted on very strong ground and occupying log houses with 190 cavalry and 80 infantry is a proof of that spirit and those talents" that have served his country so well, with further contributions to come.

On November 25, Tarleton wrote to Cornwallis again, with further encouraging news. "Sumter," he wrote, "is now reported dead." This was wishful thinking.

CHAPTER SEVENTEEN

"Men in the Right Indian Style"

Once Greene had moved his army the seventy-five miles from Charlotte to Cheraw, in December 1780, he told his wife not to worry about him. "I am posted in the Wilderness, on a great river, endeavoring to reform the army and improve its [discipline]," he told Caty, who was still in Newport. The weather "is mild and the climate moderate, so much so that we all live in [tents] without the least inconvenience." His tentmate was Colonel Otho Holland Williams of Maryland. The two officers had endured the horrendous conditions at Morristown the previous year, when it was "intensely cold and freezing," in General Washington's words, and the troops went "5 or Six days together without bread, at other times as many days without meat—& and once or twice two or three days—without either." Greene and Williams "have many agreeable moments," Nathanael told Caty, "recapitulating the pleasures and diversions" of that grim season.

This, of course, was facetious nonsense, concocted to put Caty's mind at ease. Yes, Williams shared Greene's tent, and they probably talked about their shared struggles at Morristown. But any suggestion that the new commander of the Continental army's Southern Department had it easy in the new camp along the Pee Dee River was balderdash, too. The weather was a little more forgiving, but hardly pleasant. Rains turned the roads to thick, brown sludge, which had made the march from Charlotte difficult, and upon their arrival at the next camp, Greene faced new hardships, which he bore almost sole responsibility for overcoming. There was not much General Washington up in New Jersey could do, and Greene's efforts to persuade the governors to help were appalling disappointments. Governor Jefferson in Virginia had been no help at all, Greene reported. There were shortages of nearly everything, including men. And the more men who could be recruited would mean even more shortages in supplies. The "condition of this Army," Greene wrote to Washington, was so bleak that he questioned whether "it deserves the name of one."

"Nothing can be more wretched and distressing than the condition of the troops, starving with cold and hunger—without tents and camp equipage," Greene wrote. "Those of the Virginia line are literally naked, and a great part totally unfit for any kind of duty," though it should be understood that in the military lexicon of the day "naked" did not mean "nude." But the men did lack the clothing they needed, especially if they were expected to go into battle, provided they were in sufficiently good health to do so. And restoring them to health would be impossible if they shivered every night and day, without enough to eat. Greene was going to have to send some of the Virginians home, he told Jefferson, "into some secure place and warm quarters, until they can be furnished with clothing." A soldier's life was difficult enough, "but where they are aggravated by a want of provision and clothing his condition becomes intolerable." The results are also predictable: "deaths, desertion, and the hospital must soon swallow up an army under such circumstances."

The men "are in want of everything," Greene told Jefferson. Clothing "is but a small part of the expense in raising, equipping, and subsisting an army, and yet on this alone the whole benefit of their service depends." Please send stores of all kinds, he implored Virginia's governor, and troops, too, but only those "as are fit for actual duty, as all others will rather distress than promote the service." Greene sent along the good news of such victories as the rebels had achieved in the closing weeks of the year—especially that of Sumter's triumph at Blackstock's—but hoped "these little flashes of success will not relax the exertions of the State to give us support." And the rumor that Tarleton had passed along to Cornwallis had no basis in fact: Sumter, far from dead, would be in action again, though months would pass before he would be healthy enough to take the field.

Greene was in no position to relax his own exertions, however. He had moved his hungry army from an area whose farms had been picked clean of crops and cattle to one that had so far escaped such wanton plunder. Even so, provisions were still scanty. Detachments of his men were sent to forage along the Pee Dee, but with too little to show for it. They were faring better at Cheraw than in Charlotte, which had been ravaged, but the men still were not getting enough to eat, and too many were beginning to plunder the farms near their new camp to feed themselves. Greene told Daniel Morgan that he was reminded of Abraham in the Bible, who survived the famine in the land of Canaan by emigrating, but Cheraw, South Carolina, he said, "is no Egypt."

The need to feed his army was only one factor in making the decision Greene was soon to make, though maybe not the most urgent one. His most pressing need—if he were to mount any kind of resistance to the British—was simply to keep an army in the field, rebuilding it while he could. Put bluntly, Greene would have to make sure that Cornwallis, whose men already outnumbered his own, did not strike his vulnerable army and annihilate it. Greene would also need to achieve some measure of battlefield success just to prevent the hard-pressed and increasingly demoralized citizens from abandoning the cause altogether. This need not be a major victory, but he had to do something.

And the decision he made—without calling a council of war— flew in the face of everything Greene had been taught about military strategy, during a lifetime of studying the subject. When faced with a larger, stronger enemy that is capable of defeating your army in its entirety, you should never divide it into weaker parts, lest it be even more easily destroyed "in detail," as it was called. Greene was not ignorant of this maxim of wartime theory and practice, but he set it aside, nonetheless—and did so with confidence that bordered on bravura. With Cornwallis's army bearing down on him with 2,500 men, many of them redcoated regulars, Greene could muster at most about eighteen hundred, and many of these were not yet fit for service. Despite this numerical disparity, he would keep some eleven hundred men with him at Cheraw, while dispatching six hundred who had been with him at Charlotte, southwest toward the Broad and Pacolet Rivers along the border of the two Carolinas. When they arrived at their destination, the detachment would be 120 miles from Greene's main army—with Cornwallis enviably positioned between them.

But Greene had good reasons, or thought he did, for taking such a risk. First, it would be less burdensome to provision the men in separate locations, especially when the detachment sent toward the backcountry could now forage where the British had been feeding themselves. When the opportunity arose, Greene's men could also disrupt and pillage their supply lines. More important than that, however, were more strategic considerations. If the British moved against Greene's main force, it would leave the important British posts at Ninety Six and Augusta vulnerable to the smaller detachment; but if Cornwallis moved against the smaller detachment, Greene's main army could advance on occupied Georgetown and Charles Town. Handled with proper skill, the gambit could force Cornwallis to respond by dividing his own army.

The key to the whole operation, however it would play out, was the man Greene put in charge of the smaller force. This was Daniel Morgan. No one now knows where Morgan was born or when—he seems never to have said—but it was probably in Pennsylvania or New Jersey, around 1736. This would have made him three or four years younger than George Washington and that much older than Greene. His upbringing was considerably rougher than theirs. The grandson of a Welshman and, by some accounts, a cousin of Daniel Boone's, Morgan left home at seventeen after an argument with his father and headed south, settling—in a sense—in Virginia's Shenandoah Valley. There, in late adolescence, he worked on neighbors' farms and drove wagons for them. He also drove wagons for British General Edward Braddock in his expedition against the French, and there he met Washington.

Morgan was a big man, like Washington, and a tough one. He once struck a British officer and had to take five hundred lashes for punishment. The drummer lost count during the ordeal, Morgan liked to tell people, so he had to remind the forgetful young man that he owed him one more. By one account, Morgan, hearing the drummer miscount, said he "did not think it worthwhile to tell him of his mistake, and let it go." Morgan would then show people his scars. Another time, as a militia captain on a two-man scouting party, he was shot through the neck by Indians. The musket ball hit the cheek, dislodged the teeth on one side, and left a ghastly scar. His companion was scalped and killed. By another account, he killed four Indians in as many minutes, using his rifle, knife, and bare hands.

Daniel Morgan.
Portrait by Charles Willson Peale, ca. 1794.
Independence National Park

Back in Virginia, Morgan worked a farm of his own, but never stayed out of trouble for long. He was hauled before the county courts for nonpayment of debts more than twenty times, repeatedly charged with assault and battery, and arrested for "Feloniously" burning down a tobacco warehouse; charges were dropped when witnesses against him declined to testify. By 1751, he seems to have been prospering in a modest way, and store records from an establishment near Winchester, Virginia, show that he bought a "gentleman's hat" and a watch. He also purchased items a woman might like: silk cloth, ribbon, a lady's handkerchief, and shoes. These, it would seem, were for the nineteen-year-old daughter of a Frederick County planter. By the early 1760s, the "confirmed Libertine" and the "plain, sensible and pious" helpmeet were living together without benefit of clergy; she bore Morgan two daughters and taught him to read.

But Morgan was not cut out for the quiet life of a tobacco farmer, and in the years leading up to the War of Independence, he was an eager member of militia companies, at least one of which elected him as their captain. In the summer of 1775, as captain of a Virginia rifle company, he recruited almost one hundred men in ten days and led them six hundred miles to the lines outside Boston. That fall, subsisting on soup made from lip salve and shaving soap and, when fortunate, dog meat, his volunteer company marched to Canada, reaching Quebec City's stone ramparts in early December.

The invasion of Canada, led by Richard Montgomery and Benedict Arnold and ending in disaster for the American forces, only added to Morgan's reputation for courage under fire. On the morning of the last day of the year, in a blinding snowstorm, the Continentals began their assault on the walled city. Just inside the Lower Town, a musket ball ripped through Arnold's leg, and, at the request of high-ranking field officers, Morgan took command. Facing a barricade fortified by two cannons at the far end of a narrow street, Morgan scrambled forward and threw a ladder against the barricade. When one of his soldiers hesitated, Morgan scaled the ladder himself. The moment he reached the top, musket fire and grapeshot tore through his hat and grazed his cheek. He fell backward, climbed the ladder a second time, and leaped over. On the other side, he fell, his back landing on one of the cannons.

By now, with darkness having fallen, Morgan managed to avoid the bayonets that were thrust his way by crouching under the cannon. With the other riflemen pouring over the barricade, the British and French Canadian defenders gave way, and Morgan led his men forward. Bravery alone could not overcome the enemy's superior numbers, however, and most of the rifles and muskets the Americans carried were now too wet to fire. Fearing for their lives, they began to throw down their weapons. An eerie quiet settled in, and before long, the streets began to fill with civilians. When the other officers huddled together, agreeing to surrender, Morgan—backed against a wall—refused. When the British threatened to shoot him and his men begged him to give up, he handed his sword to a passing French priest. "Not a scoundrel of those cowards," Morgan declared through tears, "shall take it out of my hands."

Among almost four hundred Continentals captured in the doomed assault on Quebec City, Morgan was released to American authorities in late September 1776 and returned to Virginia. When finally exchanged, Morgan rejoined the Continental army in 1777, where—in recognition for his exploits in Canada—he had been promoted to colonel. More than that, Washington had prevailed upon John Hancock, president of the Continental Congress, to secure a special command for Morgan. He was given his own special corps of five hundred men, mostly from his own regiment. Exempt from the routine duties of camp life, Morgan's unit would operate independently.

They would have their own uniform, if uniform is a proper description of what they were to wear. "It occurs to me," Washington wrote to Morgan, "that if you were to dress a Company or two of true Woods men in the right Indian style and let them make the Attack accompanied with screaming and yelling as the Indians do it would have very good consequences especially if as little as possible was said, or known about the matter before hand." Washington also made sure Morgan's men were equipped with scalping knives.

Morgan and his men—as an independent company but also as regulars—acquitted themselves admirably at Saratoga and in the action around Monmouth. In June 1779, afflicted with what he described as rheumatism and sciatica, but also bitter because he had been passed over for a promotion, Morgan went back to his farm in Virginia. The following summer, Horatio Gates—whom historians give credit for too little—asked Morgan to return, arranging for his promotion to brigadier general. Having recovered from his various ailments, and with his pride restored, Morgan was back in action, though too late to have helped minimize, if not prevent, the disaster at Camden. He was given command of a corps of light troops, and it was this corps, consisting of about 320 battle-hardened Maryland and Delaware Continentals and two hundred far less experienced Virginians under Lieutenant Colonel William Washington, that Greene sent west, toward the mountains.

Their assignment, Greene said, was "to give protection" to supporters of independence and "spirit up the people." Loyalists in the Ninety Six District, where the British had established a major outpost, were making life miserable for families who supported independence and were now "like sheep among wolves," as one of the men said. Their loyalist neighbors were taking all their "horses, Cows, Sheep, Clothing . . . in fine Everything that sooted them, Until we were Stript Naked." There was brutality on both sides, of course, as Greene had told his commander in chief shortly after his arrival in the Carolinas. After the war, loyalists in the area would file a petition with the British House of Lords, listing the names of three hundred men "massacred in this province" by their independence-minded neighbors; in fact, the petitioners claimed, "thrice that number" had met their deaths in this backcountry civil war.

Once the armies were divided and Morgan's force had marched to the west, Morgan in late December 1780 sent William Washington and some three hundred dragoons and mounted infantry after a party of about the same number of loyalist marauders. Washington chased them for twenty miles before catching them at a Bush River crossroads known as Hammond's Store, almost a hundred miles west of Camden. Washington had been a seminary student before the war, and the Anglican priesthood seems an unlikely vocation, if contemporary descriptions of him are any indication. He was an impressive physical specimen, tall like his more famous kinsman, but "corpulent," according to Henry Lee III. Washington's "occupations, and his amusements applied to the body," Lee said, "rather than the mind," preferring "the heat of action to the collection and sifting of intelligence" and "better fitted for the field of battle than for the drudgery of camp and the watchfulness of preparation."

When William Washington caught up with the loyalists at Hammond's Store, his abilities were fully engaged, and his sympathies activated. "The Distress of the Women and Children, stripp'd of every thing by plundering Villains," he told Greene, "cries aloud for redress." The villains got it good and hard, too. "We had a long hill to descend and another to rise," Thomas Young, one of the South Carolina militiamen who fought that day, recalled. "Col. Washington and his dragoons gave a shout, drew swords, and charged down [the] hill like madmen." Then, without the loss of a single man, they killed or wounded 150 loyalists—a slaughter comparable to Tarleton's so-called massacre at the Waxhaws. The loyalists "fled in every direction without firing a gun," Young said. One boy fighting with Washington was "fourteen or fifteen, a mere lad," who had fallen off his horse crossing a river and been jeered at by his older colleagues. Young said the indignant young soldier "swore that boy or no boy, he would kill a man that day or die. He accomplished the former. I remember very well being highly amused at the little fellow charging round a crib after a tory, cutting and slashing away with his puny arm, til he brought him down."

Until this point, Cornwallis had been aware of Morgan's movements but not terribly concerned. The departure of a significant part of Greene's army to the west in one regard might make it easier for the

British army to move into North Carolina as Cornwallis had been itching to do. But the skirmish at Hammond's Store made him reconsider. He now realized that Morgan might move on the outposts at Ninety Six and Augusta, which could not be allowed to happen. At this time, Tarleton, still smarting from the thrashing he had taken from Sumter at Blackstock's Plantation, was about forty miles south of Morgan's camp, halfway between Ninety Six and Winnsboro, in a routine patrol of the backcountry. On the second day of the new year, however, Tarleton received a new assignment, which he welcomed. If Morgan is "any where within your reach," Cornwallis wrote, "I [wish] you to push him to the utmost." Ninety Six "is of so much consequence," he said, "that no time is to be lost." By the end of the day, Tarleton had crossed the Broad River toward Kings Mountain, tracking his prey.

Tarleton as usual seems to have made good time in his pursuit of Morgan, though conditions were far from advantageous. Soaking winter rains turned the roads to sludge and caused the Pee Dee River to rise, but by January 16, Tarleton had closed within five miles of Morgan, who was growing concerned. Hoping to consolidate his meager forces, he had recalled William Washington and his men, who were joined on their march back from Hammond's Store by another group of militia. This group was under the command of Colonel Andrew Pickens, maybe the single most peculiar character next to Francis Marion fighting for the rebels. Pickens made the dour, vinegar-sipping Marion seem like a hail-fellow-well-met. The taciturn and long-faced Presbyterian elder, one bemused acquaintance said, "would take the words out of his mouth between his fingers, and examine them before he uttered them." The Cherokees he fought against in 1761 called him the "Wizard Owl." Captured after surrendering a fort in the wake of Charles Town's fall, Pickens renounced his parole when loyalists plundered his plantation and—just as Sumter had done—took up arms once again.

Morgan saw ability in the unlikely Pickens, whom he described as "a valuable, discreet, and attentive officer, and he has the full confidence of the militia." This was no small consideration. What distinguished Morgan from Washington and Greene and almost every other Continental officer was that he had confidence in the militia, and they did not, at least at first. Morgan had been a militiaman himself. He spoke their language. He was well aware of their tendency to panic when the shooting started and to flee at the sight of ranks of redcoats rushing down on them with gleaming bayonets.

But Morgan believed that they could be effective if properly led, and within days he would be able to put this belief to the test. And if Pickens "had the confidence of the militia," this probably meant that he had confidence in them. It seems clear that Tarleton had nothing but contempt for them. The British officers had little or no faith in their own militiamen, which Lieutenant Colonel Alexander Innes, of one of South Carolina's provincial regiments, called a "useless, disorderly, destructive banditti." Tarleton, who had some idea of the composition of the enemy's forces, was eager to take them on. By the time he caught up with them, Morgan would have his men in position.

By midafternoon on January 16, with Tarleton closing ground rapidly, Morgan had chosen the place where he would make his stand. Officers who knew the countryside directed him to a high, gently sloping expanse of pasturelands and open woods where farmers grazed their cattle. About twenty miles west of Kings Mountain, Cowpens, as it was called, was clear of dense woods and swamps. A couple of ridges ran across the ground, and past them was a plains. Just beyond the plains were woodlands of oak and hickory, and behind the woods, about five miles to the north and west of the position Morgan selected, ran the Broad River. The terrain would give him ample room to maneuver his troops, but it would also confine them to the spot: they were stuck on this side of the river; their only alternative to standing their ground was death by drowning. Even Tarleton liked what he saw when he reached Cowpens. Part of his British Legion were horse soldiers, and horse soldiers need open ground. In his memoirs, in which he referred to himself in third person, he called it "as proper a place for action as Lieutenant colonel Tarleton could desire. America does not produce many more suitable to the nature of the troops under his command."

Morgan prepared his men for battle, physically and psychologically, and the plan he had worked out for positioning them on the field of battle was rooted in his astute, seemingly instinctive, assessment of their abilities. Well aware of the tendency of inexperienced and poorly trained men to panic, he believed he could turn that weakness into a strength. While unorthodox and baffling to his own officers, Morgan's plan is studied to this day.

Morgan would put about 150 militiamen with rifles in a skirmish line, concealed where possible behind the trees that dotted the pastures.

About 150 yards behind this first line, he established a second line of about three hundred more men, these under Pickens. There was yet a third line, another 150 yards or so from the second, composed mainly of some 450 of Morgan's Delaware and Maryland Continentals—the most experienced troops under his command that day. A reserve of William Washington's dragoons supplemented by mounted Georgia militia—about 120 of these—waited in the woods half a mile behind the main field of battle. (Military historians argue about the precise numbers, and Tarleton said he faced a larger force than this—but as of this writing these figures are generally accepted.)

Morgan, who would position himself with the Delaware and Maryland regulars, was up all night, hobbling from campfire to campfire, taking great pains to tell his soldiers—especially the young and inexperienced militiamen—exactly what he would expect of them when dawn came. But he also took the opportunity to rouse their spirits and assure the most fainthearted among them that he had full confidence that they would surprise even themselves by what they could achieve. "And long after I had laid down," Thomas Young recalled, "he was going about among the soldiers encouraging them and telling them that the 'Old Wagoner' would crack his whip over Ben [Tarleton] in the morning, as sure as they lived."

But for that to happen, Morgan would count on them to do their part, and he would ask only what he knew they were capable of doing. The ones on the first and second lines were not expected to hold their position at all costs. But they were to stand their ground until the redcoats were within fifty paces of their line, then fire once, twice, and if at all possible three times, at the command of their officers. Then they were to fall back to the second line, but do so in good order. "Just hold up your heads, boys," he would say, "three fires, and you are free! And then when you return to your homes, how the old folks will bless you, and the girls will kiss you for your gallant conduct."

Once they had fired, the 150 in the first line were to merge with the bulk of the militia in the second. There the action would be repeated—one, two, three shots, dropping officers wherever possible—and then, as soon as the British surged forward with their bayonets, all the militiamen were to leave the field, heading around the left flank of the Delaware and Maryland regulars. There they would reassemble, acting as a reserve.

Greene gave no such exhortations to Delaware and Maryland regulars. This would have been an insult. But as he rode from line to line, he joked with them all—and reminded them in dead earnest to look for the officers as the British charged. He wanted their officers taken out of the action, knowing that disorder in their ranks would follow. "Look for the epaulets!" Morgan told them. "Pick off the epaulets." That, anyway, was the plan.

CHAPTER EIGHTEEN

"A Devil of a Whippin'"

At 2 a.m. on January 17, Tarleton sounded reveille. An hour later, his men broke camp, and at 6:45, about fifteen minutes before sunrise, his advance patrol made its first contact with Morgan's pickets. Shots were exchanged, and the Americans scrambled back to their camp. Fifteen minutes after that, the drums rolled, then Tarleton's redcoats gave what Morgan called a "prodigious yell, and came running at us as if they Intended to eat us up." Morgan's men were in position and waiting, but they did not have to wait for long. Tarleton's men "came on like a thunder storm," James Potter Collins recalled, "as if certain of victory." Pickens made sure that his men did not fire until the British were within fifty yards—his order was "executed with great firmness"— and then "it was pop, pop, pop, and then the whole volley," Thomas Young said. "It seemed like one sheet of flame from right to left." More than half the British officers dropped to the ground, and things were developing even more favorably than Morgan had hoped. The militia had performed admirably. Having inflicted more damage than anyone could have anticipated, they were also filing off as instructed, which the overconfident British interpreted as panicked flight.

Battles are messy affairs, however. Even the most well-planned and ably executed meet with unforeseen complications, and that was the case this day. In its giddy rush toward the line of Continental regulars, the British infantry had become overconfident, confused, and disorganized. Tarleton saw that his men were breaking formation and sent his Legion cavalry, until then in reserve, charging into the Americans' right flank, which was under the command of the capable John Eager Howard of Maryland. Howard responded by ordering the Virginians to pivot to the right to meet the charge. Unfortunately, the order was misunderstood, and the Virginians began to pull back. Other officers saw this, figured they had missed an order to retreat, and began to withdraw as well, emboldening Tarleton's oncoming horsemen. With the momentum suddenly shifting to the British, Collins felt something akin to horror. "Now," he thought, "my hide is in the loft."

William Washington, meanwhile, was also witnessing this worrisome turn of events and got a message to Morgan. "They're coming on like a mob," Washington reported. "Give them a fire, and I'll charge them." Morgan, watching as well, rushed to Howard, demanding an explanation for why his men were withdrawing. Assuring his commander that his men were still under his control, Howard told Morgan that they could repulse Tarleton's men, if given a position on which to reform and make a stand. Morgan selected one, and Howard's men converged there, turned, and at a mere thirty yards "commenced a very destructive fire, which [the British] little expected, and a few rounds occasioned great disorder in their ranks. While in this confusion, I ordered a charge with the bayonet." Washington and his dragoons came crashing out of the woods toward Tarleton and his mounted men, and the momentum shifted yet again. They came on "like a whirlwind," Collins said, and the British "began to keel from their horses, without being able to remount. The shock was so sudden and violent, they could not stand it, and immediately betook themselves to flight; there was no time to rally, and they appeared to be as hard to stop as a drove of wild Choctaw steers."

Tarleton, whose horse had already been shot from beneath him, grabbed another, and ordered his Legion to follow him into the worst of it and reverse the tide. This at least some of them did, though there was clearly more fight left in Tarleton than in his Legionnaires, many of whom, he quickly discovered, had already left Cowpens, heading back to Cornwallis's camp at Winnsboro. Swinging their sabers, those who were still with their commander "began to make a few hacks" at Howard and Washington's men, Collins said, "without doing much injury." There was also a good deal of fight left in Washington, who, while slashing away at a British officer, had his saber break near the handguard.

This rendered Washington vulnerable to the blows of his intended victim, and a fourteen-year-old bugler used his pistol to shoot the redcoat in the shoulder, thereby rescuing his commander. Washington was not out of danger yet, however, because now Tarleton himself charged him. Washington flailed away with his broken saber, and Tarleton pulled his pistol and fired. "The ball missed Washington," Robert D. Bass wrote in *The Green Dragoon,* his biography of Tarleton, "but wounded his horse," though not badly enough to prevent him from galloping back to camp and from there to follow the Legionnaires who had fled.

The British by this point were "falling very fast [and] could not stand it long," Collins wrote. They too appeared to panic, and some "began to throw down their arms, and surrender themselves prisoners of war." Others continued to run, and as the Marylanders gave chase, Howard spotted one of Tarleton's cannons, a highly mobile, horse-carried "grasshopper," so-called because of its tendency to recoil upon firing. Howard ordered one of his captains to seize it, but another of his junior officers heard the command too, and "both being emulous for the prize," they scrambled toward it. The second placed the business end of his spontoon—a long, steel-tipped spike—into the ground and "made a long leap which bought him upon the gun and gave him the honor of the prize."

When Tarleton got back to camp, he found that the men left to guard the wagons had fled, and even their horses, cut free, had gone. Rebel militia, who were gleefully plundering the wagons, fled at his approach, and the few men Tarleton had with him burned the wagons, then set out to rejoin Cornwallis at Winnsboro. Mounted men under Washington and Pickens chased Tarleton for two miles, taking prisoners along the way, before calling off the pursuit.

The battle ended well before noon, and the more Greene learned, the more evident it became that his plan, even with hitches and complications and momentary setbacks, had worked. Thinking they would have "another Fishing creek frolic," in Collins's words, the overconfident redcoats had acted exactly as Greene had envisioned. Just as they believed they had routed the Americans, they had been driven back and then cut to pieces, courtesy of quick thinking and decisive action by Washington and Howard.

When "the fight was over," Collins recalled, "the sight was truly melancholy." Scores of redcoated corpses lay in straight lines where they had run into rifle fire. "The dead on the side of the British, exceeded the number killed at the battle of King's Mountain, being if I recollect aright, three hundred or upwards," Collins would write. "The loss, on the side of the Americans, was only fifteen or sixteen, with a few slightly wounded." As is so often the case, actual totals remain in dispute, but the results were gratifyingly lopsided. "I was desirous to have a stroke at Tarleton—my wishes are gratified & [I] have given him a devil of a whippin', a more compleat victory never was obtained," Morgan crowed to a friend. Though slightly outnumbered—Morgan had one thousand men in the battle, to Tarleton's eleven hundred—British losses came to 110 killed and 830 captured, which included two hundred wounded. That compares to twelve of Morgan's men killed and sixty-one wounded.

"This day, I fired my little rifle five times, whether with any effect or not, I do not know," Collins said. "Next day after receiving some small share of the plunder, and taking care to get as much of the powder as we could, we were disbanded and returned to our old haunts, where we obtained a few days' rest." Morgan himself, still hobbling and suffering from his old and painful ailments, would be going home soon, too. He was not too exhausted, though, once the shooting stopped and victory had been achieved, to pick up a nine-year-old drummer boy and kiss him on both cheeks.

Two days after the battle, Morgan found time to report to Greene. "The troops I have the honor to command have been so fortunate as to obtain a complete victory" over Tarleton. Besides prisoners, the Americans had seized thirty-five of the enemy's wagons, two of their fieldpieces (including the aforementioned grasshopper), "and all their music." As for the prisoners, Morgan was eager to point out,

> for the honor of the American arms, that although the progress of [Tarleton's army] was marked with burning and devastation, and although they waged the most cruel warfare, not a man was killed, wounded or even insulted after he surrendered. Had not Britons during this contest received so many lessons of humanity, I should flatter myself that this might teach them a little. But I fear they are incorrigible.

News of the battle—the worst loss for the British since John Burgoyne had surrendered to Horatio Gates at Saratoga—spread rapidly. Up in Massachusetts, Abigail Adams wrote to Mercy Otis Warren that

Daniel Morgan was now "the rising Hero in the South." The spirits of independence-minded Americans soared, and for good reason. Morgan had shown that militia, used properly, could defeat the best-trained British regulars, which no one—not Washington, not Greene, not Gates or Knox, none of the members of Congress and none of the governors—had ever imagined possible. And the arrogance of the British, who would believe they were routing the enemy when they were in fact being led into a trap, could be used against them.

To what extent the British themselves learned anything from this unpleasant experience is difficult to determine. Tarleton rode into Cornwallis's camp on the day after the battle and made his report. Discussions of what had gone wrong followed, and Cornwallis in turn made his report to Sir Henry Clinton. In it, after recounting the appalling losses, Cornwallis said that the fifty-four dragoons who rode into camp with their commander, "having had time to recollect themselves, and being animated with the bravery of their officer who had so often led them to victory," still supported him. And Cornwallis still supported Tarleton. "It is impossible to foresee all the consequences that this unexpected and extraordinary event may produce," Cornwallis told Clinton. And in his report to Lord George Germain, Cornwallis again expressed his confidence in Tarleton and his dragoons. Why the outcome was so difficult to foresee was that "upon all former occasions, [his troops] behaved with the most distinguished gallantry." For all that, Cornwallis was nonetheless crestfallen by the outcome. "The late affair," he told Lord Francis Rawdon, "has almost broke my heart."

Whatever Cornwallis might say, Tarleton's reputation was damaged by the disaster at Cowpens, and rightfully so. General William Moultrie, who had been a prisoner of war since Charles Town's fall, heard British officers say the reversal "was the consequence of trusting such a command to a boy like Tarleton." Tarleton knew what others were saying and made a formal request to Cornwallis that he be allowed to retire, and that a court-martial be scheduled to assess the extent to which he could be blamed for the loss. Cornwallis dismissed the idea and responded to Tarleton with sympathy. "You have forfeited no part of my esteem as an officer by the unfortunate event of the action of the 17th," Cornwallis wrote. "The means you used to bring the enemy to action were able and masterly, and must ever do you honour."

The blame lay with his troops, who, for the first time anyone could recall, panicked, threw down their arms, and surrendered, while Tarleton and his dragoons continued to fight. "Your disposition was unexceptionable; the total misbehaviour of the troops could alone have deprived you of the Glory which was so justly your due." Two months later, *The London Chronicle,* reporting the battle, also viewed Tarleton with sympathy. "By all accounts," it reported, "Col. Tarleton was never more distinguished for spirit and gallantry than on this occasion."

In late January, Morgan received a note of well-earned congratulations from Otho Holland Williams, the thirty-two-year-old who fought with the tough Maryland line at Camden while serving as Gates's deputy adjutant general. Like Morgan, Williams had come to the attention of his superiors in rifle companies and, at the time of his writing, was sharing a tent at Cheraw on the Pee Dee River in South Carolina with his new commander in chief, Nathanael Greene.

"I rejoice exceedingly at your success," Williams wrote to Morgan.

The advantages you have gained are important and do great Honor to your little Corps. I am particularly happy that so great a share of the glory is due to the officers and men of the Light Infantry . . . Next to the happiness which a man feels at his own good fortune is that which attends his Friend. I am much better pleased that you have plucked the laurels from the brow of the hitherto fortunate Tarleton than if he had fallen by the hands of Lucifer. Vengeance is not sweet if it is not taken as we would have it. I am delighted that the accumulated honors of a young Partisan should be plundered by my Old Friend. We have had a *feu de joy,* drank all your Healths, Swear you are the finest Fellows on earth, and love you if possible more than ever.

Williams enclosed orders from Greene, "written immediately after we received the news and during the operation of some cherry bounce."

The note from Williams was no doubt appreciated, but Morgan had no time to sit back and enjoy his success. With most of the militia gone, he had only 550 men left under his command, plus the burden of prisoners. Cut off from Greene and the rest of the Continental army in the South, he was also dangerously exposed. Cornwallis, with 2,500 men, was now coming after him, determined to put things to rights after the disaster at Cowpens, destroy Morgan's troops, and free the prisoners.

Greene's decision to divide his army, sending Morgan to the west, had worked out splendidly so far. But the move was never intended to be permanent. Aware that Cornwallis was pursuing Morgan, Greene ordered him to rejoin the main army and to do so quickly. Greene also told Edward Carrington, his quartermaster general, to assemble as many boats as he could at crossings on the Catawba, Yadkin, Haw, and Dan Rivers. The last of these, the Dan, flows along the border of North Carolina and Virginia. If Greene could get his Continentals over the Dan and into Virginia, Greene believed, they would be out of the danger posed by Cornwallis and his larger army. There, in the richest and most populous of the states, where war materials were already being produced and sent farther South, his men could rest and be resupplied. Virginia had not been picked over the way the Carolinas had. There would be food for the men and forage for the horses. To that end, Greene and Morgan would reunite at Guilford Courthouse, North Carolina, a cluster of cabins with a Quaker meetinghouse about eighty miles from the Virginia border, and push on from there. Morgan was on the move, and the first phase of what became the "Race to the Dan" had begun.

Early on, Morgan made reasonably good time, considering the fact that he was traveling with some six hundred prisoners taken at Cowpens. Once he and his men crossed the Catawba, he sent the prisoners ahead under guard. Realizing that Morgan had a head start and was outpacing him, Cornwallis on January 25 stopped at Ramsour's Mill, just south of the Catawba. Here he also took measures to lighten his load, though these were more dramatic and, to his own men, disturbing. He ordered all the wagons, except those that carried ammunition and those that might be needed for the transport of the wounded, to be burned. To the horror of his already exhausted and dispirited soldiers, he destroyed kegs of rum. Then, in an act of solidarity with them, he torched his own tent while they watched. For the rest of the winter campaign, Cornwallis would sleep, as they did, rolled up in a blanket on the ground.

By the time Cornwallis reached the Catawba, heavy rains had swollen its waters, making it impossible for his army to cross. They waited two days, which enabled Morgan to put more distance between them. It wasn't until February 1 that Cornwallis could get his men across the Catawba. By then, Morgan was approaching the Yadkin, but Cornwallis—without much of his burdensome baggage train—was closing the distance between them. Night fell, and using the boats Carrington had found for them, the Americans made it to the other side of the river. Arriving just as the last of the boats crossed the Yadkin, Cornwallis took out his frustration by bombarding the far shore, to no effect. Without boats, high water prevented the redcoats from getting to the other side, and they were forced to march fifty miles upriver where shallower water enabled them to wade across. The British lost another two days by the detour.

On February 7, Morgan and his men arrived at Guilford Courthouse, where they were reunited with the rest of Greene's army that had withdrawn from Cheraw. Two days later, Cornwallis appeared at Salem, disappointed that he had failed to cut Morgan off and destroy him, but still only twenty-five miles away from Greene and his main army. The British could arrive at Guilford Courthouse the next day, Greene believed, and possibly attack. The first phase of the race was over, and the second was about to begin.

CHAPTER NINETEEN

"I Risque Every Thing"

At Guilford Courthouse, Greene, who was used to making his own decisions, held a rare council of war. He consulted only three other officers—Daniel Morgan, Otho Holland Williams, and Brigadier General Isaac Huger of South Carolina. Still seriously outnumbered by Cornwallis—they were convinced that he had three thousand men with him, when in truth it was more like 2,500—the four discussed the peril they were in, and "it was determined unanimously that we ought to avoid a general Action at all Events" and that the army should head for the Dan River, as Greene initially intended, and cross into Virginia. Success, odd as it might appear, would effectively mean abandoning North Carolina to the enemy. There would be no Continental army in either of the Carolinas now, and the only forces to prevent the British from controlling both of those states, plus Georgia, would be guerrillas, partisans, and irregulars such as Marion and others even more obscure and with far less connection to the main army. But this would be temporary. When good and ready, and bolstered by reinforcements, Greene could return to North Carolina and take on Cornwallis and his redcoats in a place of the Americans' own choosing. Greene was confident that this would be possible, though he would have to divide his army yet again, once more exposing the smaller of his forces—these commanded once again by Morgan, presumably—to considerable peril. Cornwallis, at Salem, was no farther from the Dan than Greene and Morgan were, about a hundred miles from the various crossings.

Cornwallis, for his part, was convinced that Greene could never amass enough boats to get all his men across and might well have his enemy trapped, with the Dan to their backs. "It being my business to force him to fight," Cornwallis told Lord George Germain, he would "make great expedition to get between Greene and the fords of the Dan," wherever Greene was foolhardy enough to think he could cross. Because Cornwallis believed that Greene would not have the boats he needed, he would have to attempt his crossing at the shallower fords closer to Danville, to the west. Cornwallis could trap him there. He was optimistic that this could be done, but not all of his men shared his confidence. Here they were, as General Charles O'Hara, one of the most capable of British officers, put it, "without baggage, necessaries, or provisions of any sort for officer or soldier, in the most barren, inhospitable, unhealthy part of North America, [opposing] the most savage, inveterate, perfidious, cruel enemy, with zeal and with bayonets only . . . resolved to follow Greene's army to the end of the world."

But from Greene's perspective, there was a problem, and it had nothing to do with boats or the lack thereof. Morgan, he learned, would not be leading the Flying Army—the smaller force he would again send to the west—after all. Morgan's sciatica was making life miserable for him, especially when it rained or snowed, and there were weeks of winter still ahead. Morgan was forthright about his condition, as much as it grieved him to face the consequences. It had been his "sanguine expectation to do something clever this campaign," he told Greene, but that was more and more unlikely. A "pain in the hip" made movement itself an ordeal. He had suffered in this way for three weeks now and could not in good conscience pretend otherwise or withhold this information from his commander in chief. Damp weather made his "ceatick" insufferable, and "at times when I am walking or standing still [I] am obliged to set down in the place it takes me, as quick as if I were shot." He had also come down with a fever and was spending too much time flat on his back in his tent. When "violently attck'd with the piles," meaning hemorrhoids, he found sitting in the saddle to be a form of torture.

Only rest would help, and Morgan would need a leave of absence for that to be possible. Failure to look after his health immediately would, he said, "totally disable me from further service." So on February 10, while they were still at Guilford Courthouse, Greene gave Morgan the leave of absence he requested, with the hope that he would in time regain his strength and return. Grateful but with regret, Morgan left the camp in a carriage, heading back to the Shenandoah Valley of Virginia and his home.

In Morgan's place as commander of the light infantry and the attached cavalry under Henry Lee and William Washington, Greene appointed Otho Holland Williams, his old tentmate from that grim winter at Morristown. Williams would be sent west with seven hundred men to screen the movements of the main army and deceive Cornwallis as to Greene's intentions as he headed toward Virginia. The son of Welsh immigrants who had settled in Maryland, Williams was orphaned at thirteen and, with little or no formal education, went to work in the Frederick County Clerk's Office. Precise and orderly, he held a comparable post for the city of Baltimore, but in 1775, at twenty-six years, he joined a local rifle corps, fought with the Continental army in the siege of Boston, and in November 1775 was taken prisoner when Fort Washington fell to the British. Williams, one of the Continental army's senior officers from Maryland, was badly wounded that day, though the nature of those wounds is unclear.

Williams was, as described by one of his soldiers, "about six feet high, elegantly formed; his whole appearance and conduct much beyond his years; his manner such as made friends of all who knew him." Williams was "erect and elegant in his form," Lee said, "made for activity rather than strength," which seems the case since his health deteriorated after years of campaigning, and maladies that developed during the war—most likely from his imprisonment—would nag him for the rest of his life. The one physician from our own time to look at Williams's symptoms found that they "are classic for pre-antibiotic tuberculosis."

Others suffered far worse as prisoners of war. Much of the time, Williams was on Long Island, on parole, overseen by the British but largely unrestricted in his movements. He made friends with a British major "who treated him as a fellow gentleman, and introduced him to the polite society of the British officer corps," according to John Beakes Jr. in his biography of Williams, which included visits to the "fashionable houses" in New York's Battery neighborhood. This pleasant interlude ended, however, when Williams was abruptly transferred from Long Island and locked up in Provost Prison in Manhattan on charges of communicating with George Washington and planning to help other prisoners escape. There, confined much of the time in a sixteen-foot-square room, he lived "in a state of loathsome filth," subsisting on food "of the vilest sort, and scarce enough to keep soul and body together." Conditions were so crowded that when the prisoners lay down to sleep, they would all have to turn over at the same time, upon the command of their guards.

None of this grim existence seemed to discourage Williams unduly. Ethan Allen, who was confined with him, said he "walked through the prison with an air of great disdain," asking, "Is this is the treatment which gentlemen of the Continental army are to expect from the rascally British when in their power?" His "barbarous" captors did not appreciate his attitude, and on at least one occasion, Beakes writes, Williams "was made to ride to the gallows with a rope around his neck, and seated on a coffin, as though being led to his execution," and then led back to prison. When his brother managed to get forty silver dollars to him, Williams loaned thirty of them to other inmates so they could purchase clean shirts and shoes.

Williams was released in an exchange for British prisoners in January 1778, fourteen months after his capture at Fort Washington. A friend heard from him shortly after he regained his freedom in a letter that "breathed the most extravagant joy [and] excessive friskiness." While still locked up, Williams was promoted to colonel, and once free he returned to the army. He was at Monmouth the following June, but his men were held in reserve, and he was soon serving as an aide-de-camp to von Steuben, Washington's drillmaster at Valley Forge, handling largely administrative duties not unlike those he had performed years earlier as a county clerk. On Christmas Day of 1779, he was promoted once again, this time to adjutant general of the entire Continental army, reporting directly to the commander in chief. When spring came and de Kalb was transferred to the South, Williams and the rest of the Maryland and Delaware Continentals were sent to the Carolinas, too. They fought valiantly at Camden, holding their ground when the Virginia and North Carolina militias fled in terror. Henry Lee was impressed with Williams's performance during the battle. Riding his horse, Liberty, Lee wrote, the adjutant general "was conspicuous throughout the action; cheerfully risking his valuable life out of his station, performing his assumed duties with precision and effect, volunteering his person wherever danger called."

Williams did not judge too harshly those who panicked and ran. "He who has never seen the effect of a panic upon a multitude can have but an imperfect idea of such a thing," he wrote. "The best disciplined troops have been enervated and made cowards by it. Armies have been routed by it, even when no enemy appeared to furnish an excuse. Like electricity, it operates instantaneously—like sympathy, it is irresistible where it touches." Still, the effect of their inability to stand firm could not be denied. By noon on the day after the battle, Williams wrote, "a very lengthy line of march occupied the road from Charlotte to Salisbury," as the defeated Continentals and their camp followers trudged north. "It consisted of the wretched remnant of the late Southern army," as well as Catawba Indians who had fought there, and "a great number of distressed whig families." The wounded soldiers, in a forlorn array of conveyances, Williams wrote, bounced along the rough roads,

> some in wagons, some in litters, and some on horseback—their sufferings were indescribable. The distresses of the women and children, who fled from Charlotte and its neighborhood; the nakedness of the Indians, and the number of their infants and aged persons; and the disorder of the whole line of march [presented] an image of compound wretchedness—care, anxiety, pain, poverty, hurry, confusion, humiliation, and dejection.

Even so, Williams saw cause for optimism. The country between Charlotte and Salisbury was fertile, and "the hospitality of the inhabitants" meant there was food, providing "that relief which was requisite to preserve life; besides a liberal supply of provisions for all this cavalcade."

Once what was left of the shattered American troops had made it to Horatio Gates's new headquarters at Hillsborough—"this Dirty, disagreeable hole," as Williams called it in a letter to Morgan—serious efforts to rebuild the army had begun in earnest. All that remained was enough men to constitute but one regiment, and Williams was put in command of the seven or eight hundred now in camp. In December, four months after the disaster at Camden, Greene had arrived, taken over from Gates, and divided the army, with the main force stationed at Cheraw. Williams was there, drilling his troops, when in late January an aide to Morgan rode into camp with the news of his victory at Cowpens.

. . .

On February 10, Greene and the main army left Guilford Courthouse, and three days later, Williams, now in command of the screening force, rode away with about seven hundred "of the flower of the American Army," Williams said, and the second phase of the Race to the Dan began. Because they were vastly outnumbered and were to keep as close to the British as possible while avoiding a major engagement—which they would surely lose—they would be in danger, twenty-four hours a day, the entire time. Their assignment was to act as a buffer between the armies under Cornwallis and Greene, all the while trying to make the enemy believe they actually were Greene's main force, and not a mere detachment from it, and moving ever closer to the Dan and to Virginia.

"Throughout the night," Lee wrote in his history of the southern campaign,

> the corps of Williams held a respectable distance, to thwart, as far as was practicable, the nocturnal assault. The duty, severe in the day, became more so at night; for numerous patrols and strong pickets were necessarily furnished by the light troops, not only for their own safety, but to prevent the enemy from placing himself, by a circuitous march, between Williams and Greene. Such a maneuver would have been fatal to the American army.

To prevent such a calamity, half of the troops were always on duty at night, "so that each man . . . was entitled to but six hours' repose in forty-eight." Williams "always pressed forward with the utmost dispatch in the morning, to gain such a distance in front as would secure breakfast to his soldiers, their only meal during this rapid and hazardous retreat. So fatigued was officer and soldier that each man not placed on duty" fell asleep the moment the next shift took over.

"The shoes were generally worn out, the body clothes much tattered, and not more than a blanket for four men," Lee wrote. And not all the men who were off duty had the luxury of slumber. Around every campfire, one of the four or five men who gathered was not allowed to lie down; this unfortunate soldier had to remain standing, just to keep the fire blazing. Tents were never used during the retreat. "The heat of the fires was the only protection from rain, and sometimes snow."

Through it all, they were skirmishing with detachments of Corn-wallis's army, usually involving the detachment of Lee and his dragoons. On February 11, as the screening force prepared to cross the Haw, Wil-liams told Greene that the British were no more than eight miles from his own troops, and the skirmishing was becoming more intense. Lee had led a charge when a British detachment had approached, Williams reported, "and Captured 3 or 4 Men whom I send you. They Say Ld Cornwallis & the whole British Army preceeded by Coll Tarletons Legion is close in our rear."

By this time, Greene, now approaching the Dan, worried that the British might still overtake Williams and his screening force. If that happened, they could push by him and destroy Greene's main army. "You have the flower of the army," he reminded Williams, "don't expose the men too much, lest our situation should grow more critical." Wil-liams was well aware of the responsibility on his shoulders, and the possible consequences of the decisions he had to make. He was now less than two days away from Greene's troops, and the enemy was push-ing him so hard he might find himself driven right into Greene's own camp. Thanks to Tarleton's skirmishing and the intelligence he had gained in the process, Cornwallis now knew that Williams was leading a detachment and not the main army—and that the detachment was drawing ever closer to Greene's larger body of troops.

Cornwallis knew, too, that Greene was headed for the lower cross-ings. This made the British commander more confident that he could destroy the Continentals because he believed that the boats they needed would not be there. Williams, meanwhile, was growing increasingly worried, and at 7 p.m. on February 13, he dashed off a note informing Greene just how precarious the situation had become. To prevent the British from attacking Greene, Williams might have to fight them then and there, which meant he "must risque the Troops I have the Honor to command and in so doing I risque every thing." And he no longer had as many men with him as he had when he set out. His foot soldiers were "so excessively exhausted that I am confident that I lose men every day."

These fears intensified moments later when, in the distance, Wil-liams spotted campfires. He was clearly stumbling into Greene's own camp, which left him no alternative but to turn around and fight, to keep Cornwallis at bay. It was indeed Greene's camp, Williams learned, but Greene had already pushed on, leaving the campfires for the comfort of Williams's men. Unfortunately, there was no time for them to stop, and at 4 a.m. the next day, Greene instructed Williams to follow as closely as he could to the main army's path and attempt to merge their forces, for the end of the race—however it might turn out—was fast approaching.

"Follow our route, as a division of our force may encourage the enemy to push us further than they will dare to do, if we are together," Greene wrote. "I have not slept four hours since you left me, so great has been my solicitude to prepare for the worst." Spies, moreover, were everywhere, which also made rest impossible. "I have great reason to believe," he said, "that one of Tarleton's officers was in our camp the night before last."

After pausing briefly, both armies pushed on through the darkness, and for several hours that followed, communications between Greene and Williams ceased. It was not until early afternoon on February 14 that Williams heard from his commander. He and his troops had reached the Dan, and the boats that Carrington had promised awaited them. "The greater part of our wagons are over," Greene reported at two o'clock, "and the troops are crossing." The next time Williams heard from Greene was in a dispatch written at five thirty. "All our troops are over," he said. "I am ready to receive you and give you a hearty welcome." Williams relayed the good news to his troops, and they expressed their joy with cheers so loud that the British vanguard under Charles O'Hara could hear them.

Just before 6 p.m., while Lee's Legion stood guard between the Americans at the river and the fast-approaching British, Williams and his men crossed the Dan. A couple of hours later, when darkness had fallen, Lee's cavalry climbed into the boats and, with their horses swimming alongside them, made it to the far shore. Just as the last boat, with Lee on board, pushed off, O'Hara and his troops arrived. There were no more boats on the south banks of the Dan, so the British—once they arrived—could not cross. The race was over.

General Washington, back in New York, was delighted by the news. "You may be assured," he wrote to Greene, "that your Retreat before Lord Cornwallis is highly applauded by all Ranks, and it reflects much honor upon your military Abilities." Even Tarleton, in his history of the southern campaign, expressed his admiration. "Every measure of the Americans, during the march from Catawba to Virginia, was judiciously designed and vigorously executed." Alexander Hamilton put it this way: to have retreated "in the face of so ardent a pursuit, through so great an extent of the country, through a country offering every obstacle, affording scarcely any resources, with troops destitute of every thing [and to have done so] without loss of any kind, may, without exaggeration, be denominated a masterpiece of military skill and execution."

Greene, for his part, shared the glory with Williams, whom he had trusted with the responsibility that was originally assumed to be Daniel Morgan's. The screening force, Greene told Washington, "was commanded by Col. Williams who had orders to keep as near the [enemy] as he could without exposing the party too much," retarding their progress as much as they could. "His conduct upon the occasion," Greene reported, "does him the highest honor."

Some of his men had marched more than two hundred miles since they left Cowpens, the last forty, according to Larry G. Aaron in *The Race to the Dan*, in sixteen hours. They had done so, moreover, under horrid winter conditions, as bleak as those more celebrated soldiers faced at Valley Forge and Morristown. "The miserable situation of the troops for want of clothing had rendered the march the most painfull imaginable," Greene wrote in his report to Washington. Hundreds of the men had trudged through mud and ice, "tracking the ground with their bloody feet." Even so, they were "in good spirits notwithstanding their suffering and excessive fatigue."

In Greene's camp, "joy beamed in every face," Lee wrote, "and as if every man was conscious of having done his duty, the subsequent days [of] the reunion of the army on the north of the Dan were spent in mutual gratulations." Around the campfires, they recalled "the hopes and fears which agitated every breast during the retreat." When they heard the news, Americans—civilians and soldiers alike—celebrated, not least by poking fun at the British and their inability to catch their prey. The tune was "Yankee Doodle," but the words were new:

> *They rambled up and rambled down,*
> *Joined hands and off they ran, sir,*
> *And General Greene was like to drown*
> *Cornwallis in the Dan, sir.*

CHAPTER TWENTY

"I Am Wedded to My Sword"

It was no coincidence that one of the last men to cross the cold and muddy waters of the Dan River was also one of the first to get back on the other side. This was Henry Lee III, and he was what later generations came to call "a young man in a hurry." Harry Lee was never the sort of soldier who saw much percentage in sitting around in camp, gaining back the weight one lost in long marches with scant provisions or polishing sabers and bayonets. Lee liked action, and just two days after he had crossed the river the first time, he proposed to Greene that he be allowed to return to North Carolina immediately to make trouble for the British. So he was by all evidence delighted when Greene decided to send him and his cavalry—"Lee's Legion," it was called—with two companies of Maryland Continentals back over the river. There they were to link up with Andrew Pickens and his men, who, on Greene's orders, were "to pursue the Enemy and harass them as much as possible." Having repeatedly demonstrated his knack for maneuvering quickly and quietly, Lee would also shadow the enemy, gathering intelligence for Greene and the other officers still back in Virginia. His assignment, also, was to "check the audacity" of the British and their loyalist allies and "rouse the drooping spirits" of their friends.

Lee recrossed the Dan on February 18—four days before Greene did—but it wasn't until the morning of the 23rd that he and Pickens found each other, and there was a moment when their meeting almost proved calamitous. Lee's men were outfitted—like Tarleton's—with short green jackets and plumed helmets—and when soldiers in Pickens's rear guard first spotted Lee and his mounted troops, they assumed they had stumbled onto the enemy. They hurriedly sent word back to the main camp, at a farm, where the others were roused from their slumber and told to form up for battle. "Too late to retreat," a captain under Pickens recalled, "so [we] prepared to fight."

Before shots were fired, however, Pickens's men and Lee's recognized each other, and disaster was averted. Such confusion was not uncommon in this war. Uniforms were in short supply, and those that existed varied so widely and idiosyncratically that calling them uniforms seems at times almost comical. On both sides, quasi-civilians fought in the clothes they wore on their farms and served alongside members of state militias and duly constituted "regulars" of Greene's Continentals and Lord Cornwallis's redcoats. About the only thing distinguishing the Americans who fought against each other at Kings Mountain was what they stuck in their hats: loyalists favored sprigs of evergreen, and the rebels used pieces of white cloth or paper. That way, in almost no other, they could tell friend from foe. This was a problem much of the time during the war in the South, and just two days after Pickens's men almost opened fire on Lee's, there was more confusion when two small forces stumbled into each other, and this time the encounter would end with considerable loss of life.

The man in the middle of this—an incident that looked to survivors as well as observers like an unforgivably bloody mess—was Lee, known to family and friends as Harry and to history as "Light Horse Harry." Born in 1756, he was from one of the "long-tailed" families of Virginia that, under different circumstances, might well have remained loyal to the Crown. The Lees of Virginia, who had their own coat of arms, were nevertheless deeply enmeshed in the drive for independence. When the first Henry Lee landed in the Old Dominion, he made a fortune in tobacco on his plantation, which he called "Leesylvania," and his descendants established themselves down the road at Stratford Hall, which stood, fortress-like, on a cliff overlooking the Potomac River.

Lees had been in Virginia for more than a century by the time Henry III took up arms against the British, establishing great plantations and assuming positions of influence in the colony and, in time, in the Congresses that represented all thirteen colonies. His father, Henry Lee II, served in the Virginia House of Burgesses, its legislature, as did

Richard Henry Lee, a first cousin. This Richard Henry Lee was the author of what became known as the "Westmoreland Resolves," named for the county where Stratford Hall overlooked the Potomac. A full decade before the fighting at Lexington and Concord, the Westmoreland Resolves—signed by four Lees as well as James Monroe's father, and George Washington's—called for Virginia's separation from England. Richard Henry Lee was also a delegate to the First and Second Continental Congresses, where in June 1776 he introduced a resolution calling on the other colonies to support separation. The following month, he signed the Declaration of Independence. Forced by illness to leave Congress and return to Virginia, he served in the Virginia House of Delegates. In April 1781, when British gunboats were raiding along the Potomac, a forty-nine-year-old Richard Henry reactivated his commission in the Virginia militia, returned to his Northern Neck plantation, and defended Stratford Landing from the marauding redcoats. "In a late engagement," he crowed in a letter to Samuel Adams, "the enemy landed under a cover of heavy cannonade from three vessels of war . . . a small body of militia [were] well posted. After a small engagement, we had the pleasure to see the enemy, though superior in number, run to their boats and precipitously re-embark, having sustained a small loss of killed and wounded." Richard Henry Lee had every reason to be proud of his involvement: while he was a tall and imposing physical specimen, he was also prone to debilitating illnesses, including epilepsy.

Arthur Lee, one of Richard Henry's younger brothers, while consequential in the history of the War of Independence, is not viewed with much admiration by historians; his own contemporaries did not regard him much more highly, either. *The Encyclopedia of the American Revolution* introduces Arthur, with evident distaste, as "American diplomat, troublemaker." That esteemed reference work refers to him, further on, as a "marplot." Benjamin Franklin, who worked closely with Lee representing colonial interests in Europe, called him a "Genius," but a troubled one. He "must either find or make a quarrel wherever he is," Franklin wrote. "The only excuse for him that his conduct will admit of, is his being at times out of his Senses." If some of the "many Enemies he provokes do not kill him sooner he will die in a madhouse."

While not without some basis in fact, these characterizations detract from Lee's role, as a law student and later a propagandist in London, in shaping the opposition to the war that, as early as 1775, was mounting among Whig members of Parliament. Highly intelligent, Arthur was without doubt a complicated, maybe neurotically thin-skinned character, orphaned at ten and sent by older siblings and one of his Lee uncles across the Atlantic that same year. At Edinburgh he studied medicine and finished first in his class, but practiced only briefly, in London. The first time he observed an actual surgical operation induced "so severe a shock" that he said he never again wished to witness anything so unpleasant. He never married and believed that one cause of his brother Richard Henry's epilepsy—or any man's—could be "too frequent enjoyment of women."

Arthur practiced law too, also in London, but found diplomacy and impassioned journalism more to his liking. Taxation without representation, he told his readers, was "absurd, monstrous, stupid, iniquitous, and evil." With a marked gift for intrigue, Arthur helped to negotiate the treaty under which France entered the war and to expose the financial improprieties of his fellow diplomat Silas Deane, whom Congress in response ordered back to America. It was through his friend James Boswell, Samuel Johnson's biographer, that Arthur Lee in 1768 met the rabble-rousing British politician John Wilkes, then locked up in King's Bench Prison for his anti-government activities. Lee worked with characteristic panache to persuade the radical Whig controversialist of the justice of the American cause. It would be Wilkes, along with William Pitt the Elder and, most notably, Edmund Burke, who argued with greatest eloquence in Parliament that the war was not only unjust but also unwinnable.

The Lees, while scholarly and philosophical advocates of independence, were also exuberant in their support of it. They made a kind of art of open-handed generosity, and Harry Lee had grown up in their comfortable and convivial world. He had learned to ride, it was said, as a toddler, and kept his own horse with him when he went away to study the classics at the College of New Jersey (later Princeton) and prepare for a career in the law. It was hard to maintain one's enthusiasm for *Blackstone's Commentaries* with war coming on, especially given his family's festive, even giddy, involvement in the cause. A college classmate who had come down from New Jersey to serve as a tutor at a neighboring plantation left an account of a party he attended at Lee Hall, the plantation of another Richard Lee, an uncle of Harry's known as "the Squire." The party—more than a year before the fighting started—began on a

Major General Charles Lee.
Engraving by James Neagle after Barham Rushbrooke,
London, ca. 1813

Monday and did not end until the following Thursday, when, to the Squire's dismay, guests began to climb back into their carriages and ride away. He was expecting them to stay another day.

"The Ladies were Dressed Gay," the young tutor reported. There was music—a French horn and two violins—and dancing. When the women moved across the ballroom floor, "their Silks & Brocades rustled and trailed behind them!" There was also "drinking for Pleasure," with lemon punches, toddies, and hard cider. The more the men drank, the more enthusiastic they were to fight for independence, and there in the Lee Hall ballroom—before the hard realities of war disturbed their cozy lives—defeating the redcoats would be no more difficult than riding to hounds. Some of the men were "toasting the Sons of america," the tutor wrote in his journal. Others sang "Liberty Songs, as they call'd them, in which six, eight, ten or more would put their Heads near together and roar." The result, though spirited, was also "unharmonious."

But Harry Lee had also learned something of the more sober business of war, as understood at the highest levels. In April 1775, he had dined at Mount Vernon with Washington himself. The only other guest at Washington's plantation that afternoon was a former officer in the British army who had fought in the Seven Years' War. This rather odd-looking gentleman—he had a big nose, weak chin, potbelly, and gangly arms and legs—was Charles Lee, who, remarkably enough, was not one of Harry's relatives. But he was the same Charles Lee who, in the not-too-distant future, would be captured by Banastre Tarleton. (Tarleton, of course, was the same Tarleton who would try to capture Harry Lee and fail.)

A professional soldier, Charles Lee had served as a major general and aide-de-camp to Poland's King Stanislaus and in the Russian military under the Empress Catherine II in the second Russo-Turkish War. Charles Lee would become, by Washington's own admission, "the first Officer in Military Knowledge and experience we have in the whole Army," though the two would have a falling-out at Monmouth, where the commander in chief relieved Lee of his command, and he would later be dismissed altogether. John Adams told Abigail that he, John, "had read as much on the military Art and much more of the History of War" as any of the American officers—except for Charles Lee.

Familiar with the topography of the American colonies—he owned a farm in Virginia's Shenandoah Valley—Charles Lee had definite ideas about how the looming war should be prosecuted, and he was not reluctant to share then. He favored a so-called Fabian strategy, a war of attrition, of mobility and surprise, of "harassing and impeding" the enemy, interrupting its supply lines, and wearing down its will to win. Lee also believed that militiamen and even irregulars could be highly effective in such campaigns. Washington had little use for such undisciplined amateurs, but the kind of warfare Charles Lee championed was what Harry Lee, when he joined Washington's army, would excel at.

On April 19, 1775, just three days after the dinner at Mount Vernon, British regulars and Massachusetts militiamen clashed at Lexington and Concord. In mid-June, Congress had appointed Washington as commander in chief of the Continental army, and two days after that, Charles Lee was named second in command and head of the army's Southern Department. The following month, Harry—abandoning his studies—wrote to Charles, referring to "the familiarity with which you treated me" during their dinner, asked to serve under him "to acquaint myself with the art of war." There is no record of a response, and there might not have been one; a year later, in March 1776, Harry wrote to Charles a second time, but again, if there was a response, it has not survived. Whatever the case, within a matter of weeks, Harry rode to the capital at Williamsburg, signed on with the 5th Troop of Virginia Light Horse, and was elected by the other men to be their captain. Blond-haired and blue-eyed, Light Horse Harry looked impressive in the saddle, "with a form light and agile [and] a quick and penetrating glance."

In early 1777, Harry Lee and his unit were sent north to Washington's army, and while patrolling outside British-occupied Philadelphia in August, the men under Lee's command took twenty-four prisoners. In November, they surprised an enemy foraging party, again taking captives. The redcoats "ran without giving one fire," Lee reported. He was proving so adept at these raids that the following month, Washington made sure Lee had all the dragoons he needed. "He is so enterprising and useful an Officer that I should wish him not to be Straitened for want of men," the commander in chief wrote. Given more men to work with, Lee proved even more effective. In mid-January, *The New-Jersey Gazette* reported that, "though seldom having more than 25 men and horses fit for duty," Lee's little band had taken more than one hundred prisoners, "with the loss of only one horse."

There can be costs to calling attention to oneself in this way, and by the time Harry and his dragoons had taken that first clutch of prisoners back in August, other officers—"offended by his ambition and arrogance," according to one of his biographers—accused him of insubordination. The details are sketchy, but he was formally charged and later that month faced a court-martial. The court found "that Capn. Henry Lee is not guilty of the charge exhibited against him, and do acquit him with honor." But fellow officers eager for promotion were not the only ones following his escapades. So were the British. Hessian Captain Johann Ewald complained that Lee's dragoons "constantly alarmed our outposts," and in January 1778 the British devised a plan to put an end to these alarms—and to Light House Harry himself. They assembled a special unit of mounted troops, estimated at up to two hundred men, the sole mission of which was to hunt down Harry Lee and kill him. The mission failed.

Throughout the spring, Lee continued his raids on British supply lines, again earning Washington's praise for his "zealous activity." In late March, Washington offered Lee a coveted staff position, comparable to Alexander Hamilton's, as an aide-de-camp. This was a great honor and a perfect spot for one who wished, as Harry had told Charles Lee back in 1775, "to acquaint myself with the art of war." Light Horse Harry's response was prompt and surprising. He declined. While flattered, he said, his first reason for turning down the offer was that he was determined to continue the work he was doing, on the field of combat. "I am wedded to my sword," he wrote. He sought "military reputation," which could not be earned behind a desk in a general's tent—even as great a general as Washington:

> To have possessed a post about your Excellency's person . . . affords a field for military instruction, would lead me into an intimate acquaintance with the politics of the States, and might present more immediate opportunities of manifesting my high respect and warm attachment to your Excellencys character and person. I know it would also afford true and unexpected joy to my parents and friends.

Lee felt other, equally strong attachments, however. "I possess a most affectionate friendship" for his his soldiers, "a fraternal love" for his officers, and "a zeal for the honor of the Cavalry," all of which convinced him that he could render more "real service to your Excellency's arms" not at staff headquarters, but in the field.

One might imagine that Light Horse Harry's refusal would have offended Washington, a proud man who did not take rejection well. But rather than taking offense, Washington was impressed. The "undisguised manner in which you express yourself cannot but strengthen my good opinion of you," the commander in chief replied. The offer "was purely the result of a high Sense of your merit, and as I would by no means divert you from a Career in which you promise yourself greater happiness, from its affording more frequent opportunities of acquiring military fame, I entreat you to pursue your own Inclinations, as if nothing had passed on this Subject."

Their relationship firmly established on grounds of mutual respect, the two men seem to have understood each other perfectly. In early

April, informing Congress that Harry Lee and his men had "uniformly distinguished themselves by a conduct of exemplary zeal, prudence and bravery," Washington asked that Lee be given "an independent partisan Corps" and a promotion to major. "Capt. [Lee's] genius particularly adapts him to a command of this nature," Washington told Congress, and Congress dutifully complied. In November 1780, "Lee's Legion," as it became known, had been sent to the South, to support Greene's army.

In late February 1781, Lee's Legion recrossed the Dan River and returned to North Carolina, to harass the British and their Tory allies. Cornwallis, meanwhile, had established his base of operation at Hillsborough, about fifty miles south of the crossing—but another two hundred miles from his main base of supply at Camden. From Hillsborough, he implored "all loyal subjects to repair to the King's standard, and to take an active part in assisting him to restore order and constitutional government." Hundreds of loyalists responded, but when they got to the camp, most of them took one look and left. The bedraggled appearance of the emaciated British regulars made them doubt whether Cornwallis would be able even to feed them. And feeding the troops at Hillsborough was a challenge. Before long, they were slaughtering and eating their best draft horses.

Lee's old nemesis Tarleton was at camp with Cornwallis, too, and knew firsthand the increasing reluctance of the loyalists to fight for the cause. Tarleton's British Legion was made up of Americans in the main, and he knew how they thought. Cornwallis had not done enough to support them, and now he expected them to support him. For five years now, the loyalists of North Carolina had endured "a variety of calamities [that] had not only reduced their numbers and weakened their attachment," but was also convincing them that the British could not win. Another of Cornwallis's officers—Lieutenant Colonel John Hamilton of the Royal North Carolina Regiment, a provincial unit—said they expected Greene's imminent return, and, still horrified by what had happened at Cowpens in January, "the dread of violence and persecution prevented their taking a decided part in a cause which yet appeared dangerous."

Sympathetic Americans came to the camp "to stare at us," Brigadier General Charles O'Hara, the second in command, said. "Their curiosity once satisfied, they returned to their Homes." In their march of more than one thousand miles, "in almost as many directions, thro' every part of North Carolina," O'Hara recalled, "tho every means possible was taken to persuade our Friends as they are called . . . we never had with us at any one time One Hundred men in arms."

There were exceptions, however. There was Dr. John Pyle. Born in England in 1723, he attended medical school in London but, in 1766, moved with his family to North Carolina. Pyle was in his late fifties when Cornwallis was in Hillsborough and had been an ardent and energetic loyalist since the war broke out. Five years earlier, at Moore's Creek Bridge, near Wilmington, Pyle with other local loyalists fought under Cornwallis, whose redcoats suffered a stinging defeat, resulting in the collapse of royal government in the state. Fifty of the British loyalists were killed or wounded—compared to two casualties on the part of the patriots—and 850 were taken prisoner. One of these was Pyle, who managed to escape and make his way home. He took an oath of allegiance to the new state government, which allowed him to remain free. Unlike so many of his North Carolina neighbors, he believed that the British would prevail, and, breaking his parole, he began to raise troops. By the time Cornwallis was in Hillsborough, Pyle commanded a force of four hundred mounted loyalists. Informed of this encouraging development, Cornwallis promised to send troops under Tarleton to escort these recruits to camp. Pyle would have to move quickly, however, because Lee's Legion was heading their way.

CHAPTER TWENTY-ONE

"You Are Killing Your Own Men!"

On February 23, Tarleton set out to rendezvous with John Pyle and his militia. The following day, learning that Lee and his cavalry had joined forces with Andrew Pickens, for the sole purpose of "intimidating or dispersing the King's friends," Tarleton sent word for Pyle to hurry; if he did so, together they could attack Lee before he was reinforced by yet more men, in the form of a Virginia militia known to be in the area. When Pyle and his men did not appear, Tarleton sent another message; again they did not show. "Though forewarned of their danger," Tarleton said, they visited friends and family along the way, and "inspired by whiskey and novelty of their situation, they unfortunately prolonged their excursions," which they would soon regret.

What happened next was as confusing to the survivors as it has been to historians ever since. No one today even knows exactly where it took place, though most agree it was on a country lane somewhere in present-day Alamance County, North Carolina. Lee and Tarleton, in their memoirs, put their own spin on the episode, as one might expect, but there are discrepancies even in their own respective accounts. What everyone seems to agree on is that the uniforms worn by Lee's men and by Tarleton's were suspiciously similar, and this might have been intentional on Lee's part. There is reason to suspect that Lee, envying Tarleton's reputation for bravery, copied the British Legion's short green coats and plumed helmets. It might also be relevant to remember that the accents of Englishmen and Americans at this time were considerably more similar than they are today. Americans were often recent immigrants from England, and if they weren't, their parents or grand-parents were. Many Americans probably grew up speaking what we might now think of as British English.

On February 24, Pyle and his loyalists were making their way along that country lane in Alamance County, intending to hook up with Tarleton, who would lead them safely to the British camp some twenty miles east at Hillsborough. Tarleton wasn't sure where Pyle was, and Pyle wasn't sure where Tarleton was. They were approaching one another, and the three small forces—Pyle's, Lee's, and Tarleton's—might converge at any moment, whether they intended to do so or not. This became even more likely when Pickens discovered that the countryside through which he and his men were moving was loyalist territory, and that the locals, never suspecting that a detachment of rebels was in their midst, "seemed prodigiously rejoiced" at the sight of his troops. They imagined that "we were a fresh party of British," Pickens wrote. Many of them, he noticed, were armed "and prepared to join Tarleton that evening." Tarleton, Pickens learned, was only four miles away.

Lee's advance guard, meanwhile, came upon "two well-mounted young countrymen" who also assumed that the newcomers were part of Tarleton's British Legion. They said they were with Pyle, who had sent them ahead to find Tarleton's camp. The men were escorted to Lee, whom they addressed as Tarleton. Told where Pyle's main force was, Lee sent one of the men back to their commander, with Tarleton's best wishes—and with one request. Lee asked that Pyle pull his men to the left side of the lane, "so as to give convenient room for his much fatigued troops to pass without delay," as Lee wrote in his memoirs. He would take the other man with him as they began their advance. His confidence in the ruse that was developing gained strength, thanks to "the overflowing of respect and devotion falling incessantly from the lips" of the loyalist riding alongside him.

Lee also sent Pickens ahead, ordering him to move his troops as unobtrusively as possible into a thick wood to the left of the lane. There they were to wait, with their rifles at the ready. When Lee reached the rear of Pyle's column, he found them mounted and drawn up to the side of the lane just as he had requested. Spotting the young officer in the green jacket and plumed helmet, accompanied by one of their own men, Pyle's loyalists also assumed that Tarleton had arrived. Some of the loyalists toward the end of the line actually greeted him as such, and Lee responded in character. As he trotted along, he nodded to the men he passed, congratulating them for the fine-looking soldiers they were. He moved up the lane, he would recall, "with a smiling countenance, dropping occasionally, expressions complimentary to the good looks and commendable conduct of his loyal friends." Making his way to the head of the column and to its commander, Lee noticed that the loyalists' rifles were on their shoulders. This was fortuitous. It meant the muzzles of their weapons were pointed away from him and his men, and, if the ruse were detected, they could not readily be brought into position for firing.

When Lee reached the end of the line, he rode up to Pyle, "and the customary civilities were promptly interchanged." Lee took Pyle by the hand and was preparing to reveal his true identity and inform him of his options. He could immediately switch sides and fight with Lee and his Legion, or Pyle could dismiss the company he had assembled and send them home with the assurance that they would never again take up arms against the cause of independence. Should he choose to do the latter, there would be no unpleasant repercussions. They would be free to go in peace. These seem to be generous terms, and if so, it would become apparent in due course why that was the case.

But Lee never got the chance to extend this offer. At the far end of the line, something happened, and exactly what that was varied depending on who told the story. Even Lee's account—based not only on his own understandable desire to portray himself in the best possible light but also on what the men at the end of the line would have told him—contains inconsistencies. This much is clear: words were exchanged, and it became apparent to Pyle's men that they had been tricked.

Whoever recognized whom and started firing first will probably never be known, but the sound of the guns crackled along the line, and as it did, Pickens's riflemen raked the loyalists from their position in the woods. Lee's men were flailing away with their sabers, and some of the loyalists—still unaware that the men attacking them were not with Tarleton—made no attempt to fight back. Some still thought a terrible mistake was being made. "You are killing your own men!" one shouted. Others insisted that "they were friends of King George." Still others yelled, "God save the King!" These protestations, of course, served only to encourage their attackers, who soon discovered, too, that many if not most of Pyle's men were carrying guns that had no bullets. With sabers and swords alone, Lee's men hacked their way through the virtually defenseless loyalists, and the attack was so savage that many of those "swords broke [and] others bent."

It was over within ten minutes. Though wounded in the fracas, Pyle managed to escape, and legend has it that he hid in a pond until it was safe to crawl out. He managed to survive by raising just his nose above the water to breathe. Other loyalists also fled. But the ground on and around the lane was littered with the bodies of more than ninety loyalists. Some were still breathing, but most of them had been shot or hacked to death. There were dead horses, too, a scene so ghastly that none of the survivors would ever forget it, but would also seek to understand. They would also try to explain it, to others and to posterity but also to themselves. William Lenoir, who also fought at Kings Mountain, said he had "never before witnessed the works of death carried to such an extent in so short a time." Philip Higdon, one of the loyalists fortunate enough to be captured, said the "slaughter was indiscriminate." Lee's casualties were almost negligible—a horse was shot to death, and one of his men, taken prisoner, was killed.

There were other killings, too, when evening came. Moses Hall of the North Carolina militia, who went to look at the loyalist prisoners, said he and his fellows approached six of the captives huddled together. Words were exchanged. One of the militiamen shouted, "Remember Buford!" recalling the supposed bloodbath at the Waxhaws, and, Hall continued,

> the prisoners were immediately hewed to pieces with broadswords. At first I bore the scene without any emotion, but upon a moment's reflection, I felt such horror as I never did before nor have since, and returning to my quarters and throwing myself upon my blanket I contemplated the cruelties of war until overcome and unmanned by a distressing gloom.

Lee and his men marched away from this scene of horrors before dawn the next day, in time reaching what had been Tarleton's camp, "which he had just abandoned leaving lively rail fires." Hall's mood improved along the way, and his gloom lifted, when he had discovered "lying upon the ground something like the appearance of a man."

Upon inspection, this figure "proved to be a youth about sixteen who had come to view the British through curiosity." Afraid that he might give information to Lee's troops, the men under Tarleton's command "had run him through with a bayonet and left him for dead." Although he was still able to speak, his wounds were fatal, and the sight "of this unoffending boy butchered . . . released me of my distressful feelings for the slaughter of the Tories." From that moment on, Hall "desired nothing so much as the opportunity of participating in their destruction."

Some of the survivors managed to make it to the safety of Tarleton's camp, but, still confused by what had just happened, they "complained to Tarleton of the cruelty of [his] dragoons." Learning what he could about the incident, Tarleton decried the "inhuman barbarity" of Lee's men, and Cornwallis reported to Lord George Germain that the loyalists had been "most inhumanely butchered, when begging for quarter, without making the least resistance." The impact on the loyalists in the area was immediate. Nathanael Greene told Virginia governor Jefferson that the episode "has had a very happy effect on those disaffected Persons, of which there are too many in this Country." Greene wrote to Pickens that "the defeat of the Tories was so happily timed, & in all probability will be productive of such happy consequences that I cannot help congratulating you on your success."

There is no evidence from Greene's letters that he believed Lee's men had committed atrocities or—if he believed that they had—that he was much troubled by it. What became known as Pyle's Massacre and Pyle's Hacking Match quickly entered the vocabulary of the Revolution, along with "Remember Buford!" What Tarleton had supposedly done at the Waxhaws would justify the slaughter of loyalists later, and on and on, as the violence escalated. The war in the South, much more so than in Pennsylvania, Massachusetts, New York, and New Jersey, was now a civil war and, as might be expected, increasingly unrestrained by conventions of warfare observed in the main by older commanders like Washington and Cornwallis, trained in the traditions of European warfare.

Tarleton and Lee were both in their mid-twenties at this point in the war, with independent commands, detached from the main armies, making decisions on the fly, in response to immediate—and potentially fatal—developments, often in hostile territory. Killings for retaliation and revenge were now accepted in ways they would not have been in European wars.

"Light Horse Harry" has been made the villain of Pyle's Massacre, but that might be no more justified than it had been to vilify Tarleton for what took place at the Waxhaws. "Some writers and pensioners have questioned Lee's intentions in the encounter with Pyle, even suggesting that he planned the slaughter from the outset," Jim Piecuch and John H. Beakes Jr. wrote in *"Light Horse Harry" Lee in the War for Independence.* "When the British commanders first heard of the affair, they were quick to accept that their enemies were capable of great atrocities. The specter of over ninety of their men lying dead in the road, with hardly any American casualties, seemed to be evidence of some nefarious intent." But evidence of an elaborate scheme is nonexistent. At some point, Lee clearly decided "to pass as a reinforcement sent from Hillsborough to Lieutenant-Colonel Tarleton," Major Joseph Graham of the North Carolina militia recalled. But this would have been an almost instantaneous decision, because Lee did not anticipate running into Pyle's troops at all, and, when he did, he seems to have regarded the encounter as a distraction from his immediate objective—which Pickens shared—of attacking Tarleton.

Far from exuberant about the turn of events, both Lee and Pickens "exhibited great perturbation," Graham wrote, at having to deal with Pyle at all. Pickens told Greene that the engagement "blasted" their hopes of surprising Tarleton, who now knew their whereabouts and their intention. Lee found himself needing to justify his actions—rare after a decided victory—which he attempted to do, both at the time and thirty years later in his memoirs. In his account of the action, Lee quoted that of a British officer who claimed that "between two and three hundred" loyalists were "inhumanly butchered while in the act of begging for mercy. Humanity shudders at the recital of so foul a massacre; but cold and unfeeling policy avows it as the most effectual means of intimidating the friends of royal government."

This, Lee argued, was a grotesque misinterpretation of what actually happened. His men had acted in self-defense, he wrote. They had been fired on first, "and self-preservation commanded the limited destruction which ensued. Only ninety of the loyalists were killed," and "less than ninety could not have been spared from the close condition of the dragoons, and the necessity of crushing resistance instantly." Had they wished to massacre Pyle's men, "it was only necessary to have ordered pursuit, and not a man of the enemy would have escaped." Instead, Lee let them go, and "not being pursued, they escaped." He had done what any responsible commander would have done under the circumstances, which was to defend his men in a moment of great peril to their lives.

Even the terms Lee was prepared to offer Pyle—that his men could switch sides and fight against the British or simply go home unharmed—were proof enough that he had no intent of slaughtering them. As Lee wrote to Greene on the night after the engagement, he had dealt with Pyle as efficiently as possible and then moved on, "that no time might be lost in reaching Col. Tarleton," whose camp was no more than three miles away when the shooting started. That was now impossible, because Tarleton had learned from survivors from Pyle's troops where Lee and Pickens were and the threat that they posed.

By this time, however, Cornwallis was aware that Greene and his Continentals had crossed the Dan once again and were back in North Carolina, rested, resupplied, and headed his way. Now Cornwallis wanted Tarleton to rejoin the main army and ordered him to return. The next day, when Lee reached Tarleton's camp, he found it deserted, as Tarleton had pushed on. For the next two and a half weeks, the armies and their detachments played what Joseph Graham called "their game of checkers," trying to build their forces while seeking the most advantageous position for a major confrontation.

Lee was eager for action and characteristically resourceful. In early March, just days before they would fight at Guilford Courthouse, he wrote to Greene and asked him to send along a company of mounted militia that he heard had just entered the main army's camp. Lee, who prided himself on his own troops' training and discipline, shared with the other regular officers a disdain for the reliability of untested militia. "As they will be useless," he said of the militia that he asked Greene to send along, "my sole object [is] to get their best horses for the use of my cavalry, & permit them to return home." Greene, in response, sent 170 mounted militia to Lee. What became of them once they had surrendered their horses to him remains a mystery.

CHAPTER TWENTY-TWO

"This Day of Blood"

Winter moved toward spring, and the colonies took a significant step closer to nationhood. In Philadelphia, the Second Continental Congress took final action on a proposal put forward by Virginia's Richard Henry Lee four years earlier, when he offered his resolution calling for independence, by ratifying the Articles of Confederation. Formal ratification took place on March 1, 1781, and with that, the Continental Congress officially ceased to be. It was replaced by "The United States in Congress Assembled," which would govern the country until the federal Constitution took effect, with the first Congress under that government convening in March 1789 in New York.

Meanwhile, of course, there was still a war going on. While Washington remained in Morristown, preparing to leave winter quarters, Cornwallis in North Carolina and Greene in Virginia continued to rebuild their respective armies and prepare for a major engagement. Still smarting from his inability to overtake the enemy as he raced for the Dan River, Cornwallis was disappointed by the lack of provisions in the Hillsborough area and the lack of enthusiasm among the people for helping his hungry and exhausted troops. This was loyalist territory, after all, but news of the annihilation of Pyle's men had left even the most sympathetic friends of the Crown frightened and discouraged. As Cornwallis told Lord George Germain, heavy and seemingly nonstop rain in late February had swollen the rivers between him and his prey, preventing Cornwallis from catching Greene—and Otho Holland Williams, too, of course. But the skies had cleared and the waters were subsiding, and Cornwallis remained confident in the abilities of his well-trained troops. Greene knew the rivers were shallower now than they had been, and had he waited much longer, Cornwallis might have crossed into Virginia, too, and fought him there.

For a few days, Greene's men had been able to rest, safely "enjoying wholesome and abundant supplies of food in the rich and friendly county of Halifax," provided by the generous Virginians. But this could not last. To Greene's disappointment, the supplies he hoped to collect in the Old Dominion proved to be in shorter supply than he had been led to believe, and he had been unable to recruit as many locals as he had hoped. Now, with the waters of the Dan subsiding, Greene had returned to North Carolina, he said, "without ammunition provisions or Stores of any kind."

And Greene was still outnumbered. When the Continental army recrossed the river and headed back into North Carolina, he had about two thousand men under his command, which was five hundred or so fewer than Cornwallis. Even so, Lee's victory over Pyle and his militia "almost put a total stop" to the British ability to bring in new recruits, while Greene soon had reinforcements on the way. By early March, two thousand more men arrived, mostly Virginia and North Carolina militia, but also tough characters from the battle-hardened Maryland Line came into camp. One of the newcomers was Major St. George Tucker of the Virginia militia, who expressed some of the confidence building among the American troops as they headed toward Greene's camp.

"We marched yesterday to look for Lord Cornwallis, who probably marched a different route because he did not choose to fight us," Tucker wrote to his wife. "We are now strong enough, I hope, to cope with him to advantage. Our army in strength is rather better than I expected." Once the troops in Tucker's group caught up with Greene's, he figured they would have "about six thousand men of which, I believe, fifteen hundred are regulars." This was optimistic. There would be a little more than 4,300 in Greene's army, but Tucker was close to the number of Continentals; there were just over 1,700 of them.

Unfortunately—though Cornwallis did not know this—fewer than seven hundred of Greene's troops had ever been in a battle before. Spies, turncoats, sympathetic locals, and even one's own scouts can be notoriously unreliable sources of military intelligence. Cornwallis's eyes and ears had led him to believe that, if the two armies engaged, he would face a force of ten thousand. Even so, he knew that his men were better trained and far more experienced than Greene's—and Greene, though confident as well, was characteristically wary. He moved his camp constantly, all the while planning to offer battle when the time and place were advantageous. "I rarely ever lay more than two days in a place," he told Joseph Reed, the former adjutant general in the North. "The country being much of a wilderness, obliged the enemy to guard carefully against a surprise and rendered it difficult to surprise us." Greene had also dispensed with unnecessary baggage, keeping few wagons, "and only tents enough to secure our arms in case of a wasting rain." Greene understood the strategic value of his numbers being overestimated by the enemy, and he had learned from Daniel Morgan's victory at Cowpens that if he asked of his militia only as much as could reasonably be expected, he could turn a possible liability into an asset.

Struggling to recuperate back in Virginia's Shenandoah Valley, Morgan wrote to offer encouragement but also advice. He had been hoping to return and "take the field, but I find I get worse," he confessed. "My pains are now accompanied by a fever, every day." A major engagement with Cornwallis seemed inevitable, and when that day came, the fate of Greene's army—and, quite possibly, that of the war itself—would rest with the militia. "I expect Lord Cornwallis will push you till you are obliged to fight him, on which much will depend," Morgan wrote. "You'll have from what I see, a great number of militia—if they fight, you'll beat Cornwallis, if not he will beat you and perhaps cut your regulars to pieces, which will be losing all our hopes." Morgan was unsentimental about the tendency of untested men to throw down their arms and run for cover. Greene should position riflemen behind the militia, Morgan said, "with orders to shoot down the first man that runs."

Greene decided to make his stand at Guilford Courthouse, where he had gathered his troops in early February before marching them to the Dan. So he was already familiar with the area and its possibilities. Guilford Courthouse was a cluster of small houses and other structures, around a government building that has long since disappeared. The aptly named Troublesome Creek was not far away, through dense woods and a few farm fields and pastures. A Quaker meetinghouse stood about six miles to the west down the New Garden Road, which bisected the ground where Greene would position his troops. Through late February and early March, there had been skirmishing between the two armies' detachments, as might be expected when Tarleton was screening the main British army and Lee was gathering intelligence for Greene. The energetic Otho Holland Williams was also patrolling the countryside, harassing the main British army to stall their advance.

Hoping to get Williams out of the way, Cornwallis sent twelve hundred men under Tarleton to surprise and destroy him. Williams had about six hundred militiamen with him, plus Lee and his Legion covering his rear in case they needed to retreat. Tarleton set out from camp at 3 a.m. on March 6, and by 8 a.m., his men were pushing Williams back toward Reedy Fork Creek and a ford at Wetzell's Mill. Williams got most of his men over the creek and positioned a line of some 350 Continental riflemen to protect the others and slow the enemy's advance. When Tarleton's force arrived, the riflemen opened fire, and then halted, "the first time it had done so in twelve miles, and immediately began to deploy," Joseph Graham recalled. "The riflemen kept up a severe fire, retreating from tree to tree," and both sides were soon "enveloped in smoke."

Before long, Greene's militia were "running down the hill from under the smoke," splashing across the creek wherever they could. Williams and most of his men got to safety, though some, "it was said, were drowned." The regulars, however, held their ground, firing over the heads of the fleeing militia, "which caused the advancing foe to halt and repair his line." This they did in short order and pushed on. The steady resistance of these regulars, Graham said, was "equal to anything that had been seen in the war, for they were under excellent discipline." Even so, Tarleton's men made it across the creek too, scrambled up the high banks, and forced the action, causing Williams to order a general retreat, with Lee in the rear to cover it. Tarleton chased Williams for five miles before giving up the pursuit.

Both sides lost about fifty men that afternoon, and it was a disappointment to Williams that the marksmen at the crossing, ordered to fire at British Lieutenant Colonel James Webster, had failed to kill him. Several of them aimed and fired twice, but as Lee recalled with evident regret, Webster "himself and horse were untouched." The action had served its purpose in one sense, however indecisive and discouraging it might have been to Williams and Lee: it distracted Cornwallis and bought time for Greene, who took the opportunity to get his main army to Troublesome Creek.

For the next week, the armies left each alone, while Greene at dawn on March 14 marched his men the rest of the way from their camp to Guilford Courthouse, which was about fifteen miles to the south of Troublesome Creek. Cornwallis was on the move as well, eventually settling in near the Quaker church, only twelve miles from Greene's position. Suffering from what he called a "violent inflammation of the eyes," Greene was bled, but this mainstay of eighteenth-century medical practice did no good. "The inflammation is still troublesome," he told Lee, "and my eyes weak and painful." Despite it all, Greene remained active and vigilant, moving among the troops day and night, preparing them for the battle to come. At the tent of one of his officers, Greene noticed that the man was still asleep. The exchange that followed, he said, was the greatest compliment he had received in his career as a soldier. "Good heavens, Colonel," Greene said, "how can you sleep with the enemy so near?" "Why, General," the officer replied, "I knew that you were awake."

Cornwallis got his men in motion before dawn on the frosty morning of March 15, marching these weary soldiers toward Guilford Courthouse without breakfast. Tarleton's advance guard led the way, and shortly after 7 a.m., about four miles from Greene's position, they ran into part of Lee's cavalry. They began firing at each other. Lee pulled back, to a more advantageous spot—"a long lane with high curved fences on either side," he said—and waited. When Tarleton's men came down the lane, Lee's dragoons charged, knocking several of the enemy from their horses, killing some of them, and taking a few prisoners, without suffering a loss. Then they chased the British almost all the way to their camp at the New Garden Quaker meetinghouse, before turning back. Tarleton himself was injured in the fight when a musket ball ripped into his right hand, doing serious damage to his thumb and forefinger. Tarleton's arm was put in a sling, and, although he could not hold a pistol or saber, he could still ride, and did so, throughout the battle that would begin later that day.

Greene, for his part, having learned a good deal from Morgan's disposition of his forces at Cowpens, posted the North Carolina militia in the first of three lines of troops, the first being the least experienced and therefore least reliable men under his command. There were about one thousand of these untested soldiers, but their position was a formidable one. They were situated behind a rail fence on either side of the Salisbury Road, and they would have a clear view of the British when they charged up what the previous summer had been a cornfield, but now lay fallow, with patches of mud. Unlike much of the ground where Greene had decided to make his stand, the muddy field over which the enemy would advance was free of trees, exposing them to gunfire, and a stream running through it would slow them down. Much as Morgan had instructed his militia two weeks earlier, Greene told those under his command that if they managed to fire just three times, in well-executed volleys, they would have done their job. "Three rounds, my boys," he yelled, "and then you may fall back."

The first line would be flanked on the right by William Washington's cavalry and Lee's Legion on the left, with both under orders to fall back to protect the second line when the militia withdrew. Two six-pounder guns were placed in the center of the first line, on the road, facing the open field over which the redcoats would advance. The second line, consisting of some twelve hundred Virginians, was about three hundred yards behind the first, every last one of them in the woods. A third line, some 550 yards farther back, was made up of fourteen hundred Continental regulars, mainly from North Carolina and Virginia. They were on the crest of a hill, and angled so that only about half of the men were directly behind the second line; the others were on clear, high ground just to the west of the courthouse. Two more six-pounders were in the center of the third line, with the hard-hitting Maryland Continentals. Williams commanded the left of this third line, and Greene, on his horse, would stay close by, though from this position in the woods he would be unable to see what was happening to the first and second lines. Now there was nothing to do but wait.

Around noon, when the British infantry first came into view, the two six-pounders opened up with a tremendous roar, and moments later, the Royal Artillery fired back. This cannonade lasted for half an hour, covering the field with smoke, but with negligible damage to either side. The redcoats then advanced, managing to cross the small stream, but got no farther. Then, with the smoke lifting, they paused, fired one volley, re-formed, and watched as their colonel rode to the front of the ranks and, at about 1:30 p.m., yelled, "Charge!"

The whole mass of them, "in excellent order, in a smart run," as one of their sergeants put it, hustled across the muddy field with their

gleaming bayonets pointed at the enemy. The North Carolina militiamen, panicking, fired when the British were more than one hundred yards away and therefore beyond effective range of their muskets,
which failed to break the enemy's advance. But when the British got
within forty yards of Greene's first line, they suddenly stopped. Now
they could see the Americans positioned behind the rail fence, with
their guns at the ready, resting on the fence rails. "They were taking
aim with the nicest precision," British Sergeant Roger Lamb recalled,
and for a tense moment, all movement seemed to cease. "At this awful
period, a general pause took place," as the men "surveyed each other
with the most anxious suspense." Then Lamb's commander, Lieutenant
Colonel James Webster, again rode to the front of his men, and "with
his usual commanding voice," shouted, "Come on, my brave fusiliers!"

And come on they did, as the men behind the fence—those who had
not broken and run already—fired into their onrushing ranks, again to
negligible effect. The British continued to come on, and, in Lee's words,
to "our infinite distress and mortification," the North Carolina militia,
impervious to their officers' efforts to stop them, took to flight. Though
"not a man of the corps had been killed or even wounded," they continued to flee, "throwing away arms, knapsacks, and even canteens,"
as they rushed "like a torrent headlong through the woods." Some of
them never rejoined their units. Some were not seen again until later
in life, as civilians.

Now the British entered the woods to take on Greene's second line,
and found the trees and undergrowth so thick as to render their bayonets of no use. By this time, the forces on the flanks—Lee's and William Washington's—were in the middle of the action, and the orderly
ranks that existed when the fighting began were rapidly disintegrating.
It is one of the persistent myths of the American Revolution that the
redcoats were incapable of operating except in rigid formation, and
the men under Cornwallis's command at Guilford Courthouse were
among his army's best at what their officers called "bush fighting." The
Americans have been celebrated for more than two centuries for their
ability to fight "Indian-style," a term Washington himself used. But
British foot soldiers were also trained to work in tandem, sharing a tree
from behind which they would alternately fire and step back to reload;
they were also trained to lie on their backs and bellies to fire their weapons. The command "to tree" was part of standard British military jar

gon. The Americans knew how to fight in such settings too, of course. And they were "much our superiors at wood fighting, being habituated to the woods from their infancy," Thomas Anburey, a British explorer who fought at Saratoga, would admit.

But neither had much of an advantage on this day. Greene's second line put up a determined resistance, and fighting on the flanks and in the rear would soon change the nature of the battle. As the British pushed on and the Virginians on the second line tried to hold their position, Tarleton said, "the action became more severe." Charles Stedman, a British officer born in Philadelphia and educated at the College of William & Mary in Virginia, said the Americans, taking cover behind the trees, "kept up for a considerable time a galling fire," but eventually fell back. Even before the British had pushed the Virginians out of the way and moved on to attack Greene's third line of Continentals, the battle was beginning to degenerate into smaller, sometimes simultaneous separate actions. When the Virginians in the second line suddenly found the British in their rear, this discovery, as St. George Tucker told his wife, "threw the militia into such confusion" that, "without attending in the least to their officers who endeavored to halt them, and make them turn about and engage the enemy," they "broke off without firing a single gun, and dispersed like a flock of sheep frightened by dogs."

Tucker and one of his friends, a kinsman of his wife's and a future Virginia governor named Beverley Randolph, with "infinite labour . . . rallied about sixty or seventy of our men, and brought them to the charge." Other officers were less effective in their efforts. "With the few men which we had collected we at several times sustained an irregular kind of skirmishing with the British [and] we were once successful enough to drive a party for a very small distance." Tucker saw "eight or ten men killed or wounded" all around him in the woods and "was forced to ride over a British officer lying at the root of a tree." One of the militiamen gave the fallen redcoat "a dram as he was expiring and bade him die like a brave man."

Tucker was himself wounded when one of his own men "either from design or accident held his bayonet in such a direction that I could not possibly avoid it as I rode up to stop him from running away." The blade, he said, "penetrated about an inch and a half between the bones of my leg." He "felt no inconvenience from it for several hours," he told his wife three days after the battle, "but have since been obliged to hobble with the assistance of a stick, or with some one to lead me." News of his injury, she told him, "turned her into an old Pumpkin faced, dropsical, Mope."

Tucker and the other Virginians then fell in with the Continentals of the third line, as further disordered skirmishing followed. Tarleton and his cavalry swept toward them, but the regulars "gave him so warm a reception that he retreated with some degree of precipitation." Even so, the Virginians eventually gave way, and Webster quickly realized that there was nothing but trees between his men and the main Continental line of Marylanders.

About two hundred yards from the American position, Webster charged. When his men had closed to within half that distance, the Continental defenders let loose a withering volley. Webster's "brave Fuzaleers" began to fall, momentarily leaving what was left of the once-orderly British ranks as vulnerable to being surrounded as Tarleton's had been at Cowpens. From his position, however, Greene was unable to see the opportunity before him and—always determined to avoid risking his entire army—did not order the counterattack that could have ended the battle on the spot.

The smaller, separate actions continued to rage in the woods and on the flanks, and Lee's behavior baffles historians to this day. Lee and his men seem to have absented themselves from the action, only rejoining Greene's main army the following day. William Washington's cavalry did well, though, scattering one of the British units in a deadly charge that also enshrined one of Washington's fellow Virginians in the pantheon of the Old Dominion's folk heroes. This was Peter Francisco, almost seven feet tall, who, "with his brawny arms and terrible broadsword," is said to have singlehandedly killed eleven redcoats that afternoon.

The longer the action went on, and Cornwallis saw that his enemy was putting up a much better fight than he had bargained for, the more anxious he became. When his horse was shot from under him, he resorted to riding a dragoon's horse. One of Webster's officers saw him making his way on his mount across a patch of open ground that, while treeless, was covered with bushes. "The saddlebags were under the creature's belly, which much retarded his progress, owing to the vast quantity of underwood that was spread over the ground," Sergeant Lamb reported. Cornwallis was apparently unaware that he was heading into

Peter Francisco.
Miniature portrait, unknown artist, early nineteenth century.
Virginia Museum of History & Culture

danger, but Lamb, who saw what his commander did not, "immediately laid hold of the bridle of his horse and turned his head. I then mentioned to him that if his Lordship had pursued the same direction, he would in a few moments have been surrounded by the enemy and perhaps cut to pieces or captured." Lamb "continued to run alongside the horse, keeping the bridle in my hand" until Cornwallis reached the safety of one of the regiments at the edge of the woods.

The fighting in the smoky woods was now what we would call hand-to-hand combat, with any semblance of order and coordination forgotten. Cornwallis could see by now that his men were being beaten back, and it was at this juncture that Lee, who was not there, claims the British commander in chief took action that, fairly or otherwise, has forever stained his reputation. Determined to interrupt the fighting, Cornwallis, according to Lee, ordered his artillery officer to load two three-pounders with grapeshot and fire them into the bloody free-for-all. By this account, Brigadier General Charles O'Hara, wounded and bleeding on the road where the guns had been placed, "remonstrated and begged" his commander to reconsider. Cornwallis repeated the order. The grapeshot sprayed into the thicket, aimed in a general way to hit more Americans than British, but a number of redcoats reeled about and fell too, with the intended effect. The brawling ceased, and when the smoke lifted, those of Greene's men who had survived the blast staggered back to their lines.

By midafternoon, when Greene saw the ordinarily doughty Second Marylanders give way, he ordered a general retreat. It was when the First Marylanders, in the dependable hands of Lieutenant Colonel John Eager Howard, began to withdraw, that something happened no less remarkable than what Lee recorded, but of far more reliable provenance, based as it was on eyewitness accounts. The battle had gone much more favorably where the men under Howard and Williams fought, with Williams's men, in his words, having "bayoneted and cut to pieces a great number of British Guards" and reclaimed the field-pieces the enemy had taken earlier in the day. When Williams and his men began their orderly withdrawal from this part of the field, Howard said, "many of the [redcoats] who were laying on the ground & who we supposed were wounded" jumped up and fired at their backs.

Always cautious, fully committed to the belief that keeping an army in the field was of more value, in the long run, than winning any single battle, Greene was content on this day to have inflicted as much damage on his enemy as his men had already done, without risking them further. It was clear that over two hard-fought hours, they had proved far sturdier than Cornwallis had imagined they would be, and Greene was satisfied with their performance. They had lost ground and then regained it, repeatedly, and the battle had seesawed back and forth, but they were running out of ammunition, and the fight could not proceed to a decisive victory for either side. Greene did not measure their efforts by a simpleminded standard such as that. It was quite enough, he realized, that they had dealt a serious blow to the enemy's ability to threaten his army again, much less continue to hold on to either of the Carolinas.

At 3:30 p.m., Greene ordered a retreat, leaving only enough forces—notably William Washington's cavalry—to cover their withdrawal. As a hard rain fell, Cornwallis told Tarleton to pursue the retreating Americans, but his exhausted men soon returned. Greene's army marched his weary troops for three miles before pausing on the far side of Reedy Fork, rounding up stragglers, and slogged on through the night to Troublesome Creek, where they had camped in the days before the battle. The British—who had not eaten in twenty-four hours—spent the night searching in the woods for their wounded comrades. At last, they were fed—a "repast," W. J. Wood wrote in his history of the war—"of four ounces of flour and four ounces of lean beef." Greene's men were hungry, too, and had this in common with their enemy: they had no tents and slept on the cold, wet ground. James Webster, they found, had been killed, and sometime in the hours after the battle ended, a British surgeon finally attended to Tarleton's mangled right hand, amputating two fingers. Before long, he was teaching himself to write—and wield a saber—with his left hand.

"The night succeeding this day of blood," Lee wrote, "was rainy, dark and cold; the dead unburied, the wounded unsheltered, the groans of the dying and the shrieks of the living shed a deeper shade over the gloom of nature. The victorious troops"—Lee meant Greene's men—"without tents and without food, participated in sufferings which they could not believe."

Of course, Cornwallis and his men told themselves that they had won the day because they had held the battlefield and the enemy had gone. Even so, it was reluctantly agreed that they had paid far too much for no gain, beyond the privilege of camping for two nights on the ground over which they had just fought. "Except the ground and the Artillery," Greene told Joseph Reed, "they have gained [no] Advantage, on the contrary, they are little short of being ruined." In killed and wounded, Greene estimated, the British had lost at least six hundred or seven hundred men, maybe more.

That was an exaggeration, but the final reports were not yet in, and historians dispute the tallies to this day. In two of the bloodiest hours of the war, Cornwallis lost about 500 men of the 2,100 or so engaged in the action, which was 25 percent of his army. A little more than 90 of them were killed outright; another 50 later died of their wounds, with the rest too badly maimed to return to the ranks. This compares to some 80 dead and fewer than 200 wounded from Greene's army of almost 4,500, "a trifling loss," he told Jefferson, given those of the enemy. Most of those casualties—just over 1,000—were classified as "missing" and consisted of militiamen who fled from the action and never returned.

"Our men are in good spirits, and in perfect readiness to fight another day," Greene reported to General Washington in New York. Their ability to continue to fight—as the British will to win was beginning to erode—constituted both men's measure of how well the war was going. The men in the ranks felt it, too. "Should Cornwallis attack us again," St. George Tucker told his wife, "I think he would purchase a second victory fully as dearly as the first." The rebels were learning to profit from their losses. "Like Peter the Great we shall profit by defeat," Lewis Morris Jr. told his father. One more such action, he said, "and they are ruined."

All was hardly jubilation when Greene's men regrouped at Reedy Fork, however. They had marched away as their comrades were still writhing on the ground, leaving the wounded to the care of the good men and women of the New Garden Quaker Meeting. "I was born and educated in the professions and principles of your Society; and I am perfectly acquainted with your religious sentiments and general good conduct as citizens," Greene wrote to them. He knew they were pacifists, and that the British hoped to benefit from their reluctance to support the war, and he wished they were not beguiled by such overtures. "The contest is for political liberty, without which cannot be enjoyed the free exercise of your religion," Greene reminded them. He was well aware, he said, that because of "the misconduct of a few of your own, that you are generally considered as enemies to the independence of America. I entertain other sentiments," he insisted, promising that his army would "always be ready to protect you from every violence and oppression." With all that out of the way, he said he would be "exceedingly obliged" if they would attend to the "unfortunate wounded in your neighborhood."

Three weeks after the battle, a gloomy Cornwallis was still "disposing of the sick and wounded, and procuring supplies of all kinds," as he reported to Sir Henry Clinton. Cornwallis was also looking out with mounting impatience for reinforcements from Europe that he had been led to expect, "which will be indispensably necessary to enable me to act offensively or even to maintain myself in the upper parts of the country, where alone I can hope to preserve the troops from the fatal sickness"—he meant malaria—"which so nearly ruined the army last autumn."

Cornwallis was also eager to hear what Clinton wanted him to do now, "being as yet totally in the dark" about the campaign his commander in chief intended for the coming summer. Cornwallis wanted to move the theater of war to Virginia, reasoning that the rich and populous state—the one from which so many of the Continental army's supplies were flowing—needed to be brought under British control if the rest of the South were to be secure. Cornwallis had been more forthright in a letter few days earlier to General William Phillips, then at British headquarters in New York but soon to take command of British forces in Virginia. "I am quite tired of marching about the country, in quest of adventures," Cornwallis told Phillips. They should make their stand in the Chesapeake. From there, they could use Virginia's rivers to raid the towns and plantations, cut off Greene's supply lines, and rebuild their shattered southern army.

News of the British victory at Guilford Courthouse was not well received in England, where long-simmering opposition to the war was increasing in intensity. Recalling King Pyrrhus' costly battles with the Romans in the third century BCE, Charles James Fox, a Whig and prominent opponent of the war, told the other members of the House of Commons what Cornwallis himself had come to realize. "Another such victory," Fox said, "would ruin the British Army."

CHAPTER TWENTY-THREE

"They Will Not . . . Fight Like Gentlemen"

Snow's Island was never, strictly speaking, an island at all. It was a plateau of sorts, a high ground in the middle of a swamp on the Pee Dee River near Johnsonville, South Carolina, a hundred miles north of Charles Town and seventy or so miles east of Camden. Because water levels rise and fall, Snow Island's dimensions were never stable, and it has long since disappeared. But historians say that at the time of the Revolutionary War, it was bordered to the north and northeast by Lynches River and the Pee Dee, and to the south and west by Clark's Creek, an offshoot of Lynches River. That means Snow's Island would have been made up of five square miles of dark and seemingly impenetrable woods and marshlands, which, surrounded by those shallow waterways, made it difficult to find, much less to enter. A few hardy souls had occupied the land—it was named for one of its early owners—and built a farmhouse on the highest point of the high ground, safe from any floodwaters, but that was about the extent of its development.

"Inaccessible except by water, deep within a forest of cypress and pines [and] protected by tall cane breaks, briars, and vines," as one of Francis Marion's biographers put it, Snow's Island was an ideal hideout for Marion and his men. Snow's Island was habitable, though the British would not have found it so. In summer, the heat and the insects could make life miserable. With game in the woods and fish in the river, Marion's men ate well. He was a taskmaster, but their duties were not onerous, and, once they had felled trees and torn up bridges to ensure their safety from attack, Snow's Island afforded these restless marauders an opportunity to unwind, if not actually relax. They had to keep moving, and archaeologists believe that "rather than a single, permanent Snow's Island camp, there may have been multiple camps in the same vicinity," and that Marion, "like a classic guerrilla warrior, moved constantly from one to the other" to confuse the enemy.

Marion enjoyed the cooperation of the few people who lived in the countryside around Snow's Island, and his efforts to cultivate their support added to his reputation as an American Robin Hood, hiding out in a South Carolina Sherwood Forest. Legends are still told about how Marion and his men would raid the British and their loyalist allies and distribute the plunder to the families of needy patriots.

Marion's nickname, "the Swamp Fox," is closely associated with his time at Snow's Island, though there is scant evidence that anyone called him that in his own lifetime. In his somewhat fanciful Marion biography of 1809, Parson Weems tells of two young women who refer to the partisan leader as a "vile swamp fox." William Dobein James, one of Marion's men, wrote that Banastre Tarleton once chased Marion through the swamps for twenty-five miles, before giving up in frustration. "Come, my boys!" Tarleton supposedly said, in a nod to both Thomas Sumter and Marion, "let us go back, and we will soon find the game cock, but as for this d—d old fox, the devil himself could not catch him." Tarleton thereby gave two partisan warriors their nicknames. In 1829, William Gilmore Simms published a poem, "The Swamp Fox," which reads in part:

> *We follow where the swamp fox guides,*
> *   We leave the swamp and cypress tree,*
> *Our spurs are in our coursers' sides,*
> *   And ready for the strife are we.*
> *The tory camp is now in sight,*
> *   And there he cowers within his den;*
> *He hears our shout, he dreads the fight,*
> *   He fears, and flies from Marion's men.*

Simms, who also published an 1844 biography of Marion, used the sobriquet there as well, and over the years, the nickname gained traction. (Thanks to the Walt Disney TV series, which ran from 1959 to 1961, it stuck.)

The British and their loyalist allies were not as timid as Simms would have his readers believe, and after Marion's victory at Black Mingo Creek in September 1780, they were determined to hunt him down and put an end to his depredations. By November, just before Marion established his camp at Snow's Island, the British had taken over his plantation at Pond Bluff as well as the farms of several of his men, and were in active pursuit. Marion continued his activities all the same, venturing out of Snow's Island for his raids, but always keeping a small force back at the camp for its protection. At its peak, he seems to have commanded a force of maybe 250 men; being irregulars, the men came and went, more or less as they pleased, especially when needed on their farms.

Throughout the early spring of 1781, Marion skirmished with the enemy that was pursuing him, content to sting the British and then just as suddenly to disappear. Five days after the battle at Guilford Courthouse, Marion's irregulars dealt a bloody defeat to a British force at the Sampit River outside Georgetown, about thirty miles south of Snow's Island. The British, who often viewed the Americans much as most Americans viewed Blacks and Indians, regarded these tactics—however effective—as disgraceful. "They will not . . . fight like gentlemen," the British commander, with the wonderfully posh name of John Watson Tadwell-Watson, complained. They fight "like savages," he said, "eternally firing and whooping around us by night and by day waylaying and popping at us from behind every tree!"

Marion was still at the Sampit a week later when alarming news arrived. A small loyalist force under Lieutenant Colonel John Doyle and his New York Volunteers, sent from Camden to catch Marion, were fast approaching. Snow's Island was a day's march away, so Marion could not reach it in time to support the minimal force he had left to protect it. Colonel Hugh Ervin, commanding the post, was aware that the enemy was coming on and "chose the best men from his small band of cripples, convalescents, and prisoner guards," posting them along the approaches. By the time Marion made it back, Doyle's Tories had pushed aside the men guarding Clark's Creek, killing seven as they waded onto the high ground, releasing some twenty-five prisoners. They torched the farmhouse and several outbuildings, threw whatever supplies they could find into the river, and made their way back to safety. As they headed back to Camden, the loyalists burned the farms of more than one hundred of Marion's men. "Marion's repository of stores and plunder on Snow's Island, was a few days since destroyed by a detachment of his Majesty's forces, under Lieut. Col. Doyle," *The Royal Gazette,* the loyalist newspaper in Charles Town, reported. They accomplished this feat, moreover, with no loss of life.

Upon his return, Marion surveyed the damage, realized that the Snow's Island camp was no longer of any use, and made camp about ten miles to the south, at Indiantown. Marion sent Hugh Horry to harass them as they went, experiencing grim satisfaction when his men killed nine of Doyle's loyalists as they retreated. Even so, the atmosphere in camp was now sullen. There was a limit to how effective Marion's men could be at this point. With the losses they had suffered and the desertions that were inevitable after setbacks of this kind, no more than seventy soldiers remained. The British, meanwhile, were adding to their forces.

In early April, however, a scout rode into camp, saying he had spotted "a great number of continental troops, horse and foot," headed their way as reinforcements. "The news was sudden and unexpected," William Dobein James wrote, "and to men now in a state of desperation, nothing could be more transporting. Scarce was there an eye but what was suffused with tears of joy . . . hope began to revive." Spirits rose even higher later that day when Marion's men heard the sound of drums, and a vanguard of Lee's Legion arrived, with new orders from Nathanael Greene. On April 14, Light Horse Harry himself rode into camp, where he would report to Marion.

It is hard to imagine that men as unlike each other as Lee and Marion could work well together, and whether they would or not remained to be seen. Lee—educated in the classics, eloquent and self-possessed—was just twenty-five when the two men joined forces. Marion was twice Lee's age, or close to it. He came from humble Huguenot stock and had little formal schooling. There was a great deal in Marion's character that won Lee's respect, however, as seems apparent from the description he left in his memoirs:

He was reserved and silent, entering into conversation only when necessary, and then with modesty and good sense. He possessed a strong mind, improved by its own reflections and observations, not by books or travel. His dress was like his address—plain, regarding comfort and decency only. In his meals, he was abstemious, eating generally of one dish, and drinking water mostly. He was sedulous and constant in his attention to the duties of his station, to which every other consideration yielded.

Lee, who was single but would marry well not once but twice, noted that even "the charms of the fair, like the luxuries of the table and the allurements of wealth," seemed lost on Marion. "The procurement of subsistence for his men, and the contrivance of annoyance for his enemy, engrossed his entire mind."

Upon Lee's arrival, the two men discussed their options, which were not great. The loss of ammunition that had been stored at Snow's Island limited what they could do, but they agreed to attack Fort Watson near present-day Summerton, South Carolina, on the Santee River some twenty miles to the south. Sumter had tried to take the post the previous February, but if they could succeed where the Gamecock had failed, they could replenish their supplies and deny the enemy one of its significant strongholds. They set out for Fort Watson the next day. The "war of posts," defensive in nature and Fabian in its execution, that would constitute an important part of Greene's larger strategy—already discussed with Washington—began.

A "war of posts" was a strategy Washington had long contemplated but was in no position to adopt in the North, with his army and Sir Henry Clinton's squared off against each other in New Jersey and New York. But a war fought along Fabian lines made perfect sense for Greene and his officers in the South. As early as 1776, in a letter to John Hancock, then president of the Continental Congress, Washington said he had concluded that "on our side the War should be defensive" in nature, taking the form of what has been "called a War of posts, that we should on all occasions avoid a general Action or put anything to the risque unless compelled by a necessity into which we ought never to be drawn." By 1781, with the British army still better trained and more experienced than those under Greene, whose ranks were still filled with untested Continentals, militiamen, and heedless irregulars, the strategy made more sense than ever. It "would be presumption," as Washington told Hancock, to throw such men "into open Ground against their superiors in both number and discipline."

By now, the British high command had realized that the occupation of major cities such as Boston, New York, Philadelphia, and Charles

Siege of Fort Watson.
Illustration from *The Boys of '76,*
by Charles Carelton Coffin, 1879

Town, and even smaller ones like Camden, was not enough to compel the colonists to surrender. At this point, their position in the South consisted of little more than "posts" along the rivers, stretching from Georgetown on the coast all the way to Fort Ninety Six, two hundred miles to the west, which functioned to move, store, and ship ammunition and other supplies to the armies in the interior and to convey intelligence. Now, with indications that Cornwallis seemed bent on heading north, these posts would be more vulnerable than ever, and Greene with his "flying army," aided by such able subordinates as Marion and Lee, was ideally suited to take them.

Marion and Lee reached Fort Watson on the afternoon of April 16, and after a brief exchange of fire demanded its surrender. Lieutenant James McKay, the ranking British officer, said if they wanted the fort, "they must come and take it." This was not mere bluster. Fort Watson already had withstood one attack—this from Thomas Sumter the previous February—and there was a hint of genius in its construction. It sat atop an Indian burial mound, maybe forty feet high, overlooking the river, with a commanding view of the immediate surroundings. The top had been leveled off and a stockade built on the level surface, with three rows of abattis—tree branches with their tops sharpened and facing outward—at its base. The ground around it had also been cleared of trees, denying protection to would-be attackers. Marion and Lee's men were shot down as soon as they attempted to pull apart the abattis.

This was new territory for Marion and Lee. Their specialty was the ambush. Neither had any significant experience in siege warfare, which was what taking Fort Watson seemed to require. They decided to cut off the fort's water supply, but this failed when McKay's defenders, three or four days into the siege, dug a hole inside the stockade and hit water. Intermittent firing between the two positions accomplished little, except to litter the ground around the fort with the bodies of dead attackers.

But then Hezekiah Maham, a forty-year-old planter who had represented his home district in the South Carolina legislature, offered a plan they had not thought of. They could construct a wooden tower, much like those of ancient Rome, higher than the stockade—and from there, they could simply fire into the fort. With nothing to lose by trying, Marion and Lee ordered their men to gather axes from nearby farms and start chopping down trees. For five days and nights, the men collected the materials they would need, and the tower's assembly, done out of sight of the fort, began on the night of Friday, April 20. When the structure was completed, Lee said, it formed "a large, strong oblong pen, to be covered on the top with a floor of logs, and protected on the side opposite to the fort with a breastwork of light timber." On Saturday, when the tower was just about ready, Marion asked McKay for a truce long enough for them to collect the American dead. Reminding them that their men continued to fire on the fort, McKay turned them down.

On Monday morning, McKay awoke to see "a Wooden Machine which they had built, & were busy in raising a Scaffold made of rails [nearly] level with the top of our Works for their Marksmen to pick off our Centinels." When they had reached the desired height, the riflemen in the crow's nest rained fire into the fort, whose defenders, by one account, "crawled around behind their palisade," unable to mount any kind of credible defense. Back on terra firma, the Americans stormed the exterior, this time successfully pulling the abattis away and scrambling up the mound, further terrifying the men inside the stockade. Unable to defend the fort without being raked by the riflemen on the tower, McKay's men quickly lost heart. Again, Marion and Lee demanded the fort's surrender, and McKay was "reduced to the disagreeable necessity of capitulating," thanks to "the Cowardly & Mutinous behaviour" of his men, who "grounded their Arms & refused to defend the Post any longer."

The taciturn Marion was uncharacteristically exuberant in his official report. "The officers and men of [Lee's] Legion and militia performed everything that could be expected," he wrote, "and Major Mayham [*sic*] of my Brigade had in a particular manner a great share of this success, by his unwearied diligence in erecting a tower, which principally occasioned the reduction of the fort." Marion also praised Lee for his "advice and indefatigable diligence in every part of this tedious operation against as strong a Little post as could be made on the most advantageous spot that could be wished for."

Marion and Lee next turned their attention to Fort Motte, about thirty-five miles northwest of Fort Watson. Fort Motte was what the British called Mount Joseph, the plantation where, after Camden, Thomas Pinckney had gone to recuperate from his injuries. Once he was sufficiently recovered to travel, he was shipped to Philadelphia, where, with other well-connected American prisoners, he was held until exchanged. Like other officers, Pinckney took his wife and their infant son with him. Pinckney's wife was the former Betsey Motte, whose mother— the redoubtable Rebecca Brewton Motte—was still at the plantation when the British arrived, seizing her home. Rebecca's brother, the late Miles Brewton, was South Carolina's largest slave trader and by some accounts the richest man in the colony. He built a mansion near the Charles Town waterfront and owned rice and indigo plantations outside the city. Miles Brewton had died at sea in 1775, and Rebecca's husband had died five years after that, leaving his widow the sole owner of the mansion, the plantations, and the 244 slaves who worked them.

When Charles Town fell, Sir Henry Clinton made the townhouse his headquarters, and when Clinton left, Cornwallis moved in. Eventually, Rebecca was permitted to move the family to Mount Joseph. There she thought they would be safe.

But the British seized it, too, putting up a wall of ten-foot-high wooden stakes on the "high and commanding hill," in Lee's words, on which the plantation house stood. They also erected a blockhouse on two corners of the palisade, threw abattis along the wall, and dug seven-foot-wide protective ditches, making Fort Motte—as the occupiers now called it—"obstinate and strong," Marion said. Garrisoned inside the fort were two hundred redcoats, Hessians, and loyalist militiamen, guarding the stockpile of weapons. Above all, Fort Motte served as a military depot and, as such, was of strategic importance. Rebecca Motte took refuge in one of the farm's outbuildings.

Marion and Lee arrived on May 7, a Sunday, with four hundred soldiers and a six-pound cannon, demanding the fort's surrender. Lieutenant Donald McPherson, its commanding officer, refused, in the belief that Lord Rawdon, evacuating Camden, was heading his way to reinforce Fort Motte. Marion and Lee believed that Rawdon was on his way, too, and recognizing how strong McPherson's position was, realized that they would again be forced to conduct a siege, but—in something of a contradiction—they would need to be quick about it. The urgency of the situation was apparent by Wednesday night, when they could see the distant glow of Rawdon's campfires. They figured they had about forty-eight hours to compel the fort's surrender or clear out just to save themselves and their small forces.

A conventional siege would take too long, but the weather—hot and dry—suggested an alternative. Once Marion and Lee had agreed on the plan, it fell to Lee—eloquent, educated, and comfortable in the society in which Mrs. Motte moved—to inform her of their intentions. "Lamenting the sad necessity and assuring her of the deep regret which the unavoidable act excited in his and every breast," he told her that they intended to burn the British out of her house. They would shoot flaming arrows into the mansion, knowing full well the damage they would do.

"With a smile of complacency this exemplary woman listened to the embarrassed officer," Lee wrote in third person, and "gave instant relief to his agitated feelings by declaring that she was gratified with the opportunity of contributing to the good of her country." Not only that, she presented the officers with a bow "imported from India," which she urged them to use, "as probably better adapted for the objective" than whatever else they might have.

About noon on Sunday, May 12, "the rays of the scorching sun had prepared the shingle roof for the projected conflagration," and the first arrow struck the target. The shingles began to burn, and a second arrow hit another part of the roof, and then a third still another, and "like the first, kindled a blaze." When McPherson ordered some of his men to the loft to remove the burning shingles, Marion and Lee opened fire with canister from their six-pounder, "raking the loft from end to end." The bombardment sent the soldiers scurrying downstairs, and with "no other effort to stop the flames being practicable," Lee wrote, McPherson "hung out the white flag."

When the shelling stopped and the prisoners were rounded up, McPherson and his officers joined Marion and Lee and their subordinates "in a sumptuous dinner" prepared by Mrs. Motte, "soothing in the sweets of social intercourse the ire which the preceding conflict had engendered." But that is not all that happened. While the officers dined, some of Lee's men began hanging loyalist prisoners. Marion found out about these summary executions, left the house, and, confronting the perpetrators, demanded that the hanging stop. When one of Lee's men objected, Marion would have none of it. "I will have you know, damn you, that I command here," he said, "not Col. Lee," reminding the men that Rawdon would retaliate and begin hanging prisoners he had taken. The executions ended. (In later years, Rebecca Motte's grandchildren said, she kept her knitting needles in an arrow quiver as a reminder of her contribution to the cause of independence.)

The prisoners were then paroled, with their officers allowed to rejoin Rawdon, who found the loss of Fort Motte and the weapons stored within it appalling. "The stroke was heavy upon me," he told Cornwallis. Washington, as might be expected, took a different view. The outcome, he told Greene, "does honor to General [Marion] and Colonel Lee." There was good news, too, from Orangeburg, twenty-five miles south of Fort Motte, on the north fork of the Edisto River. The British post there had fallen to a small force under Sumter on May 11, with no loss of his men. On the day after Fort Motte fell, Greene arrived, assessed the situation, and issued new orders. Lee was to attack Fort Granby, on the Congaree about thirty-five miles north-west of Fort Motte, while Marion was to attempt to retake Georgetown on the coast.

Lee reached Fort Granby in mid-May. It too was well fortified, with 350 men, most of them loyalists, garrisoned within. Major Andrew Maxwell, its commander, had an unseemly reputation as caring more for plunder than for the battles at which he collected it, and the fort contained a good deal of equipment Rawdon could use, if he could get it. Upon his arrival, Lee demanded an immediate surrender, as Greene had instructed him to do, lest Rawdon arrive with reinforcements. Maxwell refused, and the next morning he awoke to see siege lines approaching and the six-pounder positioned, as Lee put it, at "point blank shot of the fort." Maxwell agreed to give up the post, provided he could take his precious plunder with him. Aware that Rawdon was approaching, Lee with some reluctance agreed, and the fort fell without a shot fired. Taking two wagonloads of his personal belongings, Max-well rode away, abandoning two cannons as well as stores of ammuni-tion, salt, and liquor, which, Lee said, "presented a very convenient as well as agreeable supply to our army."

A week after Fort Granby's surrender, Lee, joined by militia led by Andrew Pickens and Elijah Clarke, arrived at Fort Galphin. The planta-tion of the Crown's deputy superintendent of Indian affairs, Fort Gal-phin was about twelve miles south of the British stronghold of Augusta, Georgia. Lee made quick work of Fort Galphin, seizing military equip-ment and medical supplies, stored there for distribution to friendly Native Americans. The following day, Lee crossed the Savannah River, moving closer to the bigger prize of Augusta. The two posts protecting the town from the south were Fort Grierson and Fort Cornwallis, both of which would fall over the next two weeks.

By this point, animosity between the loyalists and supporters of independence in northern Georgia had reached such a pitch that Lee urged Greene to impose martial law. Even the supporters of indepen-dence around Augusta "[ex]ceed the Goths & Vandals in their schemes of plunder murder & iniqu[ity]," Lee told Greene. "All this under pretence of supporting the virtuous cause of America." As if to prove the point, in early June, just after the fall of Fort Grierson, a Georgia militiaman serving under Pickens supposedly murdered Colonel James Grierson, the local loyalist in command of the fort, while he was held captive. By some accounts, the killing took place in front of Grierson's wife and children. When Pickens reported this "very disagreeable and Melancholy affair," Greene had Grierson's body buried with military honors, saying the murder of an officer in captivity deserved "the most exemplary punishment." To that end, Greene offered one hundred guineas to any person who would "discover & secure the perpetrator of this horid crime," though no one would claim the reward.

Fort Cornwallis, occupied by three hundred loyalists and an equal number of friendly Creek Indians, held out for two weeks longer than did Fort Grierson. Just outside the fort stood a two-story log house that Lee's riflemen hoped to occupy, as Colonel Thomas Brown, commanding Fort Cornwallis, had learned. Aware of these intentions, Brown had the house packed with gunpowder, which he planned to ignite once Lee's men were inside. On a morning in early June, before the house had been seized, a tremendous blast sent pieces of it "thirty or forty feet high," Lee wrote, "its fragments falling all over the field." Fortunately, Brown "executed his plan too early for its success, or our gallant band would have shared the fate of the house." Later that morning, when the assault on the fort was to begin, the garrison surrendered, and, with it, Augusta fell as well. The American commanders agreed to delay the official ceremonies until June 5 for reasons that today sound quaint: June 4 was George III's birthday. Lest Brown meet the same fate as Grierson, Lee had him put under special protection as the troops recrossed the Savannah River and headed back into South Carolina to rejoin Greene and the main army.

In mid-April, more than a year after Charles Town's surrender, the outlook seemed bleak. Now, after four weeks of frenzied activity, six British posts—Forts Watson, Motte, Granby, Galphin, Grierson, and Cornwallis, and with these last two Augusta itself—had fallen. The British supply lines from the coast into the southern backcountry had been severed, Greene's troops were menacing Camden, and there was cause, once again, for hope.

CHAPTER TWENTY-FOUR

"We Fight, Get Beat, and Fight Again"

In April, shortly after Marion and Lee took Fort Watson, Greene turned his attention to Camden, where, eight months earlier, the Continental army under Gates had been routed. Until the British came, Camden had been a reasonably prosperous but otherwise unremarkable town of a few hundred residents, Black and white, with only one real advantage over comparable backcountry settlements. This was its proximity to the navigable Wateree River and the "Great Wagon Road," which ran from Philadelphia to York in what is now western Pennsylvania through the backcountry all the way to Georgia. Thanks to the efforts of local merchants of rare energy and enterprise, Camden by 1770 had become a major point for the movement of finished goods coming in from Charles Town, about 130 miles to the south, and for wheat and tobacco going to the coast.

When Cornwallis and the redcoats annihilated Gates's Continentals and Camden became a British garrison, it was ideally suited to serve as the enemy's major outpost in the Carolina interior. In terms of population, it was nothing: twenty-five thousand people lived in New York then, twenty thousand or so in Philadelphia, and twelve thousand in Charles Town. But in addition to its gristmill, Camden had a sawmill, a general store, a distillery, a tobacco warehouse, a courthouse, and a jail, all of them clustered along two city blocks. When the British took over, Camden's population swelled to 2,500 people, mostly men, many of whom were loyalists fighting for the British. Before long, besides a powder magazine built by the rebels, they had erected defenses that included a stockade that surrounded the town and five small forts, or redoubts.

Even then, the town's most impressive public building—two stories high and constructed of brick—was its jail, of which the British made good use. Prisoners captured in battle were housed there, and scores of others would be locked inside, seized in the more or less nonstop skirmishing that took place in the area, as well as others from more than a day's hard march away. The jail's most illustrious inmate—though a nobody at the time—was thirteen-year-old Andrew Jackson, who in 1829 would become the seventh president of the country the war was fought to establish.

Jackson was a native of the Waxhaws, that area in the Catawba River valley along the border of the Carolinas where, in the spring of 1780, the men of Tarleton's British Legion had routed Abraham Buford's Virginia Continentals. The Scots-Irish who arrived, as the Jacksons did, at Charles Town or had come down the Great Wagon Road from Pennsylvania and settled the area were proud Presbyterians who had left Northern Ireland with an intense hatred of the British; they were a "fierce" people, in Edmund Burke's words, with a pronounced sense of their own worth and a quick trigger when they felt their rights were questioned, much less trampled on.

These backcountry settlers are remembered, mostly, despite all their grim determination to survive in the face of great hardship, as illiterate and suspicious. But as David Hackett Fischer explains in *Albion's Seed: Four British Folkways in America,* this is inaccurate and unfair. These settlers were indeed hardworking and resourceful, but not a few of them came from families "that held high rank in the Old World," Fischer wrote. "Their motive in moving to America was not to rise higher in society, but to keep from falling below the status which they had already achieved." While Old Hickory's campaign biographies—and the mythology that persists—"stressed the plebian origins of this popular leader," Fischer wrote, Andrew Jackson "did not come from poor or humble people. In his earliest youth, he was taught to think of himself as a gentleman."

Hugh Jackson, the future president's grandfather, who was "a weaver and merchant" in Carrickfergus, had been prosperous enough to leave his American grandson what Fischer estimates to have been "three or four hundred pounds sterling," or about $60,000 in 2022. While Andrew Jackson Jr. said his father "never *owned* in America one acre of land," he had owned a substantial farm near Castlereagh and was sufficiently well regarded in the area to lead a party of emigrants to the New World. Andrew Jackson Sr. died when his wife, the former Elizabeth Hutchinson, was pregnant with Andrew Jr., so the mother was by far the greater influence in his life. After her husband died, Elizabeth Jackson—known as Betty—left the farmland Andrew Sr. had planned to work and moved in with her sister Jane and Jane's husband, one James Crawford, who had come to this country as part of the same group of immigrants.

Betty came from a family of linen weavers. As Andrew Jr. said, his father's "condition in life" was "independent," a reference to the family's finances and not their political opinions, though the Scots-Irish could be independent in that way, too. She and her husband were able to pay for their passage to the Carolinas, and, unlike many other families, had the means to buy land when they arrived, rather than having to apply for a land bounty. Betty had five sisters, and all of them—with husbands and children—migrated to the Waxhaws, where in the 1760s fewer than a thousand people lived. Crawfords and Hutchinsons were important people in the settlement. There was already a Presbyterian church in the Waxhaws when the last group of immigrants arrived, whose pastor had been educated at the University of Glasgow.

It was midwinter when Betty went into labor with Andrew Jr., and she seems to have given birth at her sister Jane's house—and contin-ued to live there for fourteen years. The Crawfords were farmers, and because Jane was a semi-invalid, Betty took care of eight of Jane's chil-dren in addition to her own boisterous sons—Andrew, Robert, and Hugh (known as Huey). The boys grew up on the several hundred acres that James Crawford worked, growing flax to be made into linen, as well as corn, oats, and barley. James's brother Robert, the more prosper-ous of the two, owned a few slaves, but this was rare among the small farmers of the Waxhaws. The Jackson and Crawford boys did the work that, on the more expansive rice plantations of the lowcountry, was done by slaves.

Betty, whose father fought in the Siege of Carrickfergus, detested the British and regaled her sons with stories of the English landlords of Northern Ireland and their "oppressions on the laboring poor." She was "gentle as a dove [but] brave as a lioness," Andrew Jr. said, and when the war came to the Waxhaws, she like the other Jacksons and Crawfords was a fiery champion of independence. In June 1779, when he was at most seventeen, Huey fought at the Battle of Stono Ferry when poorly trained troops under Benjamin Lincoln were attacked by British troops retreating from their first, ill-fated attempt to take Charles Town and defeated. Huey had been sick before the battle, and William Davie, his commander, told him not to fight, but he did anyway. He died shortly afterward, not from wounds, but from "the excessive heat of the weather, and the fatigues of the day." When his body was brought back to the Waxhaws, Betty had him buried in the graveyard at the church. The following May, after Tarleton's Legion defeated Buford's Virginians in the Waxhaws, the local church was turned into a hospital, and Betty and the two sons she had left cared for the survivors.

The following summer, young Andrew volunteered with the local militia, seeing action at Hanging Rock as "a mounted orderly or messenger." But even in that limited role, he witnessed the savagery of the civil war erupting around him. He never forgot the case of one neighbor who, having found the disfigured body of a friend, set about murdering loyalists with demented abandon. Before the man regained his senses—and came to be horrified by what he had done—he had killed twenty of them.

Though a mere errand boy, Jackson was armed, and on at least one occasion he used his gun against the British while hiding out with brother Robert in a neighbor's house in an exchange of fire that did not even qualify as a skirmish. The next day, when holed up in another relative's house, the boys were taken captive, watching in terror as British soldiers wrecked the house, "breaking glasses, smashing furniture, and tearing clothes to shreds," as Robert Remini told the story in his biography of Jackson. When one of the officers demanded that Andrew polish his boots, the boy, with remarkable composure, refused. "Sir," he said, "I am a prisoner of war, and claim to be treated as such." Enraged by this insolence, the officer swung his sword at Jackson's head. The youngster threw his left hand into the air, deflecting the blow, and suffered a severe gash to the head and hand, the scars of which in later years became a badge of honor.

The two Jackson boys and some twenty other prisoners were then marched off to Camden, forty miles away, and locked up on the jail's second floor. They were allowed no food or water on the trip, and once at their destination, found there were no beds and no treatment for their wounds. Andrew's clothes, including his shoes, were taken from him. Confined with nearly three hundred other prisoners, the boys got sick—and then sicker. Smallpox raced through the jail, claiming the lives of about thirty of the inmates, and leaving the survivors with disfiguring scars for the rest of their lives. Andrew in later years recalled hearing the men "groaning in the agonies of death, and no regard was paid to them."

The despair that gripped the inmates for weeks began to lift on April 20. That Friday, through windows in the jail's second floor, the men watched as Greene's army of twelve hundred Continentals arrived and made camp on Hobkirk's Hill, two miles east of Camden. Greene found the British defenses "much stronger than I expected," he told Thomas Sumter, and decided to lay siege to the fortified town, hoping to lure Lord Rawdon, commanding the post in Cornwallis's absence, into attacking him.

A few days later, at sundown, British soldiers, no doubt aware of their captives' mounting excitement, entered the jail and boarded up the windows, telling the inmates not to get their hopes up. They told them Greene had no artillery, basing the claim on the word of a deserter from the American camp, and as such, he posed no threat to the garrison, "and they intended to make a second Gates of him, and hang us all."

But Jackson was not so easily discouraged. Using a razor blade—the only implement the men had to cut their meager provisions with—he "fell to work to cut out a pine knot, out of the plank nailed over the windows [and] with the aid of a fellow prisoner, compleated my object before day, making an aperture about an inch and a half in diameter which gave a full view of Genl Greens situation." The prisoners could also see the response from within the garrison. The British army "was seen drawn up in a column, under cover of the stockade," and just after the sun rose, the redcoats left the fort. As they made their way down the road to the south—away from Greene's army—and toward the woods to their right, the men in the jail lost sight of them.

Once Rawdon's troops made it to the woods, they hoped to conceal themselves, change directions, and surprise Greene's main force. In this, they succeeded. When the American pickets were fired on at 11 a.m.,

Baron Johann de Kalb.
Portrait by Charles Willson Peale,
1781–82.

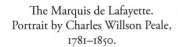

The Marquis de Lafayette.
Portrait by Charles Willson Peale,
1781–1850.

General Benjamin Lincoln.
Portrait by Henry Sargent,
early nineteenth century.

Colonel Banastre Tarleton.
Portrait by Sir Joshua Reynolds,
1782.

Horatio Gates.
Portrait by Charles Willson Peale,
1782.

Charles Cornwallis.
Portrait by Thomas Gainsborough,
1783.

"A Society of Patriotic Ladies, at Edenton in North Carolina." Printed for R. Say and J. Bennett on March 25, 1775, in London.

Henry Laurens. Portrait by John Singleton Copley, 1782.

Nathanael Greene.
Portrait by Charles Willson Peale,
ca. 1783.

Thomas Sumter.
Portrait by Rembrandt Peale,
ca. 1795.

The Battle of Cowpens.
Painting by William Tylee Ranney,
1845.

Henry "Light Horse Harry" Lee.
Portrait by Charles Willson Peale,
1782.

Rebecca Motte.
Watercolor miniature on ivory,
by Jeremiah Theus,
ca. 1758.

Mount Vernon.
Painting by Benjamin Latrobe,
ca 1796.

Surrender of Lord Cornwallis.
Painting by John Trumbull, 1819–20.
It hangs in the Rotunda of the U.S. Capitol.

John Laurens.
Watercolor miniature on ivory,
by Charles Willson Peale,
ca. 1780.

Otho Holland Williams.
Portrait by Charles Willson Peale,
ca. 1783.

some three hundred yards from the main camp, the troops back there were still cooking their morning meal; Greene was eating his breakfast. Even so, when word of the British approach reached the camp, they rallied quickly. The deserter who told Rawdon that Greene had no artillery was not lying. Greene had none when the deserter snuck away, it is true. But well before noon, Colonel Edward Carrington, Greene's quartermaster, showed up with three six-pounders and forty men who knew how to use them. When the main British column emerged from the woods, the guns—hitherto concealed by the men in the ranks—opened up with a roar, ripping holes in the onrushing line of redcoats.

The momentum could not be sustained, however. Hoping to trap Rawdon by assaulting him on both flanks, attempting a "double envelopment," Greene advanced with all of his infantry and sent William Washington and his dragoons around to the rear to attack from there, sealing off any lines of retreat. Washington's cavalry swung too far, however, and never quite caught up in time to help pull off the ambitious maneuver, which seems uncharacteristic of this generally cautious commander.

For reasons that are still unclear, the ordinarily reliable Marylanders, who had performed admirably at Cowpens and Guilford Courthouse, became disordered when one of their officers was killed. Pulling back to re-form, they left a gap in the American line, and things did not look good for Greene's army. This was exasperating, considering the advantages they had when Rawdon, taking the bait, had emerged from the town and attacked. Greene, after all, was on high ground of his own choosing. His army of fifteen hundred, including those crack Marylanders, outnumbered Rawdon's troops nearly two to one and should have been winning this battle handily. But they weren't, and Greene was becoming increasingly frustrated.

Greene, to his credit, was a model of courage throughout, though critics might have regarded his conduct as reckless. "General Greene exposed himself greatly in this action," one of his aides reported, and another officer said his conduct "resembled more that of a captain of grenadiers than that of a major general." By noon, when his army was fighting for its survival, he saw his artillerymen sweating to get the cannons out of the brush in which they had been hidden and save them from falling to the enemy, Greene dismounted and lent his own muscle to the effort. By one account, Greene "almost was taken prisoner as he personally helped to drag the cannons to safety." Rawdon's infantry had failed to find the six-pounders in the heat of the pursuit, and William Washington, sweeping behind the British lines, used his cavalry horses to haul the cannons back to Greene's main army.

All this was cold comfort, however. The British seemed to be winning everywhere, and to save his army from irreparable losses, at about 4 p.m. Greene ordered a general retreat. He pulled the troops back to Rugeley's Mill, which was where—bitter irony—Gates had positioned his army the previous August, when it was obliterated. Again deprived of the battlefield victory that he craved, Greene was disconsolate—and bitter. They could have taken Rawdon and his entire army "in three Minutes," had the Marylanders not broken as they had, he told Joseph Reed. Having to retreat, he said, left him beside himself "with vexation." Two days later, when some of his men were court-martialed for desertion and found guilty, Greene ordered five of them hanged.

The same day the men were executed for desertion, Greene wrote his report to Congress. The battle had gone well, he said, before the Marylanders broke and the others gave way. "The Troops were frequently rallied," he said, "but got into too much disorder to recover the fortune of the Day," which once seemed so promising. William Washington's cavalry had been driving the enemy back into Camden, "with the utmost precipitation," Greene claimed, when the plan fell apart. Nevertheless, his army "is in good spirits, and this little repulse will make no alteration in our general plan of operations." The war of posts would continue, and the news from other fronts—the fall of Fort Watson, primarily—was good.

In a letter to General Washington, Greene enclosed a copy of his report to Congress and summed up a pattern that seemed to be developing, after Guilford Courthouse and now Hobkirk's Hill, as the second battle of Camden would become known. "We fight, get beat, and fight again," Greene wrote. He used almost identical language in a letter to the Chevalier de la Luzerne, the French minister to the U.S.: "We fight, get beaten, rise, and fight again." Considering the outcome of the war and the performance of Greene's army in the South, what might have sounded like a sigh of resignation was becoming a rallying cry.

Greene's own losses, while not nearly so severe as those at Guilford Courthouse, were painful to accept. He suffered 250 casualties, and

Rawdon's British and loyalists lost roughly the same number. Washington offered his condolences and sought to encourage his weary subordinate. "I feel for your mortification at the loss [at Hobkirk's Hill], after it seemed so much in your favour," the commander in chief wrote, "but I hope you will have found that the enemy suffered severely as in their publication of the affair in the New York Paper they confess the loss of 200. The reduction of Fort Watson does honor to General Marion and Colonel Lee."

Even at two hundred, that was a far higher percentage of the enemy's forces than Greene's own, which proved significant in whether this tactical British victory—a victory in the sense that they held the ground while Greene's army withdrew—served their interests or that of the Americans. Even before the last man expired on the field, Hobkirk's Hill would be seen for what it was: another pyrrhic victory, on much the same order as Guilford Courthouse, more costly to the victors than to the losing side. Rawdon had been expecting reinforcements from the east and, had they arrived, he could have won handily, possibly annihilating Greene's army—meaning virtually the entire Continental army in the South—just as Cornwallis had destroyed Gates the year before.

But that did not happen. After taking Fort Watson and before moving on Fort Motte, Marion and Lee had headed west, positioning their men between the reinforcements Rawdon had been expecting and Camden. This, of course, prevented their arrival, saving Greene's army. What Greene could not know, however, was that Cornwallis, already headed for Virginia, had decided that Camden could no longer be maintained and issued instructions to Rawdon to abandon it. Rawdon was to march his army south, on the far side of the Santee River and, temporarily at least, out of immediate danger. So on the night of May 9, a Wednesday, Rawdon began evacuating the town, taking with him untold numbers of slaves and many loyalists who lived there. Before leaving, the British burned the mills, a few houses owned by known supporters of independence and, after emptying the disease-ridden jail, burned it, too. The last redcoats left Camden early in the morning of Thursday, May 10, and a few hours after that, Greene's army entered the town.

Before Andrew Jackson and his brother were released from the Camden jail, Robert Jackson had developed a full-blown case of smallpox, and was also suffering from a "severe bowel complaint." Andrew was showing symptoms of smallpox, too, sweating and shivering. It is impossible to know exactly when and under what conditions their release was secured, but at some point, Betty Jackson arrived, and as part of a general prisoner exchange, their mother led the boys out of the stockade, with Robert, too weak to walk, on horseback, and Andrew on foot. Home in the Waxhaws was forty-five miles away, and he walked the entire way, barefoot and, at least part of the time, in a miserable spring rain. By the time they arrived, Andrew was covered with sores and delirious. Two days after that, brother Robert was dead. Andrew was an invalid the rest of the year, much of which he spent without his mother's care. Once he was out of immediate danger, Betty Jackson set off for Charles Town to help care for American soldiers confined to British prison ships. That fall, while still away from home, she developed symptoms of cholera—ship fever, it was called—and died.

CHAPTER TWENTY-FIVE

"A More Noble Ambition"

Back in November 1780, after Thomas Sumter's militia routed the British Legion under Tarleton at Blackstock's, rumors had raced through the enemy camps that Sumter, shot in the fighting, had died. This was wishful thinking. The Gamecock was out of commission but back in the new year, by which time much had changed. All civil government in South Carolina had collapsed. Governor John Rutledge had departed for Philadelphia to seek support from the North in his state's efforts to oust the British, the state legislature had ceased to meet, and the courts had closed. By commission from Rutledge, Sumter was named commander in chief of the South Carolina militia, which made him—in the absence of civil government—the highest-ranking official in the state, yielding something akin to dictatorial power. Even so, he was expected to work with General Greene, as head of the Continental army's Southern Department, and Greene, of course, reported to General Washington.

Although afflicted by the wound to his shoulder, Sumter felt strong enough by the first months of 1781 to return to the field. He had commanded one thousand militia when he defeated Tarleton at Blackstock's, but many of these men had returned to their farms, and Sumter would never command such a large force again. And no sooner had he felt ready to begin what he called a "vigorous campaign" than he received a somewhat patronizing letter from Greene. In it, the commander in chief indicated, without quite saying so, that he had come to trust Marion and Lee with the Fabian tactics at which they excelled, but not the maddeningly independent, sometimes intractable Sumter. Where Greene was explicit was in reminding Sumter that he would be expected to coordinate his efforts with that of Greene's main army. He was putting Sumter on notice.

"The salvation of this country," Greene wrote,

> don't depend upon little strokes; nor should the great business of establishing a permanent army be neglected to pursue them. Partizan strokes in war are like the garnish of a table, they give splendor to the Army and reputation to the Officers, but they afford no national security—You may strike a hundred strokes, and reap little benefit from them unless you have a good Army to take advantage of your success.

Militiamen, as Sumter was well aware, come and go, and they cannot be relied on for sustained operations. Individual heroics have their place, but they should never constitute an end in themselves. "There is no mortal more fond of enterprize than myself," Greene went on, "but this is not the basis on which the fate of this country depends."

And that was not all Greene had to say. He also wanted Sumter to know how deeply he disapproved of the civil war raging in the Carolinas and the unchecked appetites of individuals who sought to profit from it. Here, too, was an only slightly disguised admonition. "Plunder and depredation prevails so in every quarter I am not a little apprehensive all this country will be laid waste," Greene wrote. "Most people appear to be in pursuit of private gain or personal glory. I persuade myself though you may set a just value upon reputation your soul is filled with a more noble ambition."

If Sumter's first efforts, upon returning to action in February, were in the slightest degree inhibited by Greene's restraining counsel, there is no evidence of it. On the contrary, his designs, motivated by a desire for what Greene called personal glory, seem downright grandiose. "The Gamecock believed that a surprise attack could carry Fort Granby," his admiring biographer Robert D. Bass wrote in *Gamecock*. "A rapid foray down the Congaree could surprise and capture Belleville. A further sweep down the Santee, Sumter convinced himself, could topple Fort Watson. A junction with Marion's brigade could give the Carolinians such overwhelming superiority that they could drive the enemy back into Charles Town. With one powerful effort they could end the war."

None of this proved true. Sumter tried to take Fort Granby in February, but that effort came to nothing for two reasons. Major Andrew Maxwell, the loyalist who commanded the fort, had been tipped off that Sumter was coming—and that he would be bringing no artillery with him. So when Sumter had his men paint logs to look like cannons, Maxwell was not fooled and therefore not intimidated. Also, Rawdon sent reinforcements to the garrison, and their approach prompted Sumter to lift the siege almost as soon as it began.

Once that was done, Sumter crossed the Congaree, and rode thirty-five miles south to Belleville, all the while hoping militiamen in the area would flock to his standard, swelling his ranks. They did not. Belleville was a plantation, much like Fort Motte, which the British had seized when Charles Town fell. They had erected a stockade around the farmhouse and used the plantation's outbuildings as part of the fortifications. The day after abandoning Fort Granby, Sumter ordered his men to open fire on Belleville and burn the outbuildings. But the British inside the fort fought back with such determination that within thirty minutes, Sumter called off the assault and again retreated, having accomplished nothing beyond exhausting his already weary and depleted ranks.

A few days later, along the Santee River, Sumter's fortunes seemed to improve. His men ambushed and captured a convoy of enemy supply wagons, allegedly killing seven members of the British escort—after they had tried to surrender. The wagons, Sumter found, contained arms, ammunition, and clothing, which his ragged men could use. They also seized locked chests that they believed contained British gold for the payment of their troops. Exactly what happened next is impossible to know at this time—accounts vary—but Sumter had the plunder loaded onto flatboats and sent across the Santee River to ship elsewhere for safekeeping. The version of events that seems to have been most widely accepted is that the pilot of the flotilla, soon believed to have been an agent of the British, steered it to Fort Watson. There the British reclaimed the plundered goods. (Others, however, took a different view. Some of his own men suspected that Sumter himself made off with the chests that were said to contain gold, and this allegation, neither proved nor disproved, persisted well into the next century.)

Eager to get the plunder back, Sumter on the last day of February ordered his assault on Fort Watson. Here too he was defeated, at a cost of eighteen American lives, a few prisoners, and a great number of horses, and the post remained in enemy hands until Marion and Lee captured it in the spring. When Sumter and his discouraged men pulled back to Farr's plantation on the Black River, some of them simply disappeared into the swamps at the river's edge. When the North Carolina men decided to leave en masse, Sumter ordered them to stay—at bayonet point.

In three weeks, Sumter had a lost a quarter of his men, and those who remained were poorly provisioned and increasingly miserable. Farr's, where they made camp, was close to Sumter's own plantation, and he further exasperated his men when he exposed them to enemy fire on a forty-mile trek made for the sole purpose of getting his own wife and son out of harm's way. With the British in hot pursuit, a "smart action ensued," Rawdon said, "in which the enemy were completely routed, leaving ten dead on the field and about forty wounded."

Sumter's men, many of whom came to believe that their commander deliberately misled them about how large a force Rawdon had sent after them, "were now exceedingly dejected," in the words of Colonel Robert Gray, a loyalist from Camden who wrote an account of the war in 1782. Sumter's great talent in the early days of his campaign had been his ability to raise troops. He seems to have been a charismatic individual, and earlier in the war, men were eager to serve under him. But now, still recovering from his injuries and smarting from a string of bloody setbacks, he was finding it difficult to keep enough men in his ranks to campaign at all. It was during this bleak period that he dreamed up and then put into practice what became known as Sumter's Law.

The plan was ingenious in a cold way, and disturbing to the more humane of his peers. Distressed by the frequency with which volunteer militia would arrive, serve for a few weeks, and then disappear, Sumter decided he needed men under him who would make a longer, more binding commitment—not the customary four- or six-week duty. Unfortunately, he had no way to pay them a bounty to enlist or to compensate them for their service. So, sometime in March 1781, he announced that he would raise several regiments of state troops consisting of men who would serve for ten months. How he would pay these men, Sumter told Marion, would involve "measures truly disagreeable, such as can only be justified by our circumstance and the necessity of the case." Their provisions—clothing, weapons, horses, tack for their horses, and the like—would be taken from the enemy or "furnished," as one of the American officers put it, from loyalists in the area. Their compensation, put differently, would consist of what they would be able to collect through plunder.

But the real reward for their service would take the form of other human beings. Sumter's men would be paid in slaves, and an elaborate system was developed to measure their worth to the soldiers who would come to own them. That way, Sumter figured, the distribution would be equitable. A "prime" slave, from eleven years of age to forty, was worth four hundred dollars; those younger than ten but older than forty were worth half as much. A colonel would receive three and one-half slaves for every year of service. Majors would get three slaves, captains two, and lieutenants one and one-half, while lowly privates would be paid one grown slave for ten months' enlistment. Of course, very few if any of these slaves had been rounded up. They would have to be captured first, just like the clothing, saddles, bridles, and weapons. Whatever else was taken from the houses and farms of loyalists would also be divvied up fairly and impartially: the men would share in two-thirds of the plunder, with one-third to remain in Sumter's hands, for the common good.

Such a plan, while disgusting to Marion, who made no secret of his contempt for it, was highly attractive to poor young men with an itch for adventure. They could join the army, fight the enemy, and come away with something they probably could not otherwise afford—a slave or two—which throughout the South conferred instant social status. Even Bass, Sumter's otherwise admiring biographer, disapproved: "At its best," he wrote, Sumter's Law "was simple plundering. At its worst, in tearing apart Negro families, it was barbaric." Marion would have nothing to do with the scheme and refused to use it to raise recruits. Pickens seems to have had no qualms about the program, but Greene was more equivocal.

"Although I am a great enemy of plundering," Greene told Sumter, "yet I think the horses belonging to the Inhabitants within the Enemy's lines should be taken away from them, especially such as are either fit from waggon or dragoon service." Of course, with horses, "or any kind of property, whether taken from Whigs or Tories, certificates ought to be given, that justice may be done hereafter." The paperwork had to be done properly, though what these certificates would be redeemed with was left unsaid, probably because no one knew. In the meantime, Greene wrote, slaves "belonging to Tories or disaffected you will apply to fulfilling your contract with the ten months' Troops." He could distribute livestock as he wished, but should not plunder food, clothes, and medicine from Tories' homes.

Sumter's men now felt they had permission to take whatever they could get their hands on, exacerbating the civil war in South Carolina, which was soon so alarming that Greene brought it to General Washington's attention. "The Whigs seem determined to extirpate the Tories, and the Tories the Whigs," Greene wrote. "Some thousands have fallen in this way in this quarter, and the evil rages with more violence than ever. If a stop cannot be put to these massacres, the country will be depopulated in a few months more, as neither Whig nor Tory can live."

Greene had repeatedly encouraged Sumter to fold his own men into the larger southern army, which he had refused to do, and in time he no longer even bothered to respond to Greene's messages. Sumter had become such a headache for Greene, according to Major William Davie of the North Carolina militia, that he had decided that the Gamecock was nothing more than a "freebooter, whose sole object was plunder." For a time, Greene even considered having Sumter arrested. But with Governor Rutledge having endorsed Sumter's Law, and civil government having almost ground to a halt in the state, Greene realized that the outcome of any such action would be difficult to predict and possibly calamitous. This, too: as the highest-ranking military officer in South Carolina, Sumter held a position that Greene had to respect—especially in the absence of civil government.

Sumter's Law seems to have done little to stimulate recruiting— the countryside was already picked clean of able-bodied young men— though it did result in more looting by the soldiers, and then in grumbling about their plunder's distribution. Discontent, which began at the top with the easily offended commander, quickly spread throughout the ranks. Sumter had apparently been unhappy since Greene, with the Gamecock laid up with injuries, had lent some of his men to Daniel Morgan in his victory over Tarleton at Cowpens. Sumter had not congratulated Morgan or Greene, he said, because of the "excessive difficulty" he experienced when writing with his injured hand. Sumter was even angrier when he learned that Lee and Marion had taken Fort Watson, where he had failed. All communications between Marion and Sumter had broken down—they were not answering one another's letters—and neither felt any obligation to the other.

When Lee took Fort Granby, which he had also failed to accomplish, Sumter was even more incensed and again complained to Greene that there, too, some of his own troops were used. This, Sumter felt, was unforgivable. Apparently, he told Greene, his services were no longer needed. "My Indisposition & Want of Capacity to be of Service to this Country," Sumter wrote, "Induces me as a friend [to it], to beg leave to Resign my command." With the letter, he enclosed his commission.

Refusing to accept Sumter's resignation, Greene returned the commission, explaining that he had no authority as a Continental officer to do so. Any such decision would be Governor Rutledge's to make. But it also seems that Greene held out some hope that Sumter, however erratic and ill-tempered, could still be of some use, if he could just figure out what that might be. Sumter had once demonstrated his ability to raise troops and deploy them effectively, and Greene evidently hoped that when Sumter recovered his health, he could put petty differences aside and return to the form that had distinguished him the previous year.

Greene could not "think of accepting [his resignation] & beg you to continue your command," he wrote. "I am sorry for your ill State of health, and shall do every thing in my power to render your command, as convenient as the nature of the service will admit." He also wished to remind Sumter

> how important your services are to the interest & happiness of this Country; and the confidence I have in your abilities [and] Zeal for the good of the service. Your continuing in command will lay the public in general and me in particular, under a very great obligation; & tho it may be accompanied with personal inconveniences, yet I hope you will have cause to rejoyce in the conclusion of the business from the consideration of having contributed so largely to the recovery of its Liberty.

Greene followed this personal letter with a formal one, reminding all concerned that the Gamecock was now in full command of the South Carolina militia, and that he had the authority to employ Marion, as of inferior rank, "in such a manner as may most effectually annoy the enemy, & at the same time cooperate with us should the occasion require it." Marion would report to Sumter—and Sumter in turn would be expected to coordinate his activities with Greene. How well this would play out, of course, was anybody's guess.

CHAPTER TWENTY-SIX

"Thunder Even at the Gates of Charles Town"

In mid-May, as Lee and Pickens began their successful campaign to retake Augusta, Sumter performed routine duties for the Southern Department's commander in chief. He and his men rode to Camden, which by this time the British had evacuated, and to Fort Motte, dismantling the rest of the enemy's defenses, which were now, he told Greene, "tolerably well demolished." Then Sumter set off for Orangeburg, the British post just south of Fort Motte and only seventy-five miles from the big prize, which was Charles Town. With a six-pounder sent by Greene, Sumter attacked the main installation at Orangeburg, a brick jail where the loyalists were holed up. The six-pounder opened up with a roar, and after four shots banged into the jail, knocking holes in its brick walls, the troops inside surrendered. Sumter took ninety prisoners, including eight officers.

Invigorated by the results, Sumter was itching to move on toward Charles Town, and the results of his efforts—and Lee's, Marion's, and Greene's—could be seen almost anywhere you looked. The roads were clogged with frightened loyalists who had either abandoned their homes or left their military companies and were fleeing toward the coast, hauling such of their belongings as they could carry, or, if they owned livestock, leading it along with them. Here too Sumter saw an opportunity for plunder. With all these refugees streaming toward Charles Town, Sumter found "every Reason to believe the Country will be Striped of every thing that is Valuable," he told Greene. "I Wish to Deprive [the loyalists] of as Many horses as possible & prevent the Inhabitance from Moving & Carrying off great Quantities of stock Which [we] are now Collecting." Sumter's efforts south of the Santee River were proving valuable in another way, too. The loyalists were staying as far away as possible from the British troops, so Lord Francis Rawdon was deprived of the intelligence ordinarily supplied by spies.

After Hobkirk's Hill, Greene headed toward the British fort at Ninety Six. On the south banks of the Saluda River, about a hundred miles west of Camden, Ninety Six remained the most important back-country post that the British still held. As such, it had to be taken if the redcoats were to be driven back to Charles Town and isolated on the coast. As described by Anthony Allaire, a loyalist officer, in his 1780 diary, it consisted of about "twelve dwelling houses, a court-house and a jail . . . situated on an eminence, the land cleared for a mile around it, in a flourishing part of the country, supplied with very good water, enjoys free open air, and is esteemed a healthy place." By the time Greene's army arrived, the British had strengthened its defenses with an earthen fort in the shape of an eight-pointed star—"the Star Fort," they called it—and surrounded the whole with a stockade fence. That "very good water" that Allaire mentioned came from a spring west of the town, protected by a small freestanding fortification of its own.

The post was garrisoned by about 550 men—Americans all but one—under the command of Lieutenant Colonel John Harris Cruger, the scion of a prominent New York family. About one hundred loyalist families took refuge inside Ninety Six, while slaves were ordered to maintain its defenses. Some two hundred men were garrisoned at the Star Fort, which contained the bulk of the post's ammunition. Ann DeLancey Cruger, the commander's wife, had refused to go to Charles Town during the siege and was staying at a farm not far from the fort. When Greene appeared with a thousand men—almost twice as many as at Ninety Six—he stationed a guard at the farm for Mrs. Cruger's protection.

Greene arrived on May 22, and conducted himself, Mercy Otis Warren wrote, with "the laconic style of the Spartan, with the spirit of a Roman, and the enthusiasm of an American." Told that a superior force of British were on their way and urged to leave while they had the chance, Greene would have none of it. "I will recover this country," he supposedly replied, "or perish in the attempt." When Thaddeus Kosciuszko, his chief engineer, determined that the post was too strong for a frontal assault to succeed, they determined that a siege was called for. If the Star Fort fell, they reasoned, the rest of Ninety Six would follow. With little or no experience with sieges, Greene relied on the advice of Kosciuszko, a man educated in European strategy and tactics at a French military academy. The sweaty and laborious digging of parallel trenches began. Cruger's loyalists, although significantly outnumbered, contested every foot of the work, which would have gone slowly under the most advantageous of circumstances because the red clay around the fort had been baked hard by the late-spring sun.

The siege "settled into a daily routine of digging, cannonading, and exchanging small arms fire," John Beakes Jr. writes in *Otho Holland Williams in the American Revolution*. "It was a gritty and dangerous type of warfare, with the Americans trying to dig their way closer to victory, and the British trying every tactic they could think of to delay what appeared to be their inevitable surrender. The only hope that Cruger and his men had was that a relief column from Charles Town could reach Ninety Six and drive the Americans away," and Charles Town was nearly two hundred miles away.

Lee arrived on June 8, during the siege's second week. Doubtful that Kosciuszko's plan would succeed, Lee told Greene they should concentrate their efforts on the fort's precarious water supply. Summer had come, and deprived of water, the garrison would have no choice but to give up. The men, meanwhile, were trying other methods to force the post to surrender. They tried what had worked at Fort Watson and erected a tower thirty yards from the Star Fort. Cruger responded by adding to its defenses, which helped, although Greene's men could still rake the fort and make life miserable for those inside it. Greene's efforts to burn it down proved ineffective, too, because the army lacked the furnaces to sufficiently heat the shells that their artillery would fire into it. His men also shot flaming arrows at the roofs of buildings in the town, as had been done at Fort Motte, but the defenders doused the flames and systematically removed wooden shingles.

Attempts to cut off the fort's water, however, were showing results. Lee directed artillery fire at the small fortification protecting the stream, preventing access to it during the heat of day. "The sufferings inside the garrison were now extreme," Roderick Mackenzie, a British officer, wrote in his account of the siege.

With infinite labour a well was dug in the Star, but water was not to be obtained, and the only means of procuring this necessary element in a torrid climate in the month of June was to send out naked Negroes, who brought scanty supply from within pistol shot of the American pickets, their bodies not being distinguishable at night from the fallen trees with which the place abounded.

Cruger began to realize that he could not hold out much longer, but a sense of urgency gripped Greene and his officers as well. Rawdon, who had left Camden for Charles Town, was now headed for Ninety Six and making good time, despite the sweltering heat. He had lost fifty men to heat exhaustion along the way. Between June 7, when he marched out of Charles Town, and June 12, Rawdon and the two thousand reinforcements he was bringing with him were at Orangeburg, just a hundred miles from Ninety Six and closing fast. If Rawdon arrived, Greene would be seriously outnumbered.

Five days later, Sumter, who had been ordered to block Rawdon's advance but failed to do so, informed Greene that the enemy was now just thirty miles from Ninety Six. Greene on June 18 ordered a direct assault on the Star Fort. At noon, his men opened fire from every position, including the tower, while foot soldiers sprang from the trenches and rushed the fort's walls. Cruger's loyalists fought back gamely, and before long, with men grappling hand-to-hand in the trenches at the foot of the fort, thirty of Greene's soldiers lay dead or dying, with "the survivors," Beakes writes, "scrambling to get back to the safety of their lines as best they could."

The final assault—on the twenty-eight-day siege—had failed, and Greene ordered a general retreat. He decided to "return to his cardinal policy," Lee wrote, "the preservation of adequate force to keep the field." Greene had saved his army so it could fight another day, but that was scant consolation for the men who made it through the ordeal with so little to show for it. That night, Lee wrote, "gloom and silence pervaded the American camp: every one disappointed—every one mortified." On the morning of June 20, Greene and his men left Ninety Six and headed north to elude Rawdon before turning southeast for the High Hills of Santee. The next day, after a brief pursuit of Greene's retreating forces, Rawdon turned back. Having already marched two hundred miles, skirmishing along the way, Rawdon's troops were too worn out to continue, and Greene was making better time than Rawdon had expected.

On June 26, Rawdon returned to Ninety Six, but many of the two thousand men he brought with him were sick from marching for two weeks in the hot sun of South Carolina's unforgiving summer. There Rawdon issued once again an order he had tried to make in May, shortly after Camden fell. Weeks earlier, he had sent messengers to Cruger instructing him to evacuate Ninety Six and fall back to Augusta, reinforcing that post which by now had also fallen. In one of those strange turns of fate so frequent in warfare, Cruger never got the message. Unfortunately for Rawdon, Greene's patrols had intercepted the orders, but unfortunately for Greene, he did not see the orders meant for Cruger, either. Unaware of his commander's wishes, Cruger held on, only to have to give up Ninety Six after all. He did so at considerable cost, but nothing like what Greene's men suffered. The loyalists lost twenty-seven killed and fifty-eight wounded at Ninety Six; estimates of Greene's losses range from about 150 to 185, the higher number being Lee's. About sixty of them were killed, and among the dead was Captain Joseph Pickens, Andrew's brother. Thaddeus Kosciuszko, who had insisted that a siege in the European tradition would succeed, suffered an "inglorious" wound that made sitting in the saddle painful for weeks to come.

Greene and his men reached the High Hills of Santee, Otho Holland Williams said, by "slow, easy marches." The troops "were placed in good quarters, and the heat of July [was] rendered tolerable by the high ground, the fine air, and good water of the selected camp," Lee wrote. "Disease began to abate, our wounded to recover, and the army to rise in bodily strength." Greene, for all his disappointment, now had the distance in time and space to reflect with some satisfaction that while a siege had failed and a battle had been lost, his overall objective had been met. The last major British base in the Carolina upcountry had fallen, just as Camden had six weeks earlier. The smaller posts—Fort Watson, Fort Motte, and the rest—had fallen, too, and the British were being pushed back to Charles Town.

While the main army rested, Lee and Marion, reporting to Sumter, were kept busy harassing the British. "No time is to be lost, therefore push your operations night and day," Greene told Sumter in mid-June, and he encouraged Light Horse Harry "to thunder even at the gates of Charles Town." Sumter, meanwhile, was to push closer to the coast as well, attacking the posts that protected the city, which the British had occupied now for more than a year. Civil government had ceased to function in Charles Town, and by now much of the once-booming port was in ruins, its citizens impoverished, and the plantations around it dilapidated.

Sumter was especially eager to attack the British post at Monck's Corner. This was the little crossroads town thirty miles north of Charles Town that Tarleton had taken a year earlier, cutting off a possible route of escape for Benjamin Lincoln's beleaguered army when it was cooped up in Charles Town. Greene gave Sumter the go-ahead to try to retake Monck's Corner, and he would be supported by both Lee and Marion in this effort. This would give the Gamecock a decided advantage, and not only in numbers. He would have about a thousand men under his command, with help from two officers who had known much more success than he had: Marion and Lee. There were about six hundred British regulars at Monck's Corner and another 150 mounted loyalists, under a Lieutenant Colonel Coates, who was sufficiently obscure and unremarkable that historians have called him James, John, and Joseph, and cannot seem to agree on what his name actually was.

But there would be no battle at Monck's Corner. Sumter drew near, and Coates slipped a few miles away to Biggin Church, a formidable brick house of worship that the British had used to store ammunition. The church was on the road that led to Charles Town, from which Coates believed he could be readily reinforced. In the early-morning hours of June 17, still outnumbered and with Sumter on his tail, Coates had the church burned and stole away once more. Lee, who was out raiding on his own but would soon rejoin Sumter, had gotten close enough to Charles Town to cause near panic there. Edward McCrady, a native of that city who in 1902 wrote one of the first major histories of the war in South Carolina, said the fighting outside the town created "the greatest alarm and confusion. The bells were rung, the alarm guns were fired, and the whole city was under arms."

When Sumter reached Biggin Church before sunup, he "found this post Avacuated," as he reported to Greene, and had no idea where Coates had headed. Lee knew, however, and made off with his cavalry to the eastern branch of the Cooper River, to the spot where his scouts told him it could be most easily forded. This would be at Quinby Bridge, where, once again, Coates hoped for reinforcements from Charles Town. Lee's cavalry chased Coates for eighteen miles, seizing his supply train and rear guard along the way. Led by Captain John Armstrong, Lee's advance troops arrived at the bridge after Coates's troops had already crossed the river and taken a defensive position on the north banks, with a highly mobile, extremely menacing howitzer, aimed at anyone who intended to follow with hostile intent. Expecting his supply train and rear guard to join him, Coates had not bothered to demolish the bridge, though his men had loosened some of the planks, intending to tear down the rest of the footing as soon as his force caught up and made the crossing.

Armstrong arrived, with Lee's instructions firmly in mind. He was "to fall upon the enemy without respect to consequences," Lee would recall. Spurring his horse, Armstrong "threw himself over the bridge," heedless of the howitzer and troops stationed there ready to fire their weapons. He came on so fast that some of the redcoats, surprised by the attack, dropped their rifles and fled. Loose planks flew off the bridge as Armstrong and his men galloped across, which, forming "a chasm in the bridge," Lee said, "presented a dangerous obstacle." The next wave of Armstrong's mounted men "took the leap," and crossed with their commander.

There they fought admirably, but Coates's infantry held them off nonetheless, while some redcoats, "appalled at the sudden and daring attack," headed for a farmhouse in their rear. This was on the plantation of Thomas Shubrick, a Charles Town slave trader, where Coates re-formed his men and took a solid defensive position, with their trusty howitzer in place. Shubrick's farmhouse was a formidable two-story structure on what one of the redcoats called "a commanding Height," considerably safer to occupy than the riverbank. There were slave quarters and other outbuildings on the plantation, which could also be occupied should Sumter and Lee and Marion and the rest of their men make it across that rickety bridge and force the issue. In the meantime, Coates hunkered down at Shubrick's and waited.

Marion and his men appeared at about three o'clock that afternoon. Lee had already arrived, and, fording the river well upstream of the bridge, he surveyed the British position. None of their options were ideal, but they rarely are in battle. There was the howitzer to consider, if they attacked from the front. If they attacked from the flanks, however, they would have to face the enemy firing at them from the relative security of the farmhouse and the outbuildings, and from behind a rail fence. Assessing the situation with some objectivity, Marion and Lee told Sumter that, without artillery, which Sumter lacked, any assault would fail. But Sumter dismissed their advice, and ordered an attack to proceed. He positioned Marion's men on the left, near a cornfield, and troops under Peter Horry, who was one of Marion's officers, on the right, with Lee's cavalry in reserve. Sumter's own men would be posted in slave quarters, which offered the only protection there was, in the center.

Just past five, Sumter told the troops under Colonel Thomas Taylor of the South Carolina militia to charge the British crouched behind the rail fence, and the fight was on. The redcoats met the charge with bayonets, repulsing Taylor's men, and when Marion plunged into the fray to support the retreat, the British themselves fell back. The redcoats behind the fence broke for the protection of the outbuildings and the farmhouse, and Marion's men found themselves, their commander said, "fired on from the stoop of the Houses & through the doors, windows & Corner."

It was over in forty minutes. Running low on ammunition and getting beaten badly, Marion pulled his troops back while, on the other side of the cornfield, Sumter retreated three miles, hoping his one piece of artillery would arrive, with a "Design of Renewing the attack in the Morning." Had he waited until the fieldpiece arrived, things might have gone differently, or so the men in the ranks believed. But, in its absence and with reinforcements yet to arrive, Coates had not only held off the attack but was now in a stronger position than before. Only six of his men had been killed, with ten times as many of Sumter and Marion's, while Lee's, in reserve, had had nothing to do but wait and watch.

Marion was livid over how Sumter had sacrificed his men in the mission from the start. The Gamecock had positioned his own soldiers in the slave quarters, which gave them some protection. Those reporting to Marion, however, had nothing to protect them from enemy fire, to which they had been needlessly exposed in an assault that—just as he and Lee had warned Sumter—could not succeed. Their soldiers were furious, too. After the guns fell silent, Taylor, as his son would tell the story, "found Gen. Sumter sitting coolly under the shade of a tree—&

said: 'Sir, I don't know why you sent me forward on a forlorn hope, promising to sustain me, & failed to do so, unless you designed to sacrifice me. I will never more serve under you' & then retired from Sumter's command." Lee and Marion did not even speak to Sumter—this was outright insubordination—before readying their troops and leaving. It was all the Gamecock could do to keep his own men from mutinying before, the next day, he too withdrew.

And that was not all. Governor Rutledge replaced Sumter as commander of the South Carolina troops with Lieutenant Colonel William Henderson, who had been taken prisoner at Charles Town but sometimes served as Sumter's second in command after his release. Upon his arrival, Henderson found Sumter's men unpaid and on the verge of revolt. They were, Henderson told Rutledge, "the most discontented men I ever saw." The "thirst for plunder" the Gamecock had encouraged "makes the command almost intolerable." Henderson, meanwhile, received an unexpected request from Sumter. Without consulting with Greene, Sumter asked that the men of his own brigade be given "a respite from service until the first of October," which meant they would be allowed to return to their homes—or do anything they wanted—for the next three months. "Have I come here only to furlough a parcel of troops," he asked Greene, "and that when the enemy is at our doors?"

Greene saw things much as Henderson did. "It would be little less than madness" to do what the Gamecock had asked, Greene told Henderson. "I have the public good, and the safety of the good people of the state, too much at heart, to think of such a measure." Lee, also outraged by Sumter's request, was not surprised. "General Sumter [has] become almost universally odious," he told Greene. "I lament that a man of his turn was ever useful, or being once deservedly great, should want the wisdom to continue so, and to preserve his reputation."

By this time, there was not much reputation to preserve, and Greene's Continental army would be moving on without the Gamecock. In late July, Sumter turned his men loose to plunder one of the cities the British had given up as they concentrated what was left of their forces in Savannah and Charles Town and the countryside around them. This was Georgetown, sixty miles north of Charles Town, which the British had evacuated in May but was still inhabited by loyalists. Sumter's men had their fun, and the British retaliated during the first week of August by firing on the town from warships offshore, burning many of its buildings and leaving Georgetown in ruins. Governor Rutledge responded by issuing a proclamation against plundering, depriving Sumter of his means of paying his men, and putting an end to Sumter's Law. Cornwallis by this time was already in Virginia, Rawdon was ill, and the Gamecock's fighting days were over.

CHAPTER TWENTY-SEVEN

"Peace Is Not Far Off"

On the evening of June 3, 1781, a Sunday, Thomas Jefferson extinguished the candles in his bedchamber at Monticello with the reasonable expectation that, come morning, a more restful chapter of his life would begin. He had now served two one-year terms as Virginia's wartime governor—a job he was not well suited for and had come to loathe—and as this day came to a close, his second term would officially end. When it did, Jefferson believed, it would bring "relief which [Virginia's constitution] has prepared for those oppressed with the labours of my office." Jefferson was by no means ready to retire from public life altogether, of course, however wearisome his life had become.

He was now thirty-eight, and before his death at eighty-three, he would go on to serve his fledgling country in roles of increasing importance: he would represent his constituents in Congress, act as minister to France, secretary of state and vice president, before two terms in the presidency. He would prove to be better in all of these offices than as a wartime governor, at which, as his fellow Virginians had come realize, he wasn't very good at all. And his performance had not seemed to show much improvement as his term came to a close, though here there might have been extenuating circumstances. Back in April, his five-month-old daughter, Lucy Elizabeth, had died—the third of his children who would not survive their infancy—and his wife, Martha, grieving the loss, was in frail health herself.

A scholar and something of an aesthete—but a better politician than he is given credit for—Jefferson did not seem to know much about war and what winning one required. By nature as well as on principle, he was reluctant to exercise the powers that are often called on during times of invasion: he did not approve of martial law or anything that resembled it, and this frustrated the generals who expected him to make quick, sometimes unpopular, decisions. Although he had served, briefly, as lieutenant of the Albemarle County militia, there is no evidence that he knew much about firearms, and he did not enjoy hunting the way so many Virginia gentlemen did.

Jefferson believed in resolving conflicts through persuasion, negotiation, and the law courts—through the exercise of Reason. Deeply committed to what has been called the "anti-authoritarianism" of the Revolution, Jefferson was reluctant to cede state power to national institutions, which were virtually nonexistent, anyway. There was the Continental Congress, of course, and Washington's army, but even the latter was largely dependent on supplies and men from the states, and the states for understandable reasons were in no hurry to put the national defense above their own. The states had their own militias, of course, and even their own small navies. They also had their own currencies, though by 1781 inflation had destroyed their value, just as it had the currency issued by the Continental Congress.

In his reluctance to relinquish power to the Continental Congress, Jefferson was not unlike state officials elsewhere, who saw themselves as representatives of a confederation that had come together to address a temporary emergency. Once that was done, they would once again operate as independent republics, and few of these officials envisioned the result of their efforts to be a great national government; that kind of thinking emerged as a result of fighting the war, not as a cause or a goal of it.

But what Jefferson possessed, and most others lacked, was an appreciation of the international nature of the war, which, conveniently, made this most enlightened of Founding Fathers optimistic about its eventual outcome. The past, with its dependence on enfeebled institutions held up on the rickety props of ignorance and superstition, must and will give way to the future. With the French and the Spanish entering the war, the English "stand alone, without a friend to support them, hated by all mankind because they are proud and unjust," Jefferson wrote shortly before planning to leave office. "But peace is not far off," he continued. "The English cannot hold out long, because all the world is against them."

The recipient of these hopeful words was John Baptiste de Coigne (sometimes Du Coigne or Ducoigne), a friendly chief of the Kaskaskia Indians, with some French blood in his background. Jefferson called him "Brother John Baptiste." The war, as Jefferson's record of his communications with de Coigne suggests, was not only international in nature, but also concerned claims to the lands west of the Appalachian Mountains. Because the war involved those lands, it involved the Native Americans who had occupied them for centuries and, while they benefited from trade with white settlers, resisted attempts to wrest their homelands from them. In 1763, after the Seven Years' War, in which the Crown wrested vast territories in North America from the French, King George III had prohibited the establishment of settlements beyond the Appalachians. This angered land speculators, including George Washington, who had invested in thousands of acres there already. But it also troubled colonists who were streaming west to settle on those lands, pushing the Indigenous people out of the way as they went.

By Jefferson's own calculations in his *Notes on the State of Virginia*, which was written in the summer of 1781, forty different Indian tribes occupied the colony between the seacoast and the mountains when the English settlers arrived in 1607; by 1669, the population of these "aborigenes" had been reduced to a third of what it had been when the white man arrived, which he attributed to "Spirituous liquors, the small-pox, war [with the settlers but also among the tribes themselves], and an abridgement of territory, to a people who lived principally on the spontaneous productions of nature." This abridgement of territory was the result of conquest but also, Jefferson insisted, by legitimate purchase. The settlers pushed on, and the "merciless Indian savages," as Jefferson in the Declaration of Independence called those who occupied the land, struck back with a fury that appalled those who, like Jefferson, seemed to expect them to abide by rules of so-called civilized warfare.

Mostly the Indians had stayed neutral in the contests between the colonists and the Crown. In the Seven Years' War, they had allied themselves with France, and now with the War of Independence, most of the tribes supported the British. Some thirteen thousand Indians would fight alongside the redcoats, whose king, after all, had tried to restrict settlement of the land between the mountains and the Mississippi; some of these Native Americans had attacked the colonists because they had been incited to do so by the British. Jefferson as governor had supported punitive expeditions against what he called the "wretches" who killed and scalped women and children along the western borders of Virginia and the Carolinas, but his attitudes toward the Indians were far more nuanced than might first appear.

Jefferson had been charmed by Indian culture since, as a boy on his father's farm, he had seen the "great Outacite, the warrior and orator of the Cherokees." The same chief known to Sumter as Ostenaco would camp there on his way to Williamsburg and as he made his way back over the mountains. Jefferson was a student in Williamsburg when Outacite sailed to England with Thomas Sumter, and he had witnessed the chief's

> great farewell oration to his people the evening before his departure for England. The moon was in its full splendor, and to her he seemed to address himself in his prayers for his own safety on the voyage, and that of his people during his absence; his sounding voice, distinct articulation, animated actions, and the solemn silence of his people at their several fires, filled me with awe and veneration, although I did not understand a word he uttered.

There were good and noble Indians who could be "civilized," as Jefferson understood the term, under the proper influences. Among these were de Coigne's Kaskaskias, from present-day Illinois, who had not only declined to fight alongside the British but at least once had defended one of the settlers' outposts against an attack by other Indians. This was unusual. Most tribes, recalling their experience in the Seven Years' War and in disputes over territory that began as soon as the colonists arrived, remained hostile.

In one of his final acts as governor, Jefferson ordered 250 Virginia militiamen to the Carolinas to "strike a decisive and memorable blow" against the hostile Chickamaugas, a splinter group of the militant Cherokees, in an ineffectual raid that would not even begin until six months after Jefferson's term expired. Virginians were so preoccupied with the Indians on their borders and with securing the lands beyond the mountains, Nathanael Greene believed, that they had failed to prepare for their defense against the British. "History affords no instance of a nation being so engaged in conquest abroad as Virginia is at a time when all her powers were necessary to secure herself from ruin at home," Greene wrote. It was an opinion that events at the end of Jefferson's time as governor seemed to confirm.

But Jefferson also found time, just days before he hoped to be relieved of his gubernatorial duties, to meet with de Coigne and a delegation of Kaskaskias, which included the chief's wife and their infant son. The two men smoked "the pipe of peace," Jefferson said. Not a smoker himself, he called this "a good old custom" handed down from the Indians' ancestors, and "as such, I respect and join in it with reverence." They exchanged gifts, and de Coigne gave Jefferson buffalo skins with intricate designs. The account Jefferson wrote after de Coigne and his party left is an eloquent expression of how Americans influenced by the Enlightenment regarded these Indigenous people and the hopes—however naive and misguided—that enlightened white men entertained about how their relationship would evolve. The record also expresses how Jefferson wished the Indians to view the war.

He thanked de Coigne for his visit, his gifts, and his tribe's help in resisting Indians allied with the British. "We, like you, are Americans," Jefferson said, "born in the same land, and having the same interests . . . You find us, brother, engaged in the war with a powerful nation. Our forefathers were Englishmen, inhabitants of a little island beyond the great water, and, being distressed for land, they came and settled here. As long as we were young and weak," there was peace.

> We were now grown up and felt ourselves strong; we knew we were free as they were, that we came here of our own accord, and not at their biddance, and were determined to be free as long as we should exist. For this reason they made war on us. They have now waged that war for six years, and have not yet won more land from us than will serve to bury the warriors they have lost . . . This quarrel, when it first began, was a family quarrel between us and the English, who were then our brothers. We, therefore, did not wish you to engage in it at all. We are strong enough of ourselves without wasting your blood in fighting our battles. The English, knowing this, have always

been suing to the Indians to help them fight. We do not wish you to take up the hatchet. We love and esteem you. We wish you to multiply and be strong. The English, on the other hand, wish to set you and us to cutting one another's throats, that when we are dead, they may take all our land.

De Coigne seems to have been eager for his people to reap the benefits of civilization, and Jefferson was eager to share these benefits with them. The chief had named his son Jefferson and asked for the governor to send schoolmasters, in Jefferson's words, "to educate your son and the sons of your people. We desire above all things, brother, to instruct you in whatever we know ourselves. We wish to learn you all our arts and to make you wise and wealthy." As soon as peace returned, "we shall be able to send you the best of school-masters, but while the war is raging," this would not be practical. "It shall be done, however, before your son is of an age to receive instruction." This was the kind of high-minded reverie—paternalistic and impractical—in which the philosophical Jefferson delighted and hoped to have more time for once he left office. But that would have to wait.

Jefferson could be patient when he wanted to be, and on the subject of slavery, he was willing to bide his time. He was one of those revolutionaries who expressed his disapproval of the institution that was, he decided, a "hideous evil." Over time, however, he concluded that slavery's abolition would have to be left to a later generation. It would await the "ripening" of public opinion, which during his lifetime had not yet occurred; toward the end of his life, Jefferson readily admitted that he had given up hope that even the generation assuming power then lacked the will—and a way—to put an end to slavery.

Born and raised in a slaveholding society, Jefferson was one of its most privileged beneficiaries. His father and mother both inherited slaves, and his wife's dowry—in addition to thousands of acres of land—consisted of 132 more of these unfortunate people. He bought and sold slaves and owned, at any one time, some 200 of them. Ironies abound. As a student at the College of William & Mary, profoundly influenced by the "rights of man" ideals of the Enlightenment, Jefferson nonetheless had a personal servant, an enslaved man named Jupiter, who would later become his coachman.

In 1768, as a member of the Virginia House of Burgesses, he drafted a plan for the voluntary manumission of slaves by their owners—illegal at that time—which received almost no support from his fellow legislators; unfortunately, the proposal's text has been lost. Six years later, in his "Summary View of the Rights of British America," published in the colonies as well as in England (but also rejected by the Virginia legislators), Jefferson made the case for independence. He also took the opportunity to blame the British for bringing slavery to America in the first place—and for preventing their subjects on this side of the Atlantic from abolishing the institution, which was, he claimed, "the great object of desire in these colonies."

His argument was ingenious as well as eloquently stated. For more than a century, he argued, the Royal African Company—Charles II was a principal stockholder—had shipped more than a million African people to America, profiting from their sale. On top of that, Jefferson argued, George III had repeatedly rejected measures passed by a number of colonial assemblies that would impose stiff—possibly prohibitive—duties on the importation of enslaved Africans. The king's Privy Council had disallowed these duties because, Jefferson wrote, they would cut into "a considerable article of British commerce." Jefferson implied that the imposition of these duties was rooted in the colonists' desire to end the "detestable" institution of slavery. Perhaps there was some truth to this; it was also true, however, that the colonial assemblies wanted to increase their own take from the slave trade. This Jefferson did not mention.

Although his "Summary View" was rejected by the Virginia House of Burgesses, it is now seen—as it was by John Adams and the other members of the Second Continental Congress who assigned the first draft to Jefferson—as a run-up to the Declaration of Independence. That ringing manifesto, drafted two years after the "Summary View," was, in Adams's words, a "vehement philippic against Negro slavery." Here too Jefferson blamed the British, again basing his argument on their prohibition against the colonies' taxing the slave trade. Finding these passages needlessly divisive and inflammatory, Congress deleted them.

A few weeks after the Declaration was adopted, Jefferson returned to Virginia and, as a member of the House of Burgesses, served on a committee to recommend revisions to state laws enacted under British subjugation. He and his fellow committee members hoped to recommend a provision for emancipating the slaves, albeit one that would not take effect for several generations. Upon emancipation, the formerly enslaved would be escorted out of the country. Even this was unacceptable to the Virginia legislators; they were, Jefferson concluded, insufficiently "refined" to adopt even this plan, which was also abandoned.

Many years later, after he had served two terms as the now-independent nation's third president, Jefferson reflected on his generation's failure to do anything about abolishing slavery or even ameliorating the harsh conditions of the enslaved. In correspondence with a young and ardent abolitionist, he confessed that it was a "mortal reproach" to his cohorts that they had done so little about slavery, concluding much earlier in life that "nothing was to be hoped" from his own generation. The institution was so deeply embedded in the culture that Virginians considered Black people "as legitimate subjects of property as their horses or cattle," and anyone who suggested otherwise was "denounced as any enemy to his country." Such a person would be "treated with the grossest indecorum," a matter of some significance to a dignified gentleman like Jefferson.

He had "always hoped," Jefferson told his young correspondent, "that the younger generation, receiving their early impressions after the flame of liberty had been kindled in every breast, and had become as it were the vital spirit of every American; that the generous temperament of youth [would have] sympathized with oppression wherever found, and proved their love of liberty beyond their own share of it." While that had not happened, Jefferson nevertheless remained confident that "the hour of emancipation is advancing on the march of time," either by "the generous energy of our own minds, or by the bloody" way shown in the French colony of Saint-Domingue, where, in 1804, the slaves had thrown off their oppressors. Until such time, Jefferson wrote, "we should endeavor, with those whom fortune has thrown on our hands, to feed and clothe them well, protect them from ill usage, require such reasonable labor only as is performed voluntarily by freeman, and be led to no repugnancies to abdicate them, and our duties to them."

In 1821, five years before his death, Jefferson again expressed his belief that emancipation was in some sense inevitable. "Nothing is more certainly written in the book of fate that [the slaves] are to be free," he wrote, but then added a chilling note to that optimistic prediction. "Nor is it less certain," he continued, "that the two races, equally free, cannot live [under] the same government. Nature, habit, opinion has drawn indelible lines of distinction between them." Acting individually, the states could "direct the process of emancipation and deportation peaceably and in such slow degree as that the evil will wear off insensibly," as "free white laborers" replaced the formerly enslaved.

Later that same month, in correspondence with Adams, Jefferson shuddered at what might happen in states "afflicted with this unfortunate population." "Are our slaves to be presented with freedom and a dagger?"

Emancipation was coming, but retribution, too, might be on the horizon. This seemingly endless war with the British was bad enough. A race war between the newly emancipated and their former owners was too awful to contemplate.

CHAPTER TWENTY-EIGHT

"British Horse Came to Monticello"

For most of his term as governor, Jefferson had been able to avoid acting as a military dictator, which is a role other men might covet. And
for the most part, the British had left Virginia alone. Back in January
1776, in a futile attempt to crush the rebellion in its crib, they had
burned Norfolk, the state's largest city at the time, but just six months
later, Lord Dunmore, the last royal governor, had hightailed it back
to England. Three years after that, by which time Jefferson had succeeded Patrick Henry as governor, the British came back to Virginia
with a vengeance. In December 1780, shortly after his plot to hand
over West Point to the British was revealed, Benedict Arnold—now
a British officer himself—sailed from New York with two thousand
troops and established a base at Portsmouth. Then, in the first week of
January, Arnold marched into a virtually defenseless Richmond, which
had replaced Williamsburg as the capital, and set it ablaze. With the
support of loyalists, Arnold and his troops demolished the ironworks
just across the James River, in hopes of depriving Greene's army farther
south of artillery, and then headed back to Portsmouth, burning plantations and carrying off slaves on their return.

That same week, General William Phillips, sent from New York
by Sir Henry Clinton, arrived at Portsmouth to reinforce Arnold with
another two thousand soldiers, doubling their number in Virginia. Well
aware of how vulnerable his native state was, Washington responded by
sending the Marquis de Lafayette to the South with about nine hundred

Continentals. Once he arrived, Lafayette was joined by about fifteen hundred Virginia militiamen—which was all that the state managed to muster—most of whom were utterly untested in battle. At this point, just two weeks before Jefferson was to retire as governor, things seemed to be shaping up to Lord Cornwallis's liking.

For months, Cornwallis had been pressing Clinton to send more of his forces to Virginia, which he hoped to make "the seat of war, even (if necessary) at the expense of abandoning New York. Until Virginia is in a manner subdued," Cornwallis argued, "our hold on the Carolinas must be difficult if not precarious." The produce of Virginia's plantations would feed the men, and moving armies around the state would be less difficult than it was in the Carolinas. As he had seen his increasingly isolated and poorly provisioned interior posts falling, one after another, Cornwallis had concluded that the shallow creeks and streams that cut through the Carolinas presented a decided advantage to the rebels defending against invasion. But he had also come to believe that Virginia, with its deep and broad waterways, gave the British the edge. "The rivers in Virginia are advantageous to an invading army," he told Clinton, while the Carolinas, precisely because the region was so spiderwebbed with what were rivers in name only, presented a "total want of interior navigation." This might be so, but Clinton, who was not ready to give up New York on a gamble elsewhere, would not budge.

When Clinton refused to do more than send Arnold and Phillips to the South, Cornwallis had simply defied his superior's wishes. In April, he set off from Wilmington, North Carolina, where he had rested and resupplied his army, and marched north, abandoning the Carolinas. By mid-May, he and his men had reached Petersburg, about twenty-five miles below Richmond. There, when Cornwallis's men were added to those under Phillips, who had taken over from Arnold, the British forces in Virginia numbered 7,200. This greatly exceeded Lafayette's small army; at its peak, when Anthony Wayne arrived with one thousand men, Lafayette would have at most 5,200, fewer than half of them Continental regulars.

By early summer of 1781, five years had passed since, as a member of the Continental Congress, Jefferson had written the Declaration of Independence. Its confidently defiant language might seem, to anyone following the war with any objectivity, a trifle premature. Yes, Greene's army in the South, with Marion and Lee and the others, had forced the British to evacuate their smaller forts in the backcountry and were being driven back toward the coast. But the enemy still held Charles Town and Savannah, and up north, while Philadelphia and Boston had been reclaimed, the redcoats continued to occupy New York. General Washington, stationed outside the town, had been unable to lure Clinton into a major engagement and, assuming he would win, retake New York.

When one thousand of Wayne's men had mutinied at Morristown, New Jersey, the previous January, just how bad conditions had gotten became common knowledge. The soldiers wanted to be paid and they wanted to be better housed, and their complaint, they insisted, was not with their officers, or with Washington, but with the toothless government in Philadelphia that was supposed to be supplying such necessities. And it wasn't only the soldiers who were suffering. In the South, once the action had shifted, the ravages of war were obvious almost everywhere you looked. Towns that had been bustling with business before the war had been reduced to smoking ruins. Bridges over the rivers that cut through the countryside had been demolished, preventing the enemy from crossing from one side to another, but also made it impossible for civilians to do so. On farms, fences had been torn down to be used as firewood, and the horses, cattle, sheep, and hogs that they had once confined had been taken away by passing armies or slaughtered on the spot. Fields lay fallow, and farms produced very little food; the owners whose farms were operating either found their corn, wheat, cattle, or hogs taken by passing troops or paid for with worthless promissory notes. On the big plantations, slaves who worked the fields had either gone over to the British or otherwise wandered off. Farmhouses, also commandeered by passing armies, had been plundered of their furnishings, and sometimes burned, just as churches had been.

Neighbors who had been friends and, sometimes, in-laws were now at war with one another. Widows and fatherless children wandered on country lanes, carrying their few belongings with them. Sickness and disease, rampant among soldiers and on prison ships, quickly spread to noncombatants. Commerce had come to a standstill, inflation was rampant, and currencies had lost their value. Civil order, in some states, had broken down altogether, and the Congress—what there was of a national government—was effectively bankrupt, getting by on loans from France, as dependent on this foreign country for money as the army was for supplies. Some armaments were being produced at iron-works in Virginia and carried by wagon into the Carolinas, and the British were determined to put a stop to that—to both their production and their movement. It was Virginia and Virginia alone that Cornwallis had come to believe was sustaining the rebel army in the Carolinas by supplying not only its food but its armaments and clothing, too.

Lafayette had no illusions about his ability to beat Cornwallis out-right and, considering the risk, decided that Richmond wasn't worth a major engagement. Almost everything of value, including military stores, had either been taken elsewhere or destroyed the first time the British ransacked the town. "I Don't believe it would Be prudent to Expose the troops for the Sake of a few Houses, most of which are empty," Lafayette reported to Washington in late May. Were Lafayette to attack Cornwallis at this point, he would "be Cut to pieces, the Mili-tia dispersed, and the Arms lost." But if he avoided any engagement, Virginians would conclude that he had given up altogether, which would demoralize the people, discourage enlistment, and result in trade and other forms of cooperation with the enemy.

Lafayette settled on a third option, which Greene had chosen months earlier. Lafayette was "determined to [skirmish], but not to Engage too far," and by all means to avoid tangling with the redcoats' increasingly formidable mounted troops, which had improved a great deal as they commandeered horses from James River plantations. The militia, Lafayette told Washington, fear those horses "like they would so many wild Beasts." Until Wayne arrived with his Pennsylvanians, Lafayette said, "I am not Strong enough even to get Beaten."

By late spring, as Richmond's townspeople resigned themselves to another attack, state legislators and other government officials rode away, agreeing to meet later in Charlottesville. There, in June, the Vir-ginia House of Delegates would choose another governor, and Jefferson would have done his duty. Encouraged by that thought, he packed up his ailing wife and their young daughters, sending them from Rich-mond to friends' plantations farther west. He would join them at Pop-lar Forest, a farm he owned almost 120 miles west of the capital at Richmond. When the immediate danger seemed to have passed, Jef-ferson brought his family back to Monticello, to wait for the legislators to arrive. His political enemies found his departure from Richmond and subsequent movements a rich source for satire. A sister-in-law of

Monticello, East Front. Photograph by William Rhodes, 1870–80

John Marshall's, who was no admirer of Jefferson's, could not contain her amusement. "Such terror and confusion you have no idea of," she wrote. "Governor, Council, everybody scampering." Nothing is "more laughable," she went on, "than the accounts we have of our illustrious Governor, who they say, took neither rest nor food for man or horse till he reached" Monticello.

This was unfair. Jefferson was not the kind of man to panic, and there is no evidence that he did so when he returned to Monticello. He had played host to a few members of Virginia's General Assembly on June 20, and there is no evidence of undue agitation the next morning when, well before sunup, he had a visitor who, by every indication, really was alarmed. This was John Jouett, known as Jack, a strapping twenty-six-year-old captain in the Virginia militia whose father ran the Swan, a tavern down in Charlottesville. Jouett had just ridden forty miles to get to Monticello, and he had news that would have alarmed less self-possessed men than the governor. Some hours earlier, Jouett told Jefferson, he had been at Cuckoo Tavern, in Louisa County, about halfway between Richmond and Charlottesville and named for its decorative clock. While there, Tarleton and 250 men on horseback rode up the lane and pulled to a halt. Because Jouett was not in uniform (militiamen rarely had them), he could listen and learn what Tarleton was doing in the area and take appropriate action.

Ordered west by Cornwallis, Tarleton was headed for Charlottesville, destroying enemy supplies along the way. Once his men had entered the temporary—and virtually defenseless—capital, they were to round up any state officials they could surprise and take them prisoner. While they carried out their orders, a detachment under Colonel John Graves Simcoe would raid and destroy military supplies at a depot at Point of Fork, about thirty-five miles southeast of Charlottesville, where two smaller rivers joined to form the James. Cornwallis, meanwhile, was headed west with Simcoe, and would make camp at Elkhill, a plantation Jefferson owned not far from Point of Fork. When Tarleton was approaching Charlottesville, yet another detachment, this under Captain Kenneth McLeod, was to ride up the mountain to Monticello, hoping to bag Jefferson himself.

How much of this Jouett knew is impossible to determine, but he knew enough to set off on his own to warn Jefferson and any legislators he could reach. He would ride to Monticello first, then into Charlottesville, and he enjoyed several advantages over Tarleton. Jouett was rested; Tarleton had driven his men hard, covering seventy miles in a day. Jouett was alone, too, and because he had grown up in this part of Virginia, he knew his way through the woods, even at night. Once Tarleton's troops were asleep, Jouett climbed into the saddle and set off "on the best and fleetest nag in seven counties," as local legend has it, and "the scars made on his face by the lashing branches of the undergrowth [would remain] with him all his life." When he arrived at Monticello and—more of the legend—Jefferson refreshed his exhausted guest "with old Madeira," Virginia's Paul Revere then galloped back down the mountain and into town to rouse the sleeping legislators.

Jouett made better time than Tarleton, but the Green Dragoon's efforts were not wholly in vain. Bloody Ban, it is said, allowed his weary horsemen to rest for three hours, and they were back in the saddle around 2 a.m. By one account, they stopped at Castle Hill, a few miles outside of Charlottesville, where, according to Dumas Malone's six-volume Jefferson biography, Tarleton "partook of a generous breakfast." Riding on, they captured and torched twelve wagons loaded with provisions for Greene's army. At the ford of the Rivanna River, they brushed by the few guards stationed there and demolished supplies of flintlocks and gunpowder, then headed into town. Somewhere along the way, they captured a few legislators and a congressman visiting from North Carolina.

The detachment under Captain McLeod, meanwhile, rode up the mountain intending to capture Jefferson, but Jouett, of course, had gotten there first. Warned that enemy troops were on the way, Jefferson prepared to send his family to a neighbor's plantation. Here, too, it is difficult to separate the facts from the legends that have been told about this eventful morning. But in her book, *The Domestic Life of Thomas Jefferson*, Sarah N. Randolph, one of his great-granddaughters, reports that Jefferson spent the morning "quietly at home collecting his most valuable papers," departing Monticello only when, using his telescope, he could see that Charlottesville's streets were "alive with British." One American soldier who seems to have arrived after Jouett left recalled the governor as "perfectly tranquil and undisturbed" as he packed his belongings. Once that was done, Jefferson rode off to meet his family, whom he joined for dinner at Blenheim, the plantation of Colonel Edward Carter, a family friend who had represented Albemarle County in the Virginia legislature.

Just after Jefferson left, McLeod and his men arrived, finding Monticello in the care of Martin Hemings, the butler, and the governor gone. Unable to fulfill their mission to capture Jefferson, McLeod and his men rode back down the mountain. Tarleton, who fancied himself a gentleman as well as a soldier, had instructed his men to leave the house and its furnishings as they found them, and they complied. Jefferson's only comment in his memorandum book was a one-line entry, suggesting his unflappable nature. For June 4, 1781, he wrote: "British horse came to Monticello."

A new governor was not chosen until June 12, when enough members of the Virginia legislature to form a quorum met in Staunton, another forty miles west of Charlottesville, in the Shenandoah Valley. Jefferson had acted as governor after his term had officially expired, and he was greatly relieved when the job was turned over to Thomas Nelson Jr. The ranking officer of the state militia, Nelson was far more willing than Jefferson to exercise powers granted to him by the legislature, which bordered on those of a military dictator. (Jefferson promised his wife "that he would never again leave her to accept any office or take part in political life," their great-granddaughter wrote, and he kept his word. Martha Jefferson died in September 1782, and Jefferson did not return to public office for more than a year, when he served in Congress.)

Cornwallis and his troops were at Jefferson's Elkhill for ten days. They might have stayed longer, but upon receiving word that Wayne had linked up with Lafayette, Cornwallis decided to head back east, toward Richmond and then Williamsburg and the coast. When Jefferson next saw the farm, he realized that Cornwallis had not exercised the gentlemanly restraint Tarleton's men had exhibited at Monticello.

Cornwallis "destroyed all my growing crops of corn and tobacco," Jefferson reported, and

> burned all my barns containing the same articles of the last year, having taken what corn he wanted; he used, as was to be expected, all my stock of cattle, sheep, and hogs, for the sustenance of his army, and carried off all the horses capable of service; of those too young for service, he cut their throats; and he burned all the fences on the plantation, so as to render it an absolute waste.

Cornwallis also left with thirty slaves, and about their departure Jefferson had mixed feelings. "Had this been to give them freedom he would have done right," Jefferson said, "but it was to consign them to inevitable death from the small-pox and putrid fever then raging in his camp. This I knew afterwards to be the fate of twenty-seven of them." These included Sam, nine years old, "who went off with the British & died," and Lucy, another child who "returned & died of the camp fever."

"History will never relate the horrors committed by the British army in the Southern States of America," Jefferson wrote. "They raged in Virginia six months only, from the middle of April to the middle of October, 1781, when they were all taken prisoners; and I give you a faithful specimen of their transactions for ten days of that time, and on one spot only."

CHAPTER TWENTY-NINE

"No Place So Proper as York Town"

For months, General Washington had persisted in his determination to force a decisive action in New York, while the crisis in Virginia deepened. The British had steadily shifted their attention from New York to Virginia, building up their troop strength there and preparing to receive more reinforcements by sea. Cornwallis had told Sir Henry Clinton that he intended to find a "proper harbour" from which he could be resupplied and had settled on Yorktown. Clinton approved of the choice, well before Cornwallis settled on it. "I know of no place so proper as York Town if it could be taken possession of, fortified, and garrisoned with 1000 men," he told Lord George Germain back in the spring. From Yorktown, with Gloucester Point across the river and Portsmouth nearby, "our cruisers might command the waters of the Chesapeak."

In time, Washington began to understand the opportunities offered by the enemy's concentration of forces in his own native state. Under the right conditions, they could be trapped. If the French fleet now in the West Indies could be induced to block off the harbor from the British, Yorktown could be surrounded, and the main British army in the South could be destroyed. In early June, while Washington was still fixated on New York, the Comte de Rochambeau, commander of the French army in North America, informed Washington that Admiral de Grasse, then in the West Indies, had agreed to come north by summer's end, and, after some deliberation, Washington and Rochambeau settled on a plan. In July, the two allied armies met near White Plains, some twenty-five miles north of New York City, where a French officer was struck by the American soldiers' "destitution. The men were without uniforms and covered with rags; most of them were barefoot. They were of all sizes, down to children who could not have been over fourteen." The notable exception, one of Rochambeau's aides observed, was the Rhode Island battalion that included Black soldiers. They were "the most neatly dressed, the best under arms, and the most precise in its maneuvers."

In mid-August, Washington learned that de Grasse was indeed headed to Virginia, and not New York, as the American commander in chief had hoped, with twenty-seven warships and 3,200 men. De Grasse's fleet could stay until mid-October at the latest, he said, so Washington and Rochambeau should "have every thing in the most perfect readiness to commence our operations" the moment the French fleet arrived. In effect, Washington's decision had been made for him. "Matters having now come to a crisis," Washington wrote in his diary, he "was obliged . . . to give up all idea of attacking New York," and head south. He and Rochambeau had only two months to march their armies—seven thousand strong—more than four hundred miles. They set off for Virginia on August 18.

Passing through Philadelphia in early September—the crowds were thrilled by the French army's splendid uniforms—Washington received the news that de Grasse had arrived in Chesapeake Bay. Had the American commander in chief known what else was taking place that day he would have been even more encouraged. In a two-and-a-half-hour battle at sea, the French under de Grasse were driving off a British fleet on its way to help their army in America. Battered and in need of repairs, the British fleet abandoned the Chesapeake altogether and hobbled back to New York, leaving Cornwallis to fend for himself.

It had been six years since Washington had seen his beloved Mount Vernon, but he got to spend four days there on his way to Yorktown. The house, outbuildings, grounds, and farms had suffered in his absence. A great deal of work would have to be done—when the war ended, and he could at last come home—to restore it to the condition it had been in when he left to take command of Continental forces in 1775. Even so, he treated Rochambeau and their party to a "princely entertainment," according to one of Washington's aides, and made the most of a tense situation. That Mount Vernon had not been burned to the ground, like some plantations along the Potomac, was remarkable.

In April, the HMS *Savage,* a British frigate with sixteen guns, slipped up the Potomac from Alexandria, Virginia, torching mansions on both sides of the river, and paused at Mount Vernon. Upon its arrival, nearly twenty of Mount Vernon's slaves escaped to the ship, whose captain then sent a boat to its docks, demanding provisions. Lund Washington, a cousin left to look after the property when the general was away, initially refused. The *Savage* pulled closer to the riverbank, which he interpreted as a threat to bombard the house, prompting a more hospitable response. Lund boarded the British ship with "a small present of poultry," which was followed by "sheep, hogs, and an abundant supply of other articles," according to the account left by the Marquis de Chastellux, a Frenchman then traveling in Virginia, who appears to have heard the story from Lafayette. The offer of these provisions, Lund hoped, would spare the farm any further losses, and possibly secure the return of the slaves.

Lund reported the news in a letter to Washington that, unfortunately, has never been found. Washington seems to have known only Lund's side of the story until early May, when Lafayette, clearly alarmed, offered what was no doubt a less generous account of the episode. What Lund had done, acting as the general's agent and complying with the enemy's request, would "certainly Have a Bad effect," Lafayette said, and was in sharp contrast to the "Spirited Answers" from neighbors whose houses had been burned.

General Washington exercised restraint in his response to his cousin. He was a "little sorry" for the losses he had sustained, he wrote, but it would have been "less painful [to] have heard, that in consequence of your non-compliance with their request, they had burnt my House, and laid the Plantation in ruins." It was bad enough that Lund, acting in his behalf, had even communicated with the enemy, "making a voluntary offer of refreshment to them," hoping "to prevent a conflagration." But "to go on board their Vessels—carry them refreshments—commune with a parcel of plundering Scoundrels—and request a favor by asking the surrender of my Negroes, was exceedingly ill-judged," and might well set a precedent for other professed patriots to do the same. What would not have surprised him, Washington wrote to his cousin, was "the loss of all my Negroes, [and] the destruction of my Houses." For that, he said, "I am prepared." But to cooperate with the enemy as Lund had done, no matter how well intentioned, surprised and appalled the general.

Such an act was not only shameful. The commander in chief also believed it increased the likelihood that the entire war might be lost, and that, as Washington made his way South, remained a real possibility. Battles were still being fought, and the outcomes were not all encouraging. That summer, as Cornwallis made his way east, Lafayette had followed at a safe distance, the two armies and their detachments engaging in a series of moves and countermoves, with intermittent raids and skirmishes. Lafayette was content to harass the British, but when facing an opportunity to strike a more decisive blow, he would take it. By early July, the British en route to Yorktown had reached the James River. Anthony Wayne with his Pennsylvania Continentals, leading the advance of Lafayette's forces, was to wait until most (but not all) of Cornwallis's forces had splashed across the river and then attack its rear. Wayne's men slogged through a quarter mile of marshland at Green Spring Plantation in James City County, then charged, killing three British guards in rapid succession.

What happened next, however, was a complete shock to the Continentals. In the late afternoon, Cornwallis counterattacked, and it became clear almost immediately that most of the British soldiers did not in fact cross the river but had been concealed in the woods. A trap had been set. Almost the whole of Cornwallis's force—seven thousand men compared to Wayne's nine hundred—was in the fight, and a general engagement, which is precisely what Lafayette had been determined to avoid, was taking place. Vastly outnumbered and facing annihilation, Wayne's men charged the numerically superior enemy, which—in a remarkable turnabout—threw the shocked British soldiers into near-chaotic confusion. By this time, it was almost sundown, which Cornwallis told Clinton prevented further action and allowed the Continentals to get away, with minimal casualties. Wayne lost about fifty men in the battle, compared to seventy-five for the British. Had it not been so late in the day, Cornwallis claimed, he could have obliterated Wayne's men, and Light Horse Harry Lee agreed. "One hour more of daylight," the latter wrote, would have "produced the most disastrous

Battle of Eutaw Springs, 8 September 1781.
Engraving from a painting by Alonzo Chappel, 1868

conclusions." Lafayette's army, while weakened, continued to make its way east. The action at Green Spring was the last significant land battle in Virginia before the siege of Yorktown. This would not be the case, however, in the Carolinas.

By the end of the summer, Greene had marched his three thousand men from their camp into the High Hills to the village of Eutaw Springs, some sixty miles northwest of Charles Town, where about an equal number of the enemy were camped. Greene had taken a circuitous route through what Lieutenant Colonel Alexander Stewart, commanding the British forces, called the "by-paths and passes through the different swamps," breaking down Stewart's intelligence system completely and managing to arrive without being detected. On September 8, Greene, with Lee, Marion, Andrew Pickens, William Washington, and Otho Holland Williams at his side, had gotten within four miles of Stewart's camp and decided to force the issue.

In what would become known as the Battle of Eutaw Springs, Greene then positioned his troops in the formation that had proved so effective at Cowpens and Guilford Courthouse. The least experienced South Carolina militia and state troops formed the first line, and behind it were Greene's own Continental regulars, although some of these men had never faced enemy fire (or bayonet), and some Carolina militia under Pickens and Marion. Greene positioned Lee's Legion on the right flank, with cavalry under William Washington in reserve. They moved through the woods until the British skirmishers detected their arrival. After an exchange of artillery fire that Williams called "bloody and obstinate," a few shots were exchanged, and when Greene ordered his men to advance, a "most tremendous fire began on both sides from right to left." His militia performed better than it ever had, unleashing seventeen rounds, holding their ground with a resolution that, their commander said, "would have graced the veterans of the great King of Prussia."

For a time, things were going well for Greene's army. They chased the British and their loyalist allies back to their camp just outside the town. At that point, however, things quickly fell apart. Racing ahead—with too few officers left to instill any order whatever—Greene's men entered the enemy's abandoned camp and began to celebrate. "The victory was now deemed certain," Williams would write, "but many joined in the shouts of victory who were still destined to bleed." A great number of those celebrants helped themselves to the provisions left behind in Stewart's camp and—Williams again—they "fastened themselves upon the liquors," and quickly became "utterly unmanageable." The result was "irretrievable confusion." The British, who were not done, managed to stop the American advance, and with ammunition running low, Greene ordered a general retreat.

The battle, while indecisive in that both sides claimed victory, was not without significance. By retreating, Greene of course abandoned the field to the enemy. But once again he had inflicted horrendous losses on the British, who were finding it increasingly difficult to replace the soldiers who had been killed, wounded, or taken prisoner. While reports filed by the two commanders disagree, military historians have concluded that Greene lost some 500 of the 2,200 men he sent into battle that day; estimates of the size of Stewart's force range from 1,800 to 2,000, and nearly 700 of these were casualties, which was the highest percentage suffered by any force on either side in the entire war. The makeup of the combatants is revealing, too. Deserters from both sides fought against each other at Eutaw Springs, leading Greene to say that this late in the war, "we fought the enemy with British soldiers and they fought us with those of America." Once again, Greene had won by losing. He was "indefatigable in collecting troops, and leading them to be defeated," a British officer said in befuddled exasperation. "The more he is beaten, the farther he advances in the end."

Rainfall the day after the battle prevented a resumption of hostilities, and Stewart led what was left of his battered army on a forlorn march back toward Monck's Corner, twenty-five miles closer to Charles Town. Their departure from Eutaw Springs meant that the British had completely lost their grip on the Carolina interior. They still held Charles Town, but that was about it.

The war's outcome would be decided, it seemed increasingly likely, in Virginia, where Washington was assembling the largest army to be brought to bear against the enemy since the war began. Under his command, with Rochambeau answering to Washington, would be more than 17,000 men, slightly more than half of whom were Americans; the rest were French. De Grasse supplied 3,300 and Lafayette and Wayne already had 5,200 in Virginia. Cornwallis, by contrast, had only about eight thousand men at Yorktown, where he was still hoping to be reinforced by sea. Washington would also be assisted by Lafayette and Baron von Steuben as well as Benjamin Lincoln, who had been captured and then exchanged when Charles Town fell.

The commander in chief arrived at Yorktown on September 14, "without any pomp or parade, attended only by a few horsemen and his own servants," St. George Tucker told his wife. To Tucker's "great surprise," Washington "recognized my features and spoke to me immediately by name." Lafayette, fresh from the action at Green Spring, rode up a few moments later and "clasped the General in his arms and embraced him with an ardor not easily described." Everything about the scene filled Tucker with hope. "Cornwallis," Tucker wrote, "may now tremble for his fate, for nothing but some extraordinary imposition of his guardian angels seems capable of saving him and his whole army from captivity."

CHAPTER THIRTY

"A Solemn Stillness"

While British and American forces began to converge on Yorktown, John Laurens was somewhere in the Atlantic, sailing from Brest to Boston with a convoy of money and supplies sent by the French government. When his work in Boston was done, he hoped to ride on to Williamsburg himself and from there—like so many others—to Yorktown.

Laurens was the son of Henry Laurens, the former president of the Continental Congress who, in October of the previous year, had been captured by the British on a diplomatic mission of his own. En route to negotiate a commercial treaty with the Dutch Republic, Henry had been held on suspicion of high treason and locked up in the Tower of London, where, as his son made his way back home, Henry remained.

John Laurens at twenty-six had seen more of the world than almost any of his countrymen. He had also packed more into his young life than the great majority of them could ever imagine. From sixteen to twenty-two, he had lived and studied in London and then, finding Oxford and Cambridge, taken together, to be nothing but "a School for Licentiousness and Debauchery," he moved to Geneva, which had been home to Calvin, Rousseau, and Voltaire. This high-minded young man found "the delightful City" much more to his liking. But when his father prevailed on him to prepare for a career—John refused to become a merchant—he returned with some reluctance to study law at London's Middle Temple. He entertained the idea of becoming a clergyman, but, following the events back in America with keen interest, he also found this unacceptable, too. He might have entered the clergy, he said, "if this did not preclude me from bearing Arms in Defense of my Country (for I can't read with Indifference the valiant acts of those, whose prudent Conduct and admirable Bravery have rescued the Liberties of their Countrymen, and deprived their Enemies of power to do them Hurt)."

When John Laurens attended the debates in Parliament and followed Britain's plans for taxing the colonies, he was infuriated by what he heard. If Parliament could do what it was preparing to do, he wrote, "we are but Slaves." Slavery was a subject Laurens took more seriously than many of his contemporaries, including those who professed to want to see it abolished. His father owned some three hundred slaves but claimed to friends and family that he disapproved of the institution. Like Jefferson and others who were influenced by the ideals of the Enlightenment, Henry Laurens found the slave trade especially repugnant. Also like Jefferson, he blamed the British for introducing slavery to its Atlantic colonies and perpetuating the slave trade. He also blamed "our Northern neighbors," who profited by the buying and selling of other human beings, despite having "censured and condemned" the practice. Henry Laurens had bought and sold people, too, until the early 1760s, when a guilty conscience seems to have trumped his desire for profit.

Mostly he kept his disapproval of slavery and the slave trade to himself, however, out of concern, apparently, for his reputation among his fellow slaveholders. In an episode difficult for us to understand today, he was once accused publicly by a political enemy of having gotten out of the slave trade from a supposed "goodness of heart." This was untrue and unfair, Laurens claimed. He had done so for business reasons only—that, in the words of his biographer, "he had no partner, business was too heavy, and he was not [at that time] seeking to embrace every gainful occupation." The "statement that he had done so from motives of goodness," moreover, "was a falsehood."

"You know, my dear son," he told John, "I abhor slavery." He wished the southern economy was not constituted as it was, but, he asked, "what can individuals do?" His other children stood to inherit the slaves, and what would they say "if I deprive them of so much estate?" It was his fervent hope that slavery would be abolished "at a future date," though he offered no plan by which that could be made to happen. Until that day came, he would content himself with ameliorating the conditions of the slaves that he owned, wishing "to bring my poor blacks to a level with the happiest peasants to be found in Europe." He opposed the separation of families, which should never be done except "in case of irresistible necessity."

None of this was sufficient for Henry's son. John Laurens was opposed to slavery in principle but also wanted to take practical steps toward its abolition. Arguments for the institution, he said, were "absurd," and ownership of slaves made a mockery of their own high-minded claims about the cause of human liberty. Blacks, too, had a rightful claim to be free, and if slaveholders believed that these unfortunate people lacked the capacity for self-government, the slaveholders had only themselves to blame. "We have sunk the Africans & their descendants below the Standard of Humanity," John said, "and almost rendered them incapable of that Blessing which equal Heaven bestow'd upon us all."

After years of study, John was eager for action—on behalf of South Carolina, and its people, enslaved as well as free. Devoting himself to "the sacred Cause of Liberty," he decided to give up his studies, return to Charles Town, and take up arms against the Crown. Concerned for the safety of his son, Henry Laurens tried to argue him out of it. "You ask me, my Dear Father, what bounds I have set to my desire of serving my Country in the Military Line," John replied. "I answer Glorious Death or the Triumph of the Cause in which I am engaged."

And he would not be dissuaded. Back in the colonies in the summer of 1777, John signed on as an aide-de-camp to General Washington, becoming fast friends with two other young men serving the commander in chief—the Marquis de Lafayette and Alexander Hamilton. But Laurens also bore arms. In his first battle, at Brandywine Creek in September, his comrades were astonished by his bravery. It was "not his fault that he was not killed or wounded," Lafayette observed, since "he did every thing that was necessary to procure one or t'other." After fighting at Germantown, he spent the winter at Valley Forge. There, given Laurens's facility with languages, Baron von Steuben relied on him to help him communicate his instructions to the troops he drilled. At Monmouth the following June, Laurens had his horse shot out from under him, and at the end of the year, defending the honor of General

Washington, which he believed had been besmirched, he fought a duel with former general Charles Lee, wounding his opponent. Hamilton acted as one of Laurens's seconds.

In late 1778 and early 1779, when the British had opened their southern campaign, Laurens proposed raising units of enslaved men, and in return for their service they would receive their freedom. Eager to lead troops himself, John asked his father to turn over his "able bodied Slaves" now, "instead of leaving me a fortune." He would train and provision these men himself, he said, accomplishing a "twofold good" with this project. The experience "would advance those who are unjustly deprived of the Rights of Mankind to a State, which would be a proper Gradation between abject Slavery and perfect Liberty," and prepare them for self-government. They would make excellent soldiers, he argued. After all, they had had from birth "the habit of Subordination almost indelibly impress'd on them." It would be his duty, Laurens continued, "to transform the timid Slave into a firm defender of Liberty and render him worthy to enjoy it himself." (Laurens even designed uniforms for his regiment. They would wear white, "a Color which is easiest kept clean and will form a good Contrast with the Complexion of the Soldier," he wrote.)

John assumed that his father, like most southern slaveholders, would consider the scheme foolhardy, if not dangerous. John was aware that he would have "that monster popular Prejudice open-mouthed against me," he said. Even so, he entertained some hope that his father would see merit in it. "I hope," John wrote, "that my plan will not appear to you the [chimera] of a young man deceived by a false appearance of moral beauty, but a laudable sacrifice of private Interest to Justice and the Public good." Henry did not see it that way at all. If John wanted to raise a regiment, he could simply return to Charles Town and recruit and equip a unit of white men. This would make more sense, since "there is not a Man in America" who would support arming slaves.

Over the eight years of the war, some five thousand to eight thousand Black soldiers had participated, though mainly in noncombatant roles. Many who had expected to bear arms ended up as laborers, waiters, cooks, and other forms of behind-the-lines support staff. This was true even of slaves who—encouraged by the 1775 proclamation of Virginia's royal governor, John Murray Dunmore, offering freedom to slaves—fled their plantations to fight for the British. The first who answered Dunmore's call fell victim to smallpox. An "Ethiopian Regiment" that the governor established was disbanded in 1776. "Dunmore's Proclamation," seen largely as a cynical ploy to wreak havoc in the South, was followed by a similar call issued by Sir Henry Clinton in 1779. All told, an estimated 100,000 slaves left their plantations, either to aid the British or to seek freedom on their own. An exception to the rule was the First Rhode Island Regiment, established in 1778, when the state found itself falling short of its quota of soldiers for the Continental army. The First Rhode Island Regiment served throughout the war, including at the siege of Yorktown.

But some white Americans—though few southerners—did support allowing Blacks into the Continental army, including in combat roles, just as John Laurens proposed. John presented to Congress a broader proposal to raise Black troops, free or enslaved, and, in the spring of 1779, Congress approved it. Congress authorized not just South Carolina but Georgia, too, to raise "three thousand able bodied negroes," who would be commanded by whites; one of these commanders would be Laurens. Under the plan, the owners of slaves who served would be paid one thousand dollars per slave; after the war, those who had served—having turned over their weapons—would receive their freedom and be paid fifty dollars. The final decision, however, was South Carolina's and Georgia's to make. If the plan was approved and executed, a congressman from New Hampshire said, "it will produce the Emancipation of a number of those wretches and lay the foundation for the Abolition of Slavery in America."

Laid before the South Carolina legislature, the proposal "was received with horror by the planters," according to the historian David Ramsay, who served in the legislature at the time. It was promptly rejected. Laurens, elected to the legislature himself, would introduce the proposal in 1779, 1780, and 1782, and it was soundly defeated each time. "White Pride & Avarice," Ramsay wrote in his history of the war, "are great obstacles in the way of Black Liberty."

The rejection of John Laurens's plan was a disappointment, but it could not have come as a shock. Laurens was a man of considerable energy, and his career as a soldier kept him busy. When the war in the South heated up, he fought in the defense of Charles Town, was taken prisoner, and, after six months of captivity in Philadelphia, was released in a general prisoner exchange. That was in November 1780, and the following month, Congress had appointed him as envoy extraordinary to France, where he spent the first months of 1781 working with Benjamin Franklin to obtain additional loans of money and grants of equipment from the friendly French government. Laurens had been reluctant to accept the diplomatic post because he would have preferred to stay in America and fight, and now—after making his report to Congress in Philadelphia—he was on his way south, where he would have that opportunity again.

Before he left Paris, John did what he could to secure his father's release from imprisonment by the British, but his efforts came to nothing. By the time John sailed back to America, Henry Laurens had been locked up for almost a year. He had managed to keep his spirits up during his incarceration, at least in the early days. Over time, however, his health suffered and his spirits sagged. When first delivered to the Tower of London, he was defiant and remained so until his gout and other ailments took their toll. Upon his arrival, he said, he was greeted with the strains of "Yankee Doodle," which "aroused sublime contempt and rather made me cheerful." He was billed for the expenses of his upkeep, including the wages of two guards who watched him day and night, which surprised him. "Whenever I caught a bird in America," he said, "I found a cage and victuals for it." He tried to keep his sense of humor here, too, saying it was almost "enough to provoke me to change my lodgings." He had assumed by now that trying to take money from men without their consent was foolish. Attempts to do so, he said, "have involved this kingdom in a bloody seven years war," and he assumed the Crown "had long since promised to abandon the project."

Somehow, Henry managed to get letters smuggled out of the prison and began to contribute articles to opposition newspapers in London. These articles were unsigned, but, as one member of Lord North's ministry said, they "smelt strong of the Tower." As Henry's biographer, David Duncan Wallace, wrote, for a time he "converted his prison into an outpost in the enemy's country." There were efforts to compromise him, which he found insulting. In February he was asked to sign a statement that, he was told, would prevent his being hanged should the Americans lose the war. He would sign no such statement, he said, that would suggest any treasonous act on his part and contribute "to the dishonor of my children."

Although son John, in Paris, found that he could do nothing for him, Benjamin Franklin took up Henry's cause, as did Edmund Burke. About the time John was returning to America, Burke and Franklin discussed exchanging Laurens for General John Burgoyne, who had been a prisoner since his defeat at Saratoga. Parliament refused, and Laurens remained in the Tower for the duration of the war.

Four days before John Laurens arrived in Williamsburg on September 14, George Washington was already there. Alexander Hamilton was there, too, having been given what Laurens himself coveted, which was a field command. But Washington had other plans for the returning diplomat, making him an aide-de-camp once again. Relying on his knowledge of the French language, Washington put Laurens to work writing dispatches to Admiral de Grasse. This was an important duty, if lacking in glamour. The French admiral had decided to leave only two vessels blocking the entrances and exits at Yorktown and would then sail off to sea with the rest of his ships. But unless de Grasse kept most of the fleet where it was, Cornwallis would surely get away. If de Grasse and his ships remained, Laurens (representing Washington) argued, the British commander would almost certainly be forced to surrender. This

Siege of Yorktown, October 1781.
From *A Pictorial History of the United States*

would "go a great way towards terminating the war, and securing the invaluable objects of it to the Allies."

De Grasse agreed to stay, and on September 28, the allies' armies had marched the thirteen miles from Williamsburg to the outskirts of Yorktown. Once the artillery arrived and the trenches were dug and redoubts constructed, the siege could begin. As the siege lines drew closer to Yorktown, the British opened up with their artillery. On the afternoon of October 9, from positions the British had abandoned, Washington responded. The commander in chief "put the match to the first gun," one of the American soldiers noted, "and a furious discharge of cannon and mortars immediately followed." The bombardment continued into the night. "The scene viewed from the camp now was grand," one of Anthony Wayne's men observed. Shells "from the works of both parties passing high in the air and descending in a curve, each with a long train of fire, exhibited a brilliant spectacle."

The British could find no refuge from the bombardment, "in or out of the town," a Hessian fighting with them said, and the townspeople "fled to the waterside," hiding in shelters along the banks, "but many of them were killed by bursting bombs, with houses utterly destroyed." British casualties mounted rapidly, and Cornwallis, who had made his headquarters in Governor Thomas Nelson's house, was forced to move to the makeshift command center down the hill at the water's edge. "My situation now becomes very critical," he reported to Clinton eight days after the bombardment began. "Experience has shown that our fresh earthen works do not resist their powerful artillery, so that we shall soon be exposed to assault in ruined works, in a bad position, and with weakened numbers. The safety of the place is, therefore so precarious that I cannot recommend that the fleet and army should run great risk in endeavoring to save us," even if that were still possible.

To complete the operation, the British defenses at Redoubts 9 and 10 would have to be taken. To that end, Washington ordered a night assault, and John Laurens—freed from his duties as Washington's amanuensis—would finally get a chance once again to fight. On the last day of September, Colonel Alexander Scammell had been captured while conducting reconnaissance on the enemy's positions, and Washington gave Laurens command of one of Scammell's battalions. The French under Lafayette were to rush Redoubt 9, while four hundred Americans under Hamilton would storm Redoubt 10. Hamilton would

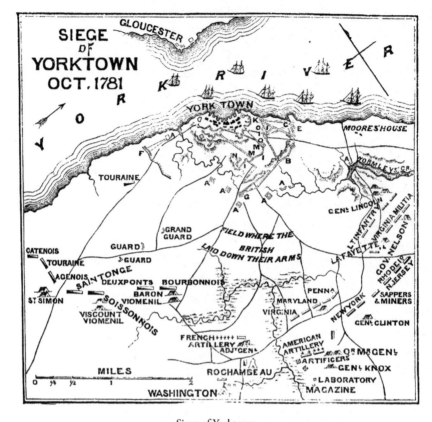

Siege of Yorktown.
Map by S. G. Goodrich, from *A Pictorial History of the United States*

lead the assault, and Laurens, with eighty men under his command, would attack the fort from behind to prevent the enemy from getting away. There were only forty-five British and Hessians inside Redoubt 10, but they were well protected behind a moat, abattis, and a palisade.

Just after dark on October 14, Hamilton's assault force moved out, while Laurens led his men to a position behind the redoubt, opposite where Hamilton's troops would charge. A plan to surprise the redcoats collapsed when British sentries, detecting Hamilton's advance, sounded an alarm. Here too what the Americans hoped would give them an edge came undone. Because they had intended to attack using fixed bayonets only, their muskets were never loaded. When the alarm was sounded, the British inside Redoubt 10 met the attack with an immediate and scalding fire. Hamilton and his men somehow pushed through it, making it over the moat, grappling their way past the punishing spearpoints of the abattis, up the palisades, and into the fort. At about the same moment, Laurens and his troops entered from the back, blocking any withdrawal and capturing Major James Campbell, the redoubt's commander. The assault was over almost before it began, with minimal casualties. Only nine of the Americans lost their lives in the assault, with twenty-five wounded. Eight of the British and Hessians were either killed or wounded; the rest were taken prisoner.

Redoubt 9 fell, too, with slightly more casualties, effectively ending any outcome other than a British surrender. The men with spades and shovels continued their grimy work, with siege lines moving ever closer to the town. The bombardment continued. Cornwallis made one last desperate attempt to escape, getting some of his troops across the river to Gloucester Point, where he had positioned Tarleton and his men, hoping his army could get away by land. A tremendous downpour that

Moore House, Yorktown, Virginia.
Photograph by Wood & Gibson, Alexander Gardner, 1862

night prevented any further movement, and the next night, Cornwallis sent a message to Washington.

"Sir," Cornwallis wrote, "I propose a cessation of hostilities for twenty-four hours, and that two officers may be appointed by each side, to meet at Mr. Moore's house, to settle terms for the surrender of the posts at York and Gloucester." The bombardment now stopped, and, as St. George Tucker told his wife the next day, it "was pleasing to contrast the last night with the preceeding—A solemn stillness prevaild—the night was remarkably clear & the sky decorated with ten thousand stars—numberless Meteors gleaming thro' the Atmosphere afforded a pleasing resemblance to the Bombs which had exhibited a noble Firework the night before, but happily divested of all their Horror."

Washington again called on John Laurens, back from the assault on Redoubt 10, to represent him in the negotiations. Lafayette's brother-in-law, the Viscount de Noailles, would speak for Rochambeau and the French. Laurens and de Noailles met with two representatives of the British at the appointed location on neutral ground along the river. The talks lasted well into the night. Both commanders agreed to most of the terms with minor modifications, but a few Cornwallis had a hard time accepting. Washington insisted, for example, that the British in the forthcoming ceremonies consent to the same humiliations they had inflicted eighteen months earlier on Benjamin Lincoln, Laurens, and all the rest of the defeated garrison at Charles Town when it fell. The defeated troops would march out of Yorktown with their colors cased, with their musicians playing a tune approved by the victors.

At 2 p.m. on Friday, October 19, the defeated British, Hessians, and loyalists—minus Cornwallis—filed out of the town, marching between the lines of the American and French soldiers who had defeated them, "their Drums in Front, beating a slow March, Their Colours furl'd and Cased," Tucker wrote. Then they "grounded their Arms & march'd back again thro' the Army a second Time into the Town. The sight was too pleasing to an American to admit of Description."

Cornwallis, saying he was ill, sent General Charles O'Hara in his place. The officers met, and among the Americans and their allies were men who might have been obscure when the war began but were no longer. There was Washington, of course, and Lafayette and Rochambeau. But there was John Laurens and Anthony Wayne and Baron von Steuben, and Henry Knox, too. And among the other men was one whose face was familiar to some of the British officers and would have been recognized by Cornwallis, had he not been back in his tent.

This was an enslaved man named James, owned by New Kent County, Virginia, farmer William Armistead. Lacking a formal education, unlike Lee or Tarleton, James did not leave written accounts of his life, so what is known about him is sketchy at best. Armistead had served as commissary of military supplies for Virginia, furnishing clothing and other provisions to the Continental army, and would have known some its officers, including, presumably, Lafayette. James, who did not use his owner's last name, is believed to have received Armistead's permission to volunteer with Lafayette's men; for all we know, Armistead offered James to the army. By at least one account, James had heard that in exchange for their service slaves could apply for their freedom, and he asked to serve. In any case, he seems to have been in his early thirties when he went to work as a courier—and eventually as a spy—for Lafayette. James, "at the peril of his life," in Lafayette's words, managed to infiltrate the British camp, where, supposedly working as a servant to Cornwallis, he "industriously collected and more faithfully delivered" intelligence valuable to the Continental army. In late August, citing an unnamed "Honest Friend" and "Servant to Lord Cornwallis" who "Has opportunities to Hear," Lafayette told Washington that Cornwallis was preparing to move his troops toward Yorktown. There's a good chance this "Honest Friend" was James, but we just don't know.

In keeping with the somber ceremonial protocols, O'Hara tried to present his sword to Washington, who declined to accept the offer from his counterpart's second in command, indicating instead that it be given to General Lincoln, who had been put through a comparable humiliation when Charles Town fell. This was done. The British officers "behaved like boys who had been whipped at school," Count Mathieu Dumas observed. "Some bit their lips, some pouted, others cried. Their broad, round-brimmed hats were well adapted to the occasion, hiding those faces they were ashamed to show."

Those "dear ragged Continentals," as Laurens called them, conducted themselves admirably during the ceremonies, despite their shabby clothing. They exhibited "an erect, soldierly air," Dumas said, "and every countenance beamed with satisfaction and joy." And that night, they could finally loosen up. Even the officers, an American colonel said, "could scarcely talk for laughing, and they could scarcely walk for jumping and dancing and singing as they went about." This had been "an illustrious day, my dear friend for our national honor and interests," Laurens wrote. At a dinner that night, a French officer was surprised at the "*sang froid* and gaiety even" of O'Hara and his lieutenants. (At some point after the surrender ceremonies, Cornwallis visited Lafayette's camp, where, upon spotting James, the enslaved man—and spy—from New Kent County, the British general reportedly said, "Ah, you rogue, then you have been playing me a trick all this time.")

"The play, sir, is over," Lafayette wrote to a friend, and a few days later, in Philadelphia, an express rider located Thomas McKean, the president of the Congress, at two in the morning. The messenger carried a letter, the cover of which read, "To be forwarded by night and by day with the utmost dispatch—Lord Cornwallis surrendered the garrison of York to General Washington, the 17th of October." The news did not reach official London until November, when Lord George Germain took a hackney coach to Downing Street to deliver the "disastrous information" to Lord North in person. The prime minister took the news as he "would have taken a ball in his breast," one witness recalled. North paced up and down, flailing his arms about, and, "under emotions of the deepest consternation and distress," cried out, "O God! It is all over!"

CHAPTER THIRTY-ONE

"God Bless You, Gentlemen!"

But the war was not "all over," and Washington was under no illusions that it was. The idea that the American Revolution ended at Yorktown is a myth, and a recently minted one at that. None of the early historians of the war, including William Gordon, John Marshall, David Ramsay, and Mercy Otis Warren—all of whom lived through it—treated Yorktown as decisive in their accounts. They were well aware that the loss of Cornwallis's army was a significant blow to the British, but also that the 7,500 enemy soldiers captured at Yorktown and Gloucester Point were only part of all British forces stationed in the colonies; there were 17,000 still in New York alone. The Continentals had lost about the same number at Charles Town as the British did at Yorktown and still fought on, as Washington expected the British to do after this setback. King George III expressed disappointment over Yorktown but hardly despair. "I have no doubt when men are a little recovered from the shock felt by the bad news, they will find the necessity of carrying on the war," he said, "though the mode of it may require alterations."

Washington was afraid that exaggerating the significance of Cornwallis's surrender would make it more difficult to finish the job and rid America of the British for good. Only ten days after the surrender, still hoping for a major engagement in New York, Washington pressed Congress to move forward with its "preparation for military Operations." He called his victory at Yorktown "an interesting event," but hardly decisive. "My greatest Fear," he wrote, "is that Congress, viewing this stroke in too important a point of Light, may think our Work too nearly closed, and will fall into a State of Languor and Relaxation." Congress responded by asking the states to provide no fewer troops than they had supplied the year before, which they would not do.

Back in the High Hills of Santee, Nathanael Greene got the news of Yorktown on October 27, the same day Washington was pressing Congress not to let down its guard. From Philadelphia, the commander in chief told Greene that he worried that the states, "taking it for granted that Great Britain will no longer support so losing a contest, will relax in their preparations for the next Campaign." Told that the British might be sending thousands of troops to South Carolina, Washington dispatched a thousand of his own men to reinforce Greene.

Eager after Eutaw Springs to push closer to Charles Town, Greene was also appealing to Congress for help. "We cannot march without Shoes," he wrote, "nor can we fight without Ammunition." The High Hills were preferable to fetid swamps for recuperating from illness and injuries but hardly ideal. Scores of "brave fellows, who had bled in the Cause of our Country, have been eat up with maggots & perished inn that miserable situation," he wrote. Others were suffering from malaria and dysentery. Basic provisions for caring for the sick and wounded, he said, "have been exceedingly scarce." Paper money was worthless, so he was relying on barter, and Robert Morris, the government's superintendent of finance, praised the former quartermaster general for his "Genius" in managing to keep the army together at all. Somehow, Morris said, Greene was making do despite "the want of Men, Money, Cloaths, Arms and Supplies." Thomas Paine sent along his encouragement, too. "How you have contrived without money to do what you have done," the author of *The Crisis* wrote, "I have scarcely a conception of." Without "an army, without Means, without anything," Henry Knox told Greene, he had "performed Wonders." If he were not still in the North, the roly-poly chief of artillery told his old friend, "I would fly to you with more rapidity than most fat men."

Greene felt much the same about the aftermath of Yorktown as Washington did. If the Americans "fold our Arms and set our selves down at ease," the British "will rally her force, and come on to a fresh attack." He was determined to get his men ready to meet any such challenge, however difficult that was proving to be. Once, when the Pennsylvanians in his army plotted a mutiny, Greene had the ringleader hanged. "I act with decision," he said. He was aware that the troops suffered and was doing what he could to ease their suffering. But they "had better be quiet." Greene also took steps to keep them from becoming unmanageably morose. With so many of his men dying of malaria, he issued an order to change the way burials were handled. "The general has observed that the custom of beating the *dead march* at Soldiers funerals has a tendency to depress the Spirits of the Sick in camp," it read, and "he is therefore pleased to order that in future this practice be discontinued." ("Pleased" was probably not the best word choice here.)

Then there was this to worry about: loyalist vigilantes were getting active in the backcountry again, and North Carolina militia had struck back with a savagery Greene found counterproductive. Resentment, Greene reminded his countrymen, is an "unsafe guide." Attacking loyalists "indiscriminately" will "drive them to a state [of] desperation," turning "a weak and feeble force" into a "sure and determined enemy." As he had reminded Sumter, it was always better "to forgive than to persecute."

Greene may have been in a generous mood around this time. His wife—the lively twenty-seven-year-old with whom General Washington had enjoyed dancing at Valley Forge—had decided to come south. Greene and his wife had not seen each other since Morristown a year and a half earlier. After weeks of parties in Philadelphia, Caty set off, with Washington promising her husband that he would "strew [her way] with flowers." She did not reach South Carolina until March 1782, but she would remain in the South until the war officially ended. During a separation from Greene, when she stayed with convalescing troops at Kiawah Island, an officer there told him they were all "very much indebted to Mrs. Greene for her vivacity and good humor. She keeps us all in good spirits . . . We laugh, sing and play backgammon." She had fallen ill herself for a time but was recovering well. "Your lady has got back her Block Island complexion," Greene was told, "and looks as she used to." By the time Caty would go back north, after seeing her husband once more, she was pregnant again.

In early November 1781, Greene's army left the High Hills, headed toward Charles Town. On December 1, he led a detachment of some four thousand men, all mounted, against a British garrison at

Dorchester, about fifteen miles northwest of the city. There were more than twice as many men in the garrison than Greene brought with him, but recognizing the general, they assumed his entire army was bearing down on them. After tossing their guns in the Ashley River, the redcoats withdrew into Charles Town. The rest of Greene's army, under Otho Holland Williams, moved on to Round O, between Charles Town and Savannah, the only other British strongholds, blocking communications and the movement of supplies and reinforcements, at least by land. Charles Town was now isolated.

About this time, Greene heard disturbing reports that the British, far from packing it in after Yorktown, were preparing to transfer thousands of troops to the South—some from New York, plus reinforcements from Ireland. It was then, hoping to build up his own troop strength, that Greene made a bold proposal, asking that Black men be allowed into the ranks. Having seen how they performed in battles in the North, he believed that they would be an asset to his army. "The natural strength of this country in point of numbers," Greene told South Carolina Governor John Rutledge, "appears to me to consist much more in the blacks, than the whites," and that "they would make good Soldiers I have not the least doubt." They should be "treated in all respects as other soldiers," and, having served, should receive their freedom. Rutledge was "alarmed" by Greene's proposal, and one South Carolina legislator—expressing a widely held view—distrusted the Rhode Islander's motives: "The northern people, I have observed, regard the condition in which we hold our slaves in a different light from us. I am much deceived indeed," he wrote, "if they do not secretly wish for a general Emancipation, if the present struggle was over."

The other soldier who had pushed for Black men to be allowed into the army was, of course, John Laurens, fresh from negotiating the surrender at Yorktown. Washington, Greene, and the others were eager for the war to end—assuming it would end in victory—but Laurens seemed to feel that his opportunities for military glory were slipping away. He had spent too much of the war as an aide-de-camp to Washington and as a diplomat in France, and too little in battle. Laurens had been pressing Greene for a field command, and when Light Horse Harry retired, Washington granted Laurens his wish, giving him command of Lee's Legion. As Gregory D. Massey writes in *John Laurens and the American Revolution,* he "had lived and prepared for such a moment," which could prove to be "the pinnacle of his military career."

Withdrawn into Charles Town, the British were now making raids into the countryside, to forage for food and, Laurens said, "to plunder and distress the inhabitants." He was determined to put a stop to this practice, even after Greene took measures to restrain him, which included moving the light troops under Laurens's command to the rear of the army. "This was little less than death to Laurens, who wishes to fight much more than I wish he would," Greene told Lee.

Laurens quickly proved to be unpopular with the men of Lee's Legion. Light Horse Harry, who could seem impetuous, had proved himself in ways Laurens had not. Lee was a careful tactician, and his men felt secure under his leadership. Under Laurens, they did not, and they made their feelings known. They have taken "a great dislike to poor Laurens," Greene told Lee, and were "determined to be removed from under his command," which Greene handled with characteristic diplomacy. He put distance between Laurens and the officers who complained by sending their commander with a small detachment on intelligence-gathering missions in the lowcountry, where he was still well regarded. In midsummer, however, when he learned that a British foraging party was heading up the Combahee River from Charles Town, Laurens abandoned his intelligence-gathering duties and, with no authorization, headed their way himself.

Before dawn on August 26, about 150 redcoats had come ashore near Beaufort and established a defensive line, while the others prepared to forage. Outnumbered three to one, Laurens nevertheless chose not to wait for reinforcements, though they were just two miles away and coming on quickly. Laurens ordered his men to charge, the British opened fire, and he was hit. The other troops arrived, "dispirited and fatigued," in time to do little but cover the retreat of Laurens's men. Two men lost their lives in the ill-conceived action. These were Laurens, who died on the ground where he fell, and a member of the cavalry that had come to help him. Nineteen others were wounded, and three were missing, compared to an "inconsiderable loss," of one British soldier dead and seven wounded. Laurens had fallen in what Greene called "a paltry little skirmish," far removed from the heroism he imagined for himself. "I wish his fall had been as glorious as his fate is much to be lamented," Greene told Otho Holland Williams. "The love of military glory made him seek it upon occasions unworthy [of] his rank. This state will feel his loss; and his father will hardly survive it."

Henry Laurens was still in England when he got the news. On

the last day of 1781, he had been released from the Tower of London. Exchanged for Cornwallis, Henry had gone to Bath to recover his health. There he remained "in deep mourning for that brave honest man, that good soldier and good Citizen, that dutiful son and sincere friend, the dear object of my present woe . . . Thank God I *had* such a son," he wrote, "who dared to die for his country." The following November, Henry Laurens received a letter from John Adams in Paris, mentioning "the melancholy Intelligence" of John's death. "I feel for you, more than I can know or ought to express," Adams said. "Our country has lost its most promising Character, in a manner however, that was worthy of her Cause."

This expression of sympathy was not the letter's main purpose, however. Adams was writing to instruct Laurens, who had been appointed by Congress to help negotiate the peace treaty with England, to make his way to Paris "as soon as possible. It would give me the highest Pleasure, and be a constant Support to have your Judgment and Advice upon the great Questions which are under Consideration." (By the time Laurens reached Paris, he found the negotiations "so far advanced" that he could be of little help; still, he tried, offering his advice on fisheries, the treatment of loyalists, and the "carrying away of negroes or other property, which I hope will lay a foundation for a future claim.")

While the surrender at Yorktown did not bring a close to the war, it had doomed Lord North's ministry, in large part because parliamentary support for the war was collapsing. There had always been opposition to the efforts to put down the rebellion in the colonies, which North's government supported. This opposition continued to mount as the war dragged on, and in March 1782, after a vote of no confidence, North resigned. His replacement was Charles Watson-Wentworth, the Second Marquess of Rockingham, whose faction in Parliament—the "Rockingham Whigs," they were called—had argued for some years that the war could be won only at too great a cost to Great Britain. Edmund Burke, the Rockingham Whigs' most eloquent spokesman, had warned that war was not only destructive to the Americans but also to "an empire so great and so distracted as ours." The war in America, after all, was only one of the wars Great Britain was fighting at that time. It was also, arguably, a minor one at that, yet another part of its ongoing struggle with France, which had erupted into war five times in the past century. America could not have forced Cornwallis's surrender—or achieved many of its victories since the French entered on the side of the Americans—without French support, including money, men, arms, and ships. Great Britain was also in a war with Spain over Gibraltar, Minorca, and Florida, which had once been a Spanish colony, as well as over islands in the West Indies; toward the war's end, Spain managed to muscle the British out of West Florida, part of its effort to control the movement of goods on the Mississippi River. British soldiers and sailors were also trying to put down a rebellion in India, and fighting with the Dutch for control of the Cape of Good Hope and the North Sea. Troops that Cornwallis could have used against the Americans were stationed all over the world, at great cost, and could not be spared.

It was in August 1782 that Great Britain, with its treasury drained, first notified General Washington of its willingness to recognize "the independency" of the colonies. Washington was still unconvinced. "That the King will push the War as long as the Nation will find Men or Money," Washington had not "a doubt in my Mind," he said in September. The following month, he told Greene he believed that the British were simply trying "to gain time by lulling us into" a defenseless complacency. Although peace talks were underway, Washington was still determined to "hold ourselves in a hostile position," prepared for war or peace.

No major battles would be fought before the British finally departed, though there were skirmishes of note—Lee's unsuccessful attack on a British garrison at John's Island, South Carolina, in January 1782, for example—and ongoing acts of domestic terrorism. A loyalist named David Fanning, afflicted with a disfiguring scalp disease called "scald head," achieved a dubious kind of notoriety that year, leading a murderous, ten-month campaign—a "small scorge," he called it— against his North Carolina neighbors. Eventually Fanning fled to Nova Scotia, managing to escape punishment after being convicted of "deliberate and wilful murder, robbery, rape or housebreaking." He denied the rape charge but asserted in his defense that there "Never was a man that been in Arms in Either Side But what Is gilty of Some of the Above Mentioned Crimes." Then there was William "Bloody Bill" Cunningham, who held independence-minded neighbors next to Fort Ninety Six responsible for whipping his lame brother to death and killing his father. Cunningham and 150 other loyalists had defeated thirty Whigs at Cloud's Creek in August 1781, killing them after they had surrendered and mutilating their bodies so badly that when the men's mothers and sisters came to bury their dead, they struggled to identify them. That November, a month after the surrender at Yorktown, one of Cunningham's men captured Andrew Pickens's younger brother, John, and other supporters of independence who were manning a convoy of supply wagons and, by one report, burned them to death.

With the British confined largely to Charles Town, Governor John Rutledge was making great strides toward restoring civil government to South Carolina. For the first time in two years, there were elections to the state legislature, which was to meet in Jacksonborough, just outside Charles Town, a site Greene had persuaded the governor to choose. The other site under consideration was Camden, but Greene felt there was more likelihood that loyalists would kidnap the lawmakers if they met that far into the backcountry. Andrew Pickens was elected to the South Carolina House of Representatives but was too busy to attend the January 1782 session. The backcountry was far from subdued, and contemporary critics said that after the murder of his brother, Pickens pursued the loyalists and their Cherokee allies with an unholy vengeance. On retaliatory "expeditions" into Georgia, his men attacked a Cherokee village, where one of his men used an oversized sword to "cleft [open] the heads of flying Indians like so many pumpkins." Pickens led two such campaigns in 1781 and 1782. In the first, in less than three weeks his troops burned thirteen towns and, with only two of his own men wounded, killed forty Cherokees. In the second, he compelled the Indians to give up claims of land in northeast Georgia.

Anthony Wayne was also active in Georgia, sent by Greene to restore American control as best he could. In the first months of 1782, Wayne's men, who included some of Thomas Sumter's old infantry, closed in on Savannah, held by the British since late 1778. Disrupting an attempt by redcoats to escort Indian reinforcements to the town, Wayne drove what remained of British forces back into Savannah, while also fighting off three hundred Creeks who hoped to surprise and overwhelm his pickets. In early July 1782, when the besieged garrison evacuated Savannah, heading for Charles Town, Wayne and his men entered the last town in Georgia occupied by the British.

By this time, the British had effectively ended active military operations in its former colonies in North America, and peace talks in Paris were well underway. In November, the American and British commissioners settled on articles that, with a few minor changes, became the preliminary agreement that would be formalized as the Treaty of Paris.

On December 12–13, with the British almost totally withdrawn into Charles Town and preparing to evacuate the city, Wayne, with about four hundred men, crossed the Ashley River, under orders from Greene to bedevil the redcoats as they left. The next morning, with a force of another four hundred, Greene and General William Moultrie—taken prisoner when Charles Town fell two years earlier—followed, meeting up with Governor John Mathews, who had succeeded John Rutledge and was eager to resume his duties when civil government could be fully restored. All these forces moved slowly toward the northern outskirts of the city, pushing past the British fortifications as guards posted there fell back. The Americans moved on, and the British withdrew "with great order and regularity," Moultrie said, "except now and then the British called to Wayne that he was [moving] too fast upon them, which occasioned him to halt a little."

Around 11 a.m. that day, Wayne marched into Charles Town, which was in some ways unrecognizable from the elegant and thriving commercial center it had been when it fell. The British had taken over the mansions of the prosperous planters and merchants as well as the plantations in the countryside, including that of Henry Laurens, who would find his townhouse in ruins. Scores of Black men, among the many runaway slaves who had fled to the city, were locked up. They were used for cleaning the streets, which had become so "exceedingly filthy" that they were "detrimental to the health of the Inhabitants." Trade had trickled to a halt, the poor of the city were more deeply impoverished, and smallpox and dysentery, originating on feverish prison ships, carried off so many city dwellers that new cemeteries had to be established. A new "Negro burying ground" was "extremely obnoxious."

By the time Wayne entered Charles Town, with Greene to follow, the British were already vacating the town, to the great relief of the inhabitants. This was especially the case, Moultrie said, of those who "had been cooped up in one room of their elegant houses for upwards of two years, whilst the other parts were occupied by British officers." By late October 1782, forty ships had sailed out of the harbor, carrying most of those officers and their soldiers as well as almost four thousand loyalists and in excess of five thousand slaves. The British also carried great quantities of loot, including the bells of St. Michael's Church, which an artillery officer called his "perquisite."

The city was strangely quiet when the Continental troops entered, and the streets were empty. The inhabitants, their liberators learned, had been instructed to stay indoors until the British had gone and the possibility of violence had passed. Escorting Governor Mathews and other city officials, Greene and his army entered the city at 3 p.m., by which time, Beatrice St. Julien Ravenel wrote in her history of the city, "hundreds made their appearance from cellars and chimneys as soon as it could be done with safety." The "balconies, the doors, and windows," Moultrie recalled, were "crowded with the patriotic fair [meaning ladies], the aged citizens and others, congratulating us on our return home," calling, "God bless you, gentlemen, you are welcome home, gentlemen!" as citizens and soldiers alike "shed mutual tears of joy." This moment "was an ample reward for the triumphant soldier," Moultrie wrote, who had suffered untold hardship to release their "fellow citizens from captivity" and restore "their liberties and possession of their city and country again." Nathanael and Caty Greene were honored at parties and balls that winter, Terry Golway writes in his biography of the general, "the toasts of Charles Town and the nation."

In April 1783, Congress proclaimed an end to the war. The Treaty of Paris was signed the following September, by which time Greene had dismissed his army and left South Carolina on his way north. He passed through Wilmington, Richmond, and Baltimore, meeting a hero's welcome along the way. At Trenton, he was reunited with Washington, and together the two rode on to Princeton. Congress was meeting in Princeton rather than Philadelphia, which was considered unsafe because unruly troops from Pennsylvania had marched there, demanding back pay. Greene submitted his resignation to Congress and headed home to Rhode Island. Washington rode on to New York, which the British had vacated two weeks earlier. There, on December 4, with "a heart full of love and gratitude," he bid farewell to his officers.

Independence from Great Britain was not an end, of course, but a beginning. A reasonably stable government had yet to be established, and Alexander Hamilton, preparing for a law career in New York, looked forward to this challenge with gusto. In July 1782, Hamilton had been chosen for the Confederation Congress, and he hoped his friend John Laurens, who was still in the army that summer, would join him in building a government worthy of the sacrifices so many Americans had made for more than a decade. "Peace made, My Dear friend, a new scene opens," Hamilton wrote Laurens on August 15, 1782. "The object then will be to make our independence a blessing. To do this we must secure our *union* on solid foundations." This is a "herculean task," he continued, "and to [accomplish it] mountains of prejudice must be leveled!"

Hamilton wanted Laurens to leave the army and commit his energies to building this new nation, which would require "all the virtue and all the abilities of the Country," Hamilton wrote. "Quit your sword my friend, put on the *toga,* come to Congress. We know each others sentiments, our views are the same: we have fought side by side to make America free, let us hand in hand struggle to make her happy." Asking to be remembered to General Greene, "with all the warmth of a sincere attachment," Hamilton closed his letter, "Yrs for ever."

Eleven days later, of course, John Laurens was dead.

The cause would go on without him.

After the War

JAMES (ARMISTEAD). In 1787, after appeals from the Marquis de Lafayette, the Virginia legislature granted James his freedom, and for the rest of his life, the liberated man called himself James Lafayette. With a pension of forty dollars a year granted by Virginia, he married, bought a farm, and raised a family. He died in 1832, in his early seventies.

ABRAHAM BUFORD. After the battle with Banastre Tarleton at the Waxhaws, Buford continued to serve in the Continental army through the surrender at Yorktown. He settled on a farm in Kentucky, where in 1833 he died at the age of eighty-five. In 2006, Tarleton's descendants sold Buford's regimental flags, captured at the Waxhaws, for more than $5 million.

CHARLES CORNWALLIS. Upon returning to England, Cornwallis served in Ireland as commander in chief and governor-general. He was also governor-general in India, where from 1790 to 1792 he led troops in the Third Anglo-Mysore War. He died in India in 1805 at the age of sixty-six.

HORATIO GATES. Despite the defeat at Camden, Gates continued to serve in the Continental army at General Washington's headquarters.

He sold his Virginia plantation, stipulating that several of its slaves be freed. Moving to present-day Manhattan, he served one term in the New York State Legislature. He died in 1806 at the age of seventy-eight and was buried in the Trinity Church graveyard on Wall Street.

NATHANAEL GREENE. After returning briefly to Rhode Island, he relocated to Mulberry Grove plantation outside of Savannah, given to him by the state of Georgia as a reward for his service. Having paid to provision his troops in the war, he was deeply in debt when he died in 1786 at the age of forty-three. He was buried in Savannah.

ANDREW JACKSON. After serving in Congress in the late 1790s, Jackson fought as a major general in the Tennessee militia during the War of 1812, defeating the British at the Battle of New Orleans. He also fought against the Seminoles in Florida three years later. Jackson returned to the Senate in 1823, and served as the seventh president of the United States from 1829 to 1837. At the age of seventy-eight, he died at "The Hermitage," his Nashville home, in 1845.

THE MARQUIS DE LAFAYETTE. This "hero of two worlds" returned to France in December 1781. He visited the United States three years later, lobbying successfully for the freedom of James (Armistead). An outspoken abolitionist, he bought a plantation in French Guiana, with the intention of freeing its enslaved population—a project for which George Washington commended him. The outbreak of the French Revolution derailed his plans, and the revolutionary government of France seized the property. Although he participated in the revolution himself, commanding an army that fought for the French republic against Austria, he had to flee to Belgium to escape the wrath of the radicals in Paris. He was imprisoned for five years but freed by Napoleon in 1800. He visited the U.S. again in 1824. When he died in Paris in 1834, at the age of seventy-six, his grave was covered in earth from Bunker Hill.

.   .   .

HENRY LAURENS. After acting as one of the peace commissioners in 1783, Laurens returned to Charles Town, where the British had burned his home, which he rebuilt. As a member of the state's constitutional convention in 1788, he supported ratification of the new federal Constitution. In 1792, at the age of sixty-eight, he died in Charles Town.

ARTHUR LEE. After he fell out of favor with French Foreign Minister Vergennes, Congress relieved Lee of his diplomatic duties. He returned to America in September 1780 and was elected to the Virginia House of Delegates and to Congress. As Northwest Indian commissioner in 1784–85, Lee helped negotiate the Treaty of Fort Stanwix. He died on his Virginia plantation in 1792 at the age of fifty-one.

HENRY LEE III. After resigning from the army in 1782, Light Horse Harry served three consecutive one-year terms as governor of Virginia but resigned to lead troops to put down the Whiskey Rebellion. In 1799, he was elected to the U.S. House of Representatives, and upon George Washington's death, Lee wrote his former commander in chief's eulogy, with the words, "First in war, first in peace, and first in the hearts of his countrymen." Disastrous investments led to his imprisonment for nonpayment of debts from 1809–10, and he used the time to write *Memoirs of the War in the Southern Department of the United States.* After returning to his impoverished family in Alexandria, Virginia, Lee left for the West Indies to recover his failing health. In 1818, he died at sixty-two at a Georgia plantation owned by a daughter of Nathanael Greene. In 1913, his remains were moved from Georgia to the chapel at Washington and Lee University in Virginia, next to those of his son, Confederate General Robert E. Lee.

RICHARD HENRY LEE. Lee served as president of Congress under the Articles of Confederation, and, after pushing successfully for adoption of the Bill of Rights, he represented Virginia in the first Senate under the new Constitution. In 1794, he died at Chantilly, a Virginia plantation, at sixty-two.

· · ·

FRANCIS MARION. After the war, Marion served in the South Carolina legislature, and in 1784, the state made him commander of Fort Johnson with a salary of five hundred dollars a year, which was seen more as sinecure than an active military assignment. He died at sixty-three in 1795 and was buried at Belle Isle, a South Carolina plantation owned by the Marion family.

DANIEL MORGAN. After resigning his commission in the army, he returned to Virginia, where he became a land speculator, amassing more than 250,000 acres. With the labor of Hessian prisoners of war, Morgan built a house near Winchester, Virginia, which he named Saratoga. In 1794, he joined with Henry Lee III to put down the Whiskey Rebellion. Two years later, he served a single term as a Federalist member of the U.S. House of Representatives. He died at his daughter's home in Winchester in 1802, in his sixties.

REBECCA BREWTON MOTTE. After the British were burned out of her plantation in 1871, Motte was still one of the richest individuals in South Carolina. She died in 1815 at the age of seventy-seven and is buried in Charleston.

WILLIAM MOULTRIE. After leading the defense of Charles Town in 1776, Moultrie was twice elected to Congress but declined to serve. Captured when the British took the city in 1780, he was exchanged two years later, was elected to the South Carolina legislature in 1783, and served two terms as governor, beginning in 1785 and 1794. He died in 1805 in Charleston at seventy-four.

ANDREW PICKENS. An Indian fighter at the end of the war, Pickens also represented South Carolina in its negotiations with local tribes over boundaries in the late 1780s. A member of the U.S. House of Representatives from 1793 to 1795, Pickens retired to a plantation called Tamassee, named for the Cherokee village that had once occupied the land. He died there in 1817 at seventy-seven. A grandson, Francis Wilkinson Pickens, was governor of South Carolina from 1860 to 1862.

ELIZA PINCKNEY. Pinckney lived a quiet life when the war ended, taking pride in the political prominence of her sons. Thomas, wounded at Camden, served as South Carolina governor and was President George Washington's minister to Great Britain; he ran unsuccessfully as the Federalist candidate for vice president in 1796. Eliza's other son, Charles Cotesworth Pinckney, was a member of the South Carolina legislature, a delegate to the Constitutional Convention, and minister to France. He was the Federalist presidential candidate in 1804 and 1808. Eliza died in 1793 at sixty-one.

FRANCIS RAWDON. As he ascended through the ranks of the British peerage, Rawdon assumed new titles and new names. By the end of his life, in 1825, when he was governor of Malta, he was known as Hastings. He had served in the Irish House of Commons, in the British House of Lords, and as governor-general of India, a position Cornwallis had held some years before. In 1826, Francis Edward Rawdon-Hastings, the First Marquess of Hastings, died. He was seventy-one.

ISAAC SHELBY. While still an active member of the North Carolina militia, Shelby served in its state legislature. He later moved to Kentucky, where in 1792 he became the state's first governor. He served a second term when he again led troops against the British in the War of 1812. He declined an appointment as secretary of war under President James Monroe and died in 1826 at the age of seventy-five.

THOMAS SUMTER. A delegate to South Carolina's Constitutional Convention—he opposed ratification—Sumter served in the state legislature for several terms. He was elected to the U.S. House of Representatives in 1789 but was defeated for reelection after being accused of speculating in government paper. He was returned to Congress in 1796, and in 1801 was elected to the Senate and served until 1810. Hounded by creditors for much of his life, he died in 1832 at the age of ninety-seven.

BANASTRE TARLETON. Paroled to England after being taken prisoner at Yorktown, Tarleton was elected to Parliament in 1790. That same year, he returned to the army and in 1815 was commissioned as a full general. He was knighted in 1820 and, at the age of seventy-eight, died in 1833.

GEORGE WASHINGTON. After resigning his commission from the army in 1783, Washington presided over the Constitutional Convention in 1787 and served two terms as the first president of the United States from 1789 to 1797. He retired to Mount Vernon, where, in 1797, he died at the age of sixty-seven.

WILLIAM WASHINGTON. Virginia-born Washington settled in Charles Town after the war and was elected to the South Carolina legislature. He served in the American army from 1798 to 1800, which included serving as a member of former President Washington's staff in the naval war with France. He died in 1810 at the age of fifty-eight and was buried at Live Oak, a South Carolina plantation.

OTHO HOLLAND WILLIAMS. Williams continued to serve in the Continental army until 1783. He was made an associate justice for Baltimore County, Maryland, and was first commissioner for the Port of Baltimore. President Washington offered him a commission as brigadier general of the army in 1792, which would have made him the second in command of the entire army. Williams declined, citing poor health. In 1793, he traveled to Barbados for his health and died the next year at the age of forty-six. He was buried in Williamsport, Maryland, a town he helped establish on land he once owned.

Acknowledgments

When it comes to friends who have helped make this book a reality, the temptation to be obsequious I find almost irresistible. Some weren't friends when I first asked for their help but became friends in the doing; others pitched in because they were friends to begin with. Still others probably have no idea they helped at all, so they might be surprised to find their names here. I owe them all a debt of gratitude for their services—personal or professional, and often both.

Most of all, I want to express my gratitude to my editor, Victoria Wilson, and to my agent, Glen Hartley. The opportunity to work with Victoria has been a great honor. Her pleasant and capable assistant, Belinda Yong, was also immensely helpful. Both, I understand, have since moved on—this was not my fault!—and the team that has taken over is also first-rate. Editor Todd Portnowitz, who has taken over from Vicky, leads a group that includes Ben Shields, who has been the assistant to both editors; Lisa Montebello, production manager; Kevin Bourke, production editor; Amy Stackhouse, copy editor; Soonyoung Kwon, text designer; Kelly Shi, publicist; Ellen Whitaker, marketer; and Ariel Harari, jacket designer.

Then, in no particular order: Robert Rayner and Robin Cheslock critiqued the manuscipt. Jim Piecuch offered his expertise on the American War of Independence, as did Jefferson scholar Mark Andrew Holowchak. Erin Hurley-Brown, whose artistic services I recommend, created the map.

Graham Dozier and Andrew Foster of the Virginia Museum of History and Culture, Zach Lemhouse of the Southern Revolutionary War Institute, and Amy Connolly and Judy Hynson of Stratford Hall were always gracious and accommodating. The author Catherine Baab-Muguira was indispensable as a professional colleague and astute reader of the manuscript. Stanley Craddock and Solomon Miles were, as always, inspirations, and I could always go to Adam Pacio in a panic, which he would unfailingly alleviate. Kent Masterson Brown, Steve Keener, and Bill Kauffman offered encouragement.

Thank you, finally, to Sally Curran, my lovely wife (and best editor by far). I couldn't have done it—or much else—without you.

Notes

INTRODUCTION

3 "distressed": John A. Krout, "The Washington Legend," *The Meaning of the American Revolution*, ed. Lawrence H. Leder (New York: Quadrangle Books, 1969), 43.

3 "was incapable of fear": Dumas Malone, "Was Washington the Greatest American?," in *The Meaning of the American Revolution*, ed. Lawrence H. Leder (New York: Quadrangle Books, 1969), 57.

3 "did nature and fortune": Ibid.

4 "George Washington's War": Leckie, *George Washington's War*.

4 "Demi-god": Lawrence H. Leder, ed., *The Meaning of the American Revolution* (New York: Quadrangle Books, 1969), 45.

6 "How is it": Edward J. Larson, *American Inheritance: Liberty and Slavery in the Birth of a Nation, 1765–1795* (New York: W. W. Norton & Co., 2023), 66.

CHAPTER ONE

8 "Here I am": Beakes, *De Kalb*, 275.

9 "The most disagreeable": Ibid.

9 "beyond anything": Peter McCandless, "Revolutionary Fever: Disease and War in the Lower South, 1775–1783," *Transactions of the American Clinical and Hematological Association* (2007): 118, 225–49.

9 "the height of madness": Ibid.

10 "I am sorry": Beakes, *De Kalb*, 383.

10 "peasant": Ibid., 6.

10 "a very effective officer": Ibid.

11 "marine infantry": Ibid., 16.

11 "All the world": Ibid., 17.

11 "more humane": Ibid., 15.

12 "inhabitants in the midst," Tocqueville, *Democracy in America,* 751.

12 "a few thousand soldiers": Ibid.

12 "first-rate fortunes": Beakes, *De Kalb,* 29.

13 "are in need of": Ibid., 40.

13 "ought to be content": Ibid., 43–44.

13 "All people here": Ibid., 46–47.

14 "You returned": Ibid., 49–50.

14 "whose experience": Ibid., 60.

14 "now in the position": Wharton, *The Revolutionary Diplomatic Correspondence of the United States,* 394.

14 "gentlemen of rank": Beakes, *De Kalb,* 72.

15 "advised him": Ibid., 90.

15 "long and painful voyage": Ibid., 107.

CHAPTER TWO

16 "was beautiful": Beakes, *De Kalb,* 109.

16 "I believe I'll bury": Ibid., 112.

17 "beggars and bandits": Ibid., 112–13.

17 "The richest man": Unger, *Lafayette,* 34.

17 "is one of the most attractive": Ibid., 35.

17 "live rapidly": Rosen, *A Short History of Charleston,* 32.

17 "grand dinner": Unger, *Lafayette,* 35.

18 "absolute power": Fraser, *Charleston! Charleston!,* 68, 51.

18 "required enormous capital": Ibid., 48.

18 "the profits were enormous": Ibid., 49, 111.

19 "was able to do": Rosen, *A Short History of Charleston,* 36.

19 "The enjoyment of a negro": Ibid., 34.

20 "to tyrannize over": Fraser, *Charleston! Charleston!,* 54.

20 "Following the sale": Ibid., 110–11.

20 "to intimidate": Ibid., 67.

21 "cutt off": Ibid., 77.

21 "absolute and unquestioned": Rosen, *A Short History of Charleston,* 34–35.

21 "Each planter": Ibid., 34–35.

21 "with that inherent right": Fraser, *Charleston! Charleston!,* 108–109.

22 "the great contests": Edmund Burke, "Speech on Conciliation with America," 22 March 1775, in Smith, *Edmund Burke on Revolution,* 57.

22 "the most adverse": Ibid., 58–60.
23 "If it be a Wild scheme": "The Marquis de Lafayette's Plan for Slavery," George Washington Library Center for Digital History, https://www.mountvernon.org/.
23 "which you propose": Ibid.
23 "be happy to join you": Ibid.
24 "would, I really believe": Wiencek, *An Imperfect God,* 263.

CHAPTER THREE

25 "Opulent and sensible": Fraser, *Charleston! Charleston!,* 143.
25 "half the best houses": Ibid., 148.
25 "A breach in the wood": Beakes, *De Kalb,* 114.
26 "astonished by their precision": Ibid., 115.
26 "though approaching sixty": Ibid., 117–18.
26 "in a more pitiable condition": Ibid., 120, 123–24.
27 "Baron de Kalb speaks": Ibid., 135.
28 "So cold": Ibid.
28 "It is odd": Ibid., 227.
29 "involve the most": Council of War, 27 March 1780, Morristown, https://founders.archives.gov.
29 "there is much reason": From George Washington to Major-Genl. Lincoln, in *The Writings of George Washington*, vol. 8, 1779–1780, ed. Worthington Chauncey Ford (New York: G. P. Putnam's Sons, 1890), 248.

CHAPTER FOUR

30 "had neither citadel": Bancroft, *History of the United States,* 302.
31 "so uncommonly broad": Maclay, *Sketches of Debate,* 341.
31 "At first": Shipton in Billias, *George Washington's Generals and Opponents,* 197.
31 "somnolency": Maclay, *Sketches of Debate,* 342.
31 "when driving": Shipton in Billias, *George Washington's Generals and Opponents,* 206.
32 "General Lincoln was never": Mattern, *Benjamin Lincoln and the American Revolution,* 13.
32 "he always frowned": Shipton in Billias, *George Washington's Generals and Opponents,* 199.
32 "The system of slaveholding": Bancroft, *History of the United States,* 329–30.
32 "Setting the example": Shipton in Billias, *George Washington's Generals and Opponents,* 199.

33   "the Effusion of Blood": Henry Clinton to Benjamin Lincoln, 11 May 1780, in Arbuthnot and Clinton, *The Siege of Charleston*, 87–88.

33   "loud wailing": Tustin, *Diary of the American War*, 260.

33   "kill all the dogs": Borick, *A Gallant Defense*, 93.

34   "mangled [him]": Ibid., 149.

34   "The precipitation": Clinton, *The American Rebellion*, 166.

35   "blustering, disagreeable Weather": Bass, *The Green Dragoon*, 72.

35   "cut the communications": To George Washington from Benjamin Harrison, 6–10 May 1780, https://founders.archives.gov.

35   "I am sorry": From George Washington to James Duane, 13 May 1780, https://founders.archives.gov.

35   "three ladies came": Diary of Lieut. Anthony Allaire, of Ferguson's Corps, Memorandum of Occurrences During the Campaign of 1780, Part I: 5 March 1780–30 June 1780, https://www.tngenweb.org/revwar/kingsmountain/allaire.html.

35   "badly cut": Ibid.

36   "whom this infamous villain": Ibid.

36   "to testify against": Ibid.

36   "there were more plunderers": Ibid.

37   "who wished to follow": Bass, *The Green Dragoon*, 77.

37   "the loss of every horse": To George Washington from Colonel Abraham Buford, 6–8 May 1780, https://founders.archives.gov.

37   "totally demolished": Borick, *A Gallant Defense*, 193.

37   "incessant": Charles Cotesworth Pinckney, *Life of Thomas Pinckney* (Boston: Houghton Mifflin and Co., 1895), 70.

37   "cannon-balls whizzing": Lincoln, quoted in Moultrie, *Memoirs of the American Revolution*, vol. 2, 96.

38   "Turkish march": Massey, *John Laurens and the American Revolution*, 162.

38   "thin, miserable, ragged": Shipton in Billias, *George Washington's Generals and Opponents*, 203.

38   "looked greatly starved": Tustin, *Diary of the American War*, 273.

38   "Large Quantities of Musket Cartridges": Franklin B. Hough, *The Siege of Charleston, by the British Fleet and Army Under the Command of Admiral Arbuthnot and Sir Henry Clinton* (Albany, NY: J. Munsell, 1867), 117–18.

38   "fixed ammunition": Roger Lamb, *An Original and Authentic of Occurrences During the Late American War, from Its Commencement to the Year 1783* (Dublin: Wilkinson & Courtney, 1809), 296.

38   "thirteen months": Bancroft, *History*, 329.

38   "were shipped to a market": Ibid., 306; Lamb, *An Original and Authentic of Occurrences*, 303, 306.

39   "exceedingly anxious": From George Washington to James Duane,

13 May 1780, George Washington Papers, Series 3, Subseries 3H, Varick Transcripts, Letterbook 2, https://tile.loc.gov.

39   "DESIRE OF THE INHABITANTS": *Royal Gazette* quoted in editorial note. From Colonel Elias Dayton to George Washington, 30 May 1780, https://founders.archives.gov.

39   "no doubt": From George Washington to the Committee at Headquarters, 11 June 1780, https://founders.archives.gov.

39   "an extraordinary blast": Tustin, *Diary of the American War*, 274.

39   "as if they would tumble": Moultrie, *Memoirs of the American Revolution*, 110.

39   "thick cloud of vapor": Tustin, *Diary of the American War*, 274.

39   "flew up into the air": Diary of Johann Hinrichs in Uhlendorf, *The Siege of Charleston*, 299.

39   "dreadful cries": Tustin, *Diary of the American War*, 274.

39   "burnt beyond recognition": Diary of Captain Ewald in Uhlendorf, *The Siege of Charleston*, 89.

39   "confoundedly frightened": Moultrie, *Memoirs of the American Revolution*, 110.

39   "a number": Tustin, *Diary of the American War*, 274.

40   "lunatics and negroes": Quoted in Joshua Shepherd, "A Melancholy Accident: The Disastrous Explosion at Charleston," *Journal of the American Revolution*, August 5, 2015.

40   "near a hundred": Ibid.

40   "The entire siege": Diary of Captain Johann Hinrichs, 13 May 1780, in Uhlendorf, *The Siege of Charleston*, 299.

CHAPTER FIVE

42   "impracticality of the design": Tarleton, *A History of the Campaigns of 1780 and 1781*, 28.

43   "rioting whalemen": Bass, *The Green Dragoon*, 12.

43   "With a volatile disposition": Ibid., 14.

43   "almost femininely beautiful": Ibid., 53.

43   "exhausted his finances": Ibid., 14.

44   "did not reconcile enemies": O'Shaughnessy, *The Men Who Lost America*, 211.

44   "a certain great man": Bass, *The Green Dragoon*, 19.

44   "eyes and ears": Ibid., 21.

45   "does not surrender": Papas, *Renegade Revolutionary*, 209.

45   "This is a most miraculous": Ibid., 22.

45   "stupid": Ibid., 32.

45   "the Green Dragoon": John Knight, "Top 10 Banastre Tarleton Myths," *Journal of the American Revolution*, August 18, 2016.

45   "for the benefit": Bass, *The Green Dragoon*, 38–40.

46   "which withered her left side": Bass, *Gamecock*, 22.

46   "Resistance being vain": Tarleton, *A History of the Campaigns of 1780 and 1781*, 79–81.

46   "articulate distinctly": Piecuch, *Blood Be Upon Your Head*, 68.

48   "went over the ground": Ibid., 69.

48   "where several had fallen," Ibid., 69.

48   "slaughter": Tarleton, *A History of the Campaigns of 1780 and 1781*, 31.

48   "received twenty-three wounds": Ibid., 70.

49   "killed on the spot": Ibid., 32.

49   "the duty he owed": Bass, *The Green Dragoon*, 83.

49   "Tarleton boasts": Ibid., 10.

50   "a vindictive asperity": Tarleton, *A History of the Campaigns of 1780 and 1781*, 32.

50   "do not contain": Piecuch, "Debating Waxhaws," *Journal of the American Revolution*, August 7, 2013.

50   "to the mistakes": Tarleton, *A History of the Campaigns of 1780 and 1781*, 32.

50   "strange behavior": Piecuch, "Debating Waxhaws."

50   "could not afford": Ibid.

50   "the terror of one side": Warren, *History of the Rise, Progress, and Termination of the American Revolution*, 311–12.

50   "Tarleton's Quarter": Boatner, *Encyclopedia of the American Revolution*, 1089.

51   "Remember Buford!": "Battle of the Waxhaws," *South Carolina Encyclopedia*, https://www.scencyclopedia.org.

CHAPTER SIX

52   "Of the violence": Beakes, *De Kalb*, 276.

52   "What a difference": Ibid., 275.

53   "immense extent": Ibid.

53   "an insurrection": Ibid., 268.

53   "I meet with no support": Ibid., 267.

53   "the Scarcity of Provisions": Ibid., 272.

53   "marauding parties of militia": Ibid., 273–74.

54   "truly alarming": Higginbotham, *Daniel Morgan*, 98–99.

54   "I am happy": Beakes, *De Kalb*, 307–308.

55   "hero of Saratoga": Mitchell, *Decisive Battles*, 170.

55 "Granny Gates": Will Monk, "The Myth of Granny Gates," *Journal of the American Revolution*, October 2, 2014.

55 "guzzling and gaming": Billias, "Horatio Gates: Professional Soldier," in Billias, *George Washington's Generals and Opponents*, 83.

56 "an Army without strength": Beakes, *De Kalb*, 306.

57 "astonished at [the] distress": Ibid., 309.

57 "is every reason to hope": Ibid., 311–12.

57 "we may as well": Ibid., 317.

57 "Desart [that] affords Nothing": Ibid., 318.

57 "not unpalatable": Ibid.

58 "The fair nymphs": Berkin, *Revolutionary Mothers*, 41.

59 "Grand Army": Ibid., 309.

59 "large numbers": Harry Schenawolf, "Road to Camden: The Southern War of the American Revolution," *Revolutionary War Journal*, November 6, 2018.

59 "little to lose": Ross, *Correspondence of Charles, First Marquis Cornwallis*, vol. 1, 2nd ed., 506.

CHAPTER SEVEN

60 "There is a theory": Lumpkin, *From Savannah to Yorktown*, 61.

60 "profoundest silence": Beakes, *De Kalb*, 349.

61 "Charge!": Ibid., 350–51.

62 "returned upon us": Ibid., 351–52.

62 "The general's astonishment": Williams, "A Narrative of the Campaign of 1780," in Johnson, *Sketches of the Life and Correspondence of Nathanael Greene*, vol. 1, Appendix B, 493.

62 "that it was his duty": Lt. Col. H. L. Landers, *The Battle of Camden, SC, August 16, 1780* (Washington, DC: U.S. Government Printing Office, 1929), 49.

64 "the most tremendous firing": Beakes, *De Kalb*, 378–79.

64 "threw the whole body of militia": Ibid., 379.

64 "the loud roar": Buchanan, *The Road to Guilford Courthouse*, 167.

64 "amongst the first": Ibid.

65 "When we had gone": Ibid.

65 "Fortune seem'd determined": To George Washington from Major General Horatio Gates, 30 August 1780, https://founders.archives.gov.

66 "The decision and the preparation": Tarleton, *A History of the Campaigns of 1780 and 1781*, 117–18.

66 "two three pounders": Ibid., 118–19.

66 "appropriation of their": Piecuch, *The Battle of Camden*, 139.

66 "perfect victory": From Major General Horatio Gates to George Washington, 30 August 1780, note 1, https://founders.archives.gov.

67 "ran like a torrent": Tarleton, *A History of the Campaigns of 1780 and 1781*, 150.

67 "broke so early": To George Washington from Major General Horatio Gates, 30 August 1780, https://founders.archives.gov.

67 "very few have fallen": Ibid.

67 "Reason sufficient": Ibid.

68 "is equal to that": Carbone, *Nathanael Greene*, 135.

68 "And was there ever": From Alexander Hamilton to James Duane, 6 September 1780, https://founders.archives.gov.

CHAPTER EIGHT

69 "villa": Glover, *Eliza Lucas Pinckney*, 126.

69 "with such regularity": Crawford, *Unwise Passions*, 127.

70 "My Treatment": Glover, *Eliza Lucas Pinckney*, 200–201.

71 "often resembled": Holton, *Liberty Is Sweet*, 630.

71 "many women": Greene and Pole, *The Blackwell Encyclopedia*, 405.

71 "War in itself": Berkin, *Revolutionary Mothers*, 28.

72 "had to assume": Clinton, *The Plantation Mistress*, 28–29.

72 "As we cannot": Berkin, *Revolutionary Mothers*, 21.

73 "The Provincial Deputies": Dr. Troy L. Kickler, "Edenton Tea Party: An American First," *North Carolina History Project*, https://northcarolina history.org/commentary/edenton-tea-party-an-american-first/.

73 "This apparently simple": Norton, *Liberty's Daughters*, 161.

74 "Is there a female Congress?": "A London Lad on the 'Edenton Ladies,'" https://boston1775.blogspot.com/2017/12/a-london-lad-on-edenton -ladies.html.

74 "A Society of Patriotic Ladies": Greene and Pole, *The Blackwell Encyclopedia*, 82.

74 "the pains and money": Glover, *Eliza Lucas Pinckney*, 28.

75 "he had kept": Ibid., 33.

75 "imployed in business": Ibid., 41.

75 "I have the business": Ibid., 42–44.

75 "schemes": Ibid., 2.

75 "What can I do": Ibid., 55.

75 "might produce something": Ibid., 56.

75 "which I look upon": Ibid., 68.

76 "Out of many": Ibid., 57.

76 "than any of the rest": Ibid., 60.

76 "In 1746": Ibid., 62.

76 "in order that": Ibid., 132.

76 "pretty extraordinary": Ibid., 117.

77 "ignorant and dishonest": Ibid., 141.

77 "lives and fortunes": Ibid., 178.

77 "and everything in it": "Letters of Eliza Lucas Pinckney, 1768–1782," *The Southern Historical Magazine* 76, no. 3 (July 1975): 158.

77 "almost ruined fortunes": Ibid., 159.

77 "dear Tom": Ibid., 157.

78 "truely generous": Ibid.

78 "I am greatly affected": Ibid.

78 "After a thousand fears": Ibid., 159.

79 "was too weak": Ibid., 200.

79 "Sully their honour": Ibid., 201.

CHAPTER NINE

80 "friends": Piecuch, *Three Peoples*, 37.

81 "High Treason": *Pennsylvania Packet*, May 13, 1778.

82 "God Almighty": Boatner, *Encyclopedia of the American Revolution*, 529.

82 "if there were 20 gods": Edgar, *Partisans & Redcoats*, 73–74.

82 "the Swearing Captain": Scoggins, *The Day It Rained Militia*, 52.

82 "two men with Rebell Uniforms": Ibid., 69.

82 "burn the rascal out": Ibid., 62.

82 "rifled the house": Ibid., 70.

82 "two aprons' full": Ibid.

83 "a Refuge for Runaways": Ibid., 77.

83 "casting swivel guns": Ibid., 59.

83 "destroy this Place": Ibid., 77.

83 "of everything": Ibid., 83.

83 "shocking massacre": Scoggins, *The Day It Rained Militia*, 145.

84 "violent rebels": Edgar, *Partisans & Redcoats*, 76.

85 "to make himself": Ibid., 74.

85 "deliberate and measured": Ibid., 77.

85 "cut her head off": Scoggins, *The Day It Rained Militia*, 106.

85 "asked for an interview": Ibid., 106–107.

85 "an honorable scar": Ibid., 107.

86 "as light as day": Ibid., 110.

87 "to raise the war-whoop": Ibid., 113.

87 "to shoot him": Ibid., 119.

87 "times began to be": Collins, *Autobiography of a Revolutionary Soldier*, 22, 24.

87 "blue barrel shot gun": Ibid., 25–26.

88 "poor hunting shirt fellows": Ibid.

88 "kind of breastwork": Scoggins, *The Day It Rained Militia*, 114.

88 "if it rained militia": Ibid.

88 "began to storm and rave": Collins, *Autobiography of a Revolutionary Soldier*, 26.

88 "fell at full length": Scoggins, *The Day It Rained Militia*, 116.

89 "Boys take the fence": Edgar, *Partisans & Redcoats*, 83.

89 "We was in full possession": Scoggins, *The Day It Rained Militia*, 117.

89 "for thirteen or fourteen": Edgar, *Partisans & Redcoats*, 83.

89 "pushed off the top": Scoggins, *The Day It Rained Militia*, 117.

89 "a fine silver-mounted gun": Ibid., 120.

89 "For my own part": Scoggins, *The Day It Rained Militia*, 117.

90 "to cut him into mincemeat": Edgar, *Partisans & Redcoats*, 84.

90 "before you perpetrate": Scoggins, *The Day It Rained Militia*, 118.

90 "one by the head": Edgar, *Partisans & Redcoats*, 85.

90 "put an end to all resistance": Ibid., 86.

CHAPTER TEN

91 "never stopped": Buchanan, *The Road to Guilford Courthouse*, 76.

92 "Overmountain Men": Dameron, *King's Mountain*, 30.

93 "We are Free Men": Richard J. Hooker, ed., *The Carolina Backcountry on the Eve of the Revolution: The Journal and Other Writings of Charles Woodmason, Anglican Itinerant* (Chapel Hill: University of North Carolina Press, 1953), viii.

93 "manufactured in Germany": Wrobel and Grider, *Isaac Shelby*, 8.

94 "the rudiments of an English education": Ibid., 9.

94 "a Very hard day": Ibid., 17.

94 "We as an army": Ibid., 18.

95 "boasted skill": Boatner, *Encyclopedia of the American Revolution*, 364.

95 "astonished all beholders": Peterson, *Arms and Armor*, 219.

96 "disgusted": Donald Norman Morgan, "Major Patrick Ferguson," https://www.americanrevolution.org/ferguson.php.

96 "It was not pleasant": Boatner, *Encyclopedia of the American Revolution*, 364.

96 "gallant and spirited behaviour": Dameron, *King's Mountain*, 15–16.

96 "His Excellency": From Robert Hanson Harrison to George Washington, 7 September 1777, in *The Writings of George Washington, from the Original Manuscript Sources*, ed. John C. Fitzpatrick, vol. 9 (Washington, DC: U.S. Government Printing Office, 1933), 195.

96 "I am not sorry": Buchanan, *The Road to Guilford Courthouse*, 198.

97 "the worms": "Ferguson, His Rifle and Brandywine: A Discussion of Patrick Ferguson, His Breechloading Ordnance Rifle, and the Battle of Brandywine," n.d., 2014, https://www.thefreelibrary.com.

97 "We come not to make war": Dr. J. B. O. Landrum, *Colonial and Revolutionary History of Upper South Carolina* (Greenville, SC: Shannon & Co., 1897), 234–35.

98 "astonished Shelby": *The Rev. James Hodge Say, Memoirs of Major Joseph McJunkin—Revolutionary Patriot*, https://onlinebooks.library.uPAedu/.

99 "There was no overall": Buchanan, *The Road to Guilford Courthouse*, 177.

99 "Huzzah for King George!": Ibid., 177–78.

CHAPTER ELEVEN

101 "as fast a sailor": Massey, *John Laurens and the American Revolution*, 165.

102 "He went to London": Wallace, *The Life of Henry Laurens*, 19.

102 "Sons of Liberty": Fraser, *Charleston! Charleston!*, 108–109.

103 "A compleat history": From John Adams to Abbe de Mabley, 15 January 1783, https://founders.archives.gov.

103 "come so tumbling": Cook, *The Long Fuse*, 1–2.

104 "borrowing more money": Ibid., 22.

104 "seditious libel": Cash, *John Wilkes*, 51.

104 "the residence of the King": Cook, *The Long Fuse*, 138.

104 "that will not roar": Ibid., 138–39.

105 "bloody, expensive": Thomas, *John Wilkes*, 169.

105 "barbarous anarchy": Weintraub, *Iron Tears*, 235–36.

105 "Wild and savage insurrection": Smith, *Edmund Burke on Revolution*, 234.

105 "an edge to life": Plumb, *England in the Eighteenth Century*, 95.

105 "grotesque extravagance": Ibid., 85.

105 "a city famous for wealth": Cook, *The Long Fuse*, 15.

106 "salutary neglect": Ibid., 3.

106 "in all things": Cook, *The Long Fuse*, 86.

106 "taking money": Ibid., 87.

106 "incurable alienation": Smith, *Edmund Burke on Revolution*, 55, 62.

106 "This fierce spirit": Ibid., 59.

107 "insisted that they were": Wood, *The American Revolution*, 58.

107 "old rotten state": Cook, *The Long Fuse*, 216.

107 "numberless and needless": Ibid., 217.

107 "corrupt and poison": Ibid.

107 "an old, wrinkled": Bailyn, *The Ideological Origins of the American Revolution*, 137.

107　"one of his Majesty's": Wallace, *The Life of Henry Laurens*, 208.

108　"to bear arms": Ibid., 209.

108　"misfortune": Cook, *The Long Fuse*, 281.

108　"is deplorable": Ibid., 294.

108　"an enormous expense": Ibid.

108　"I am not sorry": Ibid., 200.

108　"The New England": Ibid., 249.

109　"I feel a satisfaction": Massey, *John Laurens and the American Revolution*, 166.

109　"treatment immediately": Wallace, *The Life of Henry Laurens*, 363.

CHAPTER TWELVE

110　"He was below": Oller, *The Swamp Fox*, 6.

110　"black and piercing": Bass, *Swamp Fox*, 41.

110　"distinguished by small": Ibid., 40.

111　"Col. Francis Marion": Ibid.

111　"I have it": Ibid., 6.

112　"seemed to dispose": James, *A Sketch of the Life of Brigadier General Francis Marion*, 11.

112　"providentially, a dog swam": Ibid.

112　"constitution seemed renewed": Bass, *Swamp Fox*, 7.

112　"intemperate": James, *A Sketch of the Life of Brigadier General Francis Marion*, 12.

113　"When the story got about": Bass, *Swamp Fox*, 29.

113　"was obliged to sculk": Moultrie, *Memoirs of the American Revolution*, 222.

113　"crept out by degrees": Ibid.

113　"had the honour": James, *A Sketch of the Life of Brigadier General Francis Marion*, 32.

113　"partly on a pine log": Ibid.

113　"quite unarmed": Moultrie, *Memoirs of the American Revolution*, 222.

114　"was number 2 goose shot": Lumpkin, *From Savannah to Yorktown*, 69.

114　"little party": Moultrie, *Memoirs of the American Revolution*, 223.

115　"to expose his men": James, *A Sketch of the Life of Brigadier General Francis Marion*, 27.

115　"This was the first": Ibid.

116　"floated across": Bass, *Swamp Fox*, 64.

117　"Go to your families": James, *A Sketch of the Life of Brigadier General Francis Marion*, 27.

117　"burning houses": Ibid., 67.

117 "I am sorry": Ibid., 70.

117 "Whimes": Ibid.

118 "everything in their way": Ibid.

118 "The Torys are so": Ibid.

118 "shou'd certainly pay a visit": Ibid.

CHAPTER THIRTEEN

120 "desist from their opposition": Boatner, *Encyclopedia of the American Revolution*, 576.

121 "Old-Round-About": Dameron, *King's Mountain*, 36–37.

121 "Give them hell": Ibid.

121 "to get them out": Ibid.

122 "My countrymen": Alderman, *The Overmountain Men*, 83.

122 "is marching hither": Ibid.

122 "swarm of backwoodsmen": Tarleton, *A History of the Campaigns of 1780 and 1781*, 167.

123 "I arrived today": Dameron, *King's Mountain*, 42.

123 "feverish cold": Benton Rain Patterson, *Washington and Cornwallis: The Battle for America, 1775–1783* (Lanham: Taylor Trade Publishing, 2004), 248.

124 "duster": Dameron, *King's Mountain*, 44.

124 "mark [Ferguson]": Ibid.

124 "My brave fellows": Dameron, *King's Mountain*, 46.

124 "fire as quick": Ibid.

125 "When you are engaged": Moultrie, *Memoirs of the American Revolution*, 243.

125 "My feelings": Dameron, *King's Mountain*, 47.

125 "Indian war-whoops": Ibid., 57.

126 "Here they are": Ibid.

126 "took his Tomahawk": Dunkerly, *The Battle of Kings Mountain*, 18.

126 "fired until the bark": Buchanan, *The Road to Guilford Courthouse*, 231.

126 "was shot under the jaw": Dameron, *King's Mountain*, 71–72.

127 "the Bull Dog's pup": Lyman C. Draper, *King's Mountain and Its Heroes* (Baltimore, MD: Genealogical Publishing Co., 1881, 2000), 593.

127 "to throw down": Dameron, *King's Mountain*, 73.

127 "damned unfair!": Buchanan, *The Road to Guilford Courthouse*, 233.

127 "For God's sake": Dameron, *King's Mountain*, 73.

127 "We killed near a hundred": Boatner, *Encyclopedia of the American Revolution*, 581.

127 "It was some time": Ibid.

128 "Owing to these causes": Dunkerly, *The Battle of Kings Mountain*, 77–78.

128 "our men gave": Ibid., 78.

128 "almost fifty rifles": Ibid., 34.

129 "decent" burial: Draper, *King's Mountain and Its Heroes*, 321.

129 "amid the dead": Scheer and Rankin, *Rebels & Redcoats*, 420.

129 "weltering in their Gore": Dunkerly, *The Battle of Kings Mountain*, 70.

129 "exposed to the cold dew": Dameron, *King's Mountain*, 83.

129 "really distressing": Collins, *Autobiography*, 53.

129 "An unusual number": Ramsey, *The History of the American Revolution*, vol. 2, 177.

129 "Riflemen took off": Ibid.

129 "but it was badly done": Collins, *Autobiography*, 53.

130 "civilized": Jones, *Captives of Liberty*, 13.

130 "The populations": Ibid., 15.

130 "pillage, rape, and murder": Ibid.

131 "I must proceed": Dameron, *King's Mountain*, 85.

131 "sweet potato patch": Buchanan, *The Road to Guilford Courthouse*, 237.

131 "I must request": Alderman, *The Overmountain Men*, 107.

131 "near to starving": Buchanan, *The Road to Guilford Courthouse*, 237.

132 "just as farmers": Ibid.

132 "breaking open houses": Scheer and Rankin, *Rebels & Redcoats*, 420.

132 "They were either mounted": Buchanan, *The Road to Guilford Courthouse*, 239.

132 "sent into secret hiding places": Dunkerly, *The Battle of Kings Mountain*, 74.

133 "gave me": Dameron, *King's Mountain*, 86–87.

133 "No sooner had news": Pearson, *Those Damned Rebels*, 353.

133 "depression and fear": Dameron, *King's Mountain*, 87.

133 "swarm of backwoodsmen": Tarleton, *History*, 167.

CHAPTER FOURTEEN

134 "a man of industry": Golway, *Washington's General*, 15.

135 "red coats": Ibid., 44.

135 "blemish to the company": Carbone, *Nathanael Greene*, 16.

135 "I confess it is": Ibid., 16–17.

135 "too suseptible": Golway, *Washington's General*, 45.

135 "misfortune to limp": Carbone, *Nathanael Greene*, 17.

136 "the cause of liberty": George Washington Greene, *The Life of Nathanael Greene* (New York: G. P. Putnam, 1867–1871), 49.

136 "You dance stiffly": Golway, *Washington's General*, 19.

136 "Public Resort": Ibid., 39.

136 "a small brunette": Ibid., 42.

136 "Literary Accomplishments": Ibid., 15.

137 "Army of Observation": Ibid., 46.

137 "resist, expel, kill and destroy": Ibid.

137 "Though raw": Buchanan, *The Road to Charleston*, 31.

137 "dirty & nasty": From George Washington to Lund Washington, 20 August 1775, https://founders.archives.gov.

138 "To place any dependence": From George Washington to John Hancock, 25 September 1776, https://founders.archives.gov.

138 "to ruin himself": Ibid.

139 "impatient to return": From George Washington to Patrick Henry, 5 October 1776, https://founders.archives.gov.

139 "One Circumstance": Ibid.

139 "true Criterion": Ibid.

140 "came to us": Golway, *Washington's General*, 67.

140 "a first-rate military genius": From Tench Tilghman to William Duer, V.2, 870, 4 October 1776, https://digital.lib.niu.edu/.

140 "I feel mad": Golway, *Washington's General*, 103.

141 "rained, hailed and snowed," Stegeman and Stegeman, *Caty*, 40.

141 "This Gentlemen": From George Washington to John Hancock, 18 March 1777, https://founders.archives.gov.

141 "You, sir,": Golway, *Washington's General*, 140.

141 "No body ever heard": To George Washington from Major General Nathanael Greene, 24 April 1779, https://founders.archives.gov.

141 "All of you": Golway, *Washington's General*, 165.

141 "comprehensive system": Edward Paysor, "Nathanael Greene and the Supply of the Continental Army," *Quartermaster Review* (May–June 1950); Golway, *Washington's General*, 140.

142 "has undergone": Curtis F. Morgan Jr., "Nathanael Greene as Quartermaster General," *Journal of the American Revolution*, November 18, 2013.

142 "What to do": Ibid.

142 "to resign as soon": Ibid.

142 "When you were": Ibid.

143 "The fata[l] consequences": From George Washington to Samuel Huntington, 15 September 1780, https://founders.archives.gov.

143 "I cannot but remark": Ibid.

143 "exclusive of Horse": Ibid.

143 "In my absence": From George Washington to Major General Nathanael Greene, 16 September 1780, https://founders.archives.gov.

143 "cool and collected": Warren, *History of the Rise, Progress, and Termination of the American Revolution*, 324.

143 "remarkable coolness": Ibid., 308.

143 "This makes me": Golway, *Washington's General*, 22.

CHAPTER FIFTEEN

144 "What I have been dreading": Stegeman and Stegeman, *Caty*, 81.

144 "Your presence": From George Washington to Major General Nathanael Greene, 18 October 1780, https://founders.archives.gov.

144 "I am rendered": From Nathanael Greene to Catharine Littlefield Greene, *Nathanael Greene Papers*, vol. 6, Library of Congress, 415.

145 "betrayed no want of fortitude": To George Washington from Major John André, 1 October 1780, https://founders.archives.gov.

146 "talents, knowledge of service": From George Washington to Nathanael Greene, 22 October 1780, https://founders.archives.gov.

146 "is an excellent one": From John Mathews to George Washington, 14 October 1780, note 8, https://founders.archives.gov.

146 "Uninformed as I am": From George Washington to Major General Nathanael Greene, 22 October 1780, https://founders.archives.gov.

146 "that the nature": Ibid.

147 "rather than an evil": To George Washington from John Mathews, 14 October 1780, note 8, https://founders.archives.gov.

147 "You have your wish": Ibid.

147 "The common soldiers": Arnold to Germain, 7 October 1780, quoted in "Editorial Note," https://founders.archives.gov.

147 "distress and discontents": Ibid.

148 "the great pleasure": George Washington, General Orders, 26 October 1780, in *The Writings of George Washington, from the Original Manuscript Sources*, vol. 20, ed. John C. Fitzpatrick (Washington, DC: U.S. Government Printing Office, 1939), 258.

148 "On our part": Ibid., 207.

148 "If General Washington": Lockhart, *The Drillmaster of Valley Forge*, 235.

148 "They promise me": To George Washington from Nathanael Greene, 13 November 1780, https://founders.archives.gov.

149 "ever saw the face": From Thomas Jefferson to George Washington, 22 October 1780, https://founders.archives.gov.

149 "Our prospects": To George Washington from Nathanael Greene, 19 November 1780, https://founders.archives.gov.

149 "totally deranged": To George Washington from Nathanael Greene, 28 December 1780, https://rotunda.upress.virginia.edu.

149 "a magnanimous gesture": Golway, *Washington's General*, 239.

149 "I have not": Oller, *The Swamp Fox*, 101–102.

150 "I like your plan": Golway, *Washington's General*, 239.

150 "fully convinced": From Nathanael Greene to John Hancock, 26 July 1780, quoted at https://founders.archives.gov.

150 "the spirit of plundering": From Nathanael Greene to Samuel Huntington, 28 December 1780, in Showman, *The Papers of General Nathanael Greene*, 9.

151 "division among the people": To Alexander Hamilton from Major General Nathanael Greene, 10 January 1781, https://founders.archives.gov.

151 "murdered a number": From Nathanael Greene to Samuel Huntington, 28 December 1780, in Showman, *The Papers of General Nathanael Greene*, 9.

151 "It would answer": From George Washington to Major General Horatio Gates, 8 October 1780, https://founders.archives.gov.

151 "while you are so far inferior": Ibid.

151 "Tho' in general": From George Washington to Samuel Huntington, 11 October 1780, https://founders.archives.gov.

152 "so many talents": Lee, *The Revolutionary War Memoirs*, 29.

152 "There was no single": Golway, *Washington's General*, 232.

152 "our army will be": H. C. B. Rogers, *The British Army of the Eighteenth Century* (London: Routledge, 2017), 154.

152 "would in other wars": Spring, *With Zeal and With Bayonets Only*, 55.

153 "had had nine Skirmishes": To George Washington from Abner Nash, 6 October 1780, https://founders.archives.gov.

153 "Fabian": Steele Brand, "The Reluctant Warrior—How Fabius Maximus Became Rome's Greatest General by Avoiding Battle," *Military History Now*, January 29, 2020.

153 "the Delayer": Frontinus, "Strategems," in *Greek and Roman Military Writers, Selected Readings*, ed. Brian Campbell (London: Routledge, 2004), 118.

153 "rendered the embodying": From Nathanael Greene to Samuel Huntington, 7 January 1781, in Showman, *The Papers of General Nathanael Greene*, 63, 99.

154 "have spent their life": Maurice de Saxe, "Reveries on the Art of War," in Phillips, *Roots of Strategy*, 221.

154 "greatest secret": "The Instruction of Frederick the Great," in Phillips, *Roots of War*, 321.

154 "permanent army": From Nathanael Greene to Francis Marion, 4 December 1780, quoted in James S. Liles, "The Reluctant Partisan:

Nathanael Greene's Southern Campaigns," master's thesis, University of North Texas, May 2005, 222.

154 "flying army": To George Washington from Nathanael Greene, 31 October 1780, https://founders.archives.gov.

154 "I [entirely] approve": Golway, *Washington's General*, 232.

154 "a number of": From George Washington to Nathanael Greene, 8 November 1780, in *The Writings of George Washington*, vol. 9, 1780–1782, ed. Worthington Chauncey Ford (New York: G. P. Putnam's Sons, Knickerbocker Press, 1891).

CHAPTER SIXTEEN

155 "I had the honor": From Banastre Tarleton to John Tarleton, 21 August 1780, in Bass, *The Green Dragoon*, 102.

156 "one of the most": Ibid., 102–103.

156 "capacity and the vigour": Ibid., 103.

156 "To see the King": Bass, *Gamecock*, 12.

156 "became the social rage": Ibid., 13.

156 "their Behaviour": Ibid., 15.

157 "with one or both": Ibid., 19.

157 "Pray excuse": Ibid.

158 "had marched": Ibid., 46.

159 "was as precipitate": General Thomas Sumter to Major General William Smallwood, 9 November 1780, in *Papers Relating Chiefly to the Maryland Line During the Revolution*, ed. Thomas Balch (Philadelphia: T. K. and P. G. Collins, 1857), 122.

159 "Wemyss forgot": Bass, *Gamecock*, 98.

159 "being in his shirt sleeves": Ibid., 98.

159 "Knowing that should": Ibid., 99.

159 "The enemy": From Cornwallis to Sir Henry Clinton, 3 December 1780, in Ross, *Correspondence of Charles, First Marquis Cornwallis*, vol. 1, 499.

160 "there was a very large": Bass, *Gamecock*, 104.

160 "General, I won't have": Ibid., 105.

161 "men & horse fell so fast": Salley, *Col. William Hill's Memoirs of the Revolution*, 15.

161 "with bullets": See https://www.carolana.com/SC/Revolution/revolution _battle_of_blackstocks.html.

161 "with so many falling": Salley, *Memoirs,* 15.

161 "quitted the field": Bass, *Gamecock,* 109.

161 "with loud shouts": Salley, *Memoirs,* 15.

162 "General, you are wounded": Bass, *Gamecock*, 107.

162　"It is but doing": Ibid., 109.

162　"powerful corps disintegrated": Ibid., *Gamecock*, 110.

163　"did not wait": Lee, *The Revolutionary War Memoirs*, 207.

163　"Sumter is defeated": Bass, *Gamecock*, 110.

163　"fought like a gamecock": Waters, *The Quaker and the Gamecock*, 2–3.

163　"Tuck": Ibid.

163　three young men: Buchanan, *The Road to Guilford Courthouse*, 258.

163　"I have no doubt": Bass, *Gamecock*, 111.

163　"It is not easy": Commager and Morris, *The Spirit of Seventy-Six*, 1150.

163　"Sumter is now reported dead": Bass, *Gamecock*, 111.

CHAPTER SEVENTEEN

164　"I am posted": Golway, *Washington's General*, 243.

164　"intensely cold": George Washington diary, January [1870], https://founders.archives.gov.

164　"5 or Six days": From George Washington to Philip Schuyler, 30 January 1780, https://founders.archives.gov.

164　"have many agreeable": From Nathanael Greene to Catherine Greene, 29 December 1780, *The Papers of Nathanael Greene*, vol. 7, 26 December 1780–29, March 1781.

165　"condition of this Army": To George Washington from Nathanael Greene, 7 December 1780, https://founders.archives.gov.

165　"Nothing can be more": Ibid.

165　"into some secure place": To Thomas Jefferson from Nathanael Greene, 6 December 1780, https://founders.archives.gov.

165　"deaths, desertion, and the hospital": Ibid.

166　"is no Egypt": George Washington Greene, *The Life of Nathanael Greene*, vol. 3 (New York: G. P. Putnam), 92.

166　"did not think": Higginbotham, *Daniel Morgan*, 5.

168　"Feloniously": Ibid., 10.

168　"gentleman's hat": Ibid., 11.

168　"confirmed Libertine": Ibid.

169　"Not a scoundrel": Ibid., 49.

170　"It occurs to me": Washington, Orders to Colonel Daniel Morgan, 13 June 1777, https://founders.archives.gov.

170　"to give protection": Ibid.

170　"like sheep among wolves": Robert Stansbury Lambert, *South Carolina Loyalists in the American Revolution* (Columbia: University of South Carolina Press, 1987), 211–12.

170　"horses, Cows, Sheep": Edgar, *Partisans & Redcoats*, 209.

170 "massacred in this province": Ibid.

171 "corpulent": Lee, *The Revolutionary War Memoirs*, 588.

171 "The Distress": From William Washington to Nathanael Greene, 24 December 1780, *Nathanael Greene Papers*, vol. 6, Library of Congress, 611.

171 "We had a long hill": Andrew Waters, "Hammond's Store: The 'Dirty War's' Prelude to Cowpens," *Journal of the American Revolution*, December 10, 2018, https://allthingsliberty.com.

172 "any where within": From Cornwallis to Banastre Tarleton, 2 January 1781, in Tarleton, *History*, 250–51.

172 "would take the words": Higginbotham, *Daniel Morgan*, 122.

172 "Wizard Owl": Andrew, *The Life and Times of General Andrew Pickens*, 188.

172 "a valuable, discreet, and attentive": From Daniel Morgan to Nathanael Greene, 15 January 1781, *Nathanael Greene Papers*, quoted in Andrew, *The Life and Times of General Andrew Pickens*, 101.

173 "had the confidence": Ibid.

173 "useless, disorderly": Piecuch, *Three Peoples, One King*, 194.

173 "as proper a place": Tarleton, *History*, 227.

174 "And long after": Scheer and Rankin, *Rebels & Redcoats*, 418.

174 "Just hold up": Ibid.

175 "Look for the epaulets!": Axelrod, *The Real History of the American Revolution*, 321.

CHAPTER EIGHTEEN

176 "prodigious yell": Higginbothom, *Daniel Morgan*, 137.

176 "came on like a thunder storm": Collins, *Autobiography*, 56.

176 "executed with great firmness": Babits, *A Devil of a Whippin'*, 89.

176 "it was pop, pop, pop": Scheer and Rankin, *Rebels & Redcoats*, 430.

177 "Now, my hide is in the loft": Collins, *Autobiography*, 57.

177 "They're coming on": Babits, *A Devil of a Whippin'*, 117.

177 "commenced a very destructive": Ibid.

177 "like a whirlwind": Collins, *Autobiography*, 57.

177 "began to make": Ibid.

178 "The ball missed": Bass, *The Green Dragoon*, 159.

178 "falling very fast": Collins, *Autobiography*, 57.

178 "both being emulous": Howard quoted in Steele and Morris, *The Spirit of Seventy-Six*, 1157.

178 "another Fishing creek": Collins, *Autobiography*, 57.

178 "the fight was over": Ibid.

179 "I was desirous": Higginbothom, *Daniel Morgan*, 142.

179 "This day, I fired": Collins, *Autobiography*, 58.

179 "The troops I have": Scheer and Rankin, *Rebels & Redcoats*, 432.

179 "and all their music": Ibid.

179 "for the honor": Ibid.

180 "the rising Hero": Higginbothom, *Daniel Morgan*, 142.

180 "having had time": From Cornwallis to George Germain, 18 January 1781, in Tarleton, *History*, 257.

180 "It is impossible": Ibid., 258.

180 "upon all former occasions": Ibid., 253.

180 "The late affair": From Cornwallis to George Germain, 21 January 1781, in Agniel, *The Late Affair*, 99.

180 "was the consequence": Moultrie, *Memoirs of the American Revolution*, 257.

180 "You have forfeited": From Cornwallis to Banastre Tarleton, 30 January 1780 [*sic*], in Tarleton, *History*, 258.

181 "Your disposition was": Ibid.

181 "By all accounts": Bass, *The Green Dragoon*, 162.

181 "I rejoice exceedingly": From Otho Holland Williams to Daniel Morgan, *Cowpens Papers, Being the Correspondence of General Morgan and The Prominent Actors*, from the Collection of Theodorus Bailey Myers (Charleston, SC: *News and Courier*, 1881), 33.

CHAPTER NINETEEN

184 "it was determined": Carbone, *Nathanael Greene*, 172.

185 "It being my business": Ibid., 173.

185 "without baggage": From Brigadier General Charles O'Hara to the Duke of Grafton, 20 April 1781, quoted in Spring, *With Zeal and With Bayonets Only*, 24.

185 "sanguine expectation": From Daniel Morgan to Nathanael Greene, 25 January 1871, in Rebecca McConkey, *The Hero of Cowpens* (New York: A. S. Barnes & Co., 1881), 257.

185 "pain in the hip": Zambone, *Daniel Morgan*, 247.

185 "ceatick": Ibid.

185 "violently attck'd": Ibid.

185 "totally disable me": Ibid.

186 "about six feet high": Beakes, *Otho Holland Williams*, 2.

186 "are classic for": Ibid., 69.

186 "who treated him": Ibid., 45.

187 "in a state of loathsome filth": Ibid.

187 "walked through the prison": Ibid., 46–47.

187 "breathed the most": Ibid., 48.

187 "was conspicuous": Ibid., 123.

188 "He who has never": Ibid., 119, 126.

188 "a very lengthy line": Ibid., 126–27.

188 "the hospitality": Ibid., 127.

188 "this Dirty, disagreeable": From Daniel Morgan to Nathanael Greene, 31 October 1880, in James Graham, *The Life of Daniel Morgan* (Applewood Books, 2009), 244.

189 "of the flower": Beakes, *Otho Holland Williams*, 165.

189 "Throughout the night": Ibid., 163–64.

189 "so that each man": Ibid., 164.

189 "The shoes were generally worn out": Ibid.

189 "The heat of the fires": Ibid.

190 "And captured 3 or 4 Men": Ibid., 165.

190 "You have the flower": Ibid.

190 "must risque the Troops": Ibid., 165–67.

190 "so excessively exhausted": From Col. Otho Williams to Gen. Greene, 13 February 1781, in Showman, *The Papers of General Nathanael Greene*, 285–86.

191 "Follow our route": Beakes, *Otho Holland Williams*, 166.

191 "I have great reason": Ibid.

191 "The greater part": Ibid.

191 "All our troops": Aaron, *The Race to the Dan*, 32–33.

191 "You may be assured": From George Washington to Nathanael Greene, in *The Writings of George Washington, from the Original Manuscript Sources*, ed. John C. Fitzpatrick, vol. 21 (Washington, DC: Government Printing Office, 1937), 345.

191 "Every measure of the American": Tarleton, *History*, 236.

192 "in the face": Commager and Morris, *The Spirit of Seventy-Six*, 1160.

192 "was commanded by": From Nathanael Greene to George Washington, in Showman, *The Papers of General Nathanael Greene*, 15 February 1781, 293.

192 "The miserable situation": To George Washington from Nathanael Greene, 15 February 1781, https://founders.archives.gov.

192 "joy beamed": Beakes, *Otho Holland Williams*, 169.

192 "Yankee Doodle": Aaron, *The Race to the Dan*, 33.

CHAPTER TWENTY

193 "to pursue the Enemy": Bright and Dunaway, *Pyle's Defeat*, 17.

193 "check the audacity": Piecuch, " 'Light Horse Harry' Lee and Pyle's Massacre," *Journal of the American Revolution*, June 19, 2013.

194 "Too late to retreat": Babits and Howard, *Long, Obstinate, &
Bloody*, 38.

194 "long-tailed": Sydnor, *American Revolutionaries in the Making*, 63.

195 "Westmoreland Resolves": Unger, *First Founding Father*, 41.

195 "In a late engagement": Ibid., 181–82.

195 "American diplomat": Boatner, *Encyclopedia of the American Revolution*,
603–604.

195 "Genius": Potts, *Arthur Lee*, 1.

196 "so severe a shock": Ibid., 23.

196 "too frequent enjoyment": Nagel, *The Lees of Virginia*, 78.

196 "absurd, monstrous": Ibid., 48.

196 "the Squire": Nagel, *The Lees of Virginia*, 50.

197 "The Ladies were Dressed": Fithian, *Journal and Letters of Philip Vickers
Fithian*, 57.

197 "toasting the Sons": Ibid.

198 "the first Officer": Papas, *Renegade Revolutionary*, 5.

198 "had read as much": Ibid., 6.

198 "harassing and impeding": Ibid., 227.

198 "the familiarity": Cole, *"Light-Horse Harry" Lee*, 31.

199 "To acquaint myself": Royster, *Light-Horse Harry Lee*, 16.

199 "With a form": Lossing, *Recollections and Private Memoirs*, 356.

199 "ran without giving": To George Washington from Captain Henry Lee
Jr., 3 November 1777, https://founders.archives.gov.

199 "He is so enterprising". Piecuch and Beakes, *"Light Horse Harry"
Lee*, 15.

199 "though seldom": *New Jersey Gazette*, 14 January, 1778, quoted in Michael
Cecere, "Captain Lee's Genius," *The Journal of the American Revolution*,
April 28, 2014.

199 "Offended by his ambition": Cole, *Light-Horse Harry Lee*, 45.

199 "that Capn. Henry": General Orders, 25 August 1777, https://founders
.archives.gov.

199 "constantly alarmed": Buchanan, *The Road to Charleston*, 41.

200 "zealous activity": From George Washington to Brigadier General William
Smallwood, 16 February 1778, https://founders.archives.gov.

200 "to acquaint myself": Royster, *Light Horse Harry Lee*, 16.

200 "I am wedded": To George Washington from Captain Henry Lee Jr.,
31 March 1778, https://founders.archives.gov.

200 "I possess": Ibid.

200 "undistinguished manner": From George Washington to Captain Henry
Lee Jr., 1 April 1778, https://founders.archives.gov.

201 "uniformly distinguished": From George Washington to Henry Laurens,
3 April 1778, https://founders.archives.gov.

201 "all loyal subjects": Piecuch, "'Light Horse Harry Lee' and Pyle's Massacre," *Journal of the American Revolution*, June 19, 2013.

201 "a variety of calamaties": Tarleton, *History*, 231.

201 "the dread of violence": Ibid.

201 "to stare at us": Denman and Walsh, *The Pivotal Struggle*, 202.

CHAPTER TWENTY-ONE

203 "intimidating or dispersing": Tarleton, *History*, 239.

203 "Though forewarned": Ibid.

204 "seemed prodigiously rejoiced": Piecuch and Beakes, *"Light Horse Harry" Lee*, 110–11.

204 "two well-mounted": Lee, *The Revolutionary War Memoirs*, 256.

204 "so as to give": Ibid., 257.

204 "the overflowing of respect": Ibid.

205 "with a smiling countenance": Ibid., 258.

205 "and the customary civilians": Ibid.

205 "You are killing": Piecuch and Beakes, *"Light Horse Harry" Lee*, 113.

206 "swords broke": Ibid.

206 "never before witnessed": Ibid., 119.

206 "Remember Buford!": John C. Dann, ed., *The Revolution Remembered: Eyewitness Accounts of the War for Independence* (Chicago: University of Chicago Press, 1980), 202.

206 "which he had just": Ibid., 202.

206 "lying upon the ground": Ibid.

207 "had run him through": Ibid.

207 "complained to Tarleton": Tarleton, *History*, 232.

207 "inhuman barbarity": Jim Piecuch, "'Light Horse Harry' Lee and Pyle's Massacre," *Journal of the American Revolution*, June 19, 2013.

207 "most inhumanly butchered": Ross, *Correspondence of Charles, First Marquis Cornwallis*, vol. 1, 2nd ed., 519.

207 "has had a very happy effect": To Thomas Jefferson from Nathanael Greene, 2[8] February 1781, https://founders.archives.gov.

207 "the defeat of the Tories": Bright and Dunaway, *Pyle's Defeat*, 120.

207 "Remember Buford!": Ibid., 182.

208 "Some writers": Piecuch and Beakes, *"Light Horse Harry" Lee*, 116.

208 "to pass as a reinforcement": Lee, *The Revolutionary War Memoirs*, 256.

208 "exhibited great perturbation": Piecuch, "'Light Horse Harry' Lee and Pyle's Massacre."

208 "between two and three hundred": Lee, *The Revolutionary War Memoirs*, 259.

208 "and self-preservation": Ibid.

209 "it was only necessary": Ibid., 258.

209 "that no time be lost": From Lee to Greene, 25 February 1781, in Bright and Dunaway, *Pyle's Defeat*.

209 "their game of checkers": Piecuch and Beakes, *"Light Horse Harry" Lee*, 123.

209 "As they will be useless": Ibid., 125.

CHAPTER TWENTY-TWO

211 "enjoying wholesome": Lee, *The Revolutionary War Memoirs*, 249.

211 "without ammunition": Showman, *The Papers of General Nathanael Greene*, 449.

211 "almost put a total stop": Ibid.

211 "We marched yesterday": From St. George Tucker to Frances Bland Tucker, 13 March 1781, in St. George Tucker, "The Southern Campaign 1781 from Guilford Court House to the Siege of York," *The Magazine of American History*, vol. 7 (New York: A. S. Barnes and Co., 1881), 39.

212 "I rarely ever": From Nathanael Greene to Joseph Reed, 18 March 1781, in Commager and Norris, *The Spirit of Seventy-Six*, 1163.

212 "take the field": Harold Allen Skinner Jr., *A Game of Hare & Hounds: An Operational-Level Command Study of the Guilford Courthouse Campaign, 18 January–15 March 1781* (Quantico, VA: Marine Corps University Press, 2021), 88.

212 "I expect Lord Cornwallis": Golway, *Washington's General*, 255.

212 "with orders to shoot": Scheer and Rankin, *Rebels & Redcoats*, 445.

213 "the first time": Major William A. Graham, *General Joseph Graham and His Papers of North Carolina Revolutionary History* (Lincoln City, NC: Edwards and Broughton, 1904), 344.

213 "running down the hill": Babits and Howard, *Long, Obstinate, and Bloody*, 46.

213 "which caused": Graham, *General Joseph Graham*, 344.

213 "himself and horse": Lee, *The Revolutionary War Memoirs*, 267.

214 "violent inflammation": Golway, *Washington's General*, 254–55.

214 "Good heavens": Ibid., 254.

214 "a long lane": Wood, *Battles of the Revolutionary War*, 247.

215 "Three rounds": Ibid., 445.

215 "Charge!": Spring, *With Zeal and With Bayonets Only*, 226.

216 "They were taking aim": Scheer and Rankin, *Rebels & Redcoats*, 447.

216 "our infinite distress": Lee, *The Revolutionary War Memoirs*, 277.

216 "bush fighting": Spring, *With Zeal and With Bayonets Only*, 250.

216 "Indian-style": Fleming, *The Strategy of Victory*, 153.

216 "to tree": Spring, *With Zeal and With Bayonets Only*, 254.

217 "much our superiors": Ibid., 256.

217 "the action became": Tarleton, *History*, 281.

217 "kept up": Charles Stedman, *The History of the Origin, Progress, and Termination of the American War*, vol. 2 (London: Printed for the author, 1794), 339.

217 "threw the militia": From St. George Tucker to Frances Bland Tucker, 18 March 1781, in Scheer and Rankin, *Rebels & Redcoats*, 1166.

217 "infinite labour": Commager and Morris, *The Spirit of Seventy-Six*, 1166.

217 "either from design": Ibid., 40–41.

218 "turned her into": Claudia Lamm Wood, " 'With Unalterable Tenderness': The Courtship and Marriage of St. George Tucker and Frances Randolph Tucker," master's thesis, William & Mary, 1988, *Dissertations, Theses, and Master's Projects*, https://scholarworks.wm.edu/cgi/viewcontent.cgi?article=4111&context=etd.

218 "gave him so warm": Babits and Howard, *Long, Obstinate, and Bloody*, 167.

218 "with his brawny arms": Wood, W. J. *Battles of the Revolutionary War, 1775–1781*, 254.

218 "The saddlebags": Commager and Morris, *The Spirit of Seventy-Six*, 1165.

219 "remonstrated and begged": Wood, *Battles of the Revolutionary War*, 254.

220 "bayoneted and cut to pieces": Babits and Howard, *Long, Obstinate, and Bloody*, 158.

220 "many of the [redcoats]": Beakes, *Otho Holland Williams*, 206–207.

221 "repast": Wood, *Battles of the Revolutionary War*, 256.

221 "The night succeeding": Commager and Morris, *The Spirit of Seventy-Six*, 1166.

221 "Except the ground": Carbone, *Nathanael Greene*, 182.

221 "a trifling loss": Lumpkin, *From Savannah to Yorktown*, 175.

221 "Our men are in good spiritis": Golway, *Washington's General*, 260.

222 "Should Cornwallis": Ibid.

222 "I was born": Ibid.

222 "The contest": Showman, *The Papers of General Nathanael Greene*, 470.

222 "the misconduct": Ibid.

222 "disposing of the sick": Cornwallis to Henry Clinton, 10 April 1781, in Barnes and Barnes, *The American Revolution Through British Eyes*, 953.

222 "which will be indispensably": Ibid.

222 "being as yet totally": Ibid.

223 "I am quite tired": Golway, *Washington's General*, 262.

223 "Another such victory": Ibid., 260.

CHAPTER TWENTY-THREE

224 "Inaccessible": Oller, *The Swamp Fox*, 105.

225 "rather than": Ibid.

225 "vile swamp fox": Ibid., 87.

225 "Come, my boys": Collins, *Autobiography of a Revolutionary Soldier*, 34.

225 "We follow": William Gilmore Simms, "The Swamp Fox," https://digital .lib.niu.edu/islandora/object/niu-lincoln%3A37977.

226 "They will not": Bass, *Swamp Fox*, 155.

226 "chose the best": Ibid., 156.

226 "Marion's repository": Ibid., 157.

227 "a great number": Bass, *Swamp Fox*, 167.

227 "The news was sudden": James, *A Sketch of the Life of Brg. Gen. Francis Marion*, 57.

227 "He was reserved": Lee, *The Revolutionary War Memoirs*, 585.

228 "the charms of the fair": Ibid.

228 "on our side": From George Washington to John Hancock, 8 September 1776, https://founders.archives.gov.

228 "called a War": Ibid.

228 "would be presumption": Ibid.

229 "flying army": From George Washington to Nathanael Greene, 8 November 1780, quoted in Golway, *Washington's General*, 232.

230 "they must come": Ibid.

230 "a large, strong oblong pen": Lee, *The Revolutionary War Memoirs*, 332.

230 "a Wooden Machine": Piecuch and Beakes, *"Light Horse Harry" Lee*, 158.

231 "crawled around behind": Bass, *Swamp Fox*, 178.

231 "reduced to the disagreeable": Piecuch and Beakes, *"Light Horse Harry" Lee*, 158.

231 "The officers and men": Bass, *Swamp Fox*, 178–79.

232 "high and commanding hill": Lee, *The Revolutionary War Memoirs*, 345.

232 "obstinate, and strong": Buchanan, *The Road to Charleston*, 109.

232 "Lamenting the sad necessity": Lee, *The Revolutionary War Memoirs*, 347.

232 "With a smile": Ibid.

233 "as probably better": Ibid.

233 "The rays": Ibid.

233 "Raking the loft": Ibid., 348.

233 "no other effort": Ibid.

233 "in a sumptuous dinner": Lee, *The Revolutionary War Memoirs*, 348–49.

233 "I will have you know": Buchanan, *Road to Charleston*, 112.

233 "The stroke was heavy": Oller, *The Swamp Fox*, 159.

234 "point blank shot": Piecuch and Beakes, *"Light Horse Harry" Lee*, 166.

234 "presented a very convenient": Lee, *The Revolutionary War Memoirs*, 352.

235 "very disagreeable and Melancholy affair": Ibid.

235 "the most exemplary punishment" : Buchanan, *The Road to Charleston*, 137.

235 "thirty or forty feet": Lee, *The Revolutionary War Memoirs*, 366.

CHAPTER TWENTY-FOUR

237 "fierce": Smith, *Edmund Burke on Revolution*, 57.

237 "that held high rank": Fischer, *Albion's Seed*, 642.

237 "stressed the plebian": Ibid.

237 "a weaver and merchant": Ibid.

238 "never *owned* in America": Ibid., 3.

238 "condition in life": Booraem, *Young Hickory*, 2–3.

238 "oppressions on the laboring poor": Ibid., 45.

239 "gentle as a dove": Remini, *Andrew Jackson*, 11.

239 "the excessive heat": Ibid., 15.

239 "a mounted orderly": Commager and Morris, *The Spirit of Seventy-Six*, 1170.

239 "breaking glasses": Remini, *Andrew Jackson*, 21.

239 "Sir, I am a prisoner": Ibid., 22.

240 "groaning in the agonies": Ibid.

240 "much stronger": Golway, *Washington's General*, 266.

240 "and they intended": Ibid.

240 "fell to work": Ibid.

241 "double envelopment": Golway, *Washington's General*, 267.

241 "General Greene exposed": Ibid., 268.

241 "almost was taken": Lumpkin, *From Savannah to Yorktown*, 183.

242 "in three Minutes": Golway, *Washington's General*, 269.

242 "with vexation": Ibid.

242 "The Troops were": From Nathaniel Greene to Congress, 27 April 1781, Papers of the Continental Congress, M247, roll 175, vol. 2, p. 47, National Archives and Records Administration.

242 "We fight, get beat": From Nathanael Greene to George Washington, 1 May 1781, https://rotunda.upress.virginia.edu.

242 "We fight, get beaten": Golway, *Washington's General*, 271.

243 "I feel": From George Washington to Nathanael Greene, 1 June 1781, https://rotunda.upress.virginia.edu.

243 "severe bowel complaint": Remini, *Andrew Jackson*, 23.

CHAPTER TWENTY-FIVE

246 "The salvation of this country": Showman, *The Papers of General Nathanael Greene*, 74.

246 "There is no mortal": Ibid.

246 "Plunder and depredation": Bass, *Gamecock*, 120.

246 "The Gamecock believed": Ibid., 128.

248 "were now exceedingly": Waters, *The Quaker and the Gamecock*, 59.

248 "measures truly disagreeable": Ibid., 68–69.

249 "prime": Bass, *Gamecock*, 144.

249 "At its best": Ibid., 145.

249 "Although I am": Ibid., 146.

249 "belonging to Tories": Waters, *The Quaker and the Gamecock*, 118.

250 "The Whigs seem determined": George Washington Greene, *The Life of Nathanael Greene*, vol. 3 (New York: G. P. Putnam), 227.

250 "freebooter": Waters, *The Quaker and the Gamecock*, 96.

250 "excessive difficulty": Bass, *Gamecock*, 124.

251 "My Indisposition": Ibid., 175.

251 "think of accepting": Ibid.

251 "how important": Ibid.

251 "in such a manner": Ibid., 178.

CHAPTER TWENTY-SIX

252 "tolerably well demolished": Bass, *Gamecock*, 178.

252 "every Reason to believe": Ibid.

252 "twelve dwelling houses": Buchanan, *The Road to Charleston*, 141.

252 "very good water": Ibid.

252 "the laconic style": Warren, *History of the Rise, Progress, and Termination of the American Revolution*, 332.

252 "I will recover": Ibid.

254 "settled into a daily": Beakes, *Otho Holland Williams*, 240.

254 "The sufferings": Commager and Morris, *The Spirit of Seventy-Six*, 1184.

255 "the survivors": Beakes, *Otho Holland Williams*, 245.

255 "return to his cardinal": Waters, *The Quaker and the Gamecock*, 135.

255 "gloom and silence": Ibid.

256 "slow, easy marches": Beakes, *Otho Holland Williams*, 254.

256 "were placed in": Buchanan, *The Road to Charleston*, 193.

256 "No time is to be lost": Greene papers, July 14, 1781, 9:8.

257 "to thunder even": Buchanan, *The Road to Charleston*, 126.

257 "the greatest alarm": Waters, *The Quaker and the Gamecock*, 144.

257 "found this post": Ibid.

258 "threw himself over": Lee, *The Revolutionary War Memoirs*, 390.

258 "a chasm in the bridge": Ibid.

258 "appalled at the sudden": Waters, *The Quaker and the Gamecock*, 146.

258 "a commanding Height": Buchanan, *The Road to Charleston*, 182.

259 "fired on from the stoop": Waters, *The Quaker and the Gamecock*, 147.

259 "Design of Renewing": Ibid.

259 "found Gen. Sumter": Ibid.

260 "the most discontented": Bass, *Gamecock*, 204.

260 "thirst for plunder": Waters, *The Quaker and the Gamecock*, 155.

260 "a respite from service": Bass, *Gamecock*, 204.

260 "Have I come here": Ibid.

260 "It would be little less": Ibid., 205.

260 "I have the public good": Ibid.

260 "General Sumter": Waters, *The Quaker and the Gamecock*, 155–56.

CHAPTER TWENTY-SEVEN

262 "relief which": To George Washington from Thomas Jefferson, 28 May 1781, https://founders.archives.gov.

263 "anti-authoritarianism": Bailyn, *The Ideological Origins of the American Revolution*, 5.

263 "stand alone": Speech to Jean Baptiste Ducoigne, [ca. 1] June 1781, https://founders.archives.gov.

263 "But peace is not far off": Ibid.

264 "Brother John Baptist": From Thomas Jefferson to Jean Baptiste DuCoigne, 21 June 1796, https://founders.archives.gov.

264 "aborigines": Thomas Jefferson, *Notes on the State of Virginia*, ed. William Peden (New York: W. W. Norton & Co., 1982), 92.

264 "Spirituous liquors": Ibid., 96.

264 "merciless Indian savages": "Declaration of Independence: A Transcription," America's Founding Documents, https://www.archives.gov.

265 "wretches": From Thomas Jefferson to John Page, 5 August 1776, https://founders.archives.gov.

265 "great Outacite": From Thomas Jefferson to John Adams, 11 June 1812, in Bergh, *The Writings of Thomas Jefferson*, vol. 13, p. 160.

265 "great farewell oration": Ibid.

265 "strike a decisive": From Thomas Jefferson to William Preston, 15 June 1780, https://founders.archives.gov.

266 "History affords": Kranish, *The Flight from Monticello*, 271.

266 "the pipe of peace": Speech to Jean Baptiste Ducoigne.

266 "We, like you": Ibid.

267   "to educate your son": Ibid.

267   "hideous evil": Crawford, *Twilight at Monticello*, 199.

267   "ripening": Jefferson, *Notes on the State of Virginia*, 87.

268   "the great object": John Chester Miller, *The Wolf by the Ears: Thomas Jefferson and Slavery* (Charlottesville: University Press of Virginia, 1991), 7.

268   "a considerable article": Ibid.

268   "detestable": Ibid.

268   "vehement philippic": Crawford, *Twilight at Monticello*, 21.

269   "refined": Ibid.

269   "mortal reproach": Ibid.

269   "nothing was to be": Ibid.

269   "as legitimate subjects": Ibid., 100–101.

269   "denounced as any enemy": Ibid., 101.

269   "treated with": Crawford, *Twilight at Monticello*, 101.

269   "always hoped": Ibid.

269   "the hour of emancipation": Ibid.

269   "the generous energy": Ibid.

269   "we should endeavor": Ibid., 102.

269   "that the two races": Ibid., 199.

270   "direct the process": Ibid.

270   "free white laborers": Ibid.

270   "afflicted with": Ibid., 199–200.

CHAPTER TWENTY-EIGHT

272   "the seat of war": From Cornwallis to Henry Clinton, 10 April 1781, quoted in John D. Grainger, *The Battle of Yorktown, 1781: A Reassessment* (Woodbridge: Boydell Press, 2005), 30.

272   "The rivers in Virginia": Ibid.

272   "total want of interior navigation": Ibid.

274   "I Don't believe": To George Washington from Marie-Joseph-Paul-Yves-Roch-Gilbert du Motier, Marquis de Lafayette, 24 May 1781, https://founders.archives.gov.

272   "be Cut to pieces": Ibid.

272   "determined to [skirmish]": Ibid.

272   "like they would": Ibid.

272   "I am not Strong": Ibid.

275   "Such terror and confusion": Dumas Malone, *Jefferson and His Time, Vol. 1: Jefferson the Virginian* (Boston: Little, Brown and Company, 1948), 358–359.

275   "more laughable": Ibid., 359.

276 "on the best and fleetest": Virginius Dabney, "Jouett Outrides Tarleton, and Saves Jefferson from Capture," *Scribner's Magazine* (June 1928): 690, quoted in Jon Meacham, *Thomas Jefferson: The Art of Power* (New York: Random House, 2013), 139.

276 "the scars made": Malone, *Jefferson the Virginian*, 356.

276 "with old Madeira": Ibid., 356.

276 "partook of a generous": Ibid.

277 "quietly at home": Sarah N. Randolph, *The Domestic Life of Thomas Jefferson* (Charlottesville: University Press of Virginia, 1978), 55.

277 "alive with British": Ibid., 56.

277 "perfectly tranquil": Malone, *Jefferson the Virginian*, 357.

277 "British horse came": Thomas Jefferson, Memorandum Books, 1781, https://founders.archives.gov.

277 "that he would never": Randolph, *The Domestic Life of Thomas Jefferson*, 57–58.

278 "destroyed all my growing": Ibid., 57.

278 "burned all my barns": Ibid.

278 "Had this been": Ibid.

278 "who went off": Julian P. Boyd, ed., *The Papers of Thomas Jefferson*, vol. 6, May 1781 to March 1784 (Princeton, NJ: Princeton University Press, 1952), 224.

278 "returned & died": Ibid.

278 "History will never relate": Randolph, *The Domestic Life of Thomas Jefferson*, 57.

CHAPTER TWENTY-NINE

279 "proper harbour": Lengel, *General George Washington*, 330.

280 "destitution": Ketchum, *Victory at Yorktown*, 146.

280 "the most neatly dressed": Acomb, *Revolutionary Journal of Baron Ludwig von Closen*, 59.

280 "have every thing": George Washington Diary, August 1781, https://founders.archives.gov.

280 "Matters having now": Ibid.

281 "princely entertainment": From the Journal of Colonel Jonathan Trumbull, Secretary to the General, 1781, quoted at https://founders.archives.gov/documents/Washington/01-03-02-0007-0005.

281 "a small present": Marquis de Chastellux, *Travels in North America in the Years 1780, 1781, and 1782*, vol. 2 (London: G. G. J. and J. Robinson, 1787), 170.

281 "certainly Have": Stanley J. Idzerda, ed., "General La Fayette to General

Washington, 23 April, 1781," in *La Fayette in the Age of the American Revolution*, vol. 4 (Ithaca, NY: Cornell University Press, 1981), 60–61.

281 "little sorry": From George Washington to Lund Washington, 30 April 1781, https://founders.archives.gov.

281 "making a voluntary offer": Ibid.

282 "the loss of all," Ibid.

282 "One hour more": Lee, *The Revolutionary War Memoirs*, 436.

283 "by-paths and passes": Golway, *Washington's General*, 280.

284 "bloody and obstinate": Beakes, *Otho Holland Williams*, 261.

284 "most tremendous fire": Golway, *Washington's General*, 281.

284 "would have graced": Commager and Morris, *The Spirit of Seventy-Six*, 1188.

284 "The victory was now": Ibid., 1189.

284 "fastened themselves": Ibid.

284 "irretrievable confusion": Ibid., 1191.

284 "we fought the enemy": Johnson, *Sketches of the Life and Correspondence of Nathanael Greene*, 220.

285 "indefatigable in collecting": Thane, *The Fighting Quaker*, 252.

285 "more he is beaten": Golway, *Washington's General*, 284.

285 "without any pomp": Ibid.

285 "Cornwallis may now tremble": From St. George Tucker to Frances Bland Tucker, 15 September 1781, in Commager and Morris, *The Spirit of Seventy-Six*, 1224.

CHAPTER THIRTY

286 "a School for Licentiousness": Massey, *John Laurens and the American Revolution*, 26, 28, 33–34.

287 "we are but Slaves": Ibid., 48.

287 "our Northern neighbors": Wallace, *The Life of Henry Laurens*, 91.

287 "goodness of heart": Ibid., 88.

287 "You know, my dear son": Ibid., 425, 445–46, 451.

288 "in case of irresistible": Massey, *John Laurens and the American Revolution*, 15.

288 "absurd": Ibid., 67.

288 "the sacred Cause": Ibid., 48, 92.

288 "not his fault": Ibid., 75.

289 "able bodied Slaves": Ibid.

289 "would advance": Ibid.

289 "to transform": Ibid., 131.

289 "a Color which": Ibid., 96.

289 "that monster popular": Ibid., 94–95.

290 "three thousand able bodied": Ibid., 132–33.

290 "was received with horror": Ibid., 141–42.

291 "Yankee Doodle": Wallace, *The Life of Henry Laurens*, 364, 367, 381–82.

291 "smelt strong of the Tower": Ibid., 365–66, 371.

293 "go a great way": Ibid., 371.

293 "put the match": Lingel, *General George Washington*, 338.

293 "The scene viewed": Scheer and Rankin, *Rebels & Redcoats*, 484.

293 "in or out of the town": Hibbert, *Redcoats and Rebels*, 328.

293 "My situation": Ross, *Correspondence of Charles, First Marquis Cornwallis*, vol. 1, 125.

293 "Experience has shown": John D. Grainger, *The Battle of Yorktown, 1781: A Reassessment* (Woodbridge: Boydell Press, 2005), 141.

296 "Sir, I propose": Commager and Morris, *The Spirit of Seventy-Six*, 1239.

296 "was pleasing to contrast": Edward M. Riley, "St. George Tucker's Journal of the Siege of Yorktown, 1781," *William & Mary Quarterly* 5, no. 3 (July 1948): 391.

296 "their Drums in Front": Ibid., 393.

297 "at the peril": Ibid., 39–40.

297 "Honest Friend": To George Washington from Lafayette, 31 July 1781, https://founders.archives.gov.

297 "behaved like boys": Scheer and Rankin, *Rebels & Redcoats*, 494.

297 "dear ragged Continentals": Massey, *John Laurens and the American Revolution*, 200.

298 "Ah, you rogue": Richard Ingram, "James Armistead Lafayette: What We Know and Don't Know," https://www.lafayettelagrange.org/james-armistead-lafayette-what-we-know-and-dont-know/.

298 "The play, sir": Scheer and Rankin, *Rebels & Redcoats*, 495.

298 "To be forwarded": John C. Fitzpatrick, ed., *The Writings of George Washington, from the Original Manuscript Sources*, vol. 23 (Washington, DC: Government Printing Office, 1937), 243.

298 "disastrous information": Commager and Morris, *The Spirit of Seventy-Six*, 1243–44.

CHAPTER THIRTY-ONE

299 "I have no doubt": Raphael, *Founding Myths*, 212.

300 "taking it for granted": From George Washington to Nathanael Greene, 15 December 1781, https://founders.archives.gov.

300 "We cannot march": Golway, *Washington's General*, 291.

300 "brave fellows": Buchanan, *The Road to Charleston*, 252.

300 "I would fly": Golway, *Washington's General*, 286, 288, 290.

300 "fold our Arms": Ibid., 292, 300–301.

301 "unsafe guide": Ibid., 293.

301 "strew [her way]": From George Washington to Nathanael Greene, 15 December 1781, https://founders.archives.gov.

301 "very much indebted": Golway, *Washington's General*, 296, 298.

302 "The natural strength": Ibid.

302 "had lived and prepared": Massey, *John Laurens and the American Revolution*, 211.

303 "to plunder and distress": Ibid., 213, 216.

303 "a great dislike": Ibid., 220.

303 "dispirited and fatigued": Ibid., 220, 228.

304 "in deep mourning": Ibid., 231.

304 "the melancholy intelligence": From John Adams to Henry Laurens, 6 November 1782, https://founders.archives.gov.

304 "as soon as possible": Ibid.

304 "an empire so great": Smith, *Edmund Burke on Revolution*, 55.

305 "the independency": To George Washington from Guy Carleton, 2 August 1782, https://founders.archives.gov.

305 "That the King": From George Washington to James McHenry, 12 September 1782, https://founders.archives.gov.

305 "to gain time": Raphael, *Founding Myths*, 214.

305 "scald head": Boatner, *Encyclopedia of the American Revolution*, 360.

305 "small scorge": Raphael, *A People's History*, 159.

305 "deliberate and wilful murder": Ibid., 160.

306 "cleft [open]": Ibid.

307 "with great order": Moultrie, *Memoirs of the American Revolution*, 360.

307 "exceedingly filthy": Fraser, *Charleston, Charleston!*, 164.

307 "had been cooped up": Ibid., 360.

308 "perquisite": Rosen, *A Short History of Charleston*, 58.

308 "hundreds made": Ravenel, *Charleston*, 675.

308 "balconies, the doors, and windows": Ibid., 360–61.

308 "the toasts of Charles Town": Golway, *Washington's General*, 303.

308 "a heart full of love": Lengel, *General George Washington*, 351.

309 "Peace made": From Alexander Hamilton to Colonel John Laurens, 15 August 1782, https://founders.archives.gov.

AFTER THE WAR

312 "First in war": Lengel, *General George Washington*, ix.

Bibliography

Aaron, Larry G. *The Race to the Dan: The Retreat That Rescued the American Revolution.* Halifax County, VA: Halifax County Historical Society, 2007.

Acomb, Evelyn M., ed. *The Revolutionary Journal of Baron Ludwig von Closen, 1780–1783.* Chapel Hill: University of North Carolina Press, 1958.

Agneil, Lucien. *The Late Affair Has Almost Broke My Heart: The American Revolution in the South, 1780–1781.* Riverside, CT: Chatham Press, Inc., 1972.

Alderman, Pat. *The Overmountain Men: Battle of King's Mountain.* Johnson City, TN: Overmountain Press, 1986.

Andrew, Rod, Jr. *The Life and Times of General Andrew Pickens: Revolutionary War Hero, American Founder.* Chapel Hill: University of North Carolina Press, 2017.

Arbuthnot, Admiral Mariot, and Sir Henry Clinton. *The Siege of Charleston: By the British Fleet and Army, Under the Command of Admiral Arbuthnot and Sir Henry Clinton, Which Terminated in the Surrender of That Place on the 12th of May, 1780.* Albany: J. Munsell, 1867.

Axelrod, Alan. *The Real History of the American Revolution: A New Look at the Past.* New York: Sterling, 2007.

Babits, Lawrence E., and Joshua B. Howard. *Long, Obstinate, and Bloody: The Battle of Guilford Courthouse.* Chapel Hill: University of North Carolina Press, 2009.

Bailyn, Bernard. *The Ideological Origins of the American Revolution.* Cambridge, MA: Belknap Press, 1967.

Baker, Thomas E. *Another Such Victory: The Story of the American Defeat at Guilford Courthouse That Helped Win the War for Independence.* New York: Eastern Acorn Press, 1992.

Bancroft, George. *History of the United States from the Discovery of the American Continent.* Vol. 10. Boston: Little, Brown and Company, 1874.

Barefoot, Daniel W. *Touring South Carolina's Revolutionary War Sites.* Winston-Salem, NC: John F. Blair, 1999.

Barnes, James J., and Patience P. Barnes, eds. *The American Revolution Through British Eyes: A Documentary Collection.* Vol. 2. Kent: Kent State University Press, 2013.

Bass, Robert D. *Gamecock: The Life and Campaigns of General Thomas Sumter.* Orangeburg, SC: Sandlapper Publishing Co., Inc., 2001.

———. *The Green Dragoon: The Lives of Banastre Tarleton and Mary Robinson.* Columbia, SC: Sandpiper Press, Inc., 1973.

———. *Swamp Fox: The Life and Campaigns of General Francis Marion.* Orangeburg, SC: Sandlapper Publishing Co., Inc., 1959.

Beakes, John H., Jr. *De Kalb: One of the Revolutionary War's Bravest Generals.* Berwyn Heights, MD: Heritage Books, 2019.

———. *Otho Holland Williams in the American Revolution.* Charleston, SC: Nautical and Aviation Publishing Co. of America, 2015.

Bear, James A., Jr., and Lucia C. Stanton, eds. *Jefferson's Memorandum Books: Account with Legal Records and Miscellany, 1767–1826.* Vol. 2. Princeton, NJ: Princeton University Press, 1997.

Berger, Carl. *Broadsides & Bayonets: The Propaganda War of the American Revolution.* San Rafael, CA: Presidio Press, 1976.

Bergh, Albert E., ed. *The Writings of Thomas Jefferson.* Washington, DC: Thomas Jefferson Memorial Association, 1907.

Berkin, Carol. *Revolutionary Mothers: Women in the Struggle for America's Independence.* New York: Alfred A. Knopf, 2005.

Betts, Edwin Morris, and Hames Adam Bear Jr., eds. *The Family Letters of Thomas Jefferson.* Charlottesville: University Press of Virginia, 1966.

Billias, George Athan, ed. *George Washington's Generals and Opponents: Their Exploits and Leadership.* Cambridge, MA: Da Capo Press, 1994.

Boatner, Mark M., III. *Encyclopedia of the American Revolution.* Mechanicsburg, PA: Stackpole Books, 1994.

———. *Landmarks of the American Revolution: People and Places Vital to the Quest for Independence.* Harrisburg, PA: Stackpole Books, 1992.

Bodle, Wayne. *The Valley Forge Winter: Civilians and Soldiers in War.* University Park: Pennsylvania State University Press, 2002.

Booraem, Hendrik. *Young Hickory: The Making of Andrew Jackson.* Dallas: Taylor Trade Publishing, 2001.

Borick, Carl P. *A Gallant Defense: The Siege of Charleston, 1780.* Columbia: University of South Carolina Press, 2003.

Bright, Jeffrey G., and Stewart E. Dunaway. *Pyle's Defeat: The Most Comprehensive Guide: Case Closed.* Morrisville, NC: Lulu.com, 2011.

Brooks, Victor, and Robert Hohwald. *How America Fought Its Wars: Military Strategy from the American Revolution to the Civil War.* Conshohocken, PA: Combined Publishing, 1999.

Buchanan, John. *The Road to Charleston: Nathanael Greene and the American Revolution.* Charlottesville: University of Virginia Press, 2019.

———. *The Road to Guilford Courthouse: The American Revolution in the Carolinas.* New York: John Wiley & Sons, 1997.

Calloway, Colin G. *The American Revolution in Indian Country: Crisis and Diversity in Native American Communities.* New York: Cambridge University Press, 1995.

Carbone, Gerald M. *Nathanael Greene: A Biography of the American Revolution.* New York: Palgrave Macmillan, 2008.

Cash, Arthur C. *John Wilkes: The Scandalous Father of Civil Liberty.* New Haven: Yale University Press, 2006.

Christie, I. R. *Crisis of Empire: Great Britain and the American Colonies, 1754–1783.* New York: W. W. Norton & Company, 1966.

Clinton, Catherine. *The Plantation Mistress: Woman's World in the Old South.* New York: Pantheon Books, 1982.

Clinton, Henry. *The American Rebellion: Sir Henry Clinton's Narrative of His Campaigns, 1775–1782, with an Appendix of Original Documents.* Edited by William Willcox. Archon Books, reprinted 1971. New Haven, CT: Yale University Press, 1954.

Cole, Ryan. *Light-Horse Harry Lee: The Rise and Fall of a Revolutionary Hero.* Washington, DC: Regnery History, 2019.

Collins, James Potter. *Autobiography of a Revolutionary Soldier.* Revised and prepared by John M. Roberts, Esq. Clinton, LA: Feliciana Democrat, 1859.

Commager, Henry Steele, and Richard B. Morris, eds. *The Spirit of Seventy-Six: The Story of the American Revolution as Told by Participants.* New York: Da Capo, 1995.

Cook, Don. *The Long Fuse: How England Lost the American Colonies, 1760–1786.* New York: Atlantic Monthly Press, 1995.

Crawford, Alan Pell. *Twilight at Monticello: The Final Years of Thomas Jefferson.* New York: Random House Trade Paperbacks, 2008.

———. *Unwise Passions: A True Story of a Remarkable Woman and the First Great Scandal of Eighteenth-Century America.* New York: Simon & Schuster Paperbacks, 2000.

Dameron, J. David. *King's Mountain: The Defeat of the Loyalists, October 7, 1780.* Cambridge, MA: Da Capo, 2003.

Dan, John C., ed. *The Revolution Remembered: Eyewitness Accounts of the War for Independence.* Chicago: University of Chicago Press, 1980.

Denman, Jeffrey A., and John F. Walsh. *Greene and Cornwallis in the Carolinas: The Pivotal Struggle.* Jefferson, NC: McFarland and Company, 2020.

Dunkerly, Robert M. *The Battle of Kings Mountain: Eyewitness Accounts.* Charleston, SC: History Press, 2007.

Dunkerly, Robert M., and Eric K. Williams. *Old Ninety Six: A History & Guide.* Charleston, SC: History Press, 2006.

Eanes, Colonel Greg. *Tarleton's Southside Raid and Peter Francisco's Famous Fight.* Crewe, VA: Eanes Group, 2014.

Edgar, Walter. *Partisans & Redcoats: The Southern Conflict That Turned the Tide of the American Revolution.* New York: Perennial, 2001.

Engle, Paul. *Women in the American Revolution.* Chicago: Follett Publishing Company, 1976.

Farish, Hunter Dickinson, ed. *Journal and Letters of Philip Vickers Fithian: A Plantation Tutor of the Old Dominion, 1773–1774.* Charlottesville: University Press of Virginia, 1990.

Ferling, John. *Almost a Miracle: The American Victory in the War of Independence.* Oxford: Oxford University Press, 2007.

———. *Winning Independence: The Decisive Years of the Revolutionary War, 1778–1781.* New York: Bloomsbury Publishing, 2021.

Fischer, David Hackett. *Albion's Seed: Four British Folkways in America.* New York: Oxford University Press, 1989.

Fleming, Thomas. *The Strategy of Victory: How George Washington Won the American Revolution.* New York: Da Capo, 2017.

Fraser, Walter J., Jr. *Charleston! Charleston!: The History of a Southern City.* Columbia: University of South Carolina Press, 1989.

Glover, Lorri. *Eliza Lucas Pinckney: An Independent Woman in the Age of Revolution.* New Haven, CT: Yale University Press, 2020.

Golway, Terry. *Washington's General: Nathanael Greene and the Triumph of the American Revolution.* New York: Henry Holt and Company, 2006.

Graham, Major William A. *General Joseph Graham and His Papers of North Carolina Revolutionary History.* Lincoln City, NC: Edwards and Broughton, 1904.

Greene, Jack P., and J. R. Pole. *The Blackwell Encyclopedia of the American Revolution.* Malden, MA: Blackwell Reference, 1999.

Harvey, Robert. *"A Few Bloody Noses": The Realities and Mythologies of the American Revolution.* Woodstock, NY: Overlook Press, 2001.

Hibbert, Christopher. *Redcoats and Rebels: The American Revolution Through British Eyes.* New York: Avon Books, 1990.

Higginbotham, Don. *Daniel Morgan: Revolutionary Rifleman.* Chapel Hill: University of North Carolina Press, 1961.

Holton, Woody. *Liberty Is Sweet: The Hidden History of the American Revolution.* New York: Simon & Schuster, 2021.

Horry, Brig. Gen. P., and Parson M. L. Weems. *The Life of General Francis Marion.* Winston-Salem, NC: John F. Blair, 2000.

Howard, Michael, George J. Andreopoulos, and Mark R. Shulman, eds. *The Laws of War: Constraints on Warfare in the Modern World*. New Haven, CT: Yale University Press, 1994.

Huggins, Benjamin L., ed. *The Papers of George Washington: Revolutionary War Series, 27, 5 July–27 August 1780*. Charlottesville: University of Virginia Press, 2019.

Huggins, Benjamin L., and Adrina Garbooshian-Huggins, eds. *The Papers of George Washington: Revolutionary War Series, 26, 13 May–4 July 1780*. Charlottesville: University of Virginia Press, 2018.

James, William Dobein. *A Sketch of the Life of Brigadier General Francis Marion*. Teddington, Middlesex, England: Echo Library, 2009.

Johnson, William. *Sketches of the Life and Correspondence of Nathanael Greene*. 2 vols. New York: Da Capo Press, 1973.

Jones, T. Cole. *Captives of Liberty: Prisoners of War and the Politics of Vengeance in the American Revolution*. Philadelphia: University of Pennsylvania Press, 2020.

Kaplan, Sidney, and Emma Nogrady Kaplan. *The Black Presence in the Era of the American Revolution*. Amherst: University of Massachusetts Press, 1989.

Ketchum, Richard M. *Victory at Yorktown: The Campaign That Won the Revolution*. New York: Henry Holt and Company, 2004.

Kranish, Michael. *The Flight from Monticello: Jefferson at War*. New York: Oxford University Press, 2010.

Lanning, Lt. Col. Michael Lee. *African Americans in the Revolutionary War*. New York: Citadel Press Books, 2000.

Leckie, Robert. *George Washington's War: The Saga of the American Revolution*. New York: HarperCollins Publishing, 1992.

Lee, Robert E., ed. *The Revolutionary War Memoirs of General Henry Lee*. New York: Da Capo Press, 1998.

Lengel, Edward G. *General George Washington: A Military Life*. New York: Random House Trade Paperbacks, 2007.

Lockhart, Paul. *The Drillmaster of Valley Forge: The Baron De Steuben and the Making of the American Army*. New York: HarperCollins Publishers, 2008.

Lossing, Benson J., ed. *Recollections and Private Memories of the Life and Character of Washington by His Adopted Son, George Washington Parke Custis*. New York: Derby & Jackson, 1860.

Lumpkin, Henry. *From Savannah to Yorktown: The American Revolution in the South*. New York: Paragon House Publishers, 1981.

Maas, John R. *The Road to Yorktown: Jefferson, Lafayette and the British Invasion of Virginia*. Charleston, SC: History Press, 2015.

Maclay, William. *Sketches of Debate in the First Senate of the United States, in 1789–90–91*. Edited by George W. Harris. Harrisburg, PA: Lane S. Hart, 1880.

Malone, Dumas. *The Sage of Monticello.* Boston: Little, Brown and Company, 1981.

Massey, Gregory D. *John Laurens and the American Revolution.* Columbia: University of South Carolina Press, 2015.

Mattern, David. *Benjamin Lincoln and the American Revolution.* Columbia: University of South Carolina Press, 1998.

Meacham, Jon. *Thomas Jefferson: The Art of Power.* New York: Random House, 2012.

Mitchell, Col. Joseph B. *Decisive Battles of the American Revolution.* St. Simons Island, GA: Mockingbird Books, 1962.

Moultrie, William. *Memoirs of the American Revolution, So Far As It Is Related to the States of North and South Carolina, and Georgia.* Vol. 2. New York: Printed by David Longworth for the author, 1802.

Nagel, Paul C. *The Lees of Virginia: Seven Generations of an American Family.* New York: Oxford University Press, 2007.

Norton, Mary Beth. *Liberty's Daughters: The Revolutionary Experience of American Women, 1750–1800.* Ithaca, NY: Cornell University Press, 1996.

Oller, John. *The Swamp Fox: How Francis Marion Saved the American Revolution.* Boston: Da Capo Press, 2016.

O'Shaughnessy, Andrew Jackson. *The Men Who Lost America: British Leadership, the American Revolution, and the Fate of the Empire.* New Haven, CT: Yale University Press, 2013.

Papas, Phillip. *Renegade Revolutionary: The Life of General Charles Lee.* New York: New York University Press, 2014.

Pearson, Michael. *Those Damned Rebels: The American Revolution as Seen Through British Eyes.* Da Capo Press, 1972.

Peterson, Harold L. *Arms and Armor in Colonial America, 1526–1783.* New York: Bramhall House, 1956.

Peterson, Merrill D., ed. *Visitors to Monticello.* Charlottesville: University Press of Virginia, 1993.

Phillips, Brig. Gen. Thomas R., ed. *Roots of Strategy: The 5 Greatest Military Classics of All Time.* Harrisburg, PA: Stackpole Books, 1985.

Piecuch, Jim. *The Battle of Camden: A Documentary History.* Charleston, SC: History Press, 2006.

———. *The Blood Be Upon Your Head: Tarleton and the Myth of Buford's Massacre.* Lugoff, SC: Southern Campaigns of the American Revolution, 2010.

———. *Three Peoples, One King: Loyalists, Indians, and Slaves in the Revolutionary South, 1775–1782.* Columbia: University of South Carolina Press, 2008.

Piecuch, Jim, and John H. Beakes Jr. *"Light Horse Harry" Lee in the War for Independence.* Charleston, SC: Nautical and Aviation Publishing Co. of America, 2013.

Plumb, J. H. *England in the Eighteenth Century.* New York: Penguin Books, 1950.

Potts, Louis W. *Arthur Lee: A Virtuous Revolutionary.* Baton Rouge: Louisiana State University Press, 1981.

Quarles, Benjamin. *The Negro in the American Revolution.* Chapel Hill: University of North Carolina Press, 1996.

Ramsey, David, MD. *The History of the American Revolution.* Vol. 1. Indianapolis: Liberty Fund, 1990.

———. *The History of the American Revolution.* Vol. 2. Carlisle, MA: Applewood Books, n.d.

Raphael, Ray. *A People's History of the American Revolution: How Common People Shaped the Fight for Independence.* New York: Free Press, 2001.

———. *Founding Myths: Stories That Hide Our Patriotic Past.* New York: MJF Books, 2004.

Ravenel, Mrs. St. Julien. *Charleston: The Place and the People.* New York: Macmillan Company, 1927.

Remini, Robert V. *Andrew Jackson: Volume One, The Course of American Empire, 1767–1821.* Baltimore: Johns Hopkins University Press, 1998.

Roberts, Cokie. *Founding Mothers: The Women Who Raised Our Nation.* New York: Perennial, 2005.

Roberts, Kenneth. *The Battle of Cowpens: The Story of 900 Men Who Shook an Empire.* Garden City, NY: Doubleday & Co., 1958.

Rosen, Robert. *A Short History of Charleston.* Columbia: University of South Carolina Press, 1997.

Ross, Charles, ed. *Correspondence of Charles, First Marquis Cornwallis.* 3 vols. London: John Murray, 1859.

Rossiter, Clinton. *The First American Revolution.* New York: Harcourt, Brace and Company, 1956.

Rouse, Parke, Jr. *The Great Wagon Road: From Philadelphia to the South.* Richmond, VA: Dietz Press, 1992.

Royster, Charles. *Light Horse Harry Lee and the Legacy of the American Revolution.* New York: Alfred A. Knopf, 1981.

Salley, A. S., Jr., ed. *Col. William Hill's Memoirs of the Revolution.* Columbia: Historical Commission of South Carolina, 1921.

Scheer, George F., and Hugh F. Rankin. *Rebels & Redcoats: The American Revolution Through the Eyes of Those Who Fought and Lived It.* New York: Da Capo, 1957.

Schulz, Emily L., and Laura B. Simo. *George Washington & His Generals.* Mount Vernon, VA: Mount Vernon Ladies' Association of the Union, 2009.

Scoggins, Michael C. *The Day It Rained Militia: Huck's Defeat and the Revolution in the South Carolina Backcountry, May–July 1780.* Charleston, SC: History Press, 2005.

Selby, John E. *The Revolution in Virginia, 1775–1783.* Charlottesville: University of Virginia Press, 2007.

Showman, Richard K., ed. *The Papers of General Nathanael Greene, Vol. VII: 26 December 1780–29 March 1781.* Chapel Hill: University of North Carolina Press, 1994.

Shy, John. *A People Numerous & Armed: Reflections on the Military Struggle for American Independence.* New York: Oxford University Press, 1976.

Smith, Robert A., ed. *Edmund Burke on Revolution.* New York: Harper & Row, 1968.

Spring, Matthew H. *With Zeal and With Bayonets Only: The British Army on Campaign in North America, 1775–1783.* Norman: University of Oklahoma Press, 2008.

Stegeman, John F., and Janet A. Stegeman. *Caty: A Biography of Catharine Littlefield Greene.* Athens: University of Georgia Press, 1997.

Sydnor, Charles S. *American Revolutionaries in the Making: Political Practices in Washington's Virginia.* New York: Free Press, 1952.

Tarleton, Banastre. *A History of the Campaigns of 1780 and 1781 in the Southern Provinces of North America.* Dublin: Colles, Exshaw, White, H. Whitestone, Burton, Byrne, Moore, Jones and Dornen, 1787.

Thane, Elswyth. *The Fighting Quaker: Nathanael Greene.* New York: Hawthorn Books, 1972.

Thomas, Peter D. G. *John Wilkes: A Friend to Liberty.* Oxford: Clarendon Press, 1996.

Tocqueville, Alexis de. *Democracy in America and Two Essays on America.* New York: Penguin Books, 2003.

Tustin, Joseph P., ed. *Captain Johann Ewald, Diary of the American War: A Hessian Journal.* Vol. 3. New Haven, CT: Yale University Press, 1979.

Uhlendorf, Bernard A. *The Siege of Charleston: Capts. Johann Ewald, Johann Hinrichs, and Maj. Gen. Johann Christoph von Huyn (Eyewitnesses Accounts of the American Revolution).* New York: Arno Press, 1938.

Unger, Harlow Giles. *First Founding Father: Richard Henry Lee and the Call to Independence.* New York: De Capo Press, 2017.

———. *Lafayette.* Hoboken, NJ: John Wiley & Sons, Inc., 2002.

Wallace, David Duncan. *The Life of Henry Laurens.* London: Forgotten Books, 2015.

Warren, Mercy Otis. *History of the Rise, Progress, and Termination of the American Revolution.* Vol. 2. New York: AMS Press, 1970.

Waters, Andrew. *The Quaker and the Gamecock: Nathanael Greene, Thomas Sumter, and the Revolutionary War for the Soul of the South.* Philadelphia: Casemate, 2019.

Weintraub, Stanley. *Iron Tears: America's Battle for Freedom, Britain's Quagmire: 1775–1783.* New York: Free Press, 2005.

Wharton, Francis, ed. *The Revolutionary Diplomatic Correspondence of the United States*. Vol. 1. Washington, DC: Government Printing Office, 1889.

Wiencek, Henry. *An Imperfect God: George Washington, His Slaves, and the Creation of America*. New York: Farrar, Straus and Giroux, 2003.

Wood, Gordon S. *The American Revolution: A History*. New York: Modern Library, 2002.

Wood, W. J. *Battles of the Revolutionary War, 1775–1781*. New York: Da Capo Press, 1995.

Wrobel, Sylvia, and George Grider. *Isaac Shelby: Kentucky's First Governor and Hero of Three Wars*. Danville, KY: Cumberland Press, 1974.

Zambone, Albert Louis. *Daniel Morgan: A Revolutionary Life*. Yardley, PA: Westholme Publishing, 2018.

Index

Page numbers in *italics* refer to illustrations.

page 4

> Edenton Ladies. Published in the Catalogue of Prints and Drawings in the British Museum, Vol V. Courtesy, Library of Congress.
>
> Henry Laurens. National Portrait Gallery.

page 5

> Nathanael Greene. Courtesy of Independence National Historical Park.
>
> Thomas Sumter. Courtesy of Independence National Historical Park.
>
> *The Battle of Cowpens.* South Carolina State House. Public domain.

page 6

> Light Horse "Harry" Lee. Courtesy of Independence National Historical Park. INDE 14041.
>
> Rebecca Motte. MET DP 169.101.jpeg, c. 1758.
>
> Mount Vernon. Mount Vernon Museum W-5307. Mount Vernon Ladies' Association.

page 7

> *Surrender of Lord Cornwallis.* Architect of the Capitol.

page 8

> John Laurens. Courtesy of Independence National Historical Park. INDE 14075.
>
> Otho Holland Williams. Courtesy of Independence National Historical Park. INDE 14164.

A NOTE ON THE TYPE

This book was set in Adobe Garamond. Designed for the Adobe Corporation by Robert Slimbach, the fonts are based on types first cut by Claude Garamond (ca. 1480–1561). Garamond was a pupil of Geoffroy Tory and is believed to have followed the Venetian models, although he introduced a number of important differences, and it is to him that we owe the letter we now know as "old style." He gave to his letters a certain elegance and feeling of movement that won their creator an immediate reputation and the patronage of Francis I of France.

Composed by North Market Street Graphics,
Lancaster, Pennsylvania

Printed and bound by Berryville Graphics,
Berryville, Virginia

Designed by Soonyoung Kwon